. BADER

The author with a few close friends.

Francis Jozwik has been intimately associated with floriculture for the past 15 years as the owner-manager of a successful greenhouse operation. Dr. Jozwik received a Ph.D. in Plant Science from the University of Wyoming and began teaching plant physiology at Wisconsin State University. Before entering the horticultural trade, Dr. Jozwik was also employed by the Commonwealth Scientific and Industrial Research Organization of Australia as a researcher and writer in plant science.

PLANTS FOR PROFIT

A Complete Guide to
Growing and Selling
Greenhouse Crops

Francis X. Jozwik

ANDMAR PRESS

Mills, Wyoming 82644

Library of Congress Catalog Card Number 84-70515
ISBN 0-916781-00-3
Printed in the United States of America

CONTENTS
PART I

CONTENTS

PART II

PREFACE

Plants for Profit may at first glance seem marginally different from other texts dealing with greenhouse culture and marketing of ornamental plants. If the book is studied thoroughly, it should become apparent that definite practical recommendations are presented in each chapter and that these recommendations are carefully organized to result in a coherent technical approach to plant production and marketing. I have attempted to educate the reader with background material and theory but yet present a simplified, concrete guide for growers to follow in their everyday work.

The chapters on soils and fertilizers should be studied carefully since a good part of the methods presented are dependent for success upon utilizing the recommended soils and fertilizers. Reference will be made throughout this book to a "growing on or general production" soil mix composed of peat moss and sand and a "cutting mix" composed of peat moss and perlite. Detailed instructions for making these mixes are presented in chapter 8, Part I. The "growing on" mix is intended for use in all crop schedules unless specific directions are given to substitute with the "cutting mix" or some other special formula. The daily fertilizer requirements of plants in my growing methods are met by injection of either a calcium nitrate-potassium nitrate combination solution or a potassium nitrate only solution into the irrigation water. The use of one or the other of these fertilizer formulas is determined mainly by the variety of plant being grown. Directions for mixing these fertilizers and instructions for use are presented in chapter 10, Part I and with discussions of specific crops.

An important point to remember when studying greenhouse crop production is that growing temperatures refer to the night temperature at plant level unless otherwise specified.

As growers increase their level of sophistication they will surely wish to experiment with different production techniques but it should be realized that seemingly small changes can vastly alter the resulting crops. Variability of crops from year to year should be expected and planned for in advance even when conditions are replicated as closely as possible. Adhering to the practical production methods and scheduling advice contained in this book will reduce the incidence of unpredicted circumstances but every grower should realize the inherent risks coincident with the culture of living organisms. Planning for the unexpected is a great step forward in establishing a successful flower and plant business.

Readers without some background in horticulture will be well advised to study this book in sequence since a complete mastery of later chapters will be dependent upon previously presented information.

The recommendations given are primarily the distillation of many years spent in daily contact with crops and are not the result of extrapolations from theory or of second hand knowledge collected from other growers or experts. It is hoped the reader will benefit from material compiled by a fellow grower who has a wide range of experience in the practical application of biological concepts.

PART I
INTRODUCTION

Can you remember your Mother and Father admonishing "dollars don't grow on trees"? For some lucky people, dollars do grow on trees and on many other plants besides. You can turn your natural bent toward gardening into a lucrative full time business or a part time retirement income. Commercial horticulture is a field where it is still possible for an individual to accumulate a small fortune if one has the willingness to work and a love of making things grow.

I started my own career as an agricultural research scientist and college teacher. It was not long, however, before I felt the itch to do something more concrete and get my fingers in the soil. I quit my job and started a small greenhouse business which, within a few years, grew to include many different aspects of horticulture. Every dollar I invested in this business has been multiplied a thousand fold. Financial reward is not the only reason for getting into the plant business. Even though you may face problems and tensions that are present in any other field of endeavor, I think you will come to realize the great sense of satisfaction that arises from growing living things. Through your work you will begin to appreciate the great harmony with which myriad facets of God's world are possessed.

My purpose in writing this book is to present an outline of how to go about starting a greenhouse business and then acquaint the reader with some of the technical knowledge needed to grow and market plants. I have placed special emphasis on relating the technical information presented to its eventual use in a business setting. There are several fine books available which can serve as references for the individual who has progressed to the point where more detailed technical material is needed. My intended audience are the people who possess no special knowledge of the plant industry and require an entry level text which combines both business and biological principles. Many readers will want to start their plant businesses without a large amount of capital; therefore, I have included material which would seem primitive to large greenhouse concerns but fits in quite well for persons wishing to run a plant business from their own backyard.

I have made a conscious effort not to go into great detail on any one technical subject so that the reader will get an overall view of the greenhouse industry. Specific information is not included concerning cut flower or vegetable and fruit production because these crops are usually profitable only if grown on a large scale and, in the case of cut flowers, the trend of United States production is downward. The list of literature and suppliers is by no means complete but should be extensive enough for a person to find out anything he or she might need to know about plants. I hope this book will in some way repay the horticultural industry for the benefits I have reaped from it over the years.

CHAPTER 1
KNOW THYSELF

Success at any endeavor depends, to a large degree, upon knowing one's own abilities and using this knowledge to formulate realistic goals and the methods of attaining these goals. A person's ambitions must correspond with the resources, preferences, and limitations possessed by that individual. Long periods of considered reflection should precede any decision to enter into a business enterprise.

The horticultural profession is, of course, populated by people who love plants but you must also possess other characteristics to enable you to be successful. Working with plants requires a person to be optimistic and patient. The numerous tragedies which can and do befall plants during their growth would discourage all but the optimist. Biological organisms take time to complete their life cycles and, within bounds, cannot be hurried. The production of healthy plants and flowers can be very rewarding but it is not a field for the impatient or easily bored person.

If a quest for easy profits is your goal, you should avoid horticultural pursuits. Many aspects of greenhouse work are strenuous or repetitive and only persons who can look ahead to the successful outcome of their work will find these tasks rewarding. I believe it is impossible to be an excellent horticulturist without possessing a special love of bringing plants into the world and caring for them until their purpose in life is achieved. The passive nature of plants demands that one must lovingly and gradually discover their requirements for sturdy growth. Animal lovers are often given intelligent indications by their charges of what is desired or needed but a plants person must patiently probe for answers from an uncommunicative subject.

The artificial greenhouse environment makes plants and flowers totally dependent upon timely and knowledgeable care. One must tend to their needs without fail if reasonable success is to be enjoyed. All aspects of your life will be centered around the responsibility entailed in the care of these helpless organisms. Plants in this alien environment cannot be expected to prosper unless the care given to them is informed by education and experience. The survival and eventual healthy growth of plants in the greenhouse may be likened to the recovery of people in hospital life support facilities. In both situations, the care given must be dedicated, expert, and complete.

Plans for operating a greenhouse business should closely reflect the goals you have set for yourself. It is possible to design a plant business which will suit a person's particular needs but it must be done before entering business; otherwise the result might be an enterprise which is not as fulfilling as it could be or even makes you unhappy. Someone who enjoys reading and other inexpensive pursuits may want to structure a business where more free time but less money is available than the person who treasures the benefits money can buy. A person's stage in life may dramatically alter business goals. Someone who is sixty years old and entering business for supplemental retirement income should have a different business plan than a younger person who requires a full income to support several children. The number of possible business objectives is endless and each goal set forth must be compatible with the business plan devised.

Available resources will help determine the scope of your greenhouse operations. Not only your material assets but also your mental and physical capabilities must be sufficient for your project. Someone who has large financial resources and is exceptionally endowed mentally and physically has few limitations placed on what can be accomplished. Unfortunately, most individuals have limitations of one sort or another and must choose niches in horticulture which emphasize their particular assets. The diversity of horticulture is such that almost anyone should be able to find an area which suits his or her abilities. Be realistic about what you can accomplish with your resources and avoid the mistake of always swimming upstream. Successful people in business or any other field are usually the ones who have learned to float with the current and are comfortable in the knowledge that they have charted a course which their abilities will allow them to follow.

One attribute a person in business must possess in ample supply is enthusiasm. It is a strong catalyst. If you pursue a greenhouse career with enthusiasm, half the battle for success will be won.

CHAPTER 2

WHAT'S IN IT FOR YOU?

Growing and selling plants and flowers may be interesting but you could satisfy your horticultural urges without making a business of it. Probably the main reason you are reading this book is that you want to make more money or would prefer to earn a living in a more rewarding manner. Why is the horticultural field better than other businesses for making money? To tell the truth, there are many endeavors which would be equally rewarding financially. Few businesses, however, can be started with less capital and, if you have been an avid gardener for several years, you probably possess much of the general knowledge necessary to get started.

Many people are interested in operating a business that can be carried on at home, will require very little money, and can be practiced only at specific times of the year. Housewives and retired people who wish to occupy their spare time fruitfully are especially well suited to a small horticultural business. Of course, it is not necessary to remain small; your business can be as large as you wish to make it. If only a small enterprise is planned and your home lot is large enough, it may cost next to nothing to get started. Many cities will permit a home business in residential areas. The materials needed to start a modest greenhouse or cold frame can be reclaimed from scrap piles or purchased economically.

The primary expenses of a greenhouse business are land and the buildings, labor, supplies, and fuel. If one or all of these expenses can be reduced significantly, your profit will increase dramatically. This is why a home greenhouse where you do most of the labor can be so profitable. Even if you cannot do all the labor yourself, there is still plenty of room for good profits. My own greenhouses are well constructed on expensive land and I do little work other than supervision, yet they yield a handsome return. The real key to making money in the greenhouse business is knowing what you are doing and actually translating this knowledge into efficient management.

A detailed picture of revenues, expenses, and profits one might expect from a small backyard greenhouse operated in the springtime is presented in Tables 1 and 2. The prices used in the model are those received by my own business in 1984 and expenses represent an honest approximation based on my recent records.

Table 1

Expenses involved in operating a small neighborhood greenhouse for the spring season. Land prices not included.

Building and equipment costs - assume new materials are purchased

1200 sq. ft. of cold frames and 384 sq. ft. of heated greenhouse constructed at an average cost of $3.00 per sq. ft., no labor included	$ 4,752.00
Miscellaneous equipment— soil mixer, wheelbarrow, pumps, etc.	1,000.00
Total building and equipment cost	5,752.00
Yearly building and equipment cost if the total is amortized at 12% interest over a 10 year usable life span	990.36

Variable product costs per unit produced

Containers	$ .30
Flats - usable for an average of 3 years	.20
Soil	.25
Seed and material for seedlings	1.00
Total variable cost per unit (flat)	1.75

Fixed greenhouse operation costs per year

Fertilizer	$ 50.00
Water	50.00
Insecticides	100.00
Miscellaneous expenses	1,000.00
Repair	200.00
Fuel for 5 months	500.00
Total fixed operating costs per year	1,900.00

Table 2

Revenues and profits from operating a small neighborhood greenhouse. Assume ½ man day for 6 months as labor for spring production.

Calculation of revenues

Greenhouse holds 256 flats and produces 2 crops for a total of 512 flats. My 1984 price per flat of vegetables is $19.62	$10,045.44
Cold frames hold 800 flats and produce 1 crop for a total of 800 flats. My 1984 price per flat of flowers is $15.48	12,384.00
Total revenues if all plants were sold at retail prices	22,429.44

Calculation of selling and production costs

Deduct for 5% crop wastage (.05 x $22,429.44)	$ 1,121.47
Cost of advertising at 5% of revenues (.05 x $21,307.97)	1,065.40
Variable costs of planting 1312 flats at $1.75 each	2,296.00
Fixed operating costs per year	1,900.00
Building and equipment costs per year at 12% interest	990.36
Total costs per year for selling and production	7,373.23

Calculation of before tax profits

Total retail revenues less total costs ($22,429.44—7,373.23)	$15,056.21

The construction costs I am projecting in Table 1 are much higher than could be expected if you were able to salvage some materials. I am assuming that you do not possess any materials and they are purchased new at normal retail prices. Costs have been purposely overestimated so I will not be accused of misleading readers. You are expected to provide all labor in construction, growing, and selling.

The term "flats" may be unfamiliar; it is a trade term used for an outer holding tray into which growing containers are placed. The flats used in this model occupy 1.5 square feet of greenhouse space. The growing plan would be to start one crop of cold tolerant pansies, snapdragons, carnations, etc. in the greenhouse in early winter and then move them to cold frames in late winter after transplanting. These would be followed by cool tolerant plants such as petunias and alyssum which should be moved to cold frames in early spring. Then you would plant a crop of tomatoes, peppers, eggplant, etc. in the heated greenhouse; these vegetables should be sold out early so that a second crop can be rotated in. It is not possible to operate a

384 square foot greenhouse without aisle space; in reality you would produce fewer flats than I have calculated, but the revenue can easily be made up by raising hanging baskets on the rafters above the benches.

You surely would want to raise more varieties than I have mentioned. However, to keep the economic model simple, I have dealt with three main classes of plants: those that can freeze moderately with no damage, those that will grow at cool temperatures but will not tolerate hard frost, and those which will not grow at cold temperatures and will not tolerate any frost. Varieties could be substituted at will but the proportion of the three main classes would have to remain pretty much the same in this particular example. An operation of the size described should keep an individual working hard about four hours a day, seven days a week during a five month period. If we assume another month would be spent planning and cleaning up each season, you would be making $60,224.84 per year based on a full time work schedule.

I expect that the price I receive for my plants can at least be matched by other growers. This should not be too difficult since I try to raise as many as the market will absorb at a reasonable price. Income could be increased by selling such things as seed, fertilizers, insecticides, and trees. Selling and growing all your plants will not be an easy task, but if you follow the guidelines presented in this book there should be no insurmountable problems.

How is the $5,752 needed for buildings and equipment to be obtained? The most obvious method is to cut costs by obtaining most materials from salvage or in a used condition. Another possibility, if you own your own home, is to finance the greenhouse as a home improvement at the bank. It could be financed with a business loan but home improvement loans are much easier to negotiate. There are other ways of getting into the plant business which require less time and almost no capital. One method is to specialize in producing potted perennials. Many of these plants can be started easily from cuttings or divisions at no cost. Some may require the purchase of a few dollars worth of seed. Thousands of perennials can be raised in a medium sized garden plot and then transplanted to pots for market. A one quart perennial should sell at retail for approximately $2.50 to $3.50; if you sell at wholesale, you should receive $1.25 to $1.75. Several thousand dollars a year can be made with little more effort and cost than is normally expended in raising a vegetable garden.

The prices obtainable for individual plants may surprise you. The following are some examples showing the retail price I receive and a higher price which more expensive florists charge:

4 inch geranium	$ 2.25	$ 4.00
6 inch geranium	5.49	10.00
6 inch poinsettia	10.98	20.00
4 inch green plant	2.98	5.00
10 inch hanging basket.	15.00	30.00

I believe I have been more successful than the great majority of florists because my philosophy is to sell a large number of plants at a moderate price. I recommend that you expect to receive the prices I charge rather than those at the higher scale.

These elementary figures demonstrate that there are lucrative financial opportunities in the horticultural field. The satisfaction of being your own boss and the healthy mix of mental and physical work are added psychological benefits you may enjoy. I feel growing and selling plants is a very secure occupation. As the pressures of modern living increase, more people turn to decorating with plants indoors and gardening to alleviate their tensions. The trend toward urbanized societies means these pressures will grow even more and thus ensure a healthy market for plants and flowers in the future.

Most of the really successful greenhouse owners I know started their enterprise as a sideline while they worked at regular jobs. After a year or two of learning the ropes and developing a clientele, they usually saw their businesses take off at an astounding rate. There are numerous extremely large greenhouse firms started only a few years ago by individuals like you. The horticultural industry is truly in a boom era and will stay that way as long as the trends of the last twenty years continue. Sales of foliage plants, potted flowers, and bedding plants have increased greatly in recent years. There is plenty of room in this expanding market for newcomers.

CHAPTER 3

GATHER INFORMATION

Today's world requires successful people to be well informed. Gathering information about your future greenhouse business can be one of the most interesting and potentially profitable uses of your time. A sure method of inviting failure is to begin spending money before you know what you are doing. Greenhouse growing and management is a highly technical field which most people can master if they put in the proper study before beginning. The fear of lacking enough knowledge should not keep a person from entering business indefinitely, but remember, "fools rush in where angels fear to tread." Many readers who are avid gardeners may already possess enough general knowledge to run a small greenhouse business. It is in the area of marketing, business management, and precision growing that most people should prepare themselves more adequately. There are many people in the greenhouse business today who work hard and long yet never attain any degree of success simply because they pay little attention to the points mentioned above.

Please don't be intimidated when I say "marketing, business management, and precision growing." All these categories can be mastered with common sense, acute observation and a few reference books for each area. Most people who like plants will find the growing end of the greenhouse business most interesting and will have no trouble becoming precision growers if they are willing to learn and pay attention to detail. "Precision growing" means crops are grown to specific market parameters which you have determined, and that they are carefully time sequenced to maintain adequate quantities of high quality merchandise on the market at all times. "Marketing" means being able to sell what you produce. It sounds easy enough to accomplish but I have seen countless crops of beautiful plants on the garbage pile simply because there was no well thought out plan of how to sell them. The selling plan should precede the growing plan. Marketing and growing are fairly self evident ingredients in a successful greenhouse business. "Business management" is not so obvious a component and is completely ignored by a large number of greenhouse owners. It means that you have a plan for where your business is going, what you want it to do, and how the different aspects of it relate to one another. The level of sophistication needed in the three areas we have been discussing depends to some degree on how large a business you intend to operate. If you run a small backyard plant business in the spring, you may need no more than a yankee farmer's instinct for the right thing to do. In the event your enterprise grew to include several million dollars worth of greenhouse and sales areas, it would be beneficial to have formal plans and records of your growing, marketing, and management.

Let us turn our attention to the information you will need and how to find it. Once you have gathered and organized enough information, it will become much easier to develop plans which will ensure success. Be sure you get in the habit of recording any information in a systematic manner, otherwise it will be virtually worthless after a short time. The human mind is not capable of remembering accurately for more than a few days.

LITERATURE SEARCH

A thorough reading of the books and papers published about greenhouse growing will give you a preliminary acquaintance with the subject. Start with more general texts and progress to specialized subjects which you feel will have importance in your particular case. Don't forget to find some books dealing with marketing and business management and be sure they are applicable to a small business setting. A great deal of information about marketing plants will be found in scattered articles published by the trade. To my knowledge, there is no text which presents a detailed analysis of marketing and business management as it pertains to the horticultural industry.

One of the best ways to start tracking down published information is to find the most recent books and publications in the field and then start working backwards from their reference lists. Another method is to obtain copies of the yearly index for trade periodicals. Almost all universities will have a set of *Biological Abstracts* which you can use to find any scientific paper published in the biological field. This source may be important if you are looking for theoretical information but it will rarely be of use to the average greenhouse businessman. After a few days of investigating the literature you will find there is more of it than you could ever get through. Be very particular as to what books and articles you choose to read in detail. If you try to read through it all, there will never be enough time to get a business started. A good supply of note cards is essential when reading the literature. Record the subject matter of each article or book very briefly and then file it for later retrieval. Articles may have to be cross indexed under several subject headings.

PERSONAL OBSERVATION

A wealth of information can be gathered by talking and looking. The weather is very important to anyone in the greenhouse business and should be observed closely. A heightened awareness of it can be obtained by recording temperatures, wind speed, cloud conditions, etc. It is not necessary to do this all the time but if you have not been in the habit of watching weather conditions this is one method of becoming accustomed to it. You will also want to observe what people are doing as it relates to gardening in different types of weather and at what time of day. A good way to do this is to drive around residential areas in the gardening season and record just what it is people are busy with at the moment. You will find there are fairly distinct tasks they do at certain times: lawn cleanup and fertilizing in early spring, garden and tree planting in mid and late spring and then mostly watering and cultivating as summer approaches. Miscalculating the planting season by two weeks can be catastrophic for the greenhouse owner who counts on garden plants being a large part of the business.

Watching the activity of several garden stores, preferably ones that handle a large number of plants, is a worthwhile activity in the spring. This will establish what time during the day people buy their gardening needs and what kind of crowds to expect during different types of weather. Pay particular attention to when ladies start wearing shorts. This is one of the most important barometers of whether or not they think it is time to plant.

While observing plant stores for traffic patterns, write the prices down they are asking for various lines of merchandise. Notes about the quality, selection, and amount of professional service available must accompany the prices. This information will be indispensable when you are trying to decide how much to charge for your own products. Remember, price is a combination of many different factors; everything you know about a particular store will aid in evaluating its pricing structure. If there is a knowledgeable sales person present, you can gather useful facts by engaging the person in conversation and discretely leading to the topic which you want to know more about.

Unless you are a gardener with long experience in an area, it will be necessary to find out what varieties to grow and in what proportions. The best way to do this is to walk through several different areas making notes of the plants encountered and their relative abundance. Don't forget to try to observe some backyards also since the type of landscaping in the back will often be quite different from that in the front yard. It will be helpful to take the same trip again in summer and fall to see things that were not apparent in the spring. Sometimes people get used to planting certain things simply because everybody else does or because a particular nursery or greenhouse is the only one present in an area. In order to discover some crops which might be very popular but are not presently grown in your town, make occasional trips for observation to other areas. When I started my own business, there were no homes displaying hanging baskets in our city. While on a buying trip in a nearby trade center, I noticed many of the homes had one or more hanging baskets displayed. I decided to introduce them in our city and eventually they became one of the biggest money makers in my operation. Apparently, the greenhouses and stores in our area had just never tried them.

Varietal information can also be gathered at local plant stores and greenhouses. This information must be analyzed carefully since some stores may be selling the wrong merchandise and, if you follow them blindly, you will perpetuate the same mistakes. Salesmen for the large seed houses will generally have a pretty good idea of what plants will sell in an area, but they have a vested interest in trying to sell you more than might be necessary and may sometimes promote the items which generate the most commissions for them. State university extension offices should have several publications that will aid in choosing varieties (especially shrubs and trees). The quality of these publications varies considerably from state to state and most of them will indicate only what grows well, not what sells well. Visiting with local garden clubs is one method of discovering new varieties since they are usually more interested in the unusual items.

While observing stores and greenhouses for pricing and traffic patterns, keep in mind that they will be either your customers, competitors, or both. A survey of potential customers and competition is very important to drawing up a logical marketing plan. Your business will have a greater chance of prospering if you select a neighborhood which really needs a greenhouse rather than one which already has several. You should also choose, if possible, to specialize in product lines which the market has not been saturated with. You may decide there is greater potential in becoming a wholesale supplier, but you probably should not follow this route unless you have the resources to produce fairly large quantities of plants.

Talking with owners of plant stores and greenhouses can be enlightening, but it may be difficult to evaluate what they say. Remember any information they give you may be biased since they view you either as a potential customer or competitor. It is usually safer to do your own observing and draw the appropriate conclusions. The very best method of gathering information for your new greenhouse is to work for someone else. All the reading and observing in the world is no substitute for on-the-job training. Besides, you get paid for working. Any amount of time you can get working in the trade would be helpful but it is best to try to complete a full year. You can gather very erroneous impressions if you know only what happens at one particular season. Working for the best establishments will teach you how a good business is operated, but, even if the greenhouse or plant store is not particularly well run, you can still pick up a great deal of information. An added bonus in working for someone else is that you will probably be able to make a more knowledgeable decision as to whether you really want to enter the plant business.

TRADE ORGANIZATIONS

Depending on where you live, there may be several horticultural trade organizations which could be sources of information. The best way to get in touch with such organizations is to inquire at the nearest horticultural supply firm. Trade organizations can vary from mostly social clubs to those that generate a good deal of useful information for their members. Generally, those sections of the country which have a large, well established horticultural trade will have much more highly developed organizations. There are several national trade organizations which distribute information, sponsor trade fairs, lobby law makers, and generally promote the industry.

Seed houses and horticultural supply firms with nation wide distribution systems have become, to some extent, trade organizations. Many publish monthly newsletters which contain new technical developments, market reports, new variety releases, etc. Most large firms have technical aid services to growers. Greenhouse and field trials are performed with new varieties by several seed houses; growers may visit these trial plantings if they happen to be in the area. The seed and supply catalogs offered are indispensable to anyone who contemplates entering the greenhouse business. You will want copies from several firms because each one contains a little different information.

SOURCES OF SUPPLY

In addition to gathering general information from suppliers, you will want to find out just what materials and services are available to you and at what cost. If you look in the yellow pages of the telephone directory under wholesale greenhouses, florists, or nursery supplies, you will find any suppliers in your area. Most supply and seed houses advertise in national trade publications and will be happy to answer your inquiries. Eventually you may find it is more economical to buy certain merchandise from more specialized smaller companies, so do not overlook sending for all types of catalogs and price lists.

PUBLIC AGENCIES AND FINANCIAL INSTITUTIONS

Most state universities have an extension horticulturist who can be very helpful if you have specific questions. Specialists in the various areas of horticulture may also be available. Soil and tissue analysis laboratories maintained by your state may be utilized free or at very little charge. In order to find what technical services are available in your area, contact the local county agent's office.

The Small Business Administration will be a source of information concerning financing; even if you don't require financial aid, this agency can help answer questions about business management. Many helpful publications are available free from the Small Business Administration. A great deal of free financial advice is also available at local banks. The officers of banks can often give important clues as to the business climate in your area. They will be aware many times of future developments in the community which could benefit or harm your new business.

Chambers of Commerce will have information about local conditions which could be useful. They are usually able to provide data concerning population, marketing studies, and per capita income, all of which can be helpful in making sales projections. Weather will be an important influence on your business and you need to obtain a complete historical weather summary from the local United States weather bureau. These publications are very detailed and, if studied precisely, can provide a great deal of useful information.

GOVERNMENTAL REGULATIONS

It is your responsibility to become aware of the various governmental regulations which will affect your business. Most federal laws which must be complied with are explained in publications issued by the Internal Revenue Service and Small Business Administration. In some cases you would be affected by laws administered by the Environmental Protection Agency and Occupational Safety and Health Act.

State laws will usually cover such things as transportation of plants across state lines, inspection of horticultural products, licensing to sell, licensing for insecticide application, and collecting state sales and use taxes. Cities will sometimes have tax regulations which must be dealt with. These often are administered jointly by the state and city. Zoning ordinances of your municipality must be thoroughly investigated before you choose a business location. If you are building or adding to facilities, you must check the local building codes. Failure to comply with zoning and building codes can become a nightmare if you have already committed capital to a certain location. Many cities will require a small fee to conduct business within their boundaries. This fee is generally supported by local merchants since it may discourage itinerant street corner salesmen.

FORMAL EDUCATION

Most state universities offer a full program of instruction in horticulture. There are also a number of technical and vocational schools throughout the country which have horticultural departments. Formal instruction can certainly help in becoming a success; you must, however, decide if there are enough practical benefits to warrant spending the time and money to attend classes. My experience is that very few schools adequately structure their programs to the needs of the work-a-day business world and commercial success is more dependent on practical experience than formal education. If classes are conveniently available, you should certainly take advantage of them but do not feel left out if you cannot attend.

HOW MUCH IS ENOUGH?

If you have followed the outline presented in this chapter, you should be adequately prepared to begin a greenhouse business and make a success of it. You must decide when the time has come to end the information gathering stage and actively begin business. The only counsel I can give is to strike a healthy balance between study and action. I started my own greenhouse operation with much less preparation than I have suggested to you. An effort to educate one's self in the initial stages will reduce the number of mistakes made in the future; don't be too timid, however, to jump in and begin business after a reasonable job of preparation. There is no way to avoid all possible pitfalls.

CHAPTER 4

PREPARE A PLAN

The research material collected should now be organized into a logical, condensed format. Once you have analyzed the information, you will be ready to make a detailed plan for your new business. Everything possible should be mapped out in advance. Well thought out plans will save money and time later.

You should now have a general idea of the size, organization, and area of specialization your proposed horticultural business will exhibit. A helpful method of making sure the business will fit your needs and resources is to draw up a list of pros and cons which your concept of the future business would possess. The objective is to devise a business plan which has very few negative attributes. A well designed business should coincide with the resources available and your long term goals. Major national economic and horticultural trade trends must be pointing the same direction as the business strategy. There is money to be made in all economic conditions but not by using a single strategy for all conditions. All businesses change and the ability to do so without disruption is one attribute of a well thought out plan.

A basic prerequisite for developing financial or greenhouse growing plans is to arrive at a marketing strategy. You can achieve goals more quickly if you have a good idea of how much material is to be sold, to whom, and at what price. This information will be of help in preparing a financial picture in which revenues, expenses, and profits are projected. Banks and other lenders will require you to present such a financial statement before they consider business loans or lines of credit. When preparing financial projections, always plan to have a contingency fund available for miscalculations and emergencies. Even if credit is not required, charge accounts with distant suppliers will be handy because it is much easier to be billed monthly than to make a cash transaction at each purchase. Suppliers will be hesitant to grant credit unless you have good banking relationships.

Greenhouse trade publications periodically report current market statistics which will help in devising a strategy. You will need to use a good deal of common sense and analytical skill to fill in and around these published data since they are very rarely complete and will almost never pertain to the immediate market area. Your banker or the Small Business Administration should have outlines of how to prepare financial statements. After devising market and financial plans, you can decide what types and quantities of crops to grow. Never grow a crop unless you have drawn a definite market plan beforehand. You should know what the date of sale is, how many you will sell, what price you will charge, and how much profit you can expect from a crop before a seed is sown. These plans may not always work exactly but they do give definite goals to work toward and will require that you collect information about the crop rather than just planting it because it sounds good.

Doing a good deal of research on a crop before attempting to grow it will eliminate many errors and increase profits. When estimating the date a particular crop will be ready for sale, be sure to adjust the published timetable to the local climate and make certain an adequate labor force will be available to complete the crop plans. It makes no sense to grow crops half way to maturity and then have no one to care for them the rest of the way. Dependable suppliers are critical to the production of high quality crops on schedule and you should choose them carefully. Record keeping is a part of every business; unfortunately, many people for years keep records that are next to worthless. Think carefully about what data is essential to preserve, then record no more or less than you have decided upon.

After completing an outline of your business plan and checking it carefully for feasibility, make certain you are capable and willing to follow it through. Also prepare a timetable of action and try to stick as closely as possible to it. Having a definite timetable usually makes a person less likely to postpone tasks that should be undertaken. The preceding pages have had little to do with actually growing plants and, to some people, most of the material may seem self-evident. I feel, however, it has been important to start out readers with a look at their motives and needs and to indicate that a successful plant business does not just happen by accident. You should do a great deal of careful thought and preparation before risking labor and money. Let us now turn our attention to the technical information which is needed to operate a greenhouse business.

CHAPTER 5
HOW PLANTS GROW

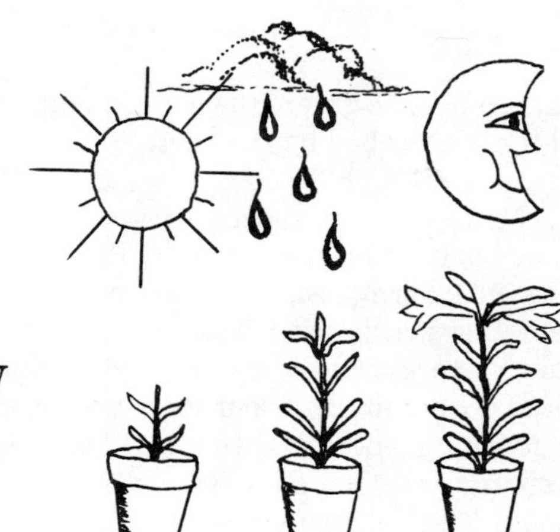

Anyone proposing to grow plants for profit should have a rudimentary knowledge of the principles underlying plant growth and development. In very simple terms, green plants are factories which process the physical energy of light into chemical energy stored in the millions of molecules making up various plant parts. Light is the energy source used by these factories but other materials and conditions are needed for the energy transfer to be completed. "Photosynthesis" is the technical term given to the chemical reaction taking place. In addition to light, carbon dioxide, oxygen, water, various mineral elements, and a proper temperature are essential for plant growth. A detailed presentation on each of these factors is beyond the scope of this chapter but brief statements concerning their functions will be given.

LIGHT - CARBON DIOXIDE - OXYGEN

Photosynthesis is a series of reactions in which light energy is used to split water (H_2O) molecules. Breaking the chemical bonds between Hydrogen (H) and Oxygen (O) releases energy which is usable in the reduction of carbon dioxide (CO_2) to sugars. Reduction means the addition of H molecules to CO_2 in the appropriate number for the formation of sugar ($C_6H_{12}O_6$). A schematic representation of the reaction is as follows:

$$6\,CO_2 + 6\,H_2O \xrightarrow[\text{chlorophyll pigment}]{\text{light energy}} C_6H_{12}O_6 + 6\,O_2$$

$$\text{carbon dioxide} + \text{water} \rightarrow \text{sugar} + \text{oxygen}$$

You must realize that this is merely a summary equation of the basic energy transfer; there are many chemical reactions actually taking place.

Carbon dioxide enters the leaf through small openings called stomates and water is absorbed by the roots.

Numerous substances present in plants are manufactured from the basic building blocks of sugar. Proteins, fats, chlorophyll (photosynthetic pigment), hormones, and vitamins are some of the more commonly known molecules synthesized. The activity of building these various molecules requires energy which is liberated during respiration, a process whereby foods are oxidized or "burned" in a somewhat analogous fashion to the use of foods for energy in animals. The energy of respiration is also used in such processes as cell division, absorption of minerals, and translocation of foods. The schematic representation of the respiration reaction is as follows:

$$C_6H_{12}O_6 \; + \; 6\,O_2 \longrightarrow 6\,CO_2 \; + \; 6\,H_2O \; + \; \text{energy}$$
$$\text{sugar} \qquad \text{oxygen} \qquad\quad \text{carbon dioxide} \qquad \text{water}$$

Again, I must emphasize that this is a simple picture of a very complex process. Oxygen is required in the reaction much as it is for a fire to burn.

At the risk of offending more precise scientific minds, I will summarize the energy relationships of plants in what I feel is a basically correct but highly simplified statement. Light energy is used to produce a photochemical reaction (photosynthesis), involving water and carbon dioxide, which converts transitory light energy into a more stable and usable energy storage packet, sugar. Energy contained in sugar remains locked up until called for to produce other molecules such as proteins or to do some form of work such as absorbing minerals. The energy of sugar is released in a chemical reaction (respiration) which is somewhat similar to the burning of fuels and is basically the reverse process of photosynthesis except that light and chlorophyll pigments are not required.

MINERAL ELEMENTS

As I mentioned, molecules other than sugars are found in plants. Carbon, hydrogen, and oxygen are the elements found in greatest abundance in these organic molecules, but many contain other elements. I term these additional ingredients mineral elements since they are generally taken up by the roots from the soil or substrate. The number of distinct molecular configurations containing these mineral elements is in the hundreds but we will limit our discussion of each mineral to prominent examples of how it is utilized.

NITROGEN (N)—Nitrogen is utilized in fairly large quantities by plants and crop yields are closely related to an adequate supply. Nitrogen is necessary for the production of proteins, chlorophyll, amino acids, and nucleic acids. When nitrogen is deficient, chlorophyll content decreases and plants will progress from light green to yellow; symptoms will appear first on older leaves. Large supplies of nitrogen result in plants that are very lush and tender and may cause delays in flowering and weak stems.

PHOSPHORUS (P)—Phosphorous needs of plants are not large in comparison to nitrogen and potassium but it is very important in plant growth. High energy phosphate compounds are basic to energy transformation within plant cells. Phosphorous promotes flowering and stiffer stems, and helps balance large nitrogen applications. It is found in particularly high concentrations in seeds. Deficiencies of phosphorous translate first into stunted growth; plant parts will eventually take on a purplish hue.

POTASSIUM (K)—Potassium is not known to be a part of any molecules in plant cells but it is extremely important in many of the metabolic processes taking place. Potassium is necessary for protein and carbohydrate synthesis and carbohydrate movement. A symptom of deficiency is the presence of necrotic (dead) spots on the edges of older leaves.

CALCIUM (Ca)—Calcium is especially important in the compounds forming cell walls and is necessary for proper development of the growing tip and roots.

SULFUR (S)—Sulfur is needed for the formation of some enzymes and vitamins in the plant.

MAGNESIUM (Mg)—Magnesium is at the center of chlorophyll molecules and, therefore, is obviously indispensable to green plants.

Several mineral elements are required by plants in minute quantities and, as such, are termed trace minerals. Iron (Fe), manganese (Mn), boron (B), copper (Cu), zinc (Zn), molybdenum (Mo), and chlorine (Cl) are the known trace elements. They are all essential for normal plant growth. The small quantities required for growth may be illustrated by chlorine which, despite years of investigation into plant nutrition, was found to be essential for plant growth only in 1954. Iron is required in the largest amounts and young leaves near the growing tip will exhibit a chlorotic yellowing between the veins if it is deficient.

WATER

Water has been shown previously to be essential for plants as a source of hydrogen and oxygen and also as a source of energy when the molecule is split. The importance of water for plants does not end here. Water serves as a universal solvent for chemical compounds, as a reagent for chemical reactions, and to maintain the turgor pressure of plant cells, which prevents wilting. Water comprises 80-90% of the fresh weight of most plants. The predominance of water in plant tissue certainly indicates the central role it plays in influencing many aspects of plant growth.

TEMPERATURE

A fundamental characteristic of chemical reactions is that they accelerate as temperatures rise. Within certain life threatening extremes of temperature, plants will normally make more rapid growth as temperatures increase. The upper and lower temperature limits beyond which plants cannot survive will vary with the species and with the particular stage of life. Winter dormant plants can survive temperatures well below the freezing point but if the same plant were subjected to frost while actively growing in summer it would quickly die. Most plant species make optimum growth at temperatures below 100° F, but certain algae (primitive photosynthetic plants) are quite at home in hot springs where temperatures may reach 200° F. Providing optimum temperatures for growth is a primary responsibility of the grower.

INTEGRATION OF PLANT REQUIREMENTS

All the various factors which have been mentioned as essential for plant growth must be present in the proper proportions. Each factor is inter-related with all other factors and the absence of only one will render the remaining ones impotent. If all factors are present within an acceptable range, the chemical reactions take place and a multitude of different molecules are manufactured. These molecules arrange themselves in an orderly fashion into the tissues which make up various plant parts and these parts will be integrated into what we know as a complete plant.

GENETIC INFLUENCE AND REPRODUCTIVE CYCLES

The method by which predetermined reactions are completed and molecules and plant parts are arranged in a harmonious fashion is governed by the particular genetic makeup of the species and individual. Tiny bits of nucleoproteins known as "genes" are the means by which the information necessary to program all the life processes of plants is transmitted from one generation to the next. These genes are information particles which direct the growth and development of plants. It is very important to recognize the central role genetic inheritance plays in the production of high quality plants and flowers. Careful provision for all the required factors by a greenhouse owner cannot turn a thistle into a rose. One must select the proper variety for the purpose in order to attain peak production.

Manipulation of the essential requirements of plants may not only speed up or slow down growth but can also dramatically alter the normal development pattern prescribed by the genes. It is thus apparent that neither environmental factors nor inheritance is predominant, but that the quality of a plant will depend upon each being given proper consideration.

The majority of green plants reproduce sexually in much the same manner as higher animals. There are minor differences, especially in structural form, but the essential process is comparable. Plants also reproduce asexually which is something higher animals are incapable of doing. The genetic makeup of offspring is affected dramatically depending on whether they were produced sexually or asexually, even though they may all come from the same mother plant. Progeny resulting from sexual reproduction have 50% of their genetic heritage from the father and 50% from the mother. Asexually reproduced offspring obtain 100% of their genetic makeup from the mother. Sexually reproduced populations are variable in their characteristics while asexually reproduced individuals of a population are exactly alike genetically. The method of reproduction is extremely important to greenhouse growers from a practical standpoint. It should be noted that under certain breeding conditions, such as self-pollinating plants or inbreeding populations, sexually reproduced plants can approximate the uniformity found in asexually reproduced populations. Table 3 is a simple diagram of a higher plant life cycle.

The preceding discussion has dealt only with some of the major concepts which are essential for a basic understanding of how plants grow. Reference to a college level botany text will satisfy the more inquisitive reader. Our purpose in this book is to concentrate on the more practical aspects of plant growth and development. A sound theoretical knowledge of plants cannot but help a greenhouse operator but is certainly not essential for success.

Table 3
Sexual and asexual life cycles of plants.

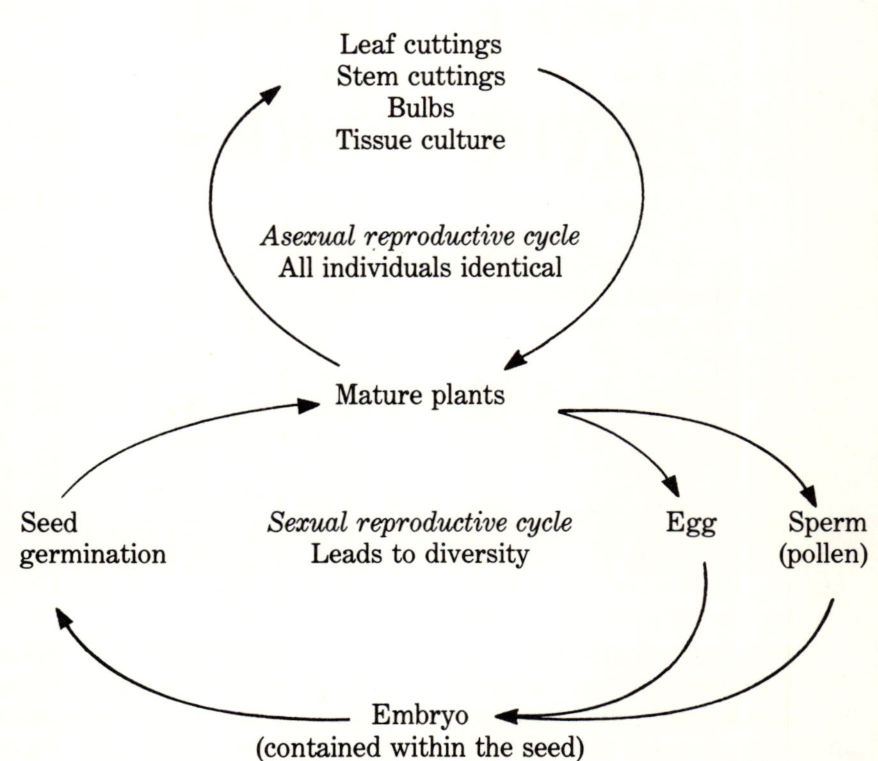

CHAPTER 6

GREENHOUSE STRUCTURES

The purpose of a greenhouse or cold frame is to provide conditions in which the life processes of plants can be carried on at the particular time desired. Architectural forms of greenhouses are unimportant as long as they accomplish their purpose in a suitable fashion. The following discussion will deal mainly with factors which must be controlled and methods of accomplishing this rather than with specific architectural details. Any greenhouse manufacturing company will supply prospective customers with construction plans of their models. They will also have information and prices for all the accessories. Many manufacturing companies have engineers available to design complete structures; this service is usually free.

If one understands how a plant grows, it should come as no surprise that the most important considerations in greenhouse construction are to provide adequate light and a proper temperature for economical culture of crops. An adequate exchange of air is also a primary consideration but normally this is easily accomplished and can be taken care of without much special design. All commercial greenhouses are a compromise between being the very best for plant growth and being economical. There is a point beyond which it does not pay to provide the ultimate in growing conditions. One important factor which must be taken into account when building a greenhouse is adequate space for workers to care for plants.

Before making any decisions about greenhouse construction, one should have a firm idea of the crops to be specialized in and at what times of the year they will be grown. It makes no sense to design greenhouses to withstand $-40°$ F if they will only be used in the late spring when temperatures never drop below $25°$ F. Provisions for heating are expensive and heat sources should be sized carefully to the particular purpose of each greenhouse.

Greenhouses may be simple structures without heating or cooling or they can be very complex with all environmental factors determined by computers. The more sophisticated operations are generally those whose owner is committed to servicing a wholesale market over a period of years. More primitive greenhouses are usually those whose owner is new to the business or is unwilling to commit capital to long term ventures. It is common in the trade to hear these extremes termed high investment and low investment construction. The type of greenhouse constructed will depend partly on how much money is available but it should also be determined by the length of time and at what seasons one plans to be in business. There is no need to construct greenhouses which will last fifty years if a person wishes to retire within ten years. Being sure of business objectives is quite important before deciding what type of greenhouse to build.

A thorough knowledge of local weather extremes is necessary before selecting a greenhouse design. Structures must be equipped for the extreme weather likely to be encountered rather than for normal conditions. There are three primary weather factors which should be considered: minimum yearly temperature, maximum likely wind speeds, and maximum snowload. If the locality has very low light intensities during growing seasons, it may be necessary to focus attention on construction details which will maximize light transmission. Low winter light can be an extreme problem in the Pacific Northwest.

GREENHOUSE COVERING MATERIALS

The material used to cover a greenhouse is, in many cases, the only thing standing between the grower and disaster. The skin of a greenhouse is quite vulnerable because it must be made of relatively flimsy, transparent material in order for light to be admitted in sufficient quality and quantity. Other factors may affect decisions somewhat, but a greenhouse cover should be chosen primarily on the basis of crop safety, light transmission, and economy.

There are three main types of covering materials utilized for greenhouses: glass, plastic films, and semirigid fiber glass or plastic panels. Glass was used almost exclusively until the 1950's when fiberglass panels became available. Fiberglass enjoyed a period, before the steep rise in energy prices, when it became the chief covering material. After the energy crunch, new construction was heavily slanted toward double layer inflated polyethylene houses because they are more energy efficient.

The need for energy efficient greenhouses which are covered with more lasting materials than polyethylene film has led to adaptations where glass and fiberglass houses are provided with movable curtains or exterior polyethylene shields. Another material introduced in this vein is double-faced plastic sheeting with air spaces between the layers.

Glass is still used in construction of new greenhouses. It is the most permanent covering available, unless damaged by hail, and retains its light transmission capabilities longer than any other material. The only logical situation where glass should be used is if a structure is to be used more than twenty-five years or if appearance is a critical factor. Glass is expensive to install and maintain. Greenhouse glass should be "double strength quality grade 'B'." Larger panes are more resistant to hail damage than smaller ones and square panes will withstand more abuse than rectangular ones. A 20 inch x 20 inch light is often used because it is large enough to withstand damage but small enough to handle with ease when installing.

When a relatively permanent covering is required, fiberglass has been the most frequent choice of growers for almost two decades. When compared to glass, it is more economical, requires less maintenance, and is more energy efficient. The biggest drawback of fiberglass has been the loss of light transmission over time. Improvements in manufacturing techniques and protection from surface degradation by special coating compounds has increased the life of fiberglass but it still cannot compete with glass in this respect. A word of caution . . . many types of fiberglass sold at retail outlets are low grade and unsuitable for greenhouse construction. Panels should be purchased from reputable greenhouse supply firms and even then specifications and guarantees must be carefully analyzed. Brand names are not sufficient proof of quality since most companies manufacture several grades of material.

Fiberglass will prevent the loss of crops from all but the most violent hailstorms. Light transmission properties are, however, seriously impaired by hail damage and the covering must often be replaced even though there are no actual holes in it. Although fiberglass transmits somewhat less light than glass, many growers believe it grows better crops, at least initially, because light is diffused as it enters and is more evenly distributed to all sections of a house.

Double-faced plastic sheeting with air spaces between the layers has been introduced recently. The chief advantage of these materials is the insulation provided and resultant savings in heating costs. These plastic panels are relatively expensive and their ability to withstand degradation with age has not been well documented in the field over many years.

Plastic film has been used for quite some time as a greenhouse covering but it was not until the 1970's that its use became widespread. The development of stronger, longer lasting films, improvements in fastening systems, and the design of greenhouse frames to accept film are some of the technical advances which led to the popularity of polyethylene houses. The increasing importance of spring bedding plants led growers to seek a greenhouse inexpensive enough to be used only for one or two spring crops. Polyethylene had not been in widespread use for long before the energy crisis arrived; at that time it became common to install two layers of plastic and inflate the airspace between them with small blower fans. This innovation saved 30-40% on fuel costs and many growers began to operate double layer plastic houses through the winter months.

I feel poly greenhouses are the logical choice for growers who want low investment houses. If you choose and install materials carefully, there is no reason to be apprehensive about growing through the winter in them. I live in Wyoming where winter winds are extremely fierce and as yet I have not had a cover blown off a house. I chose polyethylene as a cover because it is inexpensive, will protect crops from hail damage, saves fuel when used as a double layer, and, if replaced every two to three years, will provide excellent light transmission throughout the life of a structure. The only disadvantage that I can see with plastic film is the near impossibility of recovering a large house unless winds are very calm. Condensation in the ceiling can be a problem at times but is normally nothing more than an inconvenience.

If polyethylene is to be used for more than a few months, it must be manufactured with ultraviolet inhibitors added; this process slows down material degradation dramatically. I have noticed that certain tapes which I have used to cover rough spots on the frame can cause the plastic to become brittle faster. Evidently this is caused by the particular chemicals used to make the tape since other brands of tape the same color do not cause this problem. Films on the market are usually rated for two to three years of use but I have used them for up to four years in a very sunny, windy climate.

GREENHOUSE HEATING SYSTEMS

A heating system is composed of two essential parts: the heat generation component and the heat distribution portion. The most common sources of heat are hot water or steam boilers and unit heaters. The configuration and fuel sources of heat generators is limited only by the imagination. Solar heat is used in many spring crop greenhouses where the temperature is maintained only slightly above freezing.

Hot water and steam boilers are more commonly used in larger greenhouses but there are small boilers available. The heat from steam or hot water is usually distributed throughout the greenhouse by a system of metal pipes located around the perimeter of the house and under benches. Heat is transferred passively from the pipes to the surrounding air. Metal unit radiators are sometimes used as heat exchangers and will normally be equipped with a fan to aid in heat transfer and distribution. A new concept in heat distribution for hot water is the use of closely spaced, small diameter plastic hoses on bench tops. This system concentrates heat more in the immediate vicinity of plants and can be designed so that individual benches may be left unheated if they are empty. Boilers are not intrinsically more economical than unit heaters but because many of them burn coal, it often happens that they are cheaper to run than unit heaters which seldom have coal burning capability. Coal is normally the most economical fuel available. The high cost of installation and expensive heat exchange systems often offset the operating economies of coal boilers.

Unit heaters are most often fired by natural gas but can be operated with propane, fuel oil, or even coal and wood. The unit is a combination heat generator and exchanger. A fan or blower is usually attached to distribute heat away from the immediate vicinity. The self-contained nature of these units makes them especially useful for small greenhouses. Installation is simple and can be accomplished with no previous experience. Since a unit heater is located in the greenhouse, there are several safety precautions which should be observed. Always be sure heaters are properly vented and fuel lines do not leak. Even small amounts of flue gases or fuel vapors can damage crops. Observe the manufacturers' specifications for clearance from combustible materials when installing a heater. I have always made it a point to make sure the heat exchanger is fabricated from aluminum or stainless steel. Ordinary steel heat exchangers will rust out quickly in the humid greenhouse atmosphere. Pilot lights should be well protected by a series of shields to prevent their being blown out by cooling and air distribution fans. Fuel combustion requires oxygen. In relatively air tight polyethylene houses it is not uncommon for a heater to "flame out" when the oxygen supply is depleted. Normally the manufacturer's installation directions will specify how large an air opening must be provided for proper combustion.

It is extremely important to provide good air circulation in greenhouses, not only to distribute heat evenly but also to lessen the high humidity which can build up around plant surfaces when air is stagnant. Fans are the normal means of providing heat distribution. Careful placement is necessary to achieve the desired results. The distance a fan will throw air should be known and if more than one fan is used, they should be placed so that their air movements complement one another. The area directly under unit heaters is usually the coldest spot in a house and provision should be made to circulate heat under it. The best means of providing air circulation is to install a large diameter perforated plastic tube the length of a greenhouse. Air is blown into this tube and circulates out the perforations which can be placed in any desired pattern. Usually the tube is located overhead and the perforations direct air toward the sides of the greenhouse and slightly downwards. Heaters may be located to discharge warm air into these tubes.

In earlier years, unit heaters were almost universally installed overhead so that valuable floor space was not occupied and heaters were not subjected to the water and dirt present at floor level. Many units are now installed on the floor with the heat distribution ducts running underneath benches. This saves fuel because the warm air rises to heat plants rather than being circulated above plant level. An alternative arrangement is to place the heaters overhead and install ducts directing heated air to ground level. Care must be taken to assure the ducts are large enough to prevent heat backup into the heater.

Solar heat systems are normally restricted to those houses where crops will require little additional heat and the design is usually of a passive nature. Heat requirements of warm greenhouses are so large that the cost of a solar system to provide total heat would be prohibitive. A unit heater has been marketed recently which is said to direct heat via infrared rays to the plant surfaces, thus eliminating the need to heat large air masses. The cost is much greater than conventional unit heaters. I have no experience with these heaters and can neither recommend nor condemn, but it is usually best to invest your money in systems which are well proven.

Which ever heating system you may choose should be carefully sized to the greenhouse it will service. Too large a heating capacity is a waste of money and one that is too small will result in poor crops. The number of BTUs (British Thermal Units) needed to maintain a certain temperature is calculated by using an equation which takes into account the outside climatic conditions, area of exposed greenhouse surface, and type of construction materials. Firms which specialize in supplying greenhouse heating components can readily calculate your needs or supply data which will enable you to do it yourself.

I normally size heaters so they will maintain the desired crop temperature except on the very coldest nights expected. Crops will generally not be harmed if temperatures fall 15°-20° F below the optimum for a few nights. Heating systems should be designed to provide a 5-10% safety margin for calculation errors, etc. If at all possible, it is a good idea to provide heat from two units, either one of which is capable of maintaining the temperature on coldest nights above freezing. I always sleep better when I know if one heater breaks down there is another one which will prevent crop failure. Most modern heating systems rely on electricity to power fans and controls; this makes it essential to provide an emergency generator. Power failures are common; for that reason I would never recommend using electricity as a heat source. Backup generators to run air circulation fans and controls need not be very large, but, if they were to provide electricity for heat, the size and cost would escalate out of bounds.

Skyrocketing energy costs have led to a dramatic re-evaluation of how things are done in the greenhouse industry. Prior to 1973 fuel costs were a significant but not crucial cost of doing business. Many growers of marginally profitable crops have switched to more profitable crops or have gone out of business. Greenhouse construction has begun to emphasize energy conservation and a great deal of research is being done on methods of raising crops with less energy.

As I mentioned previously, one way to save 30-40% on fuel costs is to grow in inflated double-poly houses. Many growers who already have fiberglass or glass houses have taken to covering the outside with a layer of poly and inflating the air space between. Special fastener systems are sold for this job. Probably the best long term solution to high energy costs is to provide a movable system of insulation curtains within houses. Curtains are mechanically operated and drawn shut in the evening and opened in the morning. This method of fuel conservation has a high initial cost but admits more light to greenhouses than double cover techniques. Another advantage is an additional 10-20% fuel savings since curtains normally block off the upper one third of ceiling space. A similar effect is accomplished by utilizing inflatable banks of clear plastic tubes in the ceiling. When inflated, the tubes fit tight against one another, thus preventing the rise of warm air further into the ceiling. The presence of plastic tubes overhead limits light intensity and it is very difficult under most types of greenhouse construction to get a good heat seal. The main advantage of this method is the low initial cost. Growers should be aware that heat must be admitted to the outside greenhouse skin when heavy snow accumulations might cause the roof to collapse.

There are many other ways to save energy in the greenhouse but they are common sense applications such as closing up cracks and insulating any sidewall which does not admit light. I have not mentioned some methods of modifying the greenhouse skin which are in the developmental stages or have limited potential. When modifying the greenhouse structure to save fuel, one should always take note of the effect it might have on crop growth. Fuel economy at the expense of crop quality is no bargain.

One means of energy conservation everyone should practice is to select crops which will flourish at lower temperatures. In winter I try to emphasize flower crops which tolerate very cold temperatures and vice versa in summer. Of course, one cannot dictate what the market will accept but there is some latitude of choice. Research has indicated that it may be possible to lower the temperature each night for specified periods of time without affecting crop quality or timing. Many crops will tolerate colder temperatures at different stages of growth so that the grower need not maintain the higher temperatures during the entire crop cycle. It is the grower's responsibility to know the requirements of each crop and maintain the greenhouse temperature at the most economical level. Night temperatures seem to have a more pronounced effect on plants than day temperatures. When a temperature is quoted, it is commonly accepted to mean night temperature unless otherwise qualified. Daytime greenhouse temperatures should range from 5°-20° F above nighttime, the lower figure being for cloudy days and the higher for sunny conditions.

GREENHOUSE COOLING SYSTEMS

Most growers realize the need of adequate heating for crops but fail to attach the same importance to cooling systems. This is an especially common fault among inexperienced personnel. Even at northern United States latitudes, midwinter greenhouse temperatures will rise to unacceptable levels on a clear day unless some ventilation is provided. By mid spring the same greenhouse would be completely useless without a well designed cooling mechanism.

The traditional method of cooling when most houses were glass was to have vents at the roof apex, to allow rising warm air to escape. As summer approached and light intensity was not so critical, shade compounds would be applied to further reduce greenhouse temperatures. Additional vents were sometimes located in sidewalls, facilitating the entry of cool air. This system was generally adequate until the hottest months arrived, at which time crop quality suffered because greenhouse temperatures could not be lowered enough.

Today, most greenhouses are equipped with thermostatically controlled fans to evacuate warm air. This method, if properly sized, will reduce air temperatures 5°-10° F more than can be accomplished with vents relying on convection. Draft-free ventilation during the colder months can be accomplished with exhaust fans by attaching perforated polyethylene tubes to the fresh air inlets. The tube is suspended overhead by a wire support and runs the length of the greenhouse. When exhaust fans begin to run, a vacuum is created in the greenhouse and the tube inflates. Air is discharged into the greenhouse atmosphere through the perforations. The fan, tube, perforation, and inlet sizes should be carefully correlated and the entire system must be adequate for the greenhouse volume. It has been my experience that most growers fail to install large enough exhaust fans. It usually takes a summer of intolerable temperatures to convince neophytes of the importance of cooling. A system of fans should be designed so that air intake can vary from about 20% up to full load. This enables the grower to ventilate steadily on cool days without alternating rushes of cold air entering the house.

A basic principle of physics states that as water evaporates, heat is absorbed. It is not surprising then that water evaporation plays an important part in greenhouse cooling. The most common method of evaporating water is by installing large porous pads at the end of the greenhouse opposite exhaust fans. Water is circulated onto these pads when exhaust fans are running, causing rapid water evaporation as outside air is drawn through the pads. The addition of wet pads will permit a further 5°-10° F cooling of the greenhouse air as compared with fans alone. The degree of cooling will vary with outside relative humidity and light intensity. The biggest advantage of fan and pad cooling systems is that little or no shading is required, which usually results in improved crop quality. Fan and pad cooling also renders a greenhouse reasonably insect proof in the warmer months when insects can reach epidemic proportions outside. Correlating fan, pad, and water supply size is important in obtaining proper cooling. Most greenhouse manufacturers can supply a properly designed cooling system with any greenhouse ordered. Evaporative cooler units meant for mobile home service can be used in very small greenhouses; they are quite expensive for the amount of cooling received.

Another method of evaporating water to cool greenhouses is the high pressure mist system. It is used in greenhouses with vents or fans. Very fine mist is sprayed in the air above plants at pressures of 500 - 1000 pounds per square inch; most of the mist evaporates before reaching plant level. Temperatures comparable with fan and pad cooling are obtained but because of the difficulty in regulating water supply to prevent accumulations on floors and plants, mist systems are seldom used except in large ranges. Both types of evaporative cooling are more effective in areas where relative humidity is low; if incoming air is dry, more water evaporates and more cooling takes place.

Shading is an obvious method of reducing greenhouse temperatures, but it can result in decreased productivity due to reduced light intensity. Evaporative cooling permits the grower to vary the temperature independently of light. Shade compounds are readily available as a liquid concentrate which is diluted with water and sprayed on. A homemade shade can be prepared by diluting one part latex paint with five to ten parts water. Shading must normally be removed in the fall. It is quite difficult to adequately clean shade compounds from fiberglass and plastic and for this reason I would not recommend their use on these coverings unless some shade is acceptable in winter time. Shade compounds should always be white since this color reflects a great deal more sunlight than any other.

On small greenhouses, outside lath shading made from bamboo, wood, or aluminum is sometimes used. This permits some flexibility in the amount of light admitted. The cost is much higher than for shading compounds and strong winds may cause damage to both greenhouses and lath. Cloth shades of saran or cheesecloth used inside the greenhouse may reduce the temperature of plant parts and greenhouse fixtures but do not significantly alter the air temperature. Inside shading does not reduce the amount of radiant energy which penetrates the greenhouse covering.

BASIC GREENHOUSE
CONSTRUCTION CONSIDERATIONS

The choice of a greenhouse site will depend on what resources are available, the nature of the business, and several construction related factors. Wholesale greenhouses need not be located on a prime traffic site but should be easily reached from nearby main roads. Retail sales will be highly correlated with visibility, nearness to potential customers, desirability of surrounding neighbors, and ease of access and parking. The property must be well drained to prevent mud and water buildup and there should be no large trees or buildings which will shade the greenhouses. External light sources such as street lights, car headlights, and sign lighting should be evaluated carefully. Extraneous light can seriously upset flowering schedules. Level ground will permit easier construction and facilitate the movement of materials and people when the greenhouse is in production. An adequate supply of high quality water which is free of toxic materials and relatively low in soluble salts must be available. In some areas of the country attention may need to be focused on potential pollution problems. Higher wind speeds significantly increase the heating load of greenhouses; it is helpful if there are nearby natural or man-made wind barriers.

Because the site a grower chooses will be a significant part of his or her life, it should be evaluated very carefully. If a greenhouse is planned on land adjacent to the grower's home, the site should be reasonably suitable for this purpose. It is handy if a grower can live and work on the same property. About 300 hours a year would be consumed in transit if it takes the average worker one hour each day going to and from work. At $10 per hour, this is a waste of $3000, not counting vehicle use.

Whether growers choose to buy manufactured greenhouses or construct their own, there are many details which should be planned in advance. I will list some of the more important construction points which can save time and money later on.

1. If the site is at a latitude higher than 35°N and the greenhouse will be used in winter, it should be oriented longitudinally from east to west. Greenhouses with more light admitting area on one side than the other should have that side facing south. Both of these orientations provide more winter light and in general, steeper roof slopes will do the same.

2. Roof slopes of less than 25° do not allow snow to slide off readily and inside condensation will drip on plants rather than run to the sidewall.

3. Greenhouse roof beams or trusses should be engineered to support extreme local snow loads plus the anticipated load of wet hanging baskets.

4. Extremely small greenhouses are difficult to heat and cool evenly. If possible, have a floor area of at least 500 square feet.

5. Endwalls, doors, utility service, and venting are major expenses in greenhouse construction; it is usually less costly per square foot to build larger and longer greenhouses.

6. Efficient material and personnel movement should be designed into the greenhouse structure. Head space and aisle space must be adequate for free movement at a fast space.

7. The ability to add to facilities without major disruption should be planned in advance.

8. All structural members must be of aluminum, galvanized steel, or properly painted or treated lumber. The constant presence of water and the high humidity of greenhouses accelerates corrosion of metals and decay of wood.

9. Use the very highest quality paint possible; re-painting in a high-humidity greenhouse is extremely difficult and paint fumes can be damaging to crops.

10. Never use pentachlorophenol or creosote as greenhouse wood preservatives. The fumes are deadly to plants and may last for years. An acceptable wood preservative should contain copper naphthenate; one widely distributed brand is named Cuprinol.

11. An efficient work area should be provided and it must be easily accessible to all growing areas. If one plans to retail plants, customer comfort must be considered. People buying plants do not appreciate muddy walkways and clothes catching snags.

12. Air inlets must be provided for fuel combustion, especially in polyethylene houses. Heaters and boilers should be vented according to specifications and clearance from combustible materials must be observed.

13. Ventilation systems should have the ability to operate at several levels of capacity.

14. If possible, heat should be distributed near ground level so that it rises to the plants.

15. Greenhouse covering materials should be purchased from reputable supply firms.

16. Benching arrangements for plants should utilize every available square foot of space but still accommodate easy movement by workers. Benches must be at a height which workers find comfortable for working on plants.

17. Insects eventually become a problem in any greenhouse. Do not attach a greenhouse to your home. This arrangement makes it very dangerous to apply poisons for pest control.

18. Once established, weeds are difficult to eradicate from greenhouses. During construction, try to avoid bringing soil or materials onto the site if they have been located in a weed patch.

19. An alarm system to warn of power outages and temperature problems in the greenhouse after working hours should be installed.

There are several books where greenhouse construction details and plans are presented. Most helpful are the catalogs and technical bulletins published by greenhouse manufacturers. With some digging you will be able to plan heating and cooling systems for yourself. Do not blindly accept the plans a salesman presents to you. Evaluate them critically and don't be afraid to question aspects which do not satisfy your common sense. You are the one who will live with mistakes for years to come, not the salesman.

CHAPTER 7
PLANT PROPAGATION

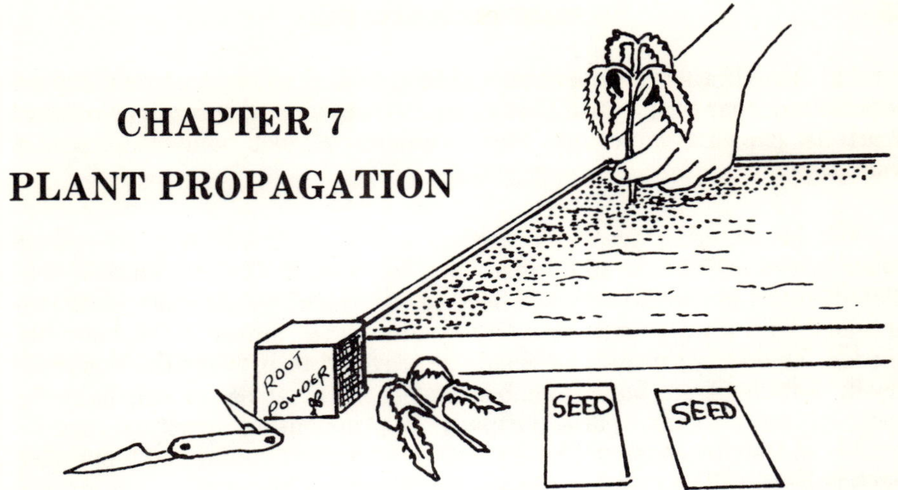

The success of every crop depends upon a grower's proficiency at producing a new population of plants from the previous generation. Propagation of new plants is generally more difficult than finishing a crop once it is well established. Because of this, a great deal of propagation is left to greenhouse firms which specialize in this particular aspect of horticulture. Young plant production requires skilled labor and carefully controlled environmental conditions. With a little effort, one can become an acceptable propagator of all but the most difficult plants. The initial stages of plant growth are often the most profitable and growers who can provide the required conditions should propagate all their own plants possible. The purchase of too many seedlings and cuttings can erode potential greenhouse profits. If your greenhouse location is away from major transportation arteries, you may have to learn propagation since minimum shipments required by suppliers may be too large for your needs or there may not be adequate transport to ship plants safely.

As mentioned previously, plants possess two very different means of propagating themselves: sexual and asexual reproduction. Both of these methods require basically the same environmental conditions and careful handling to be successful. Propagating beds or structures should normally be heated to 70°-80° F, preferably with the heat source located underneath the surface on which cuttings or seeds will be placed. Each plant species has its own temperature preferences and a few will not do well under this temperature regime. Inexpensive propagation areas may be made by laying thermostatically controlled heating cable in a bench at three to four inch centers and covering two inches deep with clean sand. Ready made heating mats are available for the same purpose and require no sand layer. Another method is to heat a small reservoir of water with either a standard home water heater or a portable tank heater and then pump warm water through plastic tubing underneath a sand bed. One must control rodent populations near propagating areas for two reasons: they cause electrical shorts by chewing cables and they can destroy much valuable seed in a short time.

If a propagating area is located in a shaded, humid tropical foliage house, there may be no additional work to do on it. If it is in a well ventilated, sunny house the area will need to be covered with a shade cloth and provided with a water mist system to maintain the almost 100% humidity needed for good propagation. Shade is provided to prevent the sun from drying out the area, but remember that there must be enough light for photosynthesis to take place normally. A propagation structure may be erected quickly by constructing a plastic covered hut containing a portable electric heater. The cost for heating these huts is high and temperatures may rise to unacceptable levels speedily on a sunny spring day. Opening the sides to prevent high temperatures allows drying out unless a mist system is installed. These huts are particularly useful for winter and early spring and when located in a house which is shaded.

Any of the different means of maintaining proper temperature and humidity can be employed in areas other than a greenhouse, but sufficient light must be provided artificially. Most people fail to provide enough light intensity and young plants turn out tall and spindly. Light fixtures must be those manufactured for growing plants; otherwise the proper wavelengths of light energy are not present for good growth. An advantage of this set up is that growth can be speeded by providing a twenty-four hour day. It is also easier to maintain a constant temperature than it is in a greenhouse.

The medium or substrate which young plants are propagated in must be loose and porous. A porous medium allows sufficient oxygen exchange to promote root growth. Root growth depends upon energy from respiration, which requires the presence of oxygen. Seedlings and cuttings can be removed from the medium with less damage if it is loose and fluffy. The container in which a propagation mixture is placed must be well drained to avoid standing water. Excess water prevents oxygen from reaching the root zone. Propagation media should be lightly fertilized. Two formulas for propagation which I use extensively are presented in Table 4.

When mixing either of these formulas, the potassium nitrate should be dissolved in five gallons of water and distributed evenly throughout the mix. Sufficient water is added to moisten the media thoroughly but not enough to cause large lumps to appear when wet particles start sticking together. The media can be stored in black, heavy duty trash bags in a cool shaded area for extended periods without appreciable chemical change. No

Table 4
Media used by the author for propagation.

Formula #1 For cuttings and coarse seed	8 cubic feet compressed sphagnum peat 3 cubic feet perlite fine grind (coarser than 8 mesh but finer than 6 mesh) $4\frac{1}{2}$ ounces potassium nitrate (KNO_3) 4 pounds ground limestone ($CaCO_3$) 10 ounces triple superphosphate or 25 ounces single superphosphate
Formula #2 For fine seed (petunias, begonias, portulaca, gloxinia, etc.)	Same ingredients as formula #1 except 3 cubic feet of fine vermiculite is substituted for the perlite

additional fertilizer should be applied unless plants are in the medium for extended periods or the variety of plant is a conspicuous fertilizer lover.

Successful propagation depends, to a large degree, upon constant cleanliness. Young plants, like human infants, are susceptible to numerous diseases and pests. Completely sterile conditions are impossible to maintain but one can make sure strict housekeeping rules are enforced. Sphagnum peat and the other ingredients of my mixtures are almost disease free and, if handled carefully to prevent contamination, will allow good success without sterilization. Most greenhouses which specialize in propagation find that media sterilization is economical if it can be done in large quantities.

Numerous propagating media on the market are clean and will do a nice job. The cost is generally much higher than that of homemade formulas. Many companies sell mixes similar to the ones just detailed. Another popular medium for starting new plants is a compressed peat pellet which swells when moistened; cuttings or seeds are then inserted. These pellets grow very nice plants but are expensive in comparison to loose mix. Recently, many propagators have started using foam blocks for rooting cuttings. These blocks do a good job of rooting and are inexpensive but, in my opinion, plants suffer more transplant shock than with other methods. Table 5 sums up the basic requirements for successful propagation. Additional details concerning propagation by sexual and asexual means follow.

Table 5
Basics of successful propagation.

A. Porous, disease free, lightly fertilized medium.	E. Control mice and plant pests.
B. Sufficient moisture at all times but never an excess.	F. Seeds and cuttings not planted too deep. Air is essential.
C. Temperature 70°-80° F. Some plants may like it cooler; check requirements.	G. Adequate light for photosynthesis.
D. Adequate skilled help to carry out sufficiently.	H. After establishment, move cuttings or seedlings to normal growing area for hardening period.

Above all—have a definite plan; propagation should be scheduled months in advance.

ASEXUAL OR VEGETATIVE REPRODUCTION

Asexual reproduction is accomplished by means of cuttings, bulbs, corms, tubers, and tissue culture. Some species are vegetatively propagated because plants do not come true from seed or, in some cases, because the seed is too expensive. Normally, adult plants can be reproduced more quickly by vegetative means than from seed. Each plant reproduced vegetatively has the same genetic make up as the mother plant and very uniform crops are the result.

Cuttings are usually taken from stem tissue but occasionally, some plants—such as certain begonias, peperomias, African violets, and others—will root more economically by means of leaf cuttings. Stem tip cuttings are used most commonly for a number of reasons. In rapidly growing plants, the stem tip may outrun viral and bacterial diseases present in older tissue. Stem tips often root faster and more uniformly, resulting in faster, more evenly developed crops. When tip cuttings are not plentiful enough, cuttings from older tissue down the stem may be taken. Because of the difference in rooting speed, tip cuttings should not be mixed in the rooting container with cuttings from more mature tissue. Cuttings must be taken only from healthy, pest free plants. Attention should be focused on obtaining groups of mother plants which possess the greatest combination of desirable characteristics. Each species is quite variable and certain plants within it will exhibit traits which are valuable to the grower.

Plants grown under the highest light intensities desirable for that species will produce the best cuttings because the tissue will contain more food than that taken from plants grown under lower light levels. The process of taking cuttings is analagous to major surgery in humans and any extra food reserves improve the chances of success. Sanitation is especially important with cuttings because of the wound produced. Moisture loss from cuttings should be minimized by taking them in early morning or late evening, then sticking (placing the part to be rooted in the medium) and watering in as soon as possible. Hard to root plants may necessitate the use of rooting hormones. In general, it is not important whether the cut is made at or between leaf nodes. Some plants root from the wounded cut, some on the sides of the stem and some at the leaf node. The latter must be inserted so that the leaf node is in firm contact with the medium. Crowding cuttings too closely in the rooting tray restricts air movement, thus encouraging fungal growth. Close spacing will also require cuttings to be transplanted on a more rigid schedule than if they are spaced further apart. Cuttings should be stuck at the normal growth orientation, in other words, upside up. The upside is not so easy to ascertain in some cases.

Leaf cuttings can be made by slicing the leaf into several pieces and inserting them into the medium or by placing the whole leaf on the medium, underside down, and cutting slits in several places. Roots will then form at the wounds if they are in contact with the medium. Only a small proportion of species will root successfully from leaves. Many plants exhibit rather unusual morphological forms and it may be difficult to distinguish between the different plant parts. Normally, if rudimentary roots have formed on a structure, closer inspection would classify it as stem tissue.

Easily rooted plants are often propagated directly in the growing container; this eliminates transplanting labor and reduces the total production cost. Some growers provide extensive propagation areas so that even harder-to-root varieties can be treated this way. The determining factor as to which method is used is whether one has more labor than money since these large propagation areas are expensive to construct and heat.

Seasonal growth rhythms may affect rooting capabilities in plants, especially trees and shrubs. Flower production usually lengthens rooting time. Tissue which has been growing rapidly but is not yet mature seems to root quickly. Some trees may be almost impossible to root unless cuttings are taken at a specific stage of growth. Generally, tree and shrub propagation is best left to specialists unless easily rooted varieties such as cottonwood or willows are the subject.

Specialized methods of taking cuttings are sometimes utilized. Plants which produce extensive runners are often propagated by placing moist soil on top of the runners in several places. Roots form at these spots and the young plants can then be separated from the mother. Air layering is accomplished by severely wounding the stem, then surrounding the wound with moist moss which is held in place and wrapped with plastic film. After roots form at the wound the stem is severed below them and the new plant potted. Rapid propagation of desirable woody varieties is often accomplished by grafting portions of stems to more common root stock. Sometimes a root stock is used not because of being readily available but because it is more suitable for particular conditions than the original root stock.

You can obtain a more detailed knowledge of propagation by cuttings by studying books which are devoted entirely to this subject, but nothing can substitute for acute observation of conditions which lead to success under your own particular circumstances. Do not despair if your first attempts fail; sometimes only a small change in procedure will lead to happier results.

Many crops are grown from bulbs, corms, or tubers but most growers purchase these from specialists. Proper treatment during shipment and after receipt is necessary. Tulips and many other bulb plants contain a small fully organized plant inside the bulb; exposure to extreme conditions such as heat can prevent the small plant from developing properly. Freezing is a common occurrence when bulbs are shipped in winter. Excess moisture and infection with diseases from adhering soil particles leads quickly to rot. Bulbs and tubers should be stored in cool, dry conditions. Certain bulbs must be subjected to specific environmental conditions before successful flowering will take place; this process can be done by the specialist or grower, but it is imperative that the grower knows whether or not the bulbs have been preconditioned.

Tissue culture has been used by experimental propagators for many years, but widespread commercial application of the technique has come only recently. New plants are started in sterile nutrient media from single cells or groups of cells. The big advantage of tissue culture is that a large number of plants can be obtained from a single mother plant, eliminating the cost of maintaining a large inventory of mother plants. Tissue culture is economical only when practiced by specialists who wholesale large numbers of small plants.

A final word of caution before leaving the subject of vegetative propagation. Many plant varieties are protected by federal patent laws. Propagating these varieties without a license from the patent holder is unlawful. It is highly unlikely that patent holders would detect a small neighborhood greenhouse infringing on patents and even more unlikely that prosecution would follow detection. Patent holders are most interested in policing large wholesale propagators, but ignorance of the law is no legal defense if you are apprehended.

SEXUAL REPRODUCTION

Seeds contain a fully developed embryo and are the result of sexual reproduction by plants. When seeds are used for propagation, the progeny are generally more variable than if one had propagated vegetatively. Large numbers of plants can usually be started much faster and more economically by seed than vegetatively. Introduction of diseases and pests into the greenhouse is less likely with one's own seedlings than if cuttings or seedlings are shipped in.

The starting point for obtaining superior seedlings is to purchase seed from a reputable seed house. Growers cannot afford to have plans upset at the last minute by poor quality seed which does not germinate or yields stunted seedlings. Seed packets should be labeled with the year of packing, germination percentage, and any special conditions necessary for germination. Conscientious seed companies will welcome any complaints you may have about failures. Same day shipping after order placement is important to growers during the busy spring season. Seed houses usually offer large discounts for quantity purchases; this practice often makes it imperative for a grower to order almost all seed from a single source. Discount schedules are published in seed catalogs but you may be able to negotiate an even more favorable rate with the salesman. Seed should be ordered only for use in the immediate season; there is no sense in tying up money in a large inventory. Most seeds will gradually lose their viability and there is always the chance of an accident causing their destruction. Leftover seeds should be stored in a cool, dry location which is mouse proof.

When sowing seed, keep a list of varieties which are in short supply so you can place new orders. A one week delay waiting for seed in the spring can mean the difference between selling a crop at regular price or specialing it out at half price.

Varieties must be selected carefully. If you are a new grower, there is little else to base a choice on except seed companys' and salesmen's recommendations. Hybrid seed is much more expensive but will return many satisfied customers because the plants generally are more vigorous and uniform. As your knowledge of varieties progresses, it will become apparent that in some cases the extra cost of hybrid seed is not justified. If at all possible, you should visit seed company trial gardens to compare varieties. All-America seed selections should be evaluated for inclusion in your crop plans because they receive heavy publicity by garden writers and seed companies. A balance must be achieved between having a large enough selection of varieties for customers and having so many varieties that one cannot keep track of them all. For medium to small growers, each additional variety decreases efficiency. One mistake you should never make is to try to grow your own seed. This is a highly specialized business.

The person responsible for seed germination is the heart of greenhouse operations in the spring. If a grower lacks the time to control germination, only the most capable employees should be entrusted with this task. Mistakes in propagation will completely negate an otherwise carefully thought out growing and marketing plan. A germination schedule should be organized well in advance and adhered to rigidly. The busy season is no time to try to figure out a plan which should have been done months ago.

The seed of each species requires a particular set of environmental conditions for optimum germination but if a grower provides adequate moisture and 70°-80° F temperatures, very few varieties will fail to germinate acceptably. In some varieties the presence or absence of light will affect germination a great deal. The only practical way one can determine if light is essential is to learn through packet labels, seed company brochures, or in the literature. Table 6 contains the main points of a germination regimen I have use for years. Optimum germination of each variety may not be achieved but much time is saved by providing only one germination environment. If particular trouble is encountered with some varieties, their requirements may be investigated more closely. The light requirements of seed are met by covering or not covering with medium.

Table 6

Practical guide for acceptable
seed germination in most species.

A. Temperature, 70°-80° F.

B. Provide adequate moisture.

C. Depth of medium not less than 1½ inches.

D. Sow to achieve approximately the following number of usable seedlings from a standard flat (11½ x 21¼ inches). Heavier sowing produces crowded, weak seedlings. Lighter sowing is a waste of space and medium.

> Petunia 800
> Marigold 700
> Tomato, pepper 500
> Alyssum, portulaca sow for 2200 and use as clumps of two to three seedlings.

E. If seeds are large, cover with 1/8 - 1/4 inch of medium unless packet says light is required.
Use #1 formula propagation mix.

(continued on page 45)

Table 6 (continued from page 44)

F. If seeds are small (petunias or smaller) leave uncovered. Spread seed on #2 formula propagation mix. Seed bed should be pressed firm with smooth board for extremely fine seed (begonia).

G. Water in well with fine spray, do not puddle water or seeds will float and concentrate together. Large water droplets will splatter seed from one flat to another.

H. Remove seedlings to normal growing area as soon as sufficient germination has occurred—before they begin to stretch.

Some seed is relatively inexpensive and some is worth more than its weight in gold; how careful you are at handling a particular variety will depend chiefly on the cost. With inexpensive seed it is often more economical to sow quickly rather than taking the time to be exacting. Certain varieties will require special treatment to break seed dormancy; depending on the species, seed may be subjected to freezing temperatures or acid baths, it may be soaked in boiling water, or the seed coat may be nicked or cracked. Tree and shrub seed often requires special dormancy treatments. Alternating day-night temperatures may increase germination in some varieties; normally it it is not economical to worry about providing this regimen unless one is germinating very expensive seed.

The foregoing discussion of seed germination requirements has been brief and slanted towards practicality. The factors influencing germination and the various combinations of them is, in reality, more complicated. Our purpose, however, is to achieve practical results rather than dwell on the possible permutations of factors.

THE PROPAGATION PLAN

Precision growing requires a grower to formulate definite plans long before the first cutting is taken or the first seed is sown. The details of crop planning will be dealt with in a later section but some mention should be made now of the major factors which will affect propagation schedules. Other than environmental influences, the propagation date will affect crop timing more than any factor and you should take great care when determining it. Whenever possible, most growers prefer to have a sequence of crops within the same variety so that all plants do not mature at the same time. Too many propagation dates for the same variety will lower efficiency but too few will result in a glut of plants at one time and not enough at other times. Only experience will enable you to determine a near perfect crop sequence but with careful planning even the neophyte can produce acceptable timing.

An added benefit of time sequencing crops is that the labor required to transplant and care for plants is spread out. Employees get tired of working on the same thing every day; they stay happier if a crop can be transplanted in a reasonable length of time. The same variety may have to be worked on in a week but there has been a break in the monotony. The total amount of work to be accomplished at a particular time must be reflected in the propagation plan. It makes no sense to germinate more seed than the labor force can handle; seedlings and cuttings are highly perishable and will decline in value quickly if not transplanted at the proper time. Available greenhouse space will also influence your propagation plan, especially for the Christmas season and springtime. Projected available space at transplanting time may force the delay of germination dates a few days; if the delay lengthens to more than a week the entire crop plan should be re-evaluated to avoid missing the expected market. Growers should label all propagation containers with waterproof markers. The variety name, date, crop number, number of finished plants to be made, pot size, and the number of propagation flats the crop includes should be clearly visible. A well documented, neat label enables employees to work independently once they have been carefully instructed on how to interpret the labels.

To aid prospective growers in timing crops, a list of germination and marketing dates is presented in Table 7. The comments about greenhouse temperatures or other significant factors should be noted carefully since they will alter maturation. This list is compiled from data collected at a latitude of 43° N and under normally high light conditions. It must be emphasized that this information is only a guide and actual results can vary considerably when any environmental factor is changed. Even if all factors appeared to be similar, no two crops ever seem to progress exactly the same from year to year. A grower should always plan to deal with some variation in timing.

Table 7

Approximate germination and marketing dates for some major crops. Latitude 43° North. Unless otherwise noted crops are grown 72 plants in 11½ inch x 21¼ inch flats.

Variety	Germination date	Growing temperature °F	Market date	Flowers present	No. plants per pot and pot size
Ageratum Blue Angel	3/22	55	5/20	yes	1
Alyssum New Carpet of Snow	4/20	55	5/30	yes	several
Alyssum Saxitile	2/21	50	5/20	no	1
Alyssum Wonderland	4/15	55	5/30	yes	several
Aster Ball Florist	4/25	55	5/30	no	1
Begonia Scarletta, Vodka, Whiskey	2/1	62	5/30	yes	1 per 3½ inch

(continued on page 47)

Table 7 (continued from page 46)

Variety	Germination date	Growing temperature °F	Market date	Flowers present	No. plants per pot and pot size
Begonia Non-Stop	12/20	62	5/30	yes	1 per 4½ inch
Broccoli Green Comet	4/10	50	5/25	no	1
Brussel Sprouts Jade Cross	4/10	50	5/25	no	1
Cabbage Golden Cross	4/10	50	5/25	no	1
Cantelope Earli Sweet	5/7	60	5/30	no	3 per 3½ inch
Carnation Grenadine	2/10	50	5/15	no	1
Cauliflower Snow King	4/10	50	5/25	no	1
Coleus Carefree	3/20	62	5/25	no	1
Cucumber Ball Early Hybrid	5/7	55	5/25	no	3 per 3½ inch
Dahlia Border Jewels	3/4	55	5/25	yes	1 per 2½ inch
Daisy Shasta Alaska	3/15	50	5/25	no	1
Dianthus Magic Charms	3/15	50	5/30	yes	1
Dianthus Barbatus Sweet William	3/1	50	5/25	no	1
Dusty Miller Maritima	3/7	50	5/25	no	1
Eggplant Dusky	4/3	60	5/25	no	1 per 3½ inch
Fushia (cuttings)	2/1	55	5/25 pinched	yes	1 per 3½ inch
Geranium (cuttings)	2/15	55	5/20 no pinch	yes	1 per 4½ inch
Geranium Smash Hit (seed)	2/10	60	5/25	yes	1 per 3½ inch
Impatiens Super Elfins	3/25	62	5/25	yes	1
Ivy Geranium (cuttings)	2/15	55	5/30 no pinch	yes	1 per 3½ inch
Lobelia Crystal Palace	3/5	50	5/25	no	several
Lupine Russell Mix	3/1	50	5/25	no	1
Marigold Apollo or Sunshot	3/1	50	5/25	yes	1
Marigold Bolero	3/20	50	5/25	yes	1
Marigold Boy Series	4/1	50	5/25	yes	1
Marigold Crackerjack	4/25	50	5/25	no	1
Marigold Queen Sophia	3/15	50	5/25	yes	1
Marigold Red Cherry	3/20	50	5/25	yes	1
Mums Garden (cuttings)	2/20	55	5/1-5/25 pinched	yes	1
Pansy Majestic Giant	2/1	50	5/20	yes	1
Pepper Early Set	3/21	55	5/25	no	1 per 3½ inch
Petunia Single Grandiflora	2/26	50	5/25	yes	1
Petunia Double Grandiflora	2/1	50	5/25	yes	1
Phlox Twinkle	3/10	50	5/30	yes	1
Poppy Oriental	2/1	50	5/25	no	1
Portulaca Double Mix	3/1	55	5/30	yes	several
Primrose	2/7	50	5/25	no	1
Pumpkin	5/1	55	5/25	no	3 per 3½ inch
Pyrethrum Robinson's Single	3/1	50	5/25	no	1
Salvia Red Hot Sally	3/22	60	5/25	yes	1
Snapdragon Floral Carpet	3/20	50	5/25	no	1
Snapdragon Rocket	3/20	50	5/25	no	1
Squash Zucchini	5/8	55	5/25	no	3 per 3½ inch
Strawberries (dormant root)	3/15	50	5/10	yes	1 per 3½ inch
Thunbergia Alata	2/15	55	5/25 pinched	yes	1 per 3½ inch
Tomato	3/20	55	5/20	no	1 per 3½ inch
Tomato	3/1	55	5/25	yes	1 per 6 inch

(continued on page 48)

Table 7 (continued from page 47)

Variety	Germination date	Growing temperature °F	Market date	Flowers present	No. plants per pot and pot size
Tomato	3/30	55	5/20	no	1 per 2¼ inch
Viola	2/7	50	5/20	yes	1
Viola Jump Ups	2/22	50	5/20	yes	1
Zinnia Thumbelina	5/8	60	5/30	no	1
Zinnia State Fair	5/7	60	5/25	no	1
Zinnia Peter Pan	3/25	60	5/25	yes	1 per 3½ inch
Begonia Non-Stop	12/20	60	5/30 no pinch	yes	3 per 6 inch
Calceolaria Brite and Early	8/22	60 early 50 late	2/1	yes	1 per 6 inch
Carnation Knight	1/7	55	6/10	yes	6 per 6 inch
Carnation Knight	4/25	55	8/18	yes	6 per 6 inch
Cineraria Improved Festival	8/22	60 early 50 late	2/18	yes	1 per 6 inch
Cineraria Improved Festival	11/7	60 early 50 late	4/10	yes	1 per 6 inch
Cyclamen Hybrid (fast crop)	3/3	60	11/15	yes	1 per 6 inch
Cyclamen Hybrid (fast crop)	4/7	60 early 50 late	3/1	yes	1 per 6 inch
Gloxinia Ultra Scarlet	11/1	65	5/10	yes	2 per 6 inch
Gloxinia Ultra Scarlet	6/17	65	12/1	yes	2 per 6 inch
Kalanchoe (cuttings)	7/7	62	12/20 no shade	yes	4 per 6 inch
Hybrid Lily Enchantment (bulbs)	1/7	60	4/1	yes	2 per 6 inch
Martha Washington Geranium	11/15	50	5/1	yes	1 per 6 inch
Christmas Pepper Holiday Cheer	5/31	60	10/20	yes	1 per 6 inch

Note: Successive crops will require less time during higher light seasons or more time in lower light seasons. To time hanging baskets or larger pots when plants are pinched, add three to four weeks crop time.

CHAPTER 8
SOILS AND
GROWING MEDIA

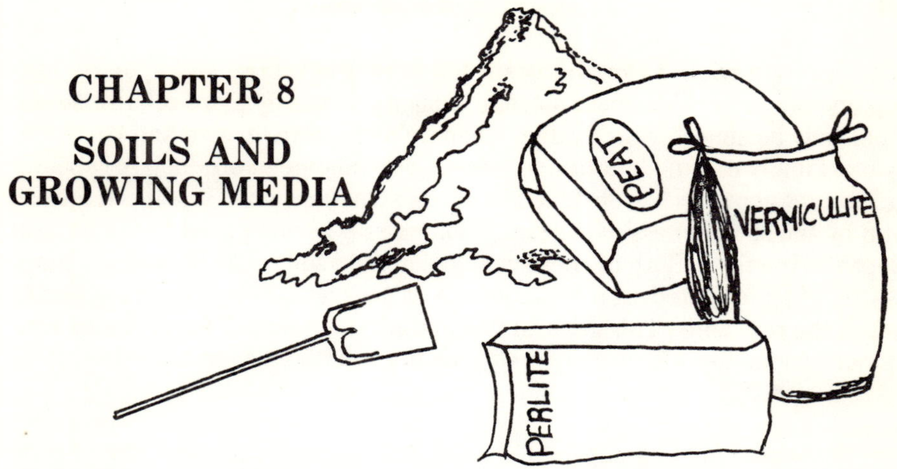

In the not too distant past, most greenhouse plants were grown in true soils and growers needed little more than a cursory knowledge of them. Today greenhouses utilize growing media composed of highly amended soil or of totally artificial components. This about-face has required successful growers to become acquainted with the elementary physical and chemical properties of different media ingredients. The possible combinations of ingredients is almost endless and growers should select the appropriate mix for their circumstances with extreme care. Slight changes in media makeup can vastly affect crop quality. In the following discussion, the term "soil" will be used as a general appellation for the substrate plants are grown in, More specific terms will be applied when necessary.

SOIL FUNCTIONS

The functions of soil are plant support, storing mineral elements and moisture, and providing an oxygen transfer route from the atmosphere to roots. A good soil should combine the various physical and chemical properties of ingredients in such a way as to carry out each function properly. Secondarily, it must be economical, readily available, uniform from batch to batch, free of diseases, insects and weed seed, and contain no harmful chemicals.

PHYSICAL AND CHEMICAL
PROPERTIES OF SOIL

The suitability of a particular soil for use in greenhouse container plant production depends chiefly upon its ability to hold adequate moisture for plant growth while maintaining sufficient root aeration, and upon its having enough mineral element storage capacity to satisfy plant requirements. Soils may be superbly productive when field crops are grown and yet be only marginally useful for container crops. This change in productive capacity is brought about by the destruction of soil structure when it is lifted for use and by the shallowness of container soil masses as compared to the natural depth in the field. Both of these changes in field soil cause it to retain more water when irrigated; as a consequence, it does not allow enough oxygen to reach the root zone. This general unsuitability of field soil for optimum container production forces growers to modify it with various amendments or to make artificial mixes containing no true soil.

The water holding capacity of soils is dependent upon the size of pore spaces between particles and upon total porosity. Large pore spaces decrease the water holding capacity. Sandy soils with big soil particles have large pore spaces and retain little water; aeration is good because water drains quickly and leaves pore spaces open for oxygen movement. Clay soils with small soil particles have small pore spaces and retain more water; aeration in them is poor. Total porosity by volume is greater in clay soils but pore size is greater in sandy soils. Soils with fine particle size, such as clay, are able to store more mineral elements than sandy soils with larger particle sizes. It should be apparent by now that the important attributes of soils as they relate to plant growth in containers are, to a large extent, determined by particle size. Water and mineral elements are held more strongly in soils with small particle size because they both exhibit residual positive electrical charges while soil particles exhibit residual negative charges on their surface. Smaller soil particles increase the quantity of negative charges exposed on the particle surface because small particles have more surface area per volume than do large particles.

An understanding of the relationship between soil particle size and moisture and mineral element retention enables a grower to postulate the effects on plant growth which may occur if certain ingredients are added to or deleted from soil mixes. Table 8 may help in visualizing the effect particle size has on various soil properties. The ideal soil mix is one in which there are enough large particles to ensure proper movement of oxygen to the root zone and sufficient numbers of small particles to retain water and mineral elements in quantities suitable for plant growth. There are many different combinations of ingredients which will approach this ideal mix; the particular combination chosen will depend on the grower's estimation of which one fits the particular situation best. All varieties of plants do not grow equally well in the same soil conditions. It is incumbent upon the grower to choose a soil mix which will meet the need of the greatest

Table 8

Characteristics of natural field soils. Total porosity is greater in clay even though pore size is smaller because there are many more pores in clay than in sand.

Natural soil types	Soil Characteristics					
	Average particle size	Average pore size	Total porosity	Water retention	Mineral element retention	Oxygen movement to roots
Clay	Small	Small	Large	High	High	Poor
Loam	↕	↕	↑	↑	↑	↕
Sandy loam						
Sand	Large	Large	Small	Low	Low	Good

number of plants. Any varieties of plants which will not grow well in the soil mix settled upon should be candidates for exclusion from the greenhouse program. It is, of course, possible to select several soil mixes for different crops but this lowers greenhouse efficiency, especially in small to medium ranges.

While particle size is the major determinant of soil mix characteristics, soil texture or structure may also have some effect. Field soils normally have a well defined structure; that is, the individual particles are arranged or aggregated into definite patterns with one another. The process of lifting these soils and mixing for greenhouse use tends to destroy their structure. Artificial structure may be given to greenhouse soils by adding such amendments as coarse peat chunks which are aggregates of finer peat particles. Soil structure is also a reflection of the degree of packing or porosity of the soil. Generally, soils which have larger aggregates will pack less tightly and consequently have more macropore space. An example of how the geometric shape of soil amendments will affect structure is illustrated by the fact that sharp sand particles will pack more tightly than dune sand particles whose edges have been rounded by wind action. This relationship is pictured in Table 9. Soils having a structure which tends to promote

Table 9

Soil structure is affected by the shape of individual particles. Pore space is greater and more regularly spaced in dune sand than in fractured sand. Pore space in black.

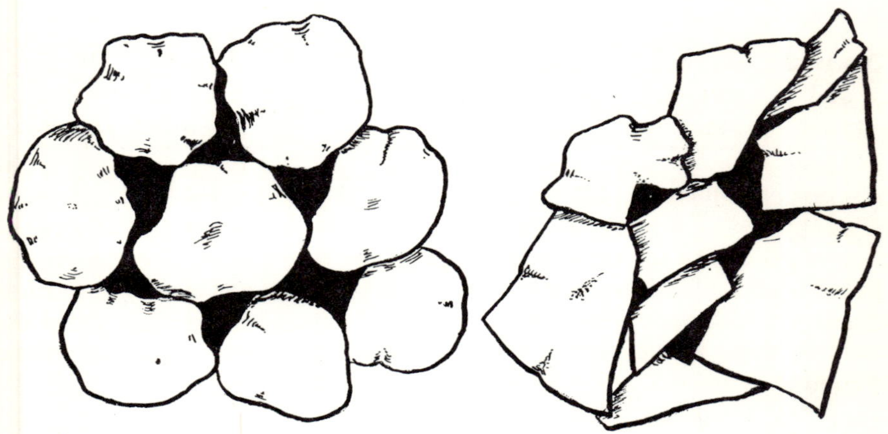

Dune or windscoured sand   *Fractured or sharp sand*

larger pore spaces will drain well and provide better oxygen exchange to the root zone. Soil structure can be modified somewhat by the mineral elements present. Calcium tends to promote formation of structural aggregates, while sodium disperses soil particles and destroys structure. Compounds containing sodium should be eliminated as much as possible from fertilizer programs.

Soil fertility is determined mainly by the extra fine particles present with a diameter of less than one micron. This portion of the soil is known as the colloidal fraction and is composed of clay and decayed organic matter. Mention has already been made of the negative charges present on the surface of soil particles; these charges attract positively charged mineral elements (cations). The capacity of a soil or soil fraction to hold mineral elements is known as the cation exchange capacity. Higher figures indicate more fertility. Sandy soils have a cation exchange capacity of perhaps 5, while clay may approach 100. Organic colloidal material is in the neighborhood of 300. These figures are very approximate and would change considerably with the particular soil or material measured; they are given solely to show the reader comparative extreme values.

A special situation may arise particularly in soils with fine particle size, where the water present in pore spaces becomes highly saturated with mineral compounds. The level of saturation is known as the soluble salts concentration. High concentrations arise when there is an excess of mineral salts in the soil initially or applied as fertilizer. These salts may be leached away by applying an excess of water, which drains through the pores and flushes the substrate. Soils with large pore spaces are obviously easier to clear of high salt levels.

The pH is a measure of the acidic or basic nature of soils; it varies with the chemical makeup of soil particles. Lower figures indicate more acid conditions and higher figures a more basic situation. A pH of 7 is neutral. Many people use the terms basic and alkaline interchangeably; this is satisfactory for general purposes but is not true in the strict scientific application. Most plants will grow in a fairly wide pH range and soils with values of 5.6 to 6.8 would be suitable for the majority of crops. Wider variations in pH can be tolerated under certain fertilizer programs but normally the pH is adjusted at the time of mixing by the addition of limestone to raise values and sulfur compounds to lower values. Special soil fertility problems can arise due to improper pH levels; more detail of these situations will be presented in the discussion of fertilizer programs.

PROPERTIES OF SOIL MEDIA INGREDIENTS

Let us now turn our attention to presenting basic information concerning the more common ingredients used in preparing greenhouse soils. Growers can then formulate specific mixes which fit their particular situation. Information presented in Table 10 summarizes some of the important attributes of commonly used ingredients.

Field Soils

Field soils may average approximately 50% pore space. The organic percentage of solid particles normally does not exceed 5% by weight, the remaining content being mineral. As mentioned previously, particle size is a prime determinant of a soil's suitability for greenhouse production. Mineral soil particles are classified according to size into gravel, sand, silt, and clay. Particles from 0.05 to 2.0 millimeters in diameter are classified as sand; gravel is anything larger than 2.0 millimeters. Silt particle diameter is 0.002 to 0.05 millimeters. Clays have a diameter of less than 0.002 millimeters.

Sandy soils, dominated by large particles, are well drained and aerated. The small surface area of large particles makes sandy soils retain little water and nutrients. Because of the small particle size with a subsequent increase in surface area and negative electrical charge, the clay fraction of

Table 10

Characteristics of commonly available materials used in greenhouse soil mixes.

	Loam	Sand	Perlite	Vermiculite	Sawdust	Ground bark	Peat moss
Uniform from batch to batch	−	+	+	+	+ −	+	+
Stable under pasteurization	+ −	+	+	+	+	+	+
Aeration good	+ −	+	+	+ −	+	+	+
Fertility low	+ −	+	+	+ −	+	+	+
Moisture retention good	+	−	−	+ −	+	+	+
Nutrient retention good	+	−	−	+ −	+	+	+
Free of weeds	−	+	+	+	+	+	+
Disease and pest free	−	+ −	+	+	+ −	+ −	+
Inexpensive	+	+	−	−	+	+ −	+ −

Note: + denotes the material possesses the characteristic.
     − denotes the material does not possess the characteristic.
     + − denotes the material possesses the characteristic in intermediate form.

---

field soils is responsible for holding the majority of nutrient minerals. Water holding capacity is large and aeration poor in clay. The plasticity and stickiness of clays make handling difficult in the greenhouse. Silt particles, being intermediate in size, have properties lying between those of sand and clay. Loam type soils are mixtures of sand, clay, and silt in varying proportions with the prefix denoting which soil particles dominate the mixture, for example "sandyloam."

In modern greenhouse production, field soils are seldom used without addition of amendments. Sandy loams or loams are the only classes which approach any degree of usability by themselves. Sandy soils can be used but require large, frequent, and precise application of fertilizer elements. Usually, field soils are mixed with the appropriate amount of organic matter and inorganic aggregates to satisfy plant requirements. The chief benefits of incorporating field soil into media mixes are that it is inexpensive if suitable local sources are available and the inherent fertility of soils containing some clay mitigates the need for growers to precisely control fertilizer application to avoid serious deficiencies. Drawbacks are the unavoidable lack of uniformity, possibility of herbicide contamination, and abundance of weed seed, soil pests, and microbes. Novice growers may find the presence of some fertility in soils a blessing because there will be less chance of crop failure due to mineral deficiencies. Experienced growers with an adequate knowledge of fertilizer needs may prefer a mix with little or no fertility so they can adjust applications to the precise needs of crops.

Organic Matter

Organic matter in various forms has been and still is the most common amendment to greenhouse soils; it is derived from dead plant tissue and, as such, will vary considerably in quality depending on what species it comes from and the state of decay. Organic matter has the beneficial attributes of adding to water and nutrient retention in sandy soils and aiding aeration in clay soils. Possession of qualities particular to both small and large soil particles makes organic matter the universal addition in greenhouse mixes. Several physical and chemical properties of organic matter should be kept in mind by the grower:

A. Organic matter generally has a good water holding capacity and good aeration.

B. Organic matter generally has a high cation exchange capacity (holds nutrients well).

C. Certain types of organic matter can cause what is known as ammonium toxicity after being pasteurized for diseases and pests.

D. Certain types of organic matter cause rapid removal of nitrogen from the substrate.

An evaluation of different organic sources follows.

PEAT MOSS—Several very different materials are commonly called peat moss. Humus and reed and sedge peats are usually almost black in color and, because of an advanced state of decay, have a large proportion of fine particles; high soluble salt contents may sometimes be encountered. These peats are unsuitable for greenhouse soils and will not be discussed further. Sphagnum and hypnum peat mosses are less decomposed and, unless ground, contain fewer fine particles. Color is from dark brown to brownish-gray. Plant cellular and tissue structure may be apparent in the higher grades if the peat has not been ground. Hypnum moss is available in

some local areas and can be obtained from distributors but it is not as widely encountered and economical as sphagnum moss.

Because of its beneficial properties, wide availability, and reasonably
low cost, sphagnum peat moss is the most popular organic constituent used
for greenhouse soils. Growers should take care that the material purchased
is labeled sphagnum peat moss and that the quality is in line with price. A
very dark brown color with numerous sticks and possibly some soil contamination indicates poor quality. Lighter greyish color with plant tissue
structure apparent and no sticks or soil contamination are indications of
high quality. Economical sources of sphagnum will usually lie somewhere in
the middle quality grades. Texture may vary from fist size chunks down to
very fine material if the peat has been mechanically ground. Small chunks
are suitable if one is growing in larger containers but finely ground peat is
desirable for soil used with small pots or propagation media.

Sphagnum peat is low in soluble salts and adds no appreciable quantities of nutrients to soils. The pH is quite acid but may be raised easily by
the addition of limestone at the time of mixing. I have personally used
sphagnum mixtures for years without incorporating limestone; crops have
been excellent. My fertilizer solutions are slightly basic, however, and if
acid fertilizers were used, pH adjustment of the mix would be mandatory.
Uniformity will change considerably from brand to brand; one should
investigate the quality and availability of a particular source carefully and
then purchase only from that source to avoid variations in crop growth.

SAWDUST—Sawdust is often available in small quantities from
lumber yards and cabinet shops; lumber processing areas have unlimited
supplies. Cost is minimal. Walnut and incense cedar sawdust are toxic to
plants, making cabinet shop sources undesirable. Redwood sawdust can be
toxic if not weathered or leached thoroughly. Sawdust compares favorably
with peat moss in most instances as a soil amendment if it is readily
available. The pH depends upon the species utilized but it is normally less
acid than peat.

A rapid depletion of nitrogen in soils is the chief drawback of using
sawdust. Adding supplemental nitrogen will ameliorate this problem but
one should realize the added cost incurred by doing so. The amount of extra
nitrogen needed will vary with source and species but it has been suggested
that 2% nitrogen by weight of the sawdust is adequate. A lookout must be
kept for toxic soluble salt levels when this much nitrogen is added. Hard-
wood sawdust from deciduous trees (oak, hickory, maple, poplar) depletes
soil nitrogen more heavily than does softwood sawdust from evergreen
needle trees (fir, redwood, pine). Nitrogen depletion may be lowered by using old sawdust which has decayed somewhat; the degree of decomposition

is hard to assess and usually takes many years to progress appreciably. Sawdust can be treated by chemical processes to eliminate the nitrogen depletion problem but this treated sawdust is not widely available and the costs become uncompetitive with peat as an organic matter source.

BARK—Tree bark is similar to sawdust as a soil additive except that available particle size is not as restricted and the problem of soil nitrogen depletion is not so severe. A partial solution to this problem is to use softwood bark which is partially decomposed. In the past few years, horticultural grade bark has become reasonably available nationwide at prices competitive with those for peat moss. In locations where there is a transport savings over peat moss, bark may be the more economical choice. I expect, however, that bark prices and availability may be subject to wide swings because it is a by-product of the lumber industry. This may make it a less predictable source of organic matter than sphagnum.

MISCELLANEOUS ORGANIC MATTER SOURCES—Manure causes a buildup of toxic ammonia when pasteurized and is not uniform from batch to batch. Pasteurization is essential because of diseases and weed seed present. It should not be used in greenhouse soils.

Wood chips cause the same nitrogen depletion as does sawdust but, because of their large particle size, do not offer the same benefits.

Ground corncobs are not readily available and cause severe nitrogen depletion of soil.

Peanut hulls may be very economical in certain areas as a source of organic matter. Nitrogen depletion of soil does occur with their use but it is much less of a problem than with sawdust. Rice hulls are comparable in quality and availability to peanut hulls.

Many other organic matter sources have been used to amend greenhouse soils but their use is limited in modern production methods by more economical, widely available and uniform sources having more desirable characteristics.

Inorganic Soil Ingredients

Inorganic materials are usually added with the purpose of increasing the proportion of large particles in soil mixes, leading to better drainage and aeration. Only the more commonly used components will be discussed individually.

SAND—Sand is the most inexpensive and readily available source of larger particled material. Weight is sometimes a drawback if one is shipping wholesale but for local growers, the extra weight may be an advantage in that it prevents pots from tipping over easily when the soil is dried out. Some sand in organic mixes also anchors plants more securely. Pure sand is more or less inert chemically but most common sand will contain small amounts of clay and silt which lend some nutrient and water holding capacity. Clay should represent less than 10% by weight of the sand used. Too much clay in soil mixes containing sand can lead to compaction because of clay particles occupying the pore spaces between sand particles. If one uses "washed" sand there should be very little clay or silt present.

There seems to be some disagreement in the literature about the size and shape of sand particles which are most useful in soil mixes. Some sources recommend sharp sand with relatively large particle size, only a small portion being less than 0.50 millimeters in diameter. Other authors are adamant that particles be no larger than 0.50 millimeters with rounded edges to avoid compaction. On a practical level, I have found that both fine dune sand and coarser "washed" sand will produce good crops when blended with the proper amount of organic material. I prefer "washed" sand because it is relatively free of clay and suppliers will deliver it to your door.

PERLITE—Perlite is a light, rather fluffy, white mineral product which is chemically inert and holds very little water; cost is moderately high. Many growers who ship long distances prefer perlite over sand because it weighs very little. It is especially suitable for propagation mixes. Perlite is sterile.

VERMICULITE—Vermiculite is a clay mineral which is physically expanded through a heating process. Being a clay, it retains the ability to hold moisture and nutrients. Vermiculite contains large amounts of potassium and magnesium so that soils mixed with it can function with reduced applications of these elements. When wetted, vermiculite breaks down easily with excessive mixing. Finer grades of vermiculite are especially suitable in mixes for germinating small seed. Vermiculite should be obtained from reputable horticultural dealers because construction grades do not absorb water well and are not handled to maintain a sterile product.

CINDERS AND SCORIA—Cinders cost very little in coal burning regions but quality may be quite variable depending on the coal grade used and how it is burned. Large quantities of sulphates may be present in cinders and these compounds must be leached out prior to use. In high rainfall areas cinders may be leached naturally if left outdoors a minimum of one year. Cinders of proper size with good porous structure are excellent additives to peat moss.

SOIL MIXTURES

The preceding discussion of soil components should enable a grower to devise plant growing media which fit a particular circumstance. For those who do not wish to make a detailed study of soil mixes, I will present some recipes which I have found to be suitable in most general applications.

Peat-Sand General Production or Growing On Mix

The growing medium I have used for general production is a sphagnum peat-sand mix. I chose this mixture mainly because of the ready availability and economy of materials and freedom from weed seed. There have been no observed problems with any crops except those which prefer an especially well drained soil. The formula is as follows:

- 2 4 cubic foot bales sphagnum peat
- 12 cubic feet washed sand
- 17 ounces triple superphosphate
- 4 ounces potassium nitrate
  (dissolved in 5 gallons of water)

Note: When peat is taken from the compressed bales it expands to nearly double the volume to yield approximately one cubic yard of total mix. This is a ratio of 55% peat - 45% sand by volume.

The peat should be finely ground if there are small bedding plant containers to fill or if propagation mixes are to be made. A coarse grind peat with fingertip size chunks would be preferable if only three-inch pots and larger were being used. This would improve drainage and aeration. Triple superphosphate (some refer to it as double superphosphate) is used because it is more economical to ship. Single superphosphate could be used instead at a rate of two and a half pounds per yard. I do not adjust pH because my growing on fertilizer (chapter 10) is slightly basic. If a less acid soil mix is preferred five pounds of calcium carbonate lime can be added. This should definitely be done if growing on fertilizers are acid in reaction. I have never pasteurized this soil mix and seldom have any serious soil borne disease problems. If facilities were available or a large greenhouse operation were envisaged, it would be preferable to pasteurize since the sand fraction is not sterile. Additional fertilization must be programmed to start soon after potting; potassium nitrate added to the medium is only a starter solution. I have never added trace elements to this soil mix. It may be necessary to do so if adequate quantities of them are not available in greenhouse water supplies and as impurities in fertilizer materials. If one wished to be certain of adequate micro nutrient supply, a fritted (slowly available) source may be added at mixing time. Mixing should be thorough with water added until the soil is well moistened.

Peat-Perlite Mix

See chapter 7 for formula. This mix is much lighter than the general production formula and is used for rooting cuttings and germinating seed. It also serves well as an alternative mix for those species which demand a fast draining soil. If one is marketing young plants for shipment, this mix is ideal because of the light weight. Many foliage plant growers use a similar recipe for general production. If used for growing on, the amount of superphosphate should be doubled and a careful watch kept for micronutrient deficiencies. Both peat and perlite are essentially sterile and no pasteurization is required if contamination is avoided. I find this mix too light for general production; dry pots continually tip over and retail customers do not seem impressed when they pick up a plant that weighs next to nothing. Commercial versions of peat-perlite media are readily available but expensive.

Peat-Vermiculite Mix

See chapter 7 for formula. Everything which was said about peat-perlite mixes applies to peat-vermiculite mixes except that they are not as well drained and, consequently, are seldom used for rooting media. I use this mix only for germinating fine seed.

Retail Potting Soil

After several years of retailing experience I came to the conclusion that most commercial retail potting mixes were either too light, too heavy, contaminated with weed seed, or too expensive. Shipping costs were also high. The following mixture was researched for customer eye and touch appeal and for suitability to the widest number of plant varieties under home conditions. Originally it was put into small sealable plastic bags but demand was very brisk so a three color, heavy duty bag was designed for packaging. The professional appearance increased sales even further. This is a very profitable use of time for any greenhouse.

2	4 cubic foot bales sphagnum peat
	(approx. 15 cubic feet loose peat)
5.25	cubic feet washed sand
1.75	cubic feet perlite
3.7	ounces potassium nitrate
4.5	pounds calcium carbonate lime
14.7	ounces triple superphosphate

Note: As in other mixes, single superphosphate can be used at slightly more than double the rate of triple superphosphate. Water should be added to the point where the mix feels slightly moist when taken from the bag. Too much water will make the bag sweat. Unless sterilized, filled bags must be in the dark when stored for prolonged periods to prevent algae growth.

Mixes Containing Field Soil

In cases where sandy loam or loam field soils of good quality are available at reasonable prices, the grower may wish to utilize them in greenhouse mixes. Sandy loams can be diluted with an equal amount of peat moss. Loam should be mixed in a 1:1:1 ratio of loam, peat moss, and coarse sand or other aggregate. When field soil is incorporated in media, it is difficult to recommend specific fertilizer additives because some fertility will already be present. A rule of thumb might be that if a mix is 50% soil, fertilizer additives could be cut by 25% from that recommended in the peat-sand production mix. Field soil should not be considered for use unless it is uniform and can be certified to be free of herbicide residues. Pasteurization of field soils is necessary because of the large number of soil organisms present. Media containing field soil generally do not require microelement application and are less sensitive to small variations in the macronutrient supply.

Mixes Containing Sawdust or Ground Bark

It should be realized that sawdust or ground bark can be substituted for sphagnum peat in most soil media. There will be some differences in soil makeup due to this change but, in general, no major alterations in plant growth should be noticed if proper attention is paid to the problem of nitrogen depletion which has been discussed previously.

SOIL PASTEURIZATION

Most large greenhouses regularly pasteurize soil media to eliminate diseases, soil pests, and weeds. Pasteurization is economical when large batches of soil are processed. In smaller greenhouses it may be more realistic to choose soil ingredients which are reasonably clean and dispense with the pasteurization process. More plants will be lost to diseases this way but omitting the cost of treating small batches of soil may make up for these losses. This is one reason I like the peat-sand growing media—good success can be achieved without pasteurization. Ingredients for propagating media should be sterile or pasteurization will be necessary.

A detailed discussion of soil pasteurization will not be given. This process, especially when steam is used, becomes quite technical. Soil is pasteurized with heat or chemicals. There are small electric units available which utilize dry heat for treatment, but steam is by far the most common method. If chemicals are used to pasteurize soil, the grower should be aware of possible toxic after effects for plants unless recommended procedures are followed carefully. Some of the chemicals are also very toxic to humans.

Choosing the proper soil mix is one of the most important decisions facing growers. Large quantities will be used and even small differences in price can be very significant over a period of years. Even more important, however, is the influence soil choice will have on crop production. Careful study must precede selection and once a medium has been chosen, changes in the formula should not be made lightly.

CHAPTER 9

TRANSPLANTING THE CROP

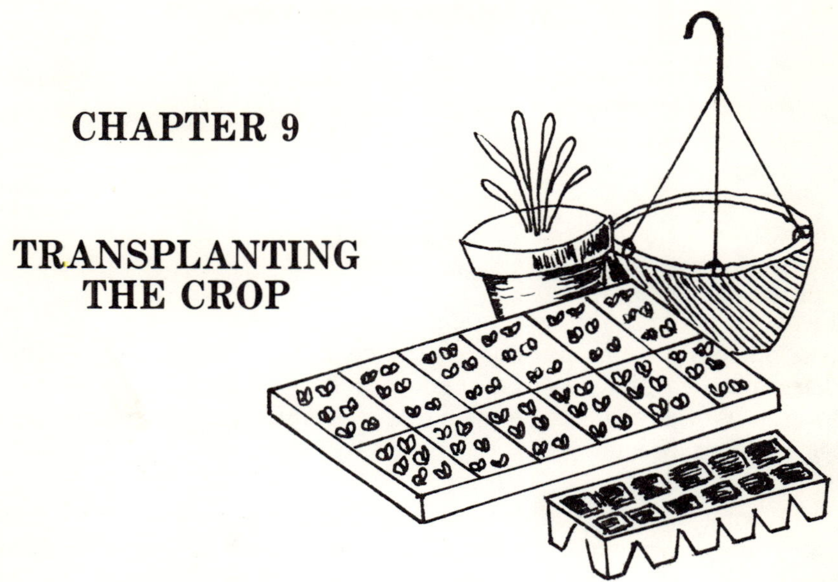

A great deal of the labor costs involved in running a greenhouse are attributed to transplanting cuttings and seedlings into growing on containers. The job must be done with care to assure plant survival and a quality crop but it must be done with speed and efficiency. Employees should be motivated to work quickly and competently. They must also be provided with the facilities and direction necessary to complement this motivation. Adequate space and a proper work layout will increase transplanting productivity greatly. The grower should analyze the entire potting process and devise a plan and layout which best fit the circumstances. If enough room is not available to assure efficient movement, thought should be given to adding on. New space is expensive, but is a one time cost; a cramped and ineffective layout costs the owner money year after year.

WORKFLOW

Most greenhouses are equipped with a structure called the potting shed or head house where the majority of soil mixing and transplanting are done. A production line sequence for these tasks should be set up in the following manner:

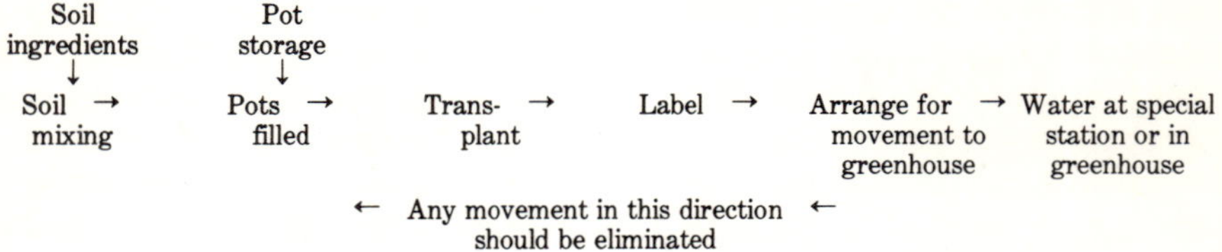

Plenty of room is the key to eliminating congestion areas. Work should flow smoothly from one stage to the next. Work bench height should be determined carefully so that employees do not suffer undue back or arm fatigue. Workers will be on their feet constantly and cement floors add to leg and foot discomfort.

Moving transplanted pots to the growing greenhouse is time consuming. Some growers feel it more efficient to do much of their planting in the greenhouse, especially when large numbers are involved. Soil is moved to the greenhouse planting station by means of tractors or large carts; moving soil is generally easier than moving pots filled with plants. One drawback to this scheme is that all pots, labels, and other work needs must also be transported to location and if something extra is needed, more trips back to the storage area will be made. Another disadvantage is the constantly changing climate in the greenhouse; it is much easier to maintain pleasant working temperatures and light conditions in a conventional building than in a greenhouse.

Major advances in machinery have come about in the past twenty years to reduce the larger grower's transplanting labor. Unfortunately large soil mixers, conveyor belts, pot filling machines, etc. are not economically justifiable for smaller establishments. If the machines cannot be utilized regularly, it is questionable if they will pay for themselves. Oftentimes, greenhouse owners will become fascinated with machines and buy them without careful consideration of whether it would be better to add extra employees who can be terminated when need for them is gone.

Transplanting work often comes in surges, which calls for seasonal employees. I have found neighborhood housewives to be the most capable and industrious source of labor for the greenhouse. They are often happy to be on "vacation" during the summer and winter holiday season when there is little planting to do. In addition, many of them work mainly to get out of the house and are concerned primarily with how they like a job rather than if it pays top wages. This is advantageous for greenhouses because most housewives are plant lovers and would rather work there than any place else. A grower can usually obtain a reliable and productive work force at reasonable wages by making the atmosphere pleasant and informal and by tolerating some of the peculiarities of housewives' schedules. Transplanting workers must be trained carefully in the fundamentals of their job. If the grower instructs them properly and has a good system of information tags in each batch of plants to be done, work will progress smoothly and efficiently with only occasional need for supervision.

PLANTING PROCEDURES

Seedlings should be transplanted when the first true leaves appear, or when they are large enough to handle. Cuttings are easiest to remove from the propagating medium when roots have begun to form but have not spread appreciably. Leaving either in the propagating trays too long will arrest growth and increase planting labor because the larger root system is more difficult to arrange in the soil. Many crops are ruined because growers have failed to provide adequate transplanting labor. Plants become stunted and flower prematurely. Seedlings which have not been planted on time should be discarded; labor and materials will be wasted when stunted plants are transplanted.

Most workers tend to be overly cautious when removing plants from the propagating tray and placing them in the growing container. If the transplanter runs a hand under the seedlings or cuttings and loosens the soil somewhat, most plants can be pulled quickly out of the tray with little lasting damage. Many roots will be broken off but the ones remaining will generate new tissue within a few days if the soil is kept well moistened. Constant availability of water until new roots are formed contributes greatly to success.

Transplanting benches must be kept clean. Old soil, plant debris, and used containers should never be allowed to contaminate new soil and plants. Another way of reducing disease losses is to plant seedlings and cuttings as shallow as possible coincident with proper anchorage. Shallow planting increases the oxygen available to roots and reduces exposure of tender stem tissue to disease organisms in the soil. Crop uniformity and ease of watering will be increased if the transplanting crew is instructed to fill containers with soil in a standardized manner. Differences in the degree of soil compaction and soil volume in pots will lead to irrigation difficulties. The number of seedlings or cuttings placed in a container will be determined by the grower's evaluation of needs. Fewer plants may be used and then cut back or "pinched" to induce branching; this method increases growing time and charges against the crop for greenhouse space will be greater. More plants in the containers reduces crop time but increases propagation costs. Except in cases where seed or cutting costs are prohibitive, I feel it is more profitable to use extra plants and reduce crop time to a minimum.

If mixed color seed formulas are used, seedlings should be taken from the seed flat indiscriminately. Choosing the larger or healthiest looking seedlings may result in a finished crop which is predominatnly one color. When the seedling or cutting is placed in containers, soil must be gently but firmly pressed around the base of the plant. This brings soil particles into close contact with roots and anchors the plant. All air holes around roots must be filled and enough empty space left at the top of pots to provide an adequate water reservoir. When plants are moved to growing areas, it is often possible to stack containers one on top of another without plant damage. This is much more efficient transport and is especially useful with bedding plant flats. Of course certain varieties must be left in a single tier or stems will be broken. Newly transplanted plants can be killed in a few minutes if left unwatered on a sunny greenhouse bench. Water should be applied frequently during the first few days but not to the point of soaking the soil through. Water absorption through the leaves is important at this stage since many roots have been lost. Some growers prefer to shade plants after transplanting but this is normally not necessary and is an expensive extra step.

Plants which have been growing for some time in containers and are ready to move up in pot size should be moistened thoroughly prior to transplanting. This eliminates the need to water the new soil mass heavily for a few days until roots are beginning to penetrate it. Roughing up the roots on older plants being transplanted stimulates new root growth and rejuvenates the plant. Extremely root bound plants will have to have the roots torn apart and some cut off to satisfactorily stimulate new growth. When roots are cut off severely it may be necessary to prune back top growth to bring the plant into balance. Whenever plants are pruned heavily, watering should be reduced until new growth becomes evident.

PLANTING CONTAINERS

Many greenhouse owners begin business using all shapes and sizes of containers which can be obtained free or at little cost. These pots are normally not sterile and do not present a professional image to customers. Disease and loss of sales due to dirty, unattractive pots are the price one pays for trying to save a few dollars. Old pots are seldom a bargain when a person's time collecting them is accounted for. This is time that could be better spent managing the greenhouse.

The main criteria one should use in choosing growing containers are economy, consumer appeal, ease of handling, freedom from disease organisms, and quality of plant growth in them. Red clay pots were the standard of the industry for many years. I believe they grow a higher quality plant and are more appealing to customers. High cost and difficulty in handling due to weight and fragility have eliminated clay pots from most greenhouses. Plastic containers have replaced clay because of economy, ease of handling and shipping, and ease of storing large numbers in a sterile condition. Growers should remember that the ultimate destination of plants and flowers is a person and container color and shape can have significant impact on whether or not this person views the product as pleasing. I think round pots are more attractive to most people than are square pots. White is more appealing than black. Containers which are almost as wide as they are tall complement most plant forms more than tall, narrow containers.

Choosing lines of containers for a growing program should be done with careful thought about the unique circumstances surrounding each crop. Spring plants for outdoors are not usually chosen with so critical an eye as are gift plants. Consequently, square pots may be preferred for spring because they hold more soil and are more amenable to handling easily in standard rectangular flats. Drain holes in all containers must be adequate. Drainage is less impeded if a portion of the drain holes are located on the extreme lower sides of containers instead of entirely on the bottom. Containers must have enough material strength for the purpose served. Hanging baskets especially should be tested for weaknesses at the juncture of hangers and container and again at the hook by which they are hung. Square pots and those with ribbed sides are preferred for long term crops such as trees; these shapes lessen the tendency of roots to circle the outside edge and supposedly stimulate roots to grow downward. Whether or not containers separate from one another readily is important to transplanting efficiency. There is nothing more aggravating to employees then struggling with pots that won't come apart when the boss is expecting top speed. Color and physical composition of containers can affect soil temperatures, especially out of doors. Black pots absorb more heat from the sun than lighter colors and plastic pots are less efficient insulators than are wood-fiber pots. Containers which fit easily and tightly into trays are much more easily transported; this is one of the big benefits of square pots. Clay and wood-fiber pots, in my estimation, are easier to grow quality plants in than plastic pots because root aeration is better. No one type of container will satisfy every growing and merchandising need. A balance must be struck between the need to standardize and the necessity of accommodating pecularities in plant growth and sales.

I will comment briefly on types of containers listed according to construction material.

PLASTIC—Pros and cons of plastic pots have already been discussed. A porous soil mix is necessary to compensate for the impermeability of pot walls to air flow. Growers will have a tendency to over water in plastic containers, more so than with containers having air-porous walls. Plastic flats filled with removable inserts having small individual cells are the standard container of the bedding plant industry. The common size of these rectangular flats is approximately 11 inches by 21 inches. Prices for different grades and weights of plastics will vary considerably and growers must choose the most economical combination which fits the need.

CLAY—Clay pots are still used to some extent in localities where a factory is located. Most consumers regard plants in clay pots as a mark of quality and would be willing to pay a slightly higher price. If the grower feels there is a market for high quality plant material with a distinctive container, clay pots may help distinguish the product clearly. I have grown poinsettias in clay pots for years because I find them particularly difficult to grow. With clay, less experienced personnel can water the crop satisfactorily. The extra cost of clay for my poinsettias is compensated for by reduced losses and because growth retardants are not needed—stiffer, shorter plant stems result when growing in containers with air porous walls.

WOOD FIBER—Fiber containers are manufactured from lumber industry by-products. The walls are somewhat air-porous so that growing in fiber pots is similar to growing in clay. Purchase price is normally reasonable but shipping is expensive due to their bulk, which also complicates storage. Pots are often difficult to separate because rough outside surfaces stick to the next pot. Flats and bedding plant containers are also available in fiber. Tree growers use the majority of fiber pots because, supposedly, a tree can be planted pot and all with the pot disintegrating in a short time and enabling roots to spread. My experience is, at least in a dry climate, that these pots do not break down fast enough to allow free movement of roots. I use a large number of fiber pots in 3½-8 inch size for spring vegetables; the public seems to associate their appearance with gardening and plants grow easier in them than in plastic. Many gardeners are ecologically minded and accept fiber pots as being biodegradable; it is questionable if this is a factor in their selection of plants.

PEAT—Peat pots are similar to wood fiber pots but because of the weaker and more porous nature of the construction material, they are used only in small sizes and root aeration is even better. Peat is also used in manufacturing pellets enclosed by a light reinforcing net. Roots of herbaceous plants will grow through the walls of these peat materials quickly. This phenomenon has led to their extensive use by propagators. Many spring bedding plants are offered in peat pots or pellets. Less damage to surrounding plants is encountered if individual pots are grouped in small plastic sales unit containers rather than in an open flat. Peat pots and pellets are easy to grow quality plants in but purchase cost is quite high, especially if they are grouped in sales unit containers.

STYROFOAM—Both pots and bedding plant packs are sometimes made from styrofoam. I can see little to distinguish them from plastic containers except they are bulkier and, depending on construction methods, could possibly lead to better aeration of the root zone. Recently, foam blocks have become extensively used as a propagation medium for cuttings. Some of them, at least, must be leached prior to usage. Cuttings planted to growing containers in foam blocks must be watered heavily until established, and, generally, shade is also required. Cuttings do root well in these blocks but establishing them in the growing container is more difficult during hot weather. In my opinion, foam blocks make the propagator's work easier but increase losses and expense for the final grower.

WOODEN—Wooden bedding plant packs and flats were once quite common but are seldom seen nowadays. In lumber country, tree boxes are used extensively but bulkiness prevents their transport to other regions. Wooden baskets are an excellent container for planting trees in. Numerous small holes in the walls and bottom allow roots to penetrate quickly into surrounding soil. Basket cost is usually somewhat higher than that of equivalent sized fiber pots. Treatment with wood preservatives increases basket life above ground but decreases usefulness as a planting container in the ground. I have used green treated baskets for years as containers for mixed porch planters. Consumers are attracted to their rustic appearance. The same plants in similarly priced plastic pots sell much more slowly.

CHAPTER 10

FERTILIZERS

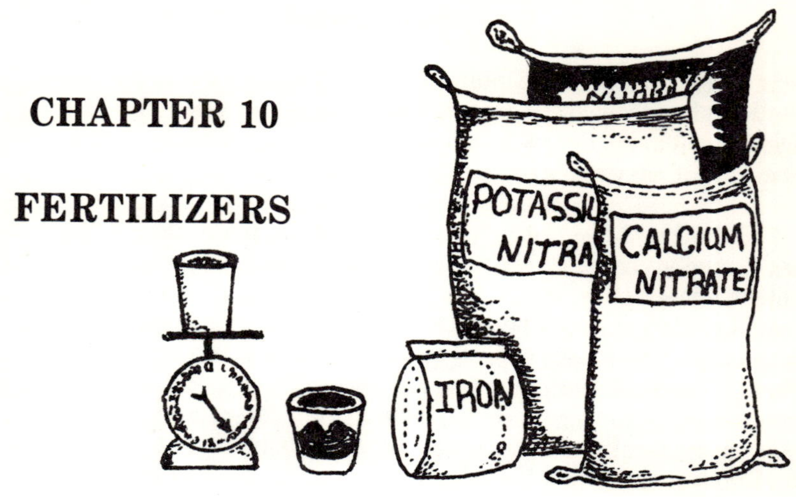

The term "fertilizer" in the following discussion shall mean those mineral elements (either free or in compound form) which were listed as essential for plant growth. Although I have alluded to them as mineral elements because their ultimate source is from the soil, they may also be provided in organic form from plant or animal remains. It has become common to speak of two different classes of fertilizers—organic and inorganic. Many people believe organic fertilizers are more effective and more natural. Plant and animal remains are no more natural than "naturally" occurring deposits of mineral fertilizer in the earth's crust. Plants absorb fertilizers in the elemental ionic form and potassium (K^+) from mineral deposits is just as effective in promoting growth as (K^+) derived from organic sources. Potassium is potassium!

FERTILIZER AVAILABILITY

It is, of course, true that potassium from one source may be less available to plants than potassium from another source. This phenomenon, however, has nothing to do with whether the source is organic or inorganic. Essential elements may be tightly bound chemically in a form which plants cannot absorb or they may be present in forms which can be directly absorbed by the plant. The amount of an element present in the soil has no direct relationship to the amount available for plant requirements. As a general rule, chemical fertilizers are more quickly available to plants than are organic fertilizers. Plant and animal tissue is composed of highly complex molecules which must be broken down before the constituent elements become available for absorption by plant roots.

Availability of nutrient elements is determined by many factors; the following are some of the more important: soil pH, soil organisms, compound stability and complexity, concentrations of other elements, and soil composition. Factors may be inter-related, as in cases where soil pH affects micro-organism populations, which in turn determine nitrogen availability to a large extent. Soil pH affects the availability of several elements other than nitrogen. High pH decreases the solubility of iron compounds and can induce iron chlorosis; the reverse occurs at a low pH and iron levels may become toxic below a pH of 5.0. A similar situation arises in the case of manganese. The concentration of one element in relation to another often affects plant growth simply because large supplies of one element will limit the physical opportunity of another element to be present near the root zone. Another effect of element concentration may be seen in the case where overdoses of phosphorus will precipitate iron from the soil solution and cause iron deficiency. The effect soil composition has on mineral element availability should be obvious since composition will affect pH, element concentration, soil organisms, and water holding capacity (remember, water is necessary for elements to enter into solution). Some mention has already been made concerning molecule complexity as it relates to element availability. Stability of compounds is another chemical attribute which vitally alters element uptake. The iron present in nails is not an especially complex form but it is very stable and is not nearly so available as is the iron in iron sulphate.

Discussion of fertilizer availability and all the inter-relationships it involves could be the subject of an entire book. For present purposes, it is enough if the reader realizes how complex the situation can become and that minor changes in soil mixes and fertilizer application programs can have unexpected and sometimes disastrous results. My purpose in presenting the following material is to elaborate practical information a grower may need to raise crops. The information is not a complete presentation of this complex field and readers should have a thorough understanding of the ramifications before they attempt to devise personal fertilizer formulas or modify existing ones.

FERTILIZER APPLICATION

Basically fertilizer may be applied in three different forms: dry, liquid, and coated with a polymeric resin membrane. Dry application is seldom made in container crops except when mixed into the soil at potting time. It is time consuming and difficult to apply a proper dosage by this method after plants are already potted. Phosphorus is almost always incorporated dry into soil mixes in the single or triple superphosphate form rather than being applied as a liquid. Reasons for this are that readily soluble forms of phosphorus are expensive and phosphorus is very tightly bound to soil particles, making it difficult to leach out. Since phosphorus is needed in relatively small quantities by plants and it doesn't leach appreciably, the amount initially incorporated into soil usually suffices for the crop cycle. Other dry fertilizers are sometimes mixed into soil, the objective usually being to provide plants with some available nutrients until liquid feeding builds up sufficient concentrations for normal plant growth.

Liquid application of fertilizer is accomplished normally by providing nutrient solutions to the root zone but foliar feeding is sometimes used, especially in the case of iron. Fertilizer injectors or proportioners are commonly used to inject concentrated stock solutions into the irrigation water. Proportioners are available in very expensive, refined models down to simple siphon devices which fit onto a garden hose. Unfortunately, only the more expensive models seem to possess the qualities of durability and accuracy. I used fertilizer injectors for years but finally started mixing diluted fertilizer directly in large tanks because the medium priced injectors I was using were constantly broken down or had to be calibrated for accuracy. When two or three fertilizers are used and growth retardants and fungicides are also applied in irrigation water, I find it much simpler to explain to unskilled employees how to use direct mix tanks than how to mix concentrated stock solutions for injectors. One limiting factor of inexpensive injectors is their inability to deliver large volumes of diluted solution.

Fertilizers used in proportioners or tanks must be easily and completely soluble and attention must be given to choosing ingredients which are compatible with one another. Many forms of phosphorus cannot be included in liquid fertilizer formulas because they precipitate out other elements. A practical method of determining if precipitation is occurring in mixtures is to observe the complete solubility of ingredients separately and then mix them together. If a residue becomes apparent at the bottom of the mixing container, precipitation has occurred. Precipitation may sometimes be overcome by using less concentrated stock solutions. Precipitation often becomes less of a problem in dilute solutions.

Fertilizer application in irrigation water will correlate roughly with the nutrient needs of plants. When plants are growing rapidly in high light and temperature conditions, the need for water is greater and consequently more fertilizer is applied. The reverse is true during the darker, colder days of winter. When applied with the irrigation water, fertilizers are diluted to extremely low ranges. This method of lightly fertilizing at every watering seems more satisfactory than less frequent but stronger applications. With stronger concentrations one runs the risk of burning tender new leaves and plants may become "hungry" between feedings. Constant liquid feed programs usually include nitrogen and potassium in the range of 100-200 ppm (parts per million) each. The term "parts per million" designates the number of parts of a fertilizer element present in one million parts of water. To obtain ppm, multiply the percentage of an element present in a fertilizer by 75. This results in the ppm of one ounce of fertilizer in 100 gallons of water. The decimal representation of percentage should be used; in other words, 44% equals 0.44. This formula is not exact but can be used for most greenhouse purposes. A few final words of caution before leaving liquid fertilizers. Concentrated stock solutions should not be made up in advance and stored. Chemical reactions can slowly take place which may significantly alter the original solution. Concentrated fertilizer solutions are often quite caustic and can severely burn tissue, especially eyes!

Fertilizers coated with polymeric resins are usually referred to as slow release fertilizers. I object to the mingling of the two meanings. Coated fertilizers may indeed be slow release but not all slow release fertilizers are coated with polymeric resin. Most slow release fertilizers are simply quite stable elemental compounds which break down slowly in the soil. Coated slow release fertilizers are those in which individual granules of fertilizers are coated with a resinous polymer membrane. This membrane acts in much the same manner as cell membranes in plant or animal tissue. When water is present, it diffuses across the membrane and dissolves the fertilizers, thus making the coated particle turgid or full of water. Dissolved fertilizer elements then diffuse through the membrane into the soil. The diffusion rate of fertilizer appears constant until about two-thirds of the fertilizer has been released. Rate of fertilizer diffusion into the soil is governed by the membrane thickness. Coated fertilizers release more fertilizers at higher temperatures than can be explained by simple physical diffusion mechanisms; apparently the physical characteristics of the membrane change with temperature.

One can readily see that soils to which coated fertilizers have been added should be used immediately and they should not be steamed after fertilizer incorporation. After a prolonged time or after steaming fertilizer concentrations may build up to toxic levels. Coated fertilizers may also be applied to soil surfaces. Some growers incorporate small amounts of coated fertilizers into the soil mix and then supply additional amounts by liquid feeding. Evidence has accumulated that this combination produces better crops than straight liquid feeding. My estimation of this phenomenon is that if one mixed sufficient starter fertilizer into the soil and added liquid fertilizer, growth would equal that obtained with the coated-liquid feed combination. Conventional dry fertilizer is much less expensive to provide than coated products. Coated fertilizers are especially useful in container production of trees. If the trees are watered by sprinkler systems, the majority of fertilizer elements in liquid feed is lost as runoff. There are several different formulations of coated fertilizers, each one being intended for particular types of crops or for specific periods of time.

My preference in applying fertilizers is to incorporate a very minimal amount into soil and feed constantly with irrigation water after potting. Some crops become very lush with only minimum fertilizer, a prime example being petunias. If any appreciable amount of fertilizer is mixed into the soil, petunias can become too rank, and, in my opinion, less suitable for garden use. One can always increase fertilizer application easily but it is sometimes difficult to reduce the amount already in soil. I feel the inexperienced grower is wiser to under fertilize slightly rather than trying to reach perfection by applying the maximum a plant can profitably use. Table 11 is a list of some important do's and don't's concerning fertilizer application.

Table 11

Fertilizer application pointers.

A.   Stronger concentrations should be applied only to moist soil.

B.   Do not store stock (concentrated) solutions.

C.   Check injector calibration frequently.

D.   Fertilizers are corrosive to common steel; line tanks with fiberglass coating.

E.   Let only reliable employees mix solutions.

F.   Some fertilizers absorb water from air if left exposed and will consequently weigh more.

G.   Do not store weed killers near fertilizer containers.

H.   Check compatibility of fertilizers before mixing.

I.   Any change of fertilizer practices should be tried on trial basis first.

J.   Avoid contact with fertilizer salts or concentrated solutions, especially on sensitive tissue.

K.   Double check all calculations.

FERTILIZER PROGRAMS

Recommending specific fertilization directions for the hundreds of circumstances a grower might encounter is clearly an impossibility. My purpose shall be to present elementary information which will enable growers to devise their own basic formulas if they wish. I will present a number of formulas which might be used if they appear to coincide with the need at hand.

The reader should review the mineral elements which were listed as being essential to plant growth in Chapter 5. In the following discussion, primary importance will be placed upon furnishing suitable levels of nitrogen, phosphorus, potassium, and occasionally iron. If a grower is lucky, these will be the only elements it is necessary to supply. The others being present as part of the major fertilizer ingredients, occurring naturally in the substrate, or present in the water supply.

PHOSPHORUS—Since phosphorus is usually added during soil mixing, specific recommendations have already been made under that heading. The superphosphate added also supplies sulfur and calcium in considerable quantities. Additional calcium is present in ground limestone if one alters soil pH with this compound. Dolomitic limestone can be substituted for altering soil pH and will supply both calcium and magnesium. I have never added dolomitic limestone and as yet have encountered no magnesium deficiencies in peat-sand soil media. This may be due to the magnesium content in the local "hard" water. Growers in areas with "soft" water should investigate the possibility of adding a magnesium source to the soil. In rare cases where additional phosphorus must be added during the growth cycle, di-ammonium phosphate may be applied at the rate of 1 ounce in 5 gallons of water.

IRON—Iron may become deficient, especially in alkaline soils or in media which contain no field soil. Iron uptake may be inadequate when soil aeration is poor. Deficiencies should be treated as they occur rather than applying iron as a matter of course. Chelated iron is often used because it does not become immobilized by attaching to soil particles. This form of iron is quite expensive. Recommendations for soil application vary considerably, ranging from 1 ounce per 10 gallons of water to 1 ounce per 25 gallons. I have always used a much more dilute solution for mild cases of iron chlorosis—1 ounce of 10% chelated iron per 50 gallons of water. Iron sulphate is a less expensive fertilizer but may become quickly unavailable; soil application is at a rate of 1 ounce per 2 gallons of water. Using iron sulphate in acid soils is not recommended because the additional amount needed and its extreme acidity will only magnify the problem. Iron is often applied as a foliar spray. I do not recommend this method for inexperienced growers because it is much easier to burn a crop if a mistake is made or conditions are not just right.

MICRONUTRIENTS—Micronutrient deficiencies were seldom a problem until the advent of completely artificial soil mixes. Even in media with no field soil content, micronutrient problems are not especially common but growers should be aware that deficiencies can arise under certain circumstances. The use of very pure fertilizers, de-ionized water, or especially clean sand could lead to micronutrient deficiencies. Most micronutrient fertilizers are very expensive and it makes no sense to apply them as a matter of course until definite problems have been encountered. Several micronutrients are toxic to plants at very low concentrations; indiscriminate use of them to cure imagined deficiencies can lead to injury from overdoses. Fritted (slow release) trace elements can be incorporated in the soil, or liquid applications may be made with soluble forms. I have made it a practice with peat-sand media to apply very dilute micronutrients approximately every 60 days. This time schedule eliminates double application to any crop. The mixing ratio is 6 ounces of Peters Soluble Trace Element Mix brand fertilizer and 4 ounces of 10% chelated iron per 300 gallons of water. Pots are given a heavy application of the solution. I have never encountered any deficiencies or overdoses with this schedule. Many growers may have no need of this micronutrient application and others may need more; each case should be decided on its own merits.

NITROGEN AND POTASSIUM—Most liquid feed programs supply only nitrogen and potassium on a regular basis. If fertilizer is applied at every watering, a solution containing approximately 100-150 ppm each of nitrogen (N) and potassium (K) is commonly used. The actual solution could vary from 75-200 ppm of each, depending upon the crop and time of year. Each grower must decide on the exact proportions of N and K suitable for the particular circumstance. When using the peat-sand soil mix formula given previously, I find the following fertilizer programs to be quite good.

A. Six ounces potassium nitrate (KNO_3)/100 gallons water. This formula is especially useful with bedding plants, tending to keep them from becoming overly lush. I also use it, after establishment, to develop large bracts and stiff stems on poinsettias. Do not use on chrysanthemums, Christmas Peppers, gloxinias, or foliage plants. There may be other varieties requiring high nitrogen for which this formula is unsuitable. Soluble salt buildup is very low with this formula because the entire molecule is usable by plants. There are 198 ppm potassium (K) and 63 ppm nitrogen (N) present in solution.

Calculation:

Potassium nitrate contains 14% nitrogen and 44% potassium.

$$75 \times 0.14 \times 6 = 63 \text{ ppm nitrogen}$$
$$75 \times 0.44 \times 6 = 198 \text{ ppm potassium}$$

B. Six ounces calcium nitrate ($CaNO_3$) and three ounces potassium nitrate (KNO_3)/100 gallons water. This formula can be used on all plants; bedding plants, especially petunias, may become more leafy than desirable. Poinsettias may develop potassium deficiencies unless formula "A" is used after establishment. Soluble salt buildup is moderate with this formula because the entire molecule is usable by plants; it is doubtful, however, if the large amount of calcium supplied is totally absorbed. There are 101.25 ppm nitrogen and 99 ppm potassium in solution.

Calculation:

Potassium nitrate contains 14% nitrogen and 44% potassium. Calcium nitrate contains 15.5% nitrogen.

$75 \times 0.155 \times 6 = 69.75$ ppm nitrogen (from calcium nitrate)

$75 \times 0.14 \times 3 = \underline{31.50}$ ppm nitrogen (from potassium nitrate)

 101.25 ppm total nitrogen

$75 \times 0.44 \times 3 = 99$ ppm potassium

Both formulas A and B have a basic pH reaction. This is desirable when the soil media is highly acid from the addition of peat. Another favorable trait of these fertilizer programs is that all the nitrogen is supplied in the nitrate form. Many plants, especially when planted in artificial media, display a disorder known as ammonium toxicity when fertilizers containing nitrogen in the ammonium form are used. Basically, nitrogen can be supplied in either the ammonium (NH_4^+) form or the nitrate form (NO_3^-). The exact reason for ammonium toxicity is debatable; certain authors contend that (NH_4^+) is unavailable for plant use and builds up toxic quantities in the soil unless converted to (NO_3^-) by soil micro-organisms. Other experts believe that (NH_4^+) is absorbable by plants and, in certain cases, utilized so fast as to disrupt normal plant functions. Whatever the case, it makes sense to use nitrate forms of nitrogen and avoid the problem altogether. In addition to being a problem with artificial media, ammonium toxicity is common when organic matter or fertilizers high in organic nitrogen are added to the soil before pasteurization. Nitrate nitrogen is easily leached from the soil while the ammonium form is more difficult to remove. Ammonium toxicity is typified by a burned appearance of the leaves. One might confuse this condition with an excess of fertilizer or soluble salts in the soil but it arises even in cases where soluble salts have been measured in a low range. Many growers were exposed to this problem when poinsettia crops were first planted in artificial mixes.

Another nitrogen related problem which can affect fertilizer programs is encountered when organic matter with a high carbon content and low nitrogen content is incorporated in soils. Mention was made of this situation when sawdust and bark were considered as organic matter sources. The problem arises because micro-organisms in the soil utilize the high carbon fraction as an energy source and their number quickly multiplies. If nitrogen is in limited supply, these organisms utilize all the available nitrogen and leave plants with none. Additional nitrogen must be supplied in soil mixes with a high carbon-to-nitrogen ratio, enough to supply both plants and micro-organisms.

Soils containing large amounts of clay or vermiculite may require less potassium because these minerals already contain large quantities of this element. Certain crops such as poinsettias and chrysanthemums seem to thrive in high potassium levels and show deficiencies quickly.

The fertilizer formulas given should not be followed blindly. Each grower must decide on particular fertilizer mixes according to soil and water chemistry and crop conditions. Observant readers may have noticed that formulas A and B are generally at the low end of the scale in ppm recommended for nitrogen and potassium. I find these fertilizer solutions do an adequate job for me; other authors usually recommend higher ppm of the two elements. Formulas A and B may be too weak if the soil medium is extremely well drained and leaching occurs at each irrigation. Growers can easily devise fertilizer recipes if the percentage of the particular element present in a fertilizer is known and the ppm formula is then used. Table 12 lists the percentage of nitrogen and potassium in some commonly used fertilizers. Blended commercial fertilizers will have the percentage of nitrogen, phosphorus, and potassium prominently displayed on the container in that order. To arrive at the ppm of a 20-10-25 fertilizer in solution perform the following calculations:

$$\begin{array}{lll}
\text{nitrogen} & 75 \times .20 = 15 \text{ ppm} \\
\text{phosphorus} & 75 \times .10 = 7.5 \text{ ppm} \\
\text{potassium} & 75 \times .25 = 18.75 \text{ ppm}
\end{array} \quad \left\{ \begin{array}{l} \text{present with 1 ounce} \\ \text{of fertilizer in} \\ \text{100 gallons of water} \end{array} \right.$$

Table 12

Important characteristics of some commonly used fertilizer materials. Composition percentages may vary slightly between sources. Higher salt indexes result in more soluble salts in solution (assume equal weights of fertilizer material.

Fertilizer material	Percent nitrogen	Percent potassium	pH reaction	Salt index
Ammonium sulphate	20	0	Acid	69
Ammonium nitrate	33.5	0	Acid	105
Sodium nitrate	16	0	Basic	100
Calcium nitrate	15.5	0	Basic	68
Potassium nitrate	14	44	Basic	74
Potassium chloride	0	62	Acid	115
Potassium sulphate	0	48	Acid	48

If 10 ounces of this 20-10-25 fertilizer were dissolved in 100 gallons of water, the resulting solution would contain 150 ppm nitrogen, 75 ppm phosphorus, and 187.5 ppm potassium.

Blended fertilizers are readily available for different soil mixes and crops. There is nothing wrong with using these ready made mixes except that the cost is much greater than for the separate ingredients. Many blended fertilizers also contain soluble phosphorus which is expensive and is not needed if phosphorus has been incorporated in the soil. Growers should make it a point to know exactly what compounds are included in premixed fertilizers; ammonium nitrogen is often the only or dominant form included in them and, as noted, this formula could result in ammonium toxicity. Readers who spend an hour reviewing the previous discussion on fertilizers will have no need for premixes and can save many dollars over the years. Growers should not be intimidated by the apparent complexity of devising fertilizer recipes; with a little study they can usually come up with better, more economical materials than those contained in premixes.

SOLUBLE SALTS

Various chemical compounds are known generically as salts. Any chemical salt which is soluble in water adds to the soluble salt level of a solution. Salts in the irrigation solution are derived from fertilizer compounds and naturally occurring minerals present in the water source. Salts in soil water come from those added in irrigation water, those minerals present naturally in the soil, and from inorganic and organic fertilizers added during soil mixing. Soluble salts in solution are determined by measuring the electrical conductivity with special instruments. Results can be specified in ppm or micromhos. Multiplying microhmos by 0.666 will convert results to ppm; multiplying ppm by 1.5 will convert results to microhmos. Soluble salts are commonly measured both in the irrigation water and soil extract solutions. Directions for preparing soil extracts and interpreting the readings obtained can be found in *The Greenhouse Environment* by John W. Mastalerz. The water is measured directly without any preparations. Table 13 provides data for interpreting water quality based on soluble salt content.

High soluble salts around plant roots subject the tissue to drought conditions even though adequate water is present. A graphic example of what takes place may be observed if a slug is immersed in a saturated salt solution. Water from the slug's body will move across the cell membranes into the saturated salt condition, leaving the slug dehydrated. If the salt concentration in solution is higher than in living tissue, water will move from the

Table 13

Water quality rating of irrigation water prior to addition of fertilizer compounds. Note: Growers should consider alternative water sources if readings are over 1000 ppm of soluble salts.

Water quality rating	Relative salt content	Reading in micromhos	Reading in ppm
Excellent	low	0-250	167
Good to fair	medium	250-750	167-500
Fair to poor	medium-high	750-2250	500-1500
Poor to unsatisfactory	excessive	2250 +	1500 +

tissue to the salt solution and vice versa. Even if the salt concentration in solution is not higher than in tissue, higher levels of salt will slow down the rate of water flow from the solution to living tissue. Thus all gradations of physiological drought may be observed, from complete desiccation to almost unobservable effects.

High soluble salt problems may never occur in the greenhouse if the water supply is good, excess fertilizers are not applied, and excess water is allowed to drain out the bottom of pots on a regular basis. The later process of allowing water to drain through the soil and out the drain holes is known as "leaching." Salts are carried out of the pot with the excess water and, as a consequence, the salt level in the soil is reduced. A grower's choice of fertilizer materials can significantly alter the salt condition of soils, even when the same quantities of nitrogen and potassium are applied. Table 12 illustrates the relative "saltiness" of common nitrogen and potassium fertilizers. It can readily be seen that ammonium nitrate contributes more than twice the nitrogen as sodium nitrate with only a slight increase in the amount of soluble salts added to a solution. One must also pay attention to how many essential elements are added by the fertilizer material. Potassium nitrate is a popular fertilizer because it is a source of both nitrogen and potassium while possessing a medium salt index. An added benefit is that the nitrogen is in the nitrate form.

All forms of salts do not appear to be equally damaging to plants. It is generally accepted that sulphate compounds are not so toxic in high concentrations as are other salts. Plant species will also differ in their response to soluble salts. Azaleas and gardenias will not tolerate high salts while carnations will grow well under relatively saline conditions. Some wild plant species which have evolved in the western United States seem to flourish under soluble salt conditions which would quickly kill the majority of species.

Table 14 lists some cultural practices which will help growers avoid salt buildup. People involved in merchandising plants to the public should convey these practices to consumers since excess soluble salts are one of the most common reasons for poor performance of plants in the home. Advanced symptoms of soluble salt injury are similar to ammonium toxicity in that marginal burning of the leaves is exhibited. Stunted growth and iron chlorosis may also indicate a soluble salt problem.

Table 14

Cultural practices which will help avoid soluble salt problems.

A.   Allow 10% of irrigation water to flow out the bottom of pots at each watering or if this is not practical, leach heavily on a regular but intermittent schedule.
B.   Choose fertilizer materials with a lower salt index when possible.
C.   Choose fertilizers which contribute more than one essential element.
D.   Do not apply more fertilizer than is needed for good growth.
E.   Soil with a high proportion of large particles will leach more rapidly and thereby reduce salt content.
F.   Maintaining a soil in a moist condition will cause less salt damage than a dry soil.
G.   Choose a water supply which does not contain excessive salts.
H.   Avoid sprinkling plants often; water less frequently but more heavily.

DIAGNOSING FERTILIZER DISORDERS

When crops are not growing properly, it is generally very difficult to pinpoint the cause especially if one does not have years of growing experience. Fertilizer and soluble salt problems should be considered as prime suspects in any plant disorders. The difficulty with diagnosing plant disorders is that plants can't tell the grower where it hurts. Growers must develop an acute sense of observation to detect unusual growth patterns early enough to remedy them before major damage is done. Unless one has observed a particular fertilizer deficiency previously, it is very difficult to read descriptions of the visual symptoms and then be reasonably sure of a diagnosis. There are simply too many plant "illnesses" which have similar symptoms. Accurate visual diagnosis comes only with long years of experience. Fertilizer deficiencies do not exhibit the same symptoms in all species; growers must keep in mind that the same disorder may look somewhat different in different species.

Tissue analysis can present the grower with more tangible evidence of fertilizer deficiencies and excesses. The trouble with tissue analysis is that the state university or private laboratories capable of performing accurate work are seldom handy to the grower. Analysis of leaf tissue can quickly confirm a grower's suspicion of particular nutrient problems. Tables are available for major crops which show the desired content of various mineral elements in leaf tissue. Brief visual symptoms of deficiencies for nitrogen, potassium, phosphorus, and iron were mentioned in Chapter 5; more detailed discussions may be found in general references listed at the end of this book. A particularly good discussion of tissue analysis is presented in *The Greenhouse Environment* by John W. Mastalerz.

Most nutrient related plant disorders can be avoided by growers having a good working knowledge of soils, fertilizers, and plant requirements. Those problems which do come up will have to be dealt with by a combination of grower knowledge of symptoms, trial and error cures, and tissue analysis data. I cannot emphasize enough the benefit a few days of study will give growers in being able to deal with nutrient problems. Table 15 presents a checklist of factors one should keep in mind when devising a fertilizer program.

Table 15

**Checklist of factors to be considered
when devising a fertilizer program.**

A. pH characteristics of fertilizers should be compatible with desired pH ranges of soils.
B. Essential fertilizer elements must be present in balanced proportions.
C. Low salt index fertilizers should be chosen whenever possible.
D. Fertilizers which supply more than one essential element are generally more desirable.
E. Nitrate forms of nitrogen are usually safer, especially in artificial soil mixes.
F. Be sure precipitation is not occurring in fertilizer solutions.
G. Double check all calculations.
H. It is safer to underfertilize slightly than to overfertilize.
I. Relatively small amounts of trace elements can be toxic to plants.
J. Ammonium toxicity and the carbon-to-nitrogen ratio of soils must be considered when deciding upon types and amounts of nitrogen to fertilize with.
K. Soil pH and other factors can alter the availability of nutrients.
L. Availability of essential elements is more important than physical concentrations.
M. The types and proportions of soil mix ingredients may affect the type and amount of fertilizers used.
N. Different species of plants may require different forms and concentrations of fertilizers.

SUMMATION OF A PARTICULAR
FERTILIZER PROGRAM

I have explained the fertilizer program I use in several different sections of this book. Recapping the essential points in a general manner may serve to clarify the overall program. One must remember this program is utilized under the conditions of an approximately 50% peat - 50% sand soil mix and irrigation water is relatively high in soluble salts (approximately 650 - 900 ppm). No limestone is incorporated into the soil mix for pH adjustment.

A weak solution of potassium nitrate is added to the soil along with adequate triple superphosphate. Plants are then fertilized at every watering with a solution of either potassium nitrate alone or potassium nitrate plus calcium nitrate. The first solution is used on all spring bedding crops and flowering baskets and on poinsettias after establishment. The latter solution is used as the general fertilizer at all other times unless the grower chooses to restrict nitrogen supplies. Petunias receive fertilizer only every third watering after they are well established. Micronutrients and chelated iron are applied every 60 days after a thorough leaching. This program is designed to ensure that fertilizer excess will not occur. Growers who can leach somewhat at each watering or who prefer plants in a lush condition may want to increase the concentrations at all stages. Low soluble salt water supplies may bring about the possibility of magnesium deficiencies and could call for increased applications of micronutrients and possibly nitrogen and potassium.

Coated polymeric resin fertilizers are incorporated at a low rate into spring flowering baskets and patio planters. A three month formulation with iron is used. These baskets and planters are also fertilized at every watering along with other crops.

Trees and shrubs planted bare root in the spring are watered heavily upon potting with the normal micronutrient and iron solution. A double rate of potassium nitrate plus calcium nitrate is applied at the same time. This fertilizer application is enough to carry plants through the early spring with straight water irrigation. If shrubs and trees are held any longer, they should receive additional fertilizations with liquids or top dressings of coated or dry slow release fertilizers.

Each grower should realize that the above program cannot be blindly followed; the same applies to other fertilizer recipes one might encounter. Growers must always observe results closely and make adjustments when necessary.

CHAPTER 11

LIGHT

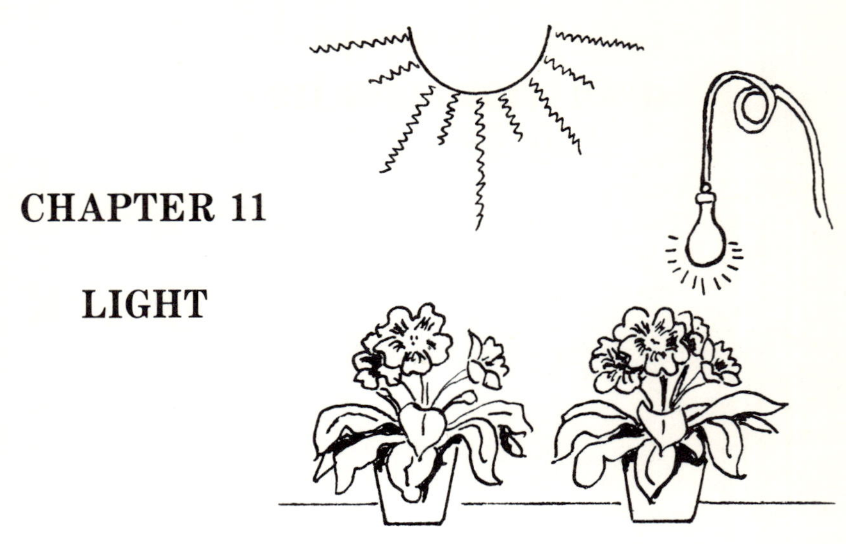

No one factor required for plant growth is more important than another but the whole being of plants is centered about the conversion of light energy into chemical energy. It is not surprising that the amount and quality of light impinging upon a plant regulates, to a great extent, its requirements for other essential ecological factors. Mineral elements and temperature can usually be regulated at will by greenhouse personnel; the ability to manipulate light energy easily is not commonplace in most greenhouses. Since it is more difficult to effect wholesale changes in light quality and intensity, most growers are content to let nature take its course. Simple operations like shading are practiced but sophisticated manipulations of light are left to more innovative growers or those whose circumstances definitely require light alteration. As a consequence, the average grower probably spends less time worrying about how to change light conditions than he does thinking about fertilizer or temperature factors. In future years economical technology will perhaps be available to alter light energy at will and greenhouse owners will take a more aggressive attitude toward its management. My own opinion is that whenever possible, growers should work within the bounds nature dictates. This philosophy generally results in lower costs and better quality crops. If certain crops do not do well at a particular time, choose one that will. This attitude cannot, of course, be carried too far. If the market absolutely demands a particular crop, it must be raised whether conditions are optimum or not. The following discussion of light will be limited to those aspects which will be necessary for non-specialized growers to have a general knowledge of the subject.

LIGHT QUALITY

Light energy is composed of wavelengths which are categorized according to the distance between successive waves. These categories are what is referred to when one speaks of light "quality." Table 16 shows the wavelength relationship between light quality categories which affect plant growth. Infrared radiation, as far as is presently known, affects plants mainly because it is absorbed by tissues and is transformed into heat. The amount of infrared radiation penetrating the greenhouse skin greatly affects temperature relationships inside the greenhouse. Ultraviolet radiation is responsible for much of the degradation occurring to plastic and fiberglass coverings. Neither ultraviolet nor infrared wavelengths pass through greenhouse coverings readily.

Table 16

Relative wavelength of different light quality categories which affect plant growth.

Light category	Effect on plant growth
Gamma X-ray	Induce genetic mutations, phytotoxic in large quantities.
Ultraviolet C Ultraviolet B	Generally phytotoxic.
Ultraviolet A	Formative effects on leaves and internodes.
Violet Blue Blue-green Green Yellow Orange Red Far-red	Visible spectrum—affects plant growth in a direct manner. Photosynthetic wavelengths.
Infrared	Affects plant growth indirectly as a source of heat.

increasing wavelength

Fortunately, the visible wavelengths which affect plant growth readily pass through the greenhouse skin. Blue and red areas of the visible spectrum have been found to account for most of the photosynthetic activity in plants. Far-red and red wavelengths are responsible for many of the flowering responses controlled by daylength. Knowledge of plant responses to different light wavelengths can be of practical importance when greenhouse covers are chosen and if plants are grown under any type of artificial light. Obviously, greenhouse covering materials should transmit the maximum amount of light possible in the red and blue wavelengths. It would not be as important for maximum transmission to occur in the green and yellow wavelengths since they are relatively weak in photosynthetic and developmental activity. Objects are perceived to be a certain color because they absorb light of that color. It should be evident that fiberglass tinted blue or red is not the best choice for greenhouse coverings because important photosynthetic rays would be filtered out.

Growers in low winter light areas can sometimes profitably provide supplemental lighting from electrical lamps. It is very important to choose lamps emitting the proper wavelengths so that growth is increased with the smallest expenditure of energy. Supplemental light is often used in the seedling stage because a large number of plants can be accelerated in growth by lighting a small area. It would obviously take more lights to accomplish the same purpose after transplanting to larger pots. Incandescent lamps emit a large proportion of red and far-red light while most fluorescent lamps are rich in blue and green wavelengths. Light strictly from incandescent sources will increase photosynthesis and growth but cause plants to become tall and spindly. Light only from fluorescent lamps does not cause extraordinary elongation of plants but neither does it result in dramatic photosynthetic increases. A combination of incandescent and fluorescent light sources provides for balanced growth because both blue and red wavelengths are present. Blue light seems to counteract the elongative effects of red light. A more energy efficient fluorescent lamp, a brand called the Wide Spectrum Gro-Lux, is now available. It combines the qualities of both incandescent and fluorescent bulbs.

Most people tend to supply artificial light in insufficient intensities to generate normal plant growth. Lamps should be placed as close as possible to plants without causing heat buildup. It has been estimated that seedlings should receive 20 - 40 lamp watts per square foot with the Wide Spectrum Gro-Lux lights located approximately one foot above plant tops. Retail customers are constantly wondering why one Gro-Lux light placed three to four feet above plants does not produce good results. A light source one foot above plants provides four times as much light as a source two feet away. One can readily see the geometric reduction of intensity which would take place at four feet.

LIGHT INTENSITY

Light intensity is a much more familiar characteristic to the average person than is light quality. If light is brighter, it is more intense. Light is often measured in units called foot-candles. Most greenhouse crops prefer full sun for maximum production. Full sun on a clear summer day in the midwestern United States might equal 10,000-12,000 foot-candles, while the reading on a cloudy winter day in the same location would be hard pressed to reach 1,000 foot-candles. Some crops are termed shade plants; the leaves of these may be burned at light intensities of 2,000-3,000 foot-candles. Individual leaves of sun plants are photosynthesizing at maximum capacity when light levels of 2,000-3,000 foot-candles are reached. Higher light levels are needed, however, to reach maximum production for the whole plant because many leaves are shaded from above and outside. Thus if inside leaves of sun plants are to receive 2,000 foot-candles, the outside ones must be exposed to considerably higher intensities. Individual leaves of shade plants become light saturated at 500-1,000 foot-candles. Shade plant leaves will not tolerate increased light intensity above the saturation point as well as do those of sun plants. Damage of plant leaves due to high light intensities is caused by photo oxidation of chlorophyll pigments.

Crop quality can be maximized with respect to light intensity in several ways: shading or supplemental lighting may be practiced, crops may be grown only at suitable times of the year, spacing between plants may be varied with seasonal light conditions, and temperature may be correlated with light intensity. Crop production is greatest at the highest light intensities possible without chlorophyll damage. When insufficient light is available for a particular variety, whether it be sun or shade, the effects are manifested in thinner, taller stems, larger, more succulent leaves, fewer flowers, less branching, and an overall reduction in dry matter weight. Too much light may damage leaf tissue quickly and be apparent as severe burns or it may show up as a gradual yellowing process as chlorophyll is destroyed.

Greenhouses are normally constructed to admit as much light as possible. Their orientation and types of coverings as they affect light were discussed previously. Rafters and roof braces can seriously impair light transmission unless they are engineered to be as small and as few in number as possible. The greenhouse interior should be covered with white paint wherever possible to increase the reflective light available for plants. Summer shading must be removed promptly in the fall or serious reductions in crop quality will result. If light intensity is to be supplemented by lamps, the design should be engineered by persons competent to determine the most economical installation. Typically, artificial light installations on a greenhouse-wide basis will not justify themselves unless a strong market exists.

Plant spacing in the greenhouse is a critical subject which every successful grower must understand completely. If plants are grown widely spaced so that no competition for light exists between them, they will achieve maximum quality. This spacing is usually not the most advantageous economically, but in a market where a strong demand for quality exists, emphasis may be placed on spacing plants to obtain maximum quality and, consequently, maximum economic return. Certain markets where quality is less of a factor than price may dictate that growers space plants closer together in order to produce more plants per square foot. Generally, growers will be best off spacing plants to a point where slight competition for light begins, resulting in complete utilization of bench space and a reasonably high quality product. Market requirements and interplant competition for light should be studied very closely; the ability of a grower to squeeze 1-2% more high quality plants out of each bench can markedly increase greenhouse profits. Recommendations for spacing can be found scattered through the literature but the final decision will always rest upon the grower's evaluation of circumstances. Latitude, local light intensities, greenhouse construction, varieties, and market demands will interact to determine the most profitable spacing densities. As a rule of thumb, many growers assume a 1 square foot spacing for the common 6 inch potted flower. Especially vigorous species may require slightly more space and less robust species a little less. I have always spaced plants somewhat closer than this because my location has a naturally high light intensity. During peak demand seasons it is extremely important to have plants spaced as closely as possible consistent with good quality. Employees must constantly be reminded of the important role spacing plays. The length of time a plant is in the greenhouse and the area it occupies are two critical factors in determining what price it should sell for.

Careful selection of plant varieties will aid growers in producing quality crops throughout the year, even though light intensity varies greatly from one season to the next. Certain plants such as cinerarias and calceolarias do well at relatively low light intensities and, as a result, are popular crops to flower from December through March. Plant breeders have developed numerous varieties within the same general groups which perform well at different seasons of the year. Chrysanthemums and snapdragons have been especially well developed in this sense. Growers who take the time to be knowledgeable about plant varieties which do well at particular times will have an edge over their competitors. Unlike machinery and materials, knowledge costs the grower nothing to acquire. It is the most important but least expensive of all the factors required for plant production. The great majority of information regarding varieties of plants which will do well under certain environmental conditions is contained in publications offered by the larger seed and plant companies which distribute their products nationwide. Reference books like this one are a poor source for varietal information because they are often out of date before publication. Plant breeding is a fast moving field and many new varieties are released each year.

A good knowledge of local light conditions is essential in growing quality plants. If you build a greenhouse in an area you are not familiar with, you must make an effort to find out the particulars of the local light situation. Light intensity will affect quality and maturation dates not only directly as a source of energy for photosynthesis but indirectly because average greenhouse temperatures are usually warmer when light is abundant. Crop timing will vary somewhat each year because of differences in solar radiation from one year to the next. Most factors except light intensity can be controlled within rather narrow bounds and, as a result, variations in crop timing from year to year will be due mostly to changing light conditions if an effort is made to hold other factors constant. Growers must evaluate published crop schedules carefully to determine how local light conditions might alter marketing dates. Crop schedules without reference to latitude and local light intensity are not as useful as those which present this information.

FLOWERING RESPONSE RELATED TO LIGHT DURATION AND QUANTITY

Flowering in plants is intricately related to light. Light energy seems to affect flowering primarily in two ways: certain plants flower only when they have been exposed to predetermined cumulative amounts of light energy while another group flowers mainly in response to the length of day regardless of total cumulative light energy received. The following presentation is arranged to acquaint the reader with basic concepts rather than becoming bogged down in detailed or qualifying remarks. Every grower must realize that although a factor such as daylength may be the primary controller of a particular plant process, this controlling factor is usually modified to some degree by other factors and may, at times, be completely overridden.

Several important crops flower primarily in response to the cumulative amount of light energy they have received. As long as a reasonable time period is allowed for normal development, flowering is independent of age. Any crop which flowers naturally year round may be suspected of possessing this cumulative energy response. Geranium seedlings planted in October have been found to require almost exactly the same cumulative light energy to flower as crops planted in February. Chronological ages for the two crops were 215 days and 126 days, respectively at flowering, but each was exposed to slightly over 55,000 gram calories per square centimeter of light energy. Carnations and gloxinias exhibit similar behavior. Experiments to determine behavior must be closely controlled to separate light responses from temperature responses. Since temperatures normally increase along with light intensity, it is sometimes difficult to find which is the controlling factor.

In the earlier part of the 20th century, scientists working with agricultural crops found that flowering in some species was controlled by the length of the day to which plants were exposed. The term "photoperiodism" was applied to this phenomenon. Extensive research over the years has shown that flowering in many species is regulated by complex photoperiodic mechanisms. Plants were divided into three basic groups: short-day plants which initiate flowers only when days are shorter than the critical daylength, long-day plants which initiate flowers only when days are longer than the critical daylength, and day-neutral plants which initiate flowers over a wide range of daylengths. It is important to point out that no specific daylength has been mentioned; a long-day plant may have a critical daylength which is shorter than is the critical daylength of a short day plant. The direction of daylength change after the critical daylength has been reached is actually the heart of the mechanism. As if this terminology were not confusing enough, it was later found that the length of the dark period was actually the controlling factor, not the daylength! The terms long-day, short-day and day-neutral were so firmly fixed in the literature, however, that plants are still referred to in this manner. Conclusive proof of the importance of the dark period is shown by the fact that brief light flashes in the dark will alter the response of short-day plants while short dark periods in the middle of the light period have no effect on the response of long-day plants. This phenomenon of short light flashes interrupting flower initiation in short-day plants is of much practical importance to growers. They need not waste energy lighting artificially until the critical daylength has been reached; short flashes provided in the middle of the night will serve the same purpose. Accidental light flashes will cause the same response. Flowering schedules may be upset by brief exposure to light when personnel enter the greenhouse at night or from automobile headlamps.

In addition to the three main photoperiodic classifications, there are less frequently manifested mechanisms of flowering response. Some plants will flower eventually regardless of the daylength but the flowering response may be speeded up or slowed down by the appropriate photoperiod. Low and high temperatures will sometimes cancel the effects of the photoperiod; temperature variations might also alter photoperiod requirements. Further refinements of photoperiodic responses have been described in short-long day plants which initiate flowers only when short days are followed by long days and long-short day plants which initiate flowers only when long days are followed by short days. Low light intensities may affect photoperiodic responses. Bud abortion is common after initiation in geraniums and Easter lilies when light levels are low and temperatures high. Low light levels will slow flower initiation in chrysanthemums. Specific response to photoperiod for important flower crops is given under the appropriate species listing in a later part of this book. Table 17 lists the effects of photoperiod on some common spring bedding plants.

Table 17

Effects of daylength on common bedding plants. Critical daylengths are not precisely located. This is a general appraisal of what takes place through the season.

Plant	Long-day	Short-day
Alyssum (annual)	None	None
Balsam	None	None
Begonia tuberous	Promotes flowering	
Begonia fibrous	None	None
Carnation	Speeds flowering	
Centaurea	Speeds flowering	
Chrysanthemum (perennial)		Induces flowering
Coleus		Induces flowering
Cosmos		Induces flowering
Dahlia		Induces flowering
Daisy Marguerite	Speeds flowering	Prevents flowering
Daisy Shasta	Induces flowering	
Gaillardia	Induces flowering	
Gypsophila	Induces flowering	
Impatiens	None	None
Lobelia	None	None
Marigold	Delays flowering	
Petunia	Increases height, speeds flowering	
Phlox (annual)	Induces flowering	
Verbena	Induces flowering	
Zinnia		Speeds flowering

Daylength also affects germination, rooting of cuttings, tuber formation, and stem elongation. The photoperiodic requirements for seed are usually not absolute. The light and dark and temperature requirements for seed germination are extensively presented in several trade books and seed companies will often distribute complimentary copies of these requirements. As I mentioned in the section on propagation, I pay little attention to these detailed presentations and have seldom had any significant germination problems.

PRACTICAL PHOTOPERIOD MANIPULATION

Many growers have little theoretical knowledge of photoperiodic responses but succeed quite well in obtaining the desired results. Most major crops have their photoperiodic requirements well documented and growers may obtain reliable light and dark schedules from large wholesale propagators of the particular crop. One must remember that these schedules will be altered by latitude because daylengths vary with latitude. If photoperiodic flowering responses are not understood well, one should follow published schedules religiously because seemingly minor details can seriously affect flowering dates.

Increasing the daylength is accomplished by providing light periods in the middle of the night with incandescent lamps. These lamps emit energy in the far-red wavelengths which are most suitable for photoperiodic induction. Certain species such as poinsettias are extremely sensitive to photoperiodic induction and low light levels will suffice. Chrysanthemums require relatively high light levels for photoperiodic induction. Sufficient light will be provided for all species if a single row of 60 watt bulbs with reflectors is spaced every 4 feet down a 4 foot wide bench. Bulbs should be less than 5 feet above the top of plants. An 8 foot wide bench would require 100 watt bulbs spaced every 6 feet. Lights are regulated by timers; most small growers can get by very well with inexpensive appliance timers available at the hardware store. Large growers can benefit from the installation of more sophisticated cyclic timing devices which reduce the total energy requirements by providing several shorter periods of light during the night.

Daylengths are reduced by drawing some type of opaque flexible material over plants at specified times. Black sateen cloth is the preferred material but 6 mil black polyethylene will suffice on temporary installations. Light levels should be reduced to two to three foot candles so the material must be checked for small holes and tears and sides must be fully down past bench level. Growers sometimes apply shade cloth too early in the day because quitting time is 5 o'clock. Early application during summer increases the heat buildup under shadecloth to levels which can be deleterious to crops. In addition, plants do not receive maximum allowable daylengths so crop quality is reduced. Black polyethylene emphasizes the heat buildup problem more than does sateen cloth. Crops requiring short days in winter may be present in the same greenhouse with plants requiring lighting for long days. In these cases the black cloth is drawn over long day plants near sundown and removed early in the morning. Periods of light are given during the night. Applying the cloth during the night prevents light leakage to short day plants.

Light from extraneous sources can seriously affect greenhouse operation if photoperiodic flower crops are grown through the winter. Poinsettias will remain vegetative at light levels of one to two foot candles. The only way to monitor light intensity adequately is with a light meter but one can gain some idea of permissible light levels by knowing that the maximum intensity of bright moonlight is 0.02 foot candles. This is not a photoperiodically inductive light level. Many localities now have ordinances against light pollution. If a grower has problems with extraneous light sources which cannot be solved by friendly persuasion, it may be possible to invoke these pollution laws. It must be remembered that short flashes of light can be just as disruptive to flowering as longer exposures. One should not become overly nervous about light pollution. I have spent many hours worrying over newly installed street lights and signs near my greenhouse but these light sources have never caused flowering schedules to be disrupted. I have also observed several greenhouses in very well lighted urban locations; they apparently have no serious problems. Buying a reliable light meter will eliminate any unwarranted worry.

Plant species will vary considerably in the number of prescribed 24 hour light/dark cycles needed to completely initiate flower buds. Certain plants will be initiated after only one cycle while others may take up to 25 days. Although flower induction may be completed within a relatively short period of time, most plants will require a longer period of appropriate cycles after initiation to make the flowering process irreversible. In the northern United States poinsettias have set bud by mid October under natural light conditions but must still receive short days until mid November to assure proper flowering.

Manipulation of the photoperiod is an added expense and worry to greenhouse operators. I have always attempted to fulfill market demand by growing plants during their natural flowering season. Not only does this practice lower expenses but it also often results in premium crops. Plants just naturally seem to grow better when it is their regular time to do so. Growers who search for appropriate natural season crops also tend to avoid the habit of growing 3 or 4 staple flowering crops all year. Seasonal crops stimulate demand because the public hasn't seen them for a year. I simply cannot sell appreciable numbers of chrysanthemums because they are in every flower shop and supermarket 365 days a year.

Although daylength manipulation will generally be a part of any year-round greenhouse operation, growers must carefully analyze whether it is more profitable to concentrate on natural season crops or to provide a selection of staples all year. If growing for small retail shops, one can influence customers to purchase what one wants to grow. If large chain stores are the primary target, one must grow what they want and that means lots of chrysanthemums. Daylength manipulation is not all a liability to growers; it can be very helpful in precisely timing large crops for particular marketing periods. Larger growers generally prefer to have crops move out entirely within a short period so that benches may be quickly refilled. Many smaller growers prefer crops to trickle out slowly as individual plants mature so that too many plants are not ready at any one time.

CHAPTER 12

TEMPERATURE

Plants require a suitable temperature range in order to carry on life processes. Most species would be killed upon exposure to temperatures of more than 150° F or less than −50° F. The temperature range for normal active growth in most plants would be approximately 40°-110° F. Certain plants originating in very cold or hot regions of the earth will extend these ranges for survival and normal growth. Acceptable growing temperatures for alpine and arctic species may lie between 25° and 85° F while tropical plants may require a range between 55° and 120° F for normal growth. Temperature not only determines the limits of survival and active growth, but also speeds up or retards the rate of growth. Within a plant's normal growth range, increases in temperature speed up chemical processes in the plant and growth accelerates. Plants may exhibit damage when temperatures fluctuate widely within a short time span even though the extreme survival limits have not been reached. This phenomenon is best illustrated by the need for plants to be exposed to gradually colder temperatures before they become winter hardy. The chemical activities taking place in plants evidently function more smoothly if temperature changes are made gradually.

TEMPERATURE AND RESPIRATION

Two basic chemical processes taking place in plants are photosynthesis and respiration. Photosynthesis is an accumulating phenomenon which contributes to the production of plant matter. Respiration, although necessary for proper growth, is a consuming process whereby plant matter is decreased. Normally, photosynthesis outpaces respiration by many times so that plants are observed to grow larger. Under some circumstances, respiration and photosynthesis may be balanced; this situation is termed the compensation point. At this point plants do not grow larger. Several factors are of major importance in determining the photosynthetic rate but temperature is the primary factor controlling respiration rates. At very low light intensities respiration can actually exceed photosynthesis and plants can decrease in mass. This may be one of the scientific principles behind the customary practice of lowering daytime temperatures in greenhouses during periods of cloudy weather. Respiration is a large contributing factor to the decline in quality of plants when they reach old age, or are placed in areas where photosynthesis cannot outpace respiration. Higher temperatures speed up respiration and the consumption of plant matter; if photosynthesis is not occurring at an equal or greater rate, a decline in quality results. One can readily understand why flowers harvested for bouquets last longer at cooler temperatures.

DAY/NIGHT TEMPERATURES

Temperatures mentioned in greenhouse literature pertain to night temperatures at plant level unless otherwise specified. This convention has come about because night temperatures normally exert a greater influence on plant growth and development than do day temperatures. Most flower crops are produced during short day seasons and it only stands to reason that the temperature to which plants are exposed for the longer length of time would affect them more. Night temperatures for important crops are given later in this book under cultural practices for each plant. It is not surprising that the majority of plant species grow better when night temperatures are lower than day temperatures. Plants have evolved for millions of years under this type of cycle and undoubtedly have physiological adaptations to it. Most experts recommend a day temperature of 10°-15° F higher than night temperatures on bright days and about 5° F higher than night temperature on cloudy days. Unless greenhouses are well equipped, it is difficult to maintain day temperatures at only 15° F higher than night temperature, especially on bright days. When light intensity is very bright in late spring, summer, and early fall, I feel day temperatures of 25° F over the night temperature will produce high quality crops. Some growers allow night temperatures to drop almost to the freezing point on selected spring crops; obviously the day temperatures cannot be held to a 10°-15° F increase if days are bright. My personal opinion is that crops can be grown faster with no decrease in quality by letting day temperatures rise 15°-25° F higher than night temperatures if light intensity is high and sufficient ventilation is possible. Certain crops for outdoor use may tolerate even wider differences.

As fuel prices have risen in past years, researchers have discovered two promising avenues of fulfilling plant temperature requirements with less energy. One of these methods involves splitting night temperatures whereby the minimum recommended temperature is maintained for perhaps only one half of the dark period. The temperature may then be lowered a few degrees during the rest of the night. The second method consists of heating soil areas as much as possible rather than the surrounding air mass. Each of these programs offers the possibility of significant fuel savings but data is not sufficient to recommend specific cultural programs for crops.

STAGE OF GROWTH AND TEMPERATURE

Many plants seem to require a higher temperature during early stages of growth than at more mature stages to reach maximum size and quality. This phenomenon has been documented in several species by controlled experiments. If temperatures are not lowered during later growth stages, plants fail to accumulate as much dry weight. Some authors feel that as plants mature, the preponderance of photosynthesis over respiration is lessened and since respiration is more directly controlled by temperature, a reduction in temperature reduces respiration more than it does photosynthesis. It has been my observation that starting plants out under warm conditions gets them strongly established in less time. Not only does this practice cut down crop time but it also reduces losses due to disease in the juvenile stage. Most of my losses due to disease occur in the first week or two after transplanting and the sooner plants grow out of this stage the better. Certain crops such as pansies, although having a shorter crop time under this regime, do not exhibit a marked increase in quality. Annual alyssum, on the other hand, has a shorter crop time and exceptional improvement in quality if grown at warm temperatures for the first week or two. Each of these species can be finished at very low temperatures but the alyssum does not like to start out cold.

Starting plants warm and finishing cooler may not only improve quality and production, but since young plants generally occupy less space than more mature ones, it also reduces fuel expenses. If an entire greenhouse cannot be filled with one crop to provide the appropriate temperatures, it may be possible to maintain one area of the greenhouse range at a higher temperature for young plant production. After being transplanted to the final container, they can be moved to cooler greenhouses.

EFFECT OF TEMPERATURE ON PLANT DEVELOPMENT

The effects temperature has on plant growth may be recognized in a general sense by people who have little more than a gardening knowledge of plants. Certain developmental processes in plants are also affected by temperature; the relationships are often less than obvious to the untrained eye.

Flower initiation in a fairly large number of species is controlled predominantly by temperature. This group of plants is not nearly so large as those where photoperiod is the controlling factor but some important crops are included. Temperature and photoperiod may interact in a number of species—one canceling, over-riding, or modifying the effect of the other under certain circumstances. The effect of temperature may be expressed in a qualitative or quantitative manner. That is, the particular temperature treatment required for flower initiation may be absolute or it may act only to speed the flowering process which would have eventually occurred anyway. Specific temperatures for a prescribed length of time may cause flowers to be initiated during that period or, in some cases, certain temperature regimes may only be the beginning in a number of factor sequences which cause flower initiation at some future date.

Many biennial and perennial plants require a period of exposure to low temperatures before flowering will occur. This low temperature exposure takes place naturally in winter time with plants that are grown outdoors. If perennial alyssum is started in the fall and then subjected to light freezes in winter, it will bloom for spring sales. Plants sown in the spring will remain vegetative through the first year. There are a number of common perennials which react in a similar manner. This low temperature exposure is not universally required for blooming in perennials. Shasta daisies and cone flowers (*Rudbeckia*) will flower a little the first summer if sown in mid-winter and perennial violas will bloom quite prolifically 12-16 weeks after sowing.

Cabbage and its close relatives are an important group of biennial bedding plants which must be subjected to cold temperatures before flower production occurs. Cabbage sown in late spring and transplanted to the garden remains in the vegetative "head" stage the first summer. If left in the field it will flower the second year, as do all biennials. Flowering in cabbage is undesirable if vegetable production is the objective. Young cabbage plants which have been spring sown and then subjected to low temperatures (45° F) for two or more weeks will flower the first growing season and lead to customer complaints. If cabbages are artificially maintained at warm temperatures, they will continue producing heads for several years. Other biennials are not so sensitive to cold treatment as is cabbage; they may require considerably more exposure to commence flowering or they may need no cold treatment at all.

Several important flower crops which are not biennials or perennials require low temperature exposure for flower initiation. Flowers are initiated when temperatures fall below the critical level for a specified period of time. After initiation, some species must remain at or below the critical temperature level to complete flower development while others can be grown at higher temperatures to accelerate flower development. Cineraria, calceolaria, Martha Washington geranium, Christmas cactus, and hydrangea are some flowering crops which require low temperature exposure at some stage of development.

Several crops require that temperatures be above a critical level for specified periods; the direction of change must be upward in relation to the critical temperature. In low temperature plants the direction of change must be downward. As it is with photoperiod, each plant has its own critical temperature. Azalea and chrysanthemum are examples of plants requiring high temperatures for flower initiation. Chrysanthemum temperature requirements are strongly inter-related with photoperiod and it is photoperiod which exerts the more dramatic and precise influence. This interaction phenomenon is not uncommon in other groups of plants. More details concerning temperature as it affects flower initiation and development will be given as the culture of individual species is discussed.

Most of the common bulb crops require rather complex temperature programs for optimum development. Fortunately for the smaller grower, many of the requirements have been met before receipt of the bulbs. Response to temperature exposure is often quantitative in nature; Easter lily bulbs stored for six weeks at 40° F force in approximately 110 days. Bulbs stored at higher temperatures require a longer forcing schedule. It is quite important that the final grower know what temperature regimes bulbs have been exposed to before shipment.

Temperature affects several developmental processes in plants other than flower initiation. Many growers are under the assumption that the cold treatment given to spring bulb crops prior to forcing is necessary for flower development. In reality, this storage period controls the degree of stem elongation and flower size. These attributes may of course be affected by forcing procedures but they are to a large degree, already determined by the pre-forcing storage period. Flower shape in several chrysanthemum varieties seems to vary depending upon greenhouse temperatures. At low temperatures some varieties exhibit a trait known as "quilling," which gives the flower a ragged, uneven appearance. Flowers may also be flattened in relation to depth. Flower color is usually improved by lowering temperatures shortly before harvest. The intensity and vibrancy of colors is enhanced by this treatment. In a few cases low temperatures may cause flower color to become less desirable. White chrysanthemums often develop a pinkish tinge under cool conditions. Many florists prefer a pure white flower. Bud abortion is common in certain crops when temperatures reach high levels, especially when light intensity is low. Easter lilies and geraniums are major crops where "bud blasting" or abortion is sometimes a problem.

TEMPERATURE AND PLANT QUALITY

Stem length and strength and the overall lushness of growth are probably the quality related characteristics growers try to manipulate most frequently by temperature control on a day to day basis. Flower initiation is certainly a major consideration in some species but the initiation period is usually only a short segment of crop time. The grower is concerned with general plant quality the entire time plants are in the greenhouse. In general, warmer temperatures result in weaker stems and lush growth. Plants that are too tall with weak stems and an over abundance of soft growth are probably the number one quality problem of floriculture today. This type of plant is not attractive to consumers and does not hold up well when removed from the greenhouse. Of course all environmental factors can contribute to this condition, but I feel temperature is normally the most important, easily modified factor which controls plant quality. Light intensity is surely as important to plant quality but is not easily controlled in critical winter months.

A great deal of emphasis has been placed recently upon producing plants faster so that additional crops may be harvested during the year. This is certainly a commendable objective but it must be accomplished without serious deterioration of quality. The high temperature, fertilizer, and moisture levels called for in these fast crop methods often result in overly lush plants, especially for garden use. Some experts contend these plants are healthier because they receive optimum growing conditions. Personally I compare them with over-fed, pampered people—they cannot stand up under rough conditions. A compromise approach is to start plants out quickly with elevated temperatures and then condition them gradually with reduced temperatures before marketing. Considerable fuel can be saved if one has a warm greenhouse where young plants are started and then moved to cooler houses for finishing.

Heating fuel is now a major greenhouse expense. At the time most greenhouse owners received their training, fuel was relatively inexpensive.

As a consequence, many cropping programs and cultural recommendations probably do not reflect the most profitable growing procedures. Much research is already being carried out in this area but it will take several years before the information finds its way into books and trade publications. Investigations should determine how far temperatures can be lowered at particular times without unacceptable reductions in crop quality and what new crops can be grown which satisfy the market and use less energy. It may be that certain crops are more profitable even though quality has been reduced slightly by energy saving measures.

I have lowered fuel consumption by maintaining approximately one-half of my greenhouse space at 45°-50° F after the poinsettia crop has been marketed. This cool space is filled with varieties which grow well at this temperature and crops which have been well started in warmer greenhouses and then moved to cooler temperatures. The combination of cool and warm houses also provides an effective ability to speed up or slow down plants for Valentine's Day and Easter. Several of the crops blooming in the cool houses during winter are grown almost to maturity during warm fall days. Foliage plants, which must be grown quite warm, occupy about one-fourth of my greenhouse space. This means that winter flower crops have a ratio of one-third warm space and two-thirds cool space. A considerable amount of fuel is saved in this manner. Such a program is not viable for every type of operation. Large wholesalers probably prefer to market plants as soon as possible rather than accumulate them for specific times. I find that I can command higher prices by having adequate material available for peak demand periods and allowing plants to accumulate somewhat between these periods by holding them cool. The somewhat reduced total production under this system is more than made up by reduced fuel costs and higher product prices. In addition, I think quality is improved by the cool temperatures. Stems are stiffer and shorter and flower color is brighter. A chart of my general crop schedule is given in Table 18.

TEMPERATURE AND CROP TIMING

The adjustment of temperatures in greenhouses or movement of plants to warmer or cooler locations is the most important tool a grower has for timing crops as the marketing date approaches. A good grower is always evaluating crop progress so that adjustments in timing may be made before a crisis has arrived. If possible, temperature changes should be made gradually. When plants are exposed to especially high temperatures to hasten flowering, bud abortion is a common occurrence. Botrytis (a mold organism) frequently appears when flowering plants are cooled to slow development. Cool air holds less water than does warm air and, as a result, high relative humidity is more of a problem in cool greenhouses. Botrytis is

Table 18

General flower and bedding plant schedule with the proportion of author's greenhouses kept cool and warm by season. Many small crops are omitted for simplicity. Foliage plants occupy 25% of total space and are heated to 65° F year around. This space is not included in the chart.

	All flower houses warm	
Fall	Grow poinsettias at 63° F until late November then cool to 58° F for fuel savings and to intensify flower color. Other Christmas flower crops are grown at the same temperatures.	
Winter and early spring	½ of flower houses warm at 60° F. Crops may be moved to cool house for delaying maturity if necessary	½ of flower houses cool at 50° F. Crops are grown to maturity here after a warm start
	Seedlings and stock plants for spring bedding plants, azaleas, begonias, chrysanthemums, Easter lilies, tulips	Calceolaria, cineraria, cyclamen, kalanchoe, Martha Washington geranium
Late spring	⅓ of flower houses warm at 58°-60° F	⅔ of flower houses cool at 50°-55° F
	Bedding plants: tomatoes, peppers, geraniums, begonias, impatiens, moss rose, salvia, zinnias, fushia, cucumbers, gerbera, ivy geraniums, garden mums, thunbergia	Bedding plants: petunias, marigolds, pansies, and other pack annuals and perennials. Also any warm grown crops in need of slowing down
Summer	½ of flowering houses warm at 62° F	½ of flower houses cool - no heat
	Propagation of young plants for fall and winter crops. Miscellaneous flower crops in progress	Summer bedding plants, night temperatures at this locality are often less than 62° F

more prevalent at high humidity and open flowers are especially susceptible. Any temperature adjustments made to influence flowering dates or
save fuel must be made with a full knowledge of the potential damages to
crop quality which might occur. Gloxinias and African violets simply will
not tolerate temperatures below 62° F for any length of time; at lower
temperatures plants become hardened, brittle, and yellowish. Impatiens
and tuberous begonias are only slightly more tolerant of cold temperatures.
On the other hand, many cool loving perennials will become lush and un-
salable if grown at over 50° F.

SOIL TEMPERATURE

It is not likely that the average grower will be able to alter substrate
temperatures appreciably unless root zone heating is installed or heated
water is used for irrigation. The effect of soil temperature on plant growth
and development has not been as thoroughly researched as has the effect of
air temperature. Unless definite data exists to indicate what effect lowering or increasing soil temperature will have, no general conclusion should
be made. Treatments should not be begun without adequate knowledge. If
a generalization must be made, it would be most appropriate to say that,
within certain ranges, warmer root zone temperatures will speed up
growth and development.

Bulb crops are frequently watered with warm water or placed on
heated surfaces to speed development. Research has been inconclusive as
to whether or not warm irrigation water has any dramatic or long lasting
effects on soil temperatures. It is certain, though, that there are no advantages to irrigating with icy cold water from the tap or well.

CHAPTER 13

WATER

Plants require water in large quantities. An average plant may require approximately 1,000 ounces of water for every ounce of dry weight added. The importance of water to plants is emphasized by the fact that young, growing tissue may be composed of 95% water. Most of the water entering a plant is lost through transpiration, in which water vapor passes out openings in the leaves called stomates. Portions of water molecules become a physical part of plant molecules, but water also serves as the background reagent in which many chemical reactions take place. The turgidity of plant cells is maintained by water; without it they become flaccid and the plant wilts. If plant cells are not full of water (turgid), expansion of cells by stretching of the cell wall does not take place. When expansion of the cell does not occur over long periods due to lack of water, the cell size becomes permanently smaller than it normally would be. This is the principle behind the common practice of withholding water to produce shorter, more compact plants.

WATER QUALITY

Water quality and its usefulness for growng plants may vary tremendously. Soluble salt content of water is the principal factor affecting quality. Classification of the usefulness of water by soluble salt content was presented in the discussion of fertilizer materials. The meaning of soluble salts, methods of measurement, and symptoms of plant damage were also presented at that time. If water is obtained from private wells or reservoirs it should be checked carefully for soluble salt levels to determine its suitability. Water from approved domestic sources will be suitable for plants because governmental regulations specify that water with a soluble salt content of 500 ppm or higher is not to be used for domestic purposes. Water from any source should be chemically analyzed to determine what mineral compounds are present and in what quantities. The mineral content of water may possibly affect what fertilizers a grower will use.

Water quality is difficult to change and every effort should be made to locate an alternative supply before one attempts to modify an unacceptable source. Soluble salt content of water may be lowered to almost zero by employing a process known as reverse osmosis. In practical usage, soluble salts need only be reduced to acceptable levels so that water derived from a reverse osmosis apparatus may be mixed with untreated water. Reverse osmosis machines are very expensive to purchase and maintain, but some greenhouses have installed them after exhausting all other possibilities. When soluble salts are in excess of 750 ppm in unfertilized irrigation water, precautions should be doubly emphasized to prevent soluble salt buildup in the soil. Personally, I would not use water having over 1000 ppm soluble salts. Water in the range of 1500-2000 ppm dissolved solids could probably be utilized if extreme precautions were taken.

Growing in a porous medium, leaching, adding only the minimum required fertilizers, and maintaining soil moisture at high levels are precautions one can take to overcome high soluble salt levels in the irrigation water. Soluble salts may vary in water sources, especially shallow wells, from season to season. Readings should be taken at several times during the year if there is reason to suspect any wide variations. When interpreting soluble salts information, one should be careful to note the exact unit of expression being used. The most common units used are parts per million and micromhos. Milliequivalents per liter (meq/l) and multiples of micromhos are less commonly employed. Micromhos times 0.666 yields ppm. Milliequivalents per liter equals ppm divided by 50. Crops may vary widely in their tolerance to soluble salts. Impatiens will do poorly at soluble salt levels which carnation plants will tolerate easily. Salt sensitive plants, such as impatiens, may serve as biological indicators of poor water quality to the grower.

One frequently hears of water being described as "hard" or "soft". Hard water is caused by the presence of large quantities of dissolved calcium and/or magnesium carbonate. These water quality terms have no direct relationship to the soluble salt content of water. Water may indeed have a high soluble salt level due to the presence of calcium and/or magnesium carbonate but it may also have a high salt level in the absence of these carbonates. The process of removing these carbonates from water is known as softening and is accomplished by the chemical exchange of sodium for magnesium and calcium. It can be seen that softening does not reduce soluble salts since it replaces one element with another. Hard water is not deleterious to plant growth unless calcium and magnesium carbonate are present in such large amounts as to render the water high in soluble salts. The residue left on leaves by these minerals can, however, cause an objectionable film or spottiness. This reside may be reduced considerably by the addition of sodium hexametaphosphate (calgon) to the water supply. When soluble salt levels are high, the addition of this compound will only magnify the problem. The carbonate residue may also be removed from leaves at market time by spraying with one of the numerous leaf-shine products available. Hard water is slightly alkaline and may sometimes cause a gradual rise in the soil pH. This is normally not a problem if soil pH is low to begin with, as it would be in high peat mixes. Alkaline water can be neutralized by utilizing a fertilizer program which acidifies the soil. Hardness is often expressed as grains per gallon; this value multiplied by 17.1 will result in ppm.

Chlorine and fluorine added to municipal water supplies normally cause no harmful effects to plants. In certain situations these elements may cause a slight tipburn on sensitive plants such as dracenas or chlorophytum. No other plants, in my experience, have shown ill effects. If the water supply comes from an open reservoir or stream, one may find that diseases such as root and stem rot (caused by fungi present in the water) will increase. Algal growth in tanks and soil surfaces may become a significant problem in these cases also. Pollution of water supplies by various industrial, domestic, and agricultural wastes is always a possibility if the water supply is from shallow wells or surface runoff. Damage due to water pollution is often very difficult to diagnose and may take some time to correctly identify. The most common cause of problems is weed killer residues from adjacent properties which either percolate down to the water table or are carried by surface runoff to streams or reservoirs.

WATER APPLICATION

No responsibility in the greenhouse will concern the grower on a day to day basis more than the irrigation of crops. Other tasks come and go with the seasons but watering is the daily religious ritual of greenhouse personnel. If irrigation is performed manually, it will comprise one of the largest labor outlays made by management. Watering is no more or less important than the regulation of other environmental factors. It is, however, less subject to a precise delineation of methods and measurement. As an example, both temperature and fertilizer elements may be measured and controlled rather easily, but there is no reasonably accurate means of quickly measuring available soil moisture. Proper water application depends entirely upon the grower's exercising careful judgment accumulated through experience. Measurement of nutrient status may sometimes be as difficult as determining available soil moisture, but nutrients are not usually monitored on a daily or even twice daily schedule as is water. Another difficulty with irrigation is communicating the grower's intentions to personnel actually performing the task. A grower may be an expert at watering but this means nothing if personnel are not thoroughly trained and motivated to carry out instructions. Only the best and most dependable greenhouse workers should be allowed to water. An old greenhouse proverb states "the person on the hose makes or breaks a crop." This saying is true because irrigators must be dependable, conscientious, and capable of developing the intuitive knowledge necessary to do a good job. Watering is more of an art than a science. If possible, a person should water the same crops regularly to acquire a "feel" for the crop's water needs.

The frequency and volume of water applied will depend on the following factors: light duration and intensity, temperature, air movement, relative humidity, soil type, pot types, plant size and stage of growth, and variety of plant. These factors will interrelate with one another to determine how much water will be used by a plant. Not only must personnel be trained to determine when and how much water is needed at a particular time, but they must also be able to project water needs into the short-term future. Inexperienced irrigators often encounter an early morning fog and decide slightly moist crops should not be watered that day; at midmorning the fog burns off and plants begin to wilt shortly thereafter. Employees must then interrupt the work day to water a second time. Experienced personnel would be familiar with this foggy morning pattern and water plants more heavily so the work day need not be interrupted. No hard and fast rules can be made about when plants should be watered because there are so many factors to consider. Retail customers always ask, "How often should I water this plant?" There is no easy answer. The best gauge of whether or not water is needed is to feel the soil. If it is reasonably moist and one judges the moisture will last through the day, no water should be applied. After a short time one will be able to anticipate how moist a soil will feel simply by looking at it. Surface appearance of soils may be misleading. In early morning, soils may be covered with a thin dew which dries up quickly with air movement and sunlight. Plants should be watered early enough in the day to allow the greenhouse to dry out before nightfall but a more accurate job can be done if one waits until the early morning dew has burned off. Soil normally dries from the top downward so it may be assumed that the soil at the bottom of pots will be more moist than that at the top. As soil dries, it shrinks and will pull away from the edge of the pot if excessively dry.

Plants may be able to go for a week or more between waterings during dark winter weather though everyday watering is needed in summer. Plants in clay and fiber pots will dry out more quickly than those in plastic pots. Certain varieties of plants are conspicuous water users while others consume very little. There is a world of difference between the water needs of hydrangeas and those of cacti. Most varieties occupy a middle ground where water use is average. Newly transplanted plants are often watered lightly but often at the start and then allowed to dry out somewhat. After this period they are usually well enough established to begin a normal watering program. Soil types will greatly influence watering frequency. Porous soils with a large particle size will require watering more often than those with a smaller particle size. The most definite indication that a plant needs water is when it wilts. This stage should seldom be allowed to occur since quality will be severely lowered if wilting is common. Some growers make it a practice to wait until a few plants wilt before watering a crop. This is not a good practice since the crop would suffer reduced quality if all plants were near the wilting stage. Another reason for not using this method is that plants on the outside edges of a bench may be very dry while those in the center are still wet.

The quantity of water one should apply is not nearly so difficult to decide as when to water. Except when plants are very small and not yet established, they should be watered heavily each time they have dried out. It may be necessary to water some plants of a crop lightly for a few days until the entire crop is ready for a thorough irrigation, but, usually, light sprinklings are a waste of time and do not promote good growth. If the soil and water system make it possible to leach easily, it is a good practice to let approximately 10% of irrigation water pass through the container drain holes. If leaching is not feasible at each watering, a schedule should be set up for heavy leachings at regular intervals. Heavy leaching will normally be imperative at 6-8 week intervals. The amount of soluble salts in the water and the concentrations of fertilizers applied will determine how often leaching must occur. It is usually difficult to get personnel into the habit of watering heavily enough. There seems to be a universal tendency for people to stand back and wave a sprinkler at plants rather than watering each pot thoroughly.

In my greenhouse, irrigators are trained with careful supervision for about a month and then allowed to water on their own. Daily spot checks of performance are made for another month. If people are not doing a satisfactory job at the end of this period, it is highly unlikely that they ever will and they should be transferred to a less critical task. I spend much time making sure that directions are understood completely. It is not easy to communicate concepts which are rather vague and have no precise definition. The grower and employee must develop to the point where each is on the same "mental wavelength." I try to explain the reasons behind each action so that irrigators eventually understand what they are doing rather than just going through the motions. Each mistake is immediately pointed out during the training period so that employees realize their performance is being critically evaluated. The importance of a careful, systematic method of watering may be illustrated by a simple example. If a crop of 100 plants will mature in 12 weeks, it takes the death of only 1 plant every week through careless watering to equal a 12% loss of gross revenue. This is a serious decline which could make the difference between a mediocre business and a highly successful business. A greenhouse selling $100,000 of plants a year would lose $12,000. That amount would make the payments on a very nice home for the owner. Even after employees have been watering for some time, the grower should make periodic inspections and suggest methods of improvement. Meticulous attention to watering is essential for good crops and it is the grower's responsibility to communicate, educate, and motivate employees to perform their very best.

WATER AND PLANT QUALITY

Watering practices will greatly affect plant appearance and quality. Judicious regulation of water applications can be a valuable tool in directing plant growth to a desirable conclusion. Reductions in quality due to overwatering are usually a result of various root and stem rots which thrive in a wet medium and the low oxygen supply to roots caused by water occupying the majority of soil pore spaces. Underwatering subjects plants to stress which leads to a smaller stature and fewer flowers. Severe water stress will cause tissue to dry up in the more succulent portions and can eventually lead to death. Generally, plants should be grown at a happy medium where root aeration is adequate but moisture stress is avoided. In the practical sense, growers usually sacrifice a small amount of plant size and flowers and maintain plants under a slight water stress. This approach lessens the chance of severe losses due to root diseases and dysfunctions.

With certain crops and under some conditions growers may deem it necessary to keep plants under a moderate water stress. Petunias are one crop which, if given plenty of water in the late season, will become too tall and spindly. Shorter, tougher plants can be produced by letting the crop dry out almost to the wilting point before irrigation. Most bedding plants transplant better into the garden if they have been subjected to periodic water stress in the greenhouse. Tissue is not so succulent and likely to be dehydrated in the hot sun. Many growers prefer to produce the more succulent plants which have been under very little water stress. I suspect there are two reasons for this: these plants are marketable in a shorter length of time and many wholesale growers never come into direct contact with disappointed customers whose plants simply expired under the rigors of garden life. During the winter flower season there is seldom any reason for placing plants under a significant water stress. Withholding water can be used to delay flowering dates, but lowering temperatures is a much more effective method of accomplishing this purpose.

WATERING SYSTEMS

Before proceeding to the different methods one may employ to apply water, we may usefully discuss the basic delivery system. A greenhouse cannot operate without a dependable and adequate supply of water. One day without water in midsummer can be catastrophic to the greenhouse operator. Water delivery systems must be sized to transport the largest amount of water which may be needed during the entire year. Obviously, this volume must be deliverable within an approximately six hour period which would constitute the normal watering day. Allowances must be made for water use in cooling systems, etc. It is always best to err on the safe side when installing delivery pipes and wells. If one is already stuck with an insufficient system, it is possible to improve the situation by installing storage tanks which can be filled during the night.

Inexperienced plumbers often install piping without an adequate number of shut off valves and union joints for easy repair. Strainers and cleanouts should be placed on pump and proportioner intakes to minimize the possibility of clogging. Strainers may also be appropriate on lines serving sprinkler and misting nozzles. If adequate pressure is unavailable from the supply source, it may be necessary to install booster pumps. Repair parts for those portions of the system which are likely to break down should be kept on hand; nothing is more aggravating than spending a busy spring day locating a 25¢ pump gasket. It is convenient if water lines are set up so that two solutions can be used in different greenhouse locations at the same time. Often it would save time if one person could be applying water to one crop while another is fertilizing a different crop. Some growers feel that a system for warming water is essential in the winter time. If water enters the delivery system straight from the tap or a cold well and pipe and hose runs are short, plants probably will benefit from warmer water. When holding tanks are employed, water usually warms up sufficiently before use.

There are several general methods by which water may be applied to crops. Manual irrigation is the most commonly employed method. When greenhouses are small and many different crops are raised, manual water application is often the most efficient. Watering can be closely regulated, especially if the grower has time to perform the task personally. With this method, greenhouse personnel are always in close contact with the crop and should notice any problems quickly. Equipment needed is minimal but labor costs are high for manual irrigation and they can double or triple if a sufficient water volume is not available for workers to move quickly. The degree of reliance a grower must place on other people to perform a critical task is the greatest disadvantage of manual irrigation. Frequent leaching is often not possible with manual irrigation; plants must be gone over several times before leaching occurs.

Whenever it is judged advantageous, automatic watering systems should be installed. Machines may be irritating at times but they are more dependable than people and do exactly as the grower instructs if they have been installed properly. A fully mechanized watering system can save a great deal in labor costs and will lower a grower's anxiety level. When greenhouses are full of plants on a hot day and key watering personnel do not show up for work, the grower with manual irrigation is under great stress. With automated systems, the grower can easily take care of such situations. The problem of weekend watering is also lessened. Many people contend that watering by hand is superior because individual plants can be watered or not depending on the need. In my own experience, if the system is designed carefully and only suitable crops are chosen, better results are obtained with mechanized watering. Under the proper circumstances, I find that automatic systems do a better job than I can do myself. The key advantage of mechanized watering is that either the grower or the more experienced employees can handle all irrigation. This substantially raises the ability to decide when to apply or not to apply water. Leaching is easily accomplished with most mechanical watering systems.

Pot plants are most often irrigated mechanically with individual tubes leading to each pot. Water is supplied to sections of greenhouses by pipeline; at each bench a polyethylene branch line is installed which runs the length of the bench. Small diameter plastic tubes are then inserted into the branch line after the appropriate holes have been punched. Different lengths of tubes are usually installed to accommodate the varying distances to the edges of the bench. A combination weight and water breaker is attached to the free end of the tube. When this weight is placed in the pot, it breaks the water stream and keeps the tube in position. This system is very effective for pots of 5 inch size and larger. Additional tubes may be placed into large pots. The weighted breakers may be equipped with simple push-pull shut off valves. This is especially handy with hanging baskets so that tubes may be shut off as baskets are harvested and water does not drain onto plants below. Several variations such as spray tubes and loop tubes are available for very large containers. It is obvious that this system is most effective when every pot on the bench is the same size and plants are uniform in growth. Solenoid water valves coupled to a timing device can make any mechanized watering system completely automatic. Soils which drain quite easily may allow water to flow primarily straight down through the soil after leaving the end of the tube. Growers not familiar with this phenomenon may have a crop severely damaged from water stress before they figure out what is taking place, especially with hanging baskets where the soil surface cannot be observed. The problem may be lessened in several ways: use larger tubes to apply water faster, decrease the number of large pores in soil, never allow soil to dry out, and do not begin tube irrigation until plant roots are established and impede the flow of water downward. Details on installation of tube irrigation systems are available from all major horticultural supply houses.

There are several methods of subirrigating plants automatically. These methods are normally used on 4 inch or smaller pots which are difficult to handle with the polyethylene tube system. The simplest set up is to place pots on a watertight, level bench with a short lip around the edge. The bench is filled with water and then allowed to drain after pots soak up sufficient moisture. A variant of this method is to set pots on a bed of moist sand which has a polyethylene film under it. Benches in this case need not have a lip or be level. The sand is kept constantly saturated with an ooze hose and the excess water flows off the side of the bench. Recently, capillary mats composed of fibers have become available to take the place of sand layers. Moisture is absorbed from both the sand beds and fiber mats by capillarity and drying out of either can break the continuity of the water transfer. Bottoms of pots must be placed in firm contact with the sand or fiber mats. Pots manufactured with small feet on the bottom may be unsuitable if good contact with the surface cannot be made. Clay pots cannot be used because water loss from them is greater than can be replaced through capillary pull. Pots over six inches deep do not water properly with capillary mats. The application of water to mats can be controlled by solenoid valves and timers to maintain constant wetness.

At first glance subirrigation would seem to be ideal, but there are several serious disadvantages to it. No leaching action occurs when water is applied from below. Crops must be either short term or periodically leached manually from above. If fertilizer is applied to capillary mats, they often become overgrown with algae; a partial solution to this problem is realized by incorporating a slow release fertilizer in the growing medium. Roots growing into the mats and sand can become a nuisance and because roots from all pots are exposed to a common water supply, diseases from one plant spread rapidly through the entire bench. Plants grown on capillary mats may be of poor quality because they always have plenty of water and become succulent. This may or may not be a problem depending on the species and market.

Sprinkler systems are the most practical way of watering bedding plants, small potted shrubs, propagation beds, and large crops of newly potted plants. Sprinklers are seldom used on potted flowers when they are spaced because of the large free area between pots and the susceptibility of flowers to rot and water spotting if watered from above. The design of sprinkler systems is limited only by a grower's imagination. The critical test of effectiveness is whether complete coverage is achieved. Overlap areas of the sprinkler patterns will receive more moisture than other sections and the area directly under sprinkler heads often receives less. Irrigations should be quite heavy so that the soil of an entire crop is brought to uniform wetness. Light sprinklings will emphasize the uneven spray patterns. Sprinkler patterns should be tested under the conditions which will exist at the time of use. Growers frequently install sprinklers and test them in winter time; when they use the sprinklers in the spring, they find the water patterns are changed. This phenomenon is usually caused by exhaust fans that are operating in the spring and distorting sprinkler patterns. Spring water use in the greenhouse is much heavier than in winter and it may be that the volume and pressure at sprinkler heads is reduced, resulting in incomplete coverage.

PITFALLS OF AUTOMATED WATERING

Growers often become over enthusiastic about the labor savings of automated water systems and install them without adequate forethought. Every crop and every situation is not amenable to automation. Even when such systems are justified, they should be analyzed carefully to provide maximum benefit per dollar invested. Changing the method of water application affects many other greenhouse operations and the interrelationships should be well understood. Soil mixtures and fertilizer applications need to be adapted to the type of watering systems installed.

The ease of irrigating with mechanical systems sometimes leads one to apply too much water. Decisions about when to water must be made more carefully with automated systems than when the task is done manually because a heavier and more general irrigation is usually given. Growers must discipline themselves to think carefully before throwing the irrigation switch. Each irrigation must be carefully monitored to make sure all elements of the system are working properly. It is not uncommon to find sprinklers which have been plugged with debris. Large plant losses can be encountered if mechanical failures are not detected quickly.

When plants are watered mechanically, the grower must institute regular inspections of crops to check on development, insect populations, timing, etc. If the grower was doing the watering by hand previously, these factors were usually taken care of at the same time. The essential point to remember about automatic watering systems is that they make life a little easier physically but do not lessen the need for careful observation and analysis of crop needs and progress. One cannot simply hook up a crop to automatic watering and come back two months later for harvest.

CHAPTER 14

REGULATING GROWTH BY NATURAL AND CHEMICAL MEANS

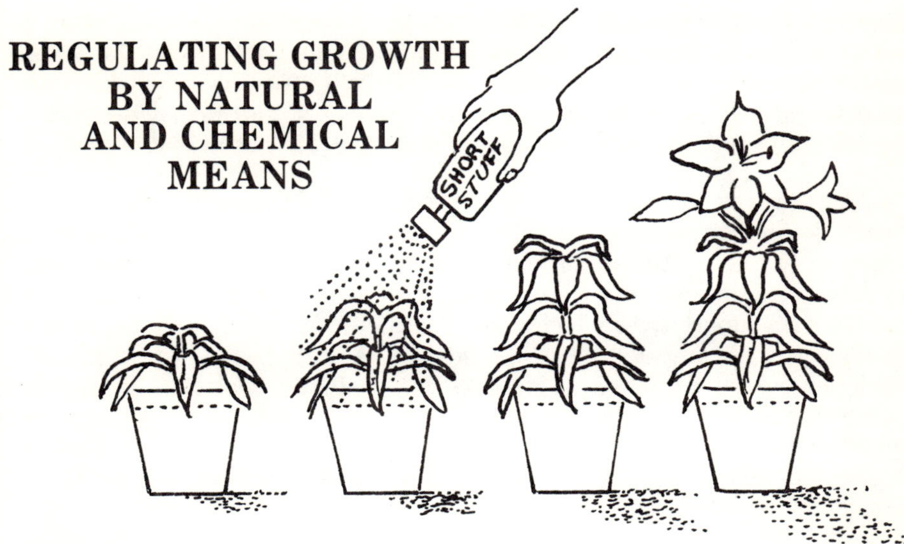

Growers must often regulate plant growth and development in different ways to produce a visually pleasing crop and to promote certain processes which make production more economical. Regulating plant growth may be approached through several avenues; selecting genetic cultivars, managing environmental factors, physically altering the plant, and applying chemicals are the basic methods available. The greater part of this book has been devoted to explaining the inter-relationships between plants and environmental factors. Readers should refer to the appropriate sections for detail in assessing the impact environmental management may have on plant growth. I will now discuss methods of growth regulation with special emphasis on chemical methods since these may not be commonly understood.

SELECTING GENETIC CULTIVARS

Ever since the advent of agriculture, man has actively practiced the selection of plants and animals possessing desirable characteristics to increase the quality and quantity of crops. This process of human directed evolution has led to thousands of varieties which, for the particular purposes of the user, are superior to wild species. Every grower should take an active interest in selecting only the most suitable varieties available for production schedules. It is generally much more economical to select appropriate varieties than it is to alter the growth of unsuitable ones to achieve the same purpose. Plant breeding has become a fast moving science in recent years and one must continually evaluate new varieties in order to stay current. Looking over the catalogs of major seed companies should convince neophytes of the importance which must be placed on the grower's selecting a proper variety. There are literally thousands of varieties offered and each one has its individual good and bad points.

A grower should list all the proposed crops and then study the varieties available for each one, eventually selecting one or several varieties which seem to fit the particular production and marketing circumstances most closely. Descriptions of varietal performance in seed catalogs tend to be loaded with superlatives which make it difficult for the uninitiated grower to choose with any degree of confidence. A well tested list of suitable varieties for local market preference is a valuable tool for the grower. Observing field trials and other growers' results and listening to recommendations from experienced seed salesmen are the best methods of choosing which varieties to grow initially. Careful observation of growth patterns in succeeding seasons will provide information enabling the grower to personally evaluate performance. Newly introduced varieties should be grown on a trial basis if they are an important crop.

Certain crops such as petunias and chrysanthemums have been extensively selected and bred so that the choice of varieties is bewildering. Seed houses and salesmen will be happy to recommend what varieties to use, but there can be no substitute for careful evaluation and selection by the grower. Many people who are primarily growers and have little contact with the ultimate consumers tend to overestimate the value of certain cultivars because they grow well and may be economical to produce. Plants have little value if they are not appealing to the public and do not fulfill the purpose for which they were purchased. Growers who also retail should listen carefully to customers' reports of plant performance and those growers who sell wholesale only must devise some means of obtaining data on customer satisfaction. Perhaps one of the best methods of evaluating varieties is to use them one's self in the home and garden. Selecting proper varieties for the market and for the growing facilities is of prime importance to success and should be given adequate consideration.

PHYSICALLY ALTERING PLANTS

Every gardener is familiar with the process of pruning and pinching plants to obtain more desirable shapes or promote vigorous growth. Many greenhouse crops require some type of physical alteration to realize their full potential as ornamentals. These alterations are usually performed by hand and can add considerably to crop expenses. As a consequence, there are numerous efforts toward using chemical applications to accomplish the same purpose. The efficacy of these chemical methods will be discussed in later sections of this chapter.

Physical alteration of plants most often falls into two broad categories: pruning or pinching and disbudding. The words pruning and pinching are not well defined and should be used carefully to make the meaning clear. The word "pruning" is normally used to denote the removal of unwanted growth. Pinching primarily means removal of the growing tip from stems to promote branching. One can readily see how the two words may overlap in meaning but the essential difference should be clear. Some plants develop too many stems to allow vigorous growth of them all. Quality is improved if the weaker shoots are removed. This allows more nutrients, water, and light for development of the remaining branches. The purpose of pruning may be to promote larger, more prolific flowers or ensure stronger, thicker stems. Occasionally one prunes to improve flower visibility or to train plants in a certain direction or form.

Many plants are not full enough to have a pleasing shape unless pinched to increase the number of branches. Employees should be trained to administer pinches in a precise fashion. The growing point may be missed if the pinch is too far up the stem and few branches result if a pinch is made too far down the stem. The terms "soft" and "hard" pinch are qualitative terms meaning those pinches made higher or lower on the stem respectively. When workers fail to excise the growing point, the main stem will continue growing upward and lateral branches are not induced. An entire crop can be ruined by improper pinching because the flowering schedule is thrown off and plants may be irregular in height. Pinching to alter plant shape must be correlated with the desired plant height and bloom date because these attributes are often affected also. Poinsettias initiate flowers naturally in late September or early October in the northern United States and delaying the pinch closer to the flower initiation date will decrease the final height of plants. In those groups of plants where flowering occurs irrespective of day length and temperature induction, the pinch date may be the primary method of regulating bloom date. Geraniums, carnations, and roses are examples of such crops.

A knowledge of the individual crop's response to pinching is essential if one is to predict the outcome accurately. Certain chrysanthemum varieties "break" or produce lateral branches quite readily and must be pinched relatively hard while other varieties must be soft pinched because lateral branches do not form easily on older tissue. Some newer poinsettia cultivars reliably produce a lateral branch at each leaf axil when pinched. If the pinch is too soft on these varieties there will be too many branches, resulting in weak stems with small flowers. Geraniums will bloom earlier with a soft pinch than with a hard pinch. The need for pinching may be overcome in some crops by increasing the number of cuttings put into a pot. I prefer this method whenever possible because it eliminates one step requiring skilled labor and generally reduces crop time. A reduction in crop time not only makes room for additional crops but, more importantly to me, shortens the response time necessary for needed alterations in inventory due to increased or decreased demand. It should be emphasized that roots are often cut to induce branching and restore vigor to newly repotted plants. It is common practice to prune tree roots the year prior to moving the trees to new locations. This induces lateral branching and a compact root system next to the trunk.

Disbudding is the practice of removing flower buds except the ones selected to remain on the stem. When all buds but the terminal one are removed, the purpose is generally to direct nutrients to that flower alone and increase the size. This method is practiced extensively with potted chrysanthemums. Many chrysanthemums are raised as sprays for filler in flower arrangements and only the terminal bud on these sprays is removed. If allowed to remain, the terminal bud will bloom earlier than the lateral buds and will reduce their size. More even flowering and an increase in size are the result of removing the terminal bud. The shape of the spray may be influenced by how early or late the terminal bud is removed. Flower buds are usually removed whenever their size permits easy handling by workers. Buds should be rolled off to the side rather than being picked like fruit. This procedure results in less damage to the plant and will break the flower stem off closer to the main stem. When the flower stem breaks too far up, there is the possibility for new bud development. One should begin disbudding with the lowest buds and progress up the stem. In this way, if the terminal bud is inadvertently removed it can be replaced by leaving the bud directly below it on the plant. When workers start disbudding at the top, the terminal bud, if broken, might have to be replaced with a bud further down the stem which would bloom at a later date than the terminal buds left on other stems. The discussion of disbudding has referred mainly to chrysanthemums since they are the main crop which requires disbudding. More detailed explanations of the effects pinching and disbudding may have are given in the references pertaining to individual crops.

ALTERING GROWTH BY CHEMICAL MEANS

Chemical means of altering plant growth have been devised mainly to lessen the costs associated with manual alteration and to produce effects which are not available by physical means or genetic selection. Much of the impetus given to chemical growth alteration was supplied in the 1920's by plant scientists who discovered that chemical compounds occurring naturally in plants were responsible for determining or regulating plant growth and development. These compounds were not used for building plant tissue or as essential ingredients for chemical reactions but as control mechanisms regulating the occurrence and speed of growth and development. Synthetic or natural regulators in use today may function in the manner just described or they may alter growth by physical alteration or destruction of the tissue organization in various plant structures.

Many natural growth regulators have been identified in plants since the initial discoveries. Their history of discovery, classification into groups, and modes of action are interesting but not especially relevant to the present discussion. The action of growth regulators depends on their concentration, their interaction with other regulators, and the tissue in which they are present. Growth regulators affect cell enlargement and division, initiation of roots, lateral bud development, fruit and leaf abscission, tropic movements, fruit set and enlargement, flower initiation, dormancy, germination, aging, growth, fruit ripening, and dwarfism. One can readily see from this list that numerous opportunities to manage the growth and development of plants exist through the judicious use of growth regulators. Synthetic compounds have been found that can be substituted for most natural growth regulators. No distinction will be made in the following presentation between natural and synthetic growth regulators.

MANAGING CROPS WITH GROWTH REGULATORS

Growers should be aware that growth regulators cannot take the place of proper culture in the production of quality plants. Growth regulators are a technical aid and cannot magically correct the errors of poor judgment and inattention to the details of crop culture. If the desired plant characteristics can be obtained by another management technique more economically, growers should use that method. My own preference is to minimize the use of chemicals in greenhouses even if it costs slightly more to do so. Not only does this choice lessen the danger of chemical contamination to employees but it also lessens the chance of crop damage from improper application. Application concentrations and interactions with other chemicals may be of extreme importance for growth regulators. One should study labels carefully to avoid crop damage and harmful effects to personnel. I will mention brand names for growth regulators only when I can aid the reader by so doing.

Stimulating Root Growth

The initiation of roots is enhanced by several compounds. Indole-3-acetic acid (IAA), indole-3-butyric acid (IBA), and alpha-naphthalene-acetic acid are the most commonly encountered. The rooting compound applied is only one factor in determining the success of propagation by cuttings.

Environmental factors and the quality of cuttings are of prime importance. Many cuttings root so quickly that there is little benefit from treatment with growth regulators while other varieties are almost impossible to propagate without this artificial stimulation. The majority of plants fall somewhere in between. Rooting compounds are applied in most cases to speed up and increase the quality of rooting. Rooting compounds may be applied as dusts or by immersing the base of the stem in a dilute solution. An effort should be made to standardize application so that cuttings root as uniformly as possible within a batch. Contamination of the rooting compound with diseased cuttings is a major problem and only healthy, clean cuttings should be used. Some commercial rooting compounds may contain fungicides to retard the spread of diseases. Active strength of compounds is generally increased for harder to root cuttings. Growers should always keep in mind whether the increased speed and quality of rooting is balanced by the added labor for application of growth regulators and the possibility of spreading diseases.

Retarding Plant Growth

The use of growth retardants to produce shorter, more desirably shaped plants has become a standard practice for many varieties. Until relatively recent times, growers could do little more than withhold water and fertilizer, lower the temperature, and prune plants to control height. Growth retardants have provided one of the most economical improvements in plant quality to be introduced in quite some time. Prior to their introduction, managing environmental factors to control plant height usually resulted in rather small, light green plants. Retarding stem elongation by chemical means has allowed growers to continue irrigating and fertilizing adequately to produce large dark green plants of a desirable height. The rise of chrysanthemums and poinsettias to pre-eminent positions in sales of flowering plants is due in no small measure to the introduction of growth retardants.

Most varieties which respond to growth retardants show no major morphological changes other than the reduction in stem length. When additional characteristics are modified, the change is evidenced often by smaller flowers, greener, thicker leaves, and a small delay in flowering. Retardants can be used as a foliar spray or as a soil drench; the application method is sometimes limited by the type of chemical used. The most common brands of growth retardants available to the industry today are A-Rest (ancymidol), B-Nine-SP (daminozide), and Cyclocel (chlormequat). Additional formulations have been used widely in the past and new ones will undoubtedly be introduced. Recommendations concerning which retardant to use will be found under the cultural information for specific varieties later in this book. Growth retardant activity may be modified by many factors and growers should treat experimental groups of plants before exposing an entire crop to an unfamiliar product.

Weed Control

Weed control is discussed under growth regulation because many of the common weed killers are synthetic growth regulating substances. The familiar 2,4-D (2,4-dichlorophenoxyacetic acid) herbicide is a growth regulator which acts by causing plants literally to grow themselves to death. Weeds must be eradicated from greenhouses mainly because they provide a haven for insects and diseases. Good insect control is impossible if numerous weeds are growing under the benches. When weeds are allowed to get out of control, they can spread to pots on the benches and cause a reduction in quality. Weed infestations throw a poor light on the capabilities of greenhouse managers when customers or business associates tour the premises. Weed control is often done by hand, which is very expensive, or sometimes by flamethrowers, which is very dangerous.

The most effective and economical means of controlling weeds is using herbicides. It is also very hazardous if not done properly. Many greenhouse owners are reluctant to use herbicides because of personal or second hand knowledge about severe crop damage caused by weedkillers. Herbicides, especially 2,4-D, should never be stored on the greenhouse grounds; many should never be used on weeds in close proximity to the greenhouse. Even the slightest presence of certain herbicide vapors can damage a crop beyond use. Generally, herbicide damage manifests itself in abnormal growth patterns; the most prominent symptoms are twisted and curled leaves and stem tips. Little remedial action can be taken. Sprayers and utensils used for herbicide application must never be used for any other purpose. No herbicide should ever be used without recommendation from reliable greenhouse experts and even then a trial application should be made safely away from major crops.

Herbicides can be classified as pre-emergence types which prevent seeds from germinating or post-emergence types which actually kill the plant. Each type is useful under certain circumstances. Many pre-emergence herbicides are non-volatile and will not harm established greenhouse plants. They do, however, remain active for quite some time and can be spread to unwanted locations by dirt particles and water movement on top of or in the soil. Contamination of seed germination areas with pre-emergence herbicides would be serious. Always make sure pre-emergence herbicides are non-volatile and that contamination of desirable areas is not possible.

Several post-emergence herbicides are suitable for use in the greenhouse but most of them remain active in the soil and can cause contamination problems. Roundup (glyphosate) is my choice of brands of weed killer for the greenhouse. It is effective, non-volatile, and deactivates upon contact with the soil, thus preventing contamination. Seeds are not affected so control must continue until the seed crop is exhausted. I have never had any damage from vapors or contamination using Roundup but each grower should thoroughly test the product to make sure damage does not occur under the particular application circumstances. Care should always be taken to prevent spray from drifting onto desirable plants when herbicides are used. When weed growth is relatively continuous, a wick applicator may be used more effectively than sprays. Rock salt applied to greenhouse floors is a safe and reasonably effective method of killing weeds. The labor cost of spreading is high and salt may be corrosive to metal posts. Applying herbicides to growing containers is not common in the greenhouse and the number of herbicides which can be used in this manner is very limited. Tree nurseries are often forced to apply herbicides to pots and several formulations have been marketed for this purpose. Whenever herbicide is applied directly to growing pots, the dosage must be measured accurately to prevent damage. I have purposely omitted recommending numerous herbicides for use because, in most cases, their use is limited to fairly specific circumstances and newly improved formulations are introduced quite often to render old ones out of date. County agricultural agents are often the best source of up to date information concerning herbicides.

Evaporative cooling pads may become overgrown with algae in summer months. Algae can be controlled in the cooling system by adding disinfectants containing benzyl ammonium chlorides to the water tanks on a weekly basis. These compounds may also be used for sanitizing tools and benches in the greenhouse, and for controlling algae on clay pots. Some damage to plants may be possible when clay pots are treated.

Pinching, Pruning, and Disbudding

Much effort has been directed toward developing chemical agents which will efficiently and reliably perform some of the time consuming tasks of pinching, pruning, and disbudding flower crops. Although many compounds show some promise, the results so far have precluded widespread greenhouse use. The only greenhouse crop which has been chemically pinched on a commercial scale is azaleas. Disbudding and pinching chrysanthemums with chemicals has made rapid progress but more effective methods are necessary before commercial applications are feasible. Excellent results are obtained with particular circumstances and varieties but only slight changes in application may cause poor response or damage to plants.

Prolonging Cut Flower Life

Although cut flowers are not the subject of this book, it is useful for anyone in the floral industry to have a passing acquaintance with their care. Cut flower life can be improved dramatically, up to three-four times, with proper handling. Flower preservatives are very economical. They perform their function by preventing stem plugging, providing respirable food sources, enabling tight buds to open, and preventing undesirable changes in flower color. The main ingredient in flower preservatives is sucrose sugar, which provides a substrate for respiration. Numerous preservative formulations which perform well are available commercially, Additional chemicals are usually added to the sucrose base to prevent stem plugging and color change.

Controlling Leaf Abscission

There are circumstances when it is beneficial to promote leaf abscission on horticultural plants. Nurserymen often use synthetic defoliants to speed up tree leaf abscission in the fall so that trees may be harvested before winter weather sets in. Hydrangeas must be subjected to cold temperatures after flowers are initiated to break dormancy. Plants are placed in dark coolers where diseases can cause severe damage unless leaves are removed before storage. Various chemicals are used to promote leaf drop. Ethylene gas is a natural product of respiration which will cause leaf abscission when critical levels are reached. Hydrangeas are commonly placed in a closed space with apples, which produce ethylene. Leaves will drop after a few days of this treatment.

Undesirable accidental leaf drop may be induced under certain circumstances. Greenhouse plants should never be placed in close proximity to ripening fruit unless adequate ventilation is provided to avoid ethylene buildup. All plants give off some ethylene gas but it is only under certain conditions that concentrations build up enough to cause damage. Large amounts of rotting plant tissue on floors or in trash bins can also cause ethylene build up. Shipping fruited decorative orange trees with other plants can lead to defoliation if ventilation is not provided. Many growers use a chemical formulation under the brand name of Vapam as a soil fumigant. Unless treated soil is properly aired out before introduction to the greenhouse, Vapam fumes may cause severe defoliation. Improperly vented or defective furnaces are often the cause of plant defoliation due to an accumulation of combustion gases.

Some chemical compounds have been found to retard abscission. This phenomenon can be useful in the growing and marketing of certain crops. Geraniums propagated from seed have become a major crop in recent years but their flowers suffer from a tendency of blooms to "shatter" (petals fall off quickly). Since flower petals are actually specialized types of leaves the same processes which prevent or increase leaf abscission will apply to them. Silver nitrate sprays are often administered to seed geraniums to prevent bloom shatter.

Promoting Flowering and Fruiting

Considerable effort has been expended towards overcoming or replacing the natural flowering responses of plants with various chemical applications. It would be very advantageous, for example, if chrysanthemum growers could simply spray crops with a chemical rather than invest in the costly shading and lighting set ups now required. Although it has become apparent that many growth regulating substances can induce, promote, or inhibit flowering under certain conditions, few widespread commercial applications have arisen. Ethylene gas has been found to induce flowering in the bromeliad (pineapple) family. Commercial pineapple farms spray field plants with alpha-naphthalene-acetic acid which induces plants to produce the flower initiating ethylene in their tissues. Many ornamental bromeliads are also brought into flower by treatment with ethylene.

Some use of growth retardants and gibberellic acid has been made in azalea culture to enhance flower production. Cyclamen have renewed their popularity in recent years and gibberllic acid applications have been useful in stimulating plants to produce large numbers of flowers at one time. The applications also cause the flower stalks to elongate so that flowers are held well above the foliage with a subsequent increase in visibility. Some chemicals have shown the capability of inhibiting flower initiation in plants. Chrysanthemum and kalanchoe are two major crops which respond in this manner to certain chemicals. Preventing flowering could, of course, be advantageous where plants are kept for purposes of vegetative propagation.

Producing fruit without pollenization is termed "parthenocarpy". Chemical treatment of flowers to induce fruit set has become widespread. Most readers will no doubt be familiar with various blossom set and berry set formulations they have seen at garden stores. Chemically induced fruit development can be advantageous for commercial growers since fruits will mature at the same time to facilitate harvest. Greater numbers of fruits may also be set by this means. Parthenocarpic fruits usually lack some of the juiciness of pollinated fruits because seeds are not formed and the reproductive fluids surrounding them are absent.

CHAPTER 15

CARBON DIOXIDE AND OXYGEN

The importance of carbon dioxide (CO_2) and oxygen (O_2) to plant growth was pointed out earlier in Chapter 5, Part I. Chapters 8 and 13, Part I concerning soils and watering further elucidated the role of oxygen in maintaining healthy plants. Selecting suitable soil components and watering properly constitute the only viable methods of manipulating oxygen supply to the plant. Growers should realize that a sufficient oxygen supply for vital plant processes is intimately related to a healthy root system. Roots cannot carry on respiration without adequate oxygen. The energy liberated in respiration is necessary for the uptake of mineral nutrients and water. Most people know that too much water is deleterious to plant growth but fail to realize that the real problem is a lack of oxygen caused by water occupying all the soil pores. A clear understanding of the problem will likely lead to better growing practices. An adequate oxygen supply is also required for good seed germination and root production on cuttings.

I have mentioned the need for adequate oxygen to support combustion in greenhouse furnaces. Plastic covered houses should be evaluated more carefully in this respect because they have very few air leaks in the skin. Lack of sufficient oxygen eventually causes a furnace flame-out, but before this point is reached, damaging carbon monoxide and ethylene gases may be produced through incomplete combustion. Recommendations have been made that two square inches of air intake area be supplied for every 5,000 BTUs of furnace capacity located in the greenhouse. An estimation of the intake area provided by door cracks and other leaks should be included in the above figure.

Carbon dioxide is of course a necessary ingredient in the photosynthetic process. Many growers, including myself, tend to overlook the critical importance of carbon dioxide to plant growth simply because it is normally present in sufficient quantities and because a deficiency is expressed by reductions in growth rather than by easily recognizable symptoms. If a greenhouse is tightly closed on a bright winter day, photosynthesizing plants can deplete the carbon dioxide supply quickly. Normal carbon dioxide concentrations in the atmosphere are about 300 ppm. When levels reach approximately 125 ppm, growth in plants ceases because respiration is occurring as fast as photosynthesis can take place at this carbon dioxide level. Carbon dioxide depletion takes place most quickly when there is little ventilation and light conditions are favorable for photosynthesis. Yield of winter time crops in many locations can be increased dramatically by the introduction of carbon dioxide into the greenhouse atmosphere. Growth has been shown to increase in many species until there are about 1,500 ppm of carbon dioxide in the atmosphere. Production increases of 50% are common.

Introducing carbon dioxide into the greenhouse atmosphere is accomplished economically by burning an open flame of natural or LP gas. Combustion of pure fuels results in the production of water vapor and carbon dioxide. One must be sure that fuels are low in contaminants, especially sulfur. Butylene and propylene may sometimes be present in fuel sources and can cause plant damage similar to that of ethylene. Flames must be adjusted properly and enough oxygen must be present to support complete combustion or incomplete combustion products will cause crop damage. Carbon dioxide generators and monitoring devices are available commercially at moderate cost.

If carbon dioxide enrichment can result in economical crop production increases, why is it that the majority of greenhouses fail to install the necessary generators? Many greenhouses could sell more plants on the important flower days than they can produce, but carbon dioxide injection cannot increase production at these times because space is the limiting factor. Bench space is filled with plants for these major selling periods and generally there is no economic advantage in hurrying the crop along or growing exceptionally large plants. It does not matter if one can grow poinsettias to mature in October because no market exists for them then. When greenhouse production is oriented toward the traditional flower days, it may be that little benefit can be realized from carbon dioxide enrichment. Easter and Mother's Day production may sometimes present tight schedules but ventilation is common at that time of year and carbon dioxide is not generally limiting. Those greenhouses which produce mainly for a daily market and could sell more than currently produced are the ones which would benefit most from carbon dioxide enrichment during winter months. When one grows for daily markets rather than holiday markets, the amount of time a crop spends on the bench is of considerable importance.

There is no evidence that the maximum levels of carbon dioxide (1,500-2,000 ppm) normally introduced into greenhouses have any deleterious effects on human beings. It has been reported that 5,000 ppm of carbon dioxide can be tolerated by people for normal work day periods.

CHAPTER 16

PLANT PESTS, DISEASES, & POLLUTION DISORDERS

Most plant damage due to pests, diseases, and pollution disorders can be minimized if growers are ever vigilant and demand cleanliness and meticulous attention to detail from employees. Poor housekeeping and carelessness cannot be tolerated in a profitable greenhouse operation. A market for flowers and plants exists because people are drawn to the aesthetic value of their beauty. Any factor which detracts from this beauty must be brought under control to insure continued existence of the market.

PLANT PESTS

Insects, mites, slugs, and rodents are the common pests which attack plants. The seemingly unlimited reproductive capacity of these pests has perhaps led to more grower frustration than any other greenhouse problem. Morale suffers under the never ending battle one faces with these animal competitors. Infestations are cleared up only to reappear in a different location a few days later. Much of the frustration engineered by plant pests can be overcome if growers assume an aggressive posture against them rather than a defensive reaction to their destructive capabilities. Obtaining a knowledge of how to control pests is the first step in gaining the upper hand; a religious implementation of this knowledge is the second step. Insects and mites are initially irritating to customers mainly because of their visual presence but the long term effects of their activity may result in permanent disfiguration or death for the plant. Entire crops can be made worthless in a short time if pests are allowed to multiply without hazard. Once a critical population level is attained, it is useless to attempt control and the crop should be discarded. Retail sales experience is helpful in convincing growers of the need never to allow infested plants into marketing channels. No other plant defect will turn customers away faster than the presence of pests.

Many types of rodents may occasionally cause damage to greenhouse plants but mice are the chief offenders. Seeds and seedlings are the main target of mice and crop schedules can be badly upset when a seed sowing is destroyed by them. Only one or two mice can play havoc with a large number of seed flats in one night. Mice are especially fond of the following seeds: pepper, marigold, pansy, cucumber, squash, melon, zinnia, tomato, asparagus sprengeri, dahlia, eggplant, and aster. Introducing a cat to the greenhouse will eliminate much of the mouse population but cats may cause more plant damage than mice unless they are trained to stay off the benches. Poison baits are quite effective in controlling mice but foul odors may result if the mice die and decay in the greenhouse. Traps will do an effective job without the drawbacks of cats or poison baits. Once the traps have served their purpose they must be removed from the greenhouse to avoid being ruined by rusting in the humid atmosphere.

Mites and insects may often seem to appear in the greenhouse as products of spontaneous generation. Entry to the greenhouse by insects is usually gained through their own locomotion or by being carried in on plants. Very few insects are introduced on personnel and supplies. The suction created by ventilating fans can sweep in any insects close to air entries. Simple precautions will eliminate the entry of most insects. Plant life outside the greenhouse should be eliminated for a distance of at least 20 feet. Screens should be installed on all air entries; mites and very small insects will not be denied entry by screens but many of the larger species will be kept out. Evaporative cooling pads not only help in bringing down greenhouse temperatures but also make entry more difficult for insects. Plants brought into the greenhouse must be carefully inspected for insects and even if they appear to be clean, treatment with a broad spectrum insecticide should follow at the earliest possible time.

Weeds on the floors are probably the largest contributor to insect populations in the greenhouse. Crops may develop infestations of insects but within a short time the crop matures and is sold or removed as dumpage. Unless growers allow old, worthless crops to occupy greenhouse space indefinitely, the insect population will be removed with the crop. If weeds are not removed on a regular schedule, a carryover insect population will remain on them even when crops have been harvested. Plants kept from one crop to the next should be inspected very carefully to prevent a carry-over of insects. Many growers are reluctant to dump crops which have passed their prime and have no reasonable prospect of being marketed. Such a crop not only occupies valuable greenhouse space but also enhances the possibilities of insect outbreaks. A well planned marketing strategy is a positive step in the control of insects. Crops which are moved in and out without carryover eliminate the transfer of insects to succeeding crops.

Insects and mites will eventually become established in any greenhouse, no matter how stringent the precautions are to prevent entry or to eliminate weeds as havens. A program of early detection and preventive sprays will ensure that major outbreaks which cause substantial plant losses never occur. Growers should make a habit of checking for infestations at least every two weeks. It will soon become apparent that certain species of plants and stages of growth are more likely to harbor an outbreak and attention should be focused on them. In my experience, Swedish ivy (*Plectranthus australis*) is almost never attacked by insects or mites while Queensland umbrella tree (*Shefflera actinophylla*) falls prey to many types of insects. I spend most of my observation time on less than ten varieties which are particularly prone to insect attacks. The grower can obtain much help from employees who are trained in the rudiments of recognizing various insects.

Preventive treatment with sprays, aerosols, fogs, etc., must be carefully monitored to eliminate undue costs and to avoid building up insect resistance to insecticides. Many authorities recommend preventive treatments every one to two weeks with alternating classes of chemical compounds. Alternating the chemical family tends to reduce the chances of insects becoming resistant to related insecticides. My personal view of preventive treatments is that regular insecticide applications at the frequency mentioned above are a waste of money and expose greenhouse workers, especially the person applying insecticides, to undue risk from residual toxic effects. My preference is to concentrate a major effort at complete insect elimination during the summer months when prolonged ventilation is possible after applications and crops are usually at the lowest numbers. Good ventilation lessens employee exposure to residual fumes and fewer crops result in fewer plants to harbor insects. Fewer crops also means weeds under benches are more visible and easier to treat.

Depending on the insect populations, one may need to wage a second but perhaps less intense effort at elimination when early spring weather allows adequate ventilation and Easter crops have been marketed. Localized treatments will, of course, be necessary between these two major treatment periods because infestations will flare up in particular crops. I have found this type of control program works quite well and is less expensive to administer. One must realize that insecticides are often very expensive and applications may require considerable skilled labor. Any unnecessary applications are a health hazard and economically unsound.

Successful control programs depend upon growers being able to quickly recognize harmful insects and the signs they leave behind. A knowledge of reproductive cycles, feeding habits, and habitat preferences is very helpful in designing control programs for insects and related pests. Many of these creatures will seldom actually be seen unless certain telltale signs of their presence are noticed. Once a grower has adequate knowledge, one can check for major insect outbreaks rather quickly. I will now present an account of the most important greenhouse pests and then follow up with specific control measures. The species described probably account for 90% of crop damage but growers should keep in mind that hundreds of pests have the potential to cause losses. Figures 1-5 depict some common greenhouse pests.

Aphids

Aphids are perhaps the most ubiquitous greenhouse pests. There are several kinds of aphids but the green peach aphid is the one most often found in greenhouses. There are winged and wingless stages of aphids but the wingless stage is by far more common. In the wingless stages the green peach aphid may be nearly 1/8 inch long, with the youngest ones being considerably smaller. The body is rather corpulent and color may range from a very light yellowish-green to tannish-red depending upon the season. When disturbed, the wingless forms move very slowly, especially the larger ones. Winged forms are brownish-black in color and can be easily distinguished from adult fungus gnats because aphids can be made to fly only with difficulty while fungus gnats fly at the least disturbance.

When aphids shed their skin, it is often easier to detect an infestation by looking for the whitish-transparent remains than it is to see the living aphid. When populations grow to epidemic proportions, glazed spots may be seen on leaves below because sugary compounds excreted by aphids will fall to lower levels. If this sugary glaze becomes widespread, a black, sooty mold will begin to grow on it. Aphids may be found on the upper or lower surface of leaves. Young stem tips are especially favored by them. When very young leaves are attacked, further growth may be malformed because of injuries to cells caused by insertion of the tubular, sucking mouthparts of aphids. More mature leaves often develop small yellowish dots as if the leaf had been pricked by a needle. When many-petaled flowers, such as

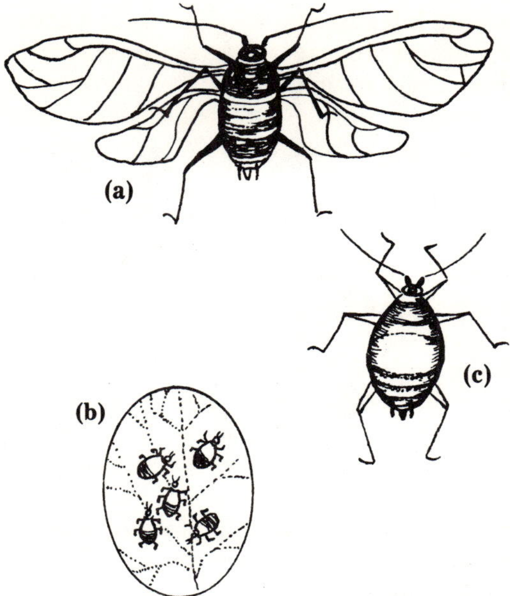

Fig. 1. Green peach aphid prevalent in greenhouses. (a) adult winged female; (b) group of wingless adults on leaf surface magnified approximately 10 times; (c) wingless adult detailed.

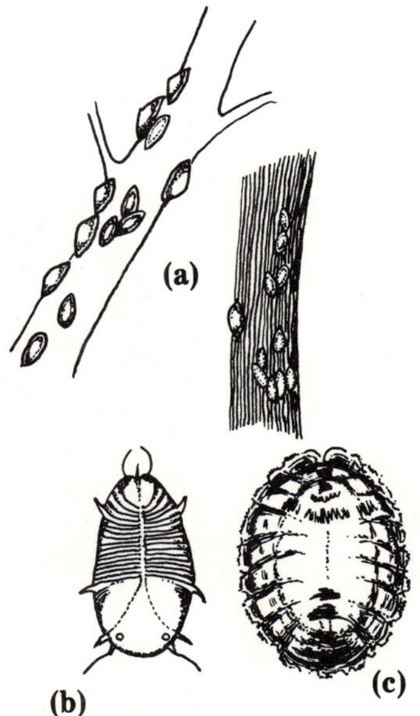

Fig. 2. Common greenhouse brown scale with rough shell. (a) armored stage attached to plant stems; (b) crawler stage before forming a shell, magnified several times in relation to the shell, (c) close up of armored shell.

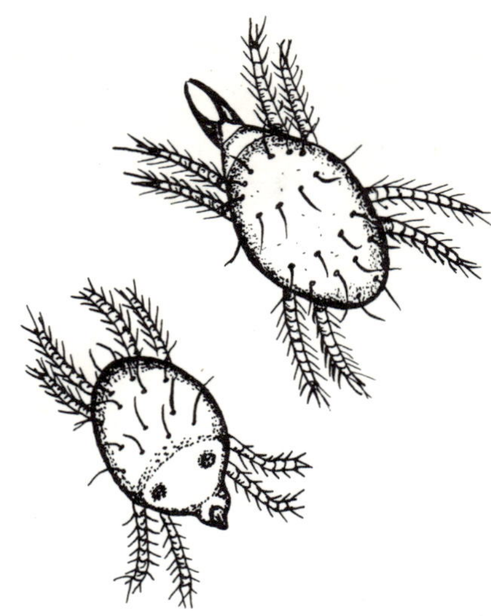

Fig. 3. Red spider, spider mite, or two spotted mite. Spots may not be evident under some conditions. Certain immature stages have less than eight legs. Some observers report pronounced mouth parts while others do not; this may be due to observing different stages of maturity or variation in populations.

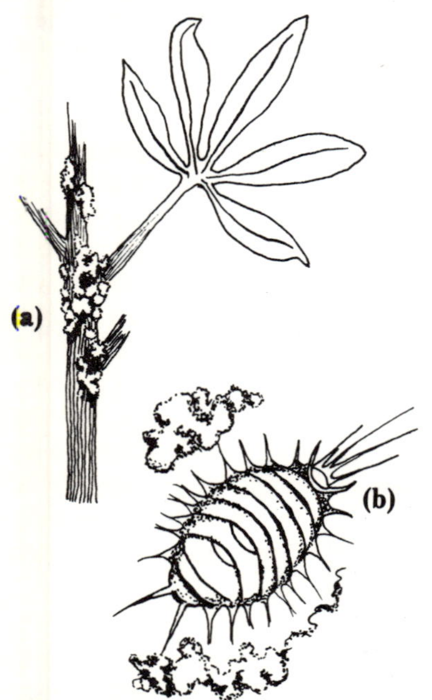

Fig. 4. (a) Cottony egg sacs deposited by mealybugs; (b) common greenhouse mealybug adult.

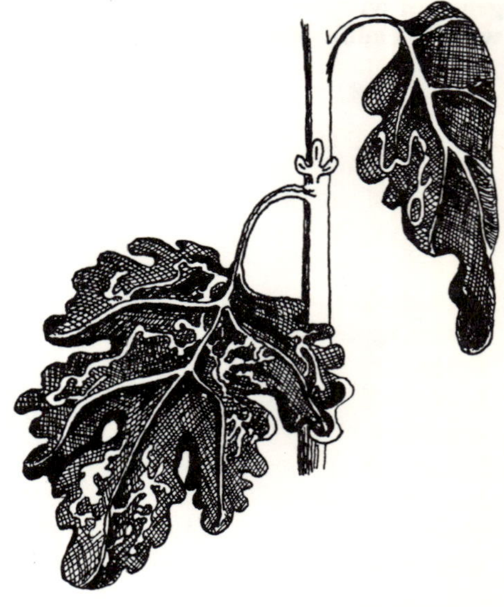

Fig. 5. Chrysanthemum leaves showing characteristic serpentine tunneling between the upper and lower epidermal layers by leaf miner larvae. Tunnels seldom cross the harder tissue at main veins.

chrysanthemums, become heavily infested, it is impossible to obtain control except with systemic insecticides.

Aphids normally do not lay eggs in the greenhouse or in more southern geographical areas. Females give birth to living offspring, the females of which can give birth to a new generation within six to ten days. The reproductive period of an aphid may give rise to three or four batches of young, with a total of 60 to 100 females. Males are not necessary for reproduction except at those times when eggs are laid. Aphids in northern latitudes will lay eggs outside the greenhouse with the approach of winter to provide an overwintering stage. When insecticides with no residual toxicity are used, application at 4 day intervals for a period of 16 days will provide good control of all aphid stages.

Mites

Mites may be somewhat less common than aphids under most circumstances but mites are perhaps the most difficult pests to control and potentially most deleterious to plant growth. Mites are, strictly speaking, not insects but belong to the spider family. Due to their small size, mites may not be detected until populations are out of control unless experienced personnel actively search for their presence. Two types of mites are particularly common in greenhouses, the red spider or two-spotted mite and the cyclamen mite.

Red spider or two-spotted mites are much more commonly present in greenhouses than are cyclamen mites. Adults of red spider mites are very small but can be seen with the unaided eye if light conditions and eyesight are good. Their color is most often a slightly transparent reddish shade but greenish or yellowish colors may be seen under particular circumstances. Two darker spots are present on the backside slightly above mid girth. These spots may be prominent to the naked eye but, especially on small mites, are sometimes less distinguishable. Adult red spiders might be confused with very immature aphids at first glance but the two spots and the tendency of spider mites to run quickly when disturbed are not shared by aphids. A fine, whitish web is spun by spider mites on the underside of leaves and when sufficient numbers are present this web becomes easily visible. In advanced outbreaks, the web may extend from branch to branch and spider mites may be seen crawling through the web.

Red spiders damage plants by inserting their sucking mouthparts into cells and feeding on the contents. Very tiny yellow puncture wounds are apparent from the topside on thinner leaved varieties. As the mite population increases, the puncture wounds may become so close together that the entire area becomes yellow. Eventually, affected portions turn brownish-yellow and die. Severely infested plants may take on the appearance of having dried out or windburned. Red spiders flourish under warm, dry conditions. The speed of reaching maturity and producing young doubles between 70°and 80° F. A complex life cycle which includes several resting stages and an egg stage make control of spider mites difficult since only the active stage may be affected by common insecticides. Several applications of insecticides are necessary to begin controlling mites unless the chemical has a good residual life.

Cyclamen mites are very small; a 10x hand lens is necessary to observe their physical presence. Their appearance under this magnification is most often a semitransparent dirty glass color. Individual body parts may be difficult to observe but movement can be discerned. The presence of cyclamen mites is usually detected by characteristic deformations of leaves and flowers rather than by observation of the mite itself.

Cyclamen mites infest very young leaf and bud tissue at the stem tip and inflict many puncture wounds with their sucking mouth parts. These wounds cause further growth of the leaf to be distorted in various ways, depending on the plant species. Sometimes growth of new leaves almost ceases and they appear hardened and dwarfed. African violets and gloxinia exhibit this type of leaf growth when affected and the crown or center of the plant becomes whitish because leaf growth has stopped but hair growth continues. Some plants, such as ivies, exhibit hardened leaves, some of which are distorted as if they were made of rubber and stretched out of shape. Infested flowers characteristically fail to open. Whenever growers begin to observe a consistent pattern of leaf or flower distortion, they should suspect cyclamen mites.

Begonias, impatiens, ivies, cyclamen, silver lace vine, African violets, and gloxinias are particularly susceptible, but other species can surely be infested. The damage caused by this pest may sometimes be attributed to chemical gaseous pollutants because of the growth distortions caused without any apparent agent visible to the naked eye. Several insecticide treatments are necessary to kill egg stages as they hatch. Life cycles may be completed in as little as two weeks.

Mealybugs

Mealybugs are oval shaped insects which are normally 1/8 to 1/4 inch long with discernible transverse lines across the back. Long tailed varieties have hair-like projections of up to ½ inch at the rear while some varieties have no easily observed tail. The body color of white to whitish-grey is imparted by a waxy powder that covers the body. Mealybugs are much like aphids in their feeding mechanism and in the honey-like substance which they excrete. Mobility is not swift but is easily discernible once the pests decide to move. Very young mealybugs tend to be slightly flesh colored because the waxy powder covering the back is thinner. Most mealybug species deposit their eggs in a cottony sac which they usually leave in leaf axils or the forks of branches. This cottony sac is often the most immediately recognizable indication that an infestation has begun. Long tailed mealybugs give birth to living nymphs and leave no egg sac. Mealybugs are easiest to kill when they are young and lack the protective powdery coat.

Scale

Scale insects are represented by several groups which vary somewhat in their color, life cycle, and type of shell. All groups are distinguishable, however, by the turtle-like shell which covers the immobile female as she lays eggs or gives birth to living young. Scale insects are often divided into hard-shelled and soft-shelled groups. Depending on the species, shells may be round, oval, or oyster shell shaped and the outer texture may be smooth or rough. Shell color will vary but brown and grey are common. The size of shells is commonly in the range of 1/8 inch but may be up to 1/4 inch.

The nymph (crawler stage) is produced through live birth or eggs and is sluggishly mobile and naked. Crawlers move about until they insert their sucking mouth parts and then begin to form a shell. Many scale insects excrete honey-like substances in the same manner as aphids and mealybugs but some do not. Shells are commonly found attached to mature plant stems but are also present on leaves. The number of shells may be few but in advanced infestations shells can cover the stem completely. Adherence of shells to the plant even after elimination of the insects makes it imperative to control scale early. Customers will not accept plants with shells attached even if there are no live insects present. Control of scale is difficult because only the short lived crawler stage is susceptible to contact insecticides.

Fungus Gnats

Fungus gnats are about 1/8 inch or less long at maturity and are greyish-back. They resemble a common gnat. Fungus gnats readily fly when disturbed; this characteristic will distinguish them easily from winged aphids which will seldom fly. Adult gnats do not harm plants but are quite irritating to customers. Fungus gnats are fond of soils and accumulations of dead organic material. Eggs are laid in moist soil where they hatch into whitish, somewhat transparent, wormlike larvae about 1/8 inch long. Larvae are difficult to see when soil is examined except when they move quickly. Larvae feed on decaying organic matter in the soil but when populations become large, they may attack roots and bulbs. Damage is seldom severe. A life cycle of about 25 days is normal.

Adult fungus gnats are readily killed by a number of insecticides but eggs, larvae, and pupae in the soil must be controlled with soil drenches. Spray applications should be made to cover soil floors which are a major breeding area. Since artificial soils high in organic matter have become prevalent, fungus gnats are more numerous. A great deal of habitat for these insects is eliminated if dead leaves and other organic trash are removed from the greenhouse and exposed soil on the floor is covered by gravel. Sufficient emphasis is probably not placed on the control of fungus gnats since they do not often injure crops physically. Consumer displeasure aroused by these insects must be considered as an important detriment to crop marketability.

Whiteflies

Whiteflies are probably the most easily recognized greenhouse insect because of their pure white color which distinguishes them immediately. Adults are approximately 1/16 inch long and will fly vigorously for short distances when disturbed from their usual resting place on the undersides of leaves. Tomatoes, lantanas, fushias, and poinsettias are particularly susceptible to white fly infestation. Although many other species are troubled by whitefly, the above four should be inspected exceptionally carefully when new plants are being introduced into the greenhouse. Many growers ship in large numbers of poinsettia cuttings each fall for Christmas marketing. Whiteflies may be introduced on a broad scale with this crop unless suppliers are warned that no infested plants will be tolerated.

Whiteflies damage plants with their sucking mouth parts in much the same manner as do aphids, mealybugs, and scale insects. Excretion of a honey-like substance with the resultant growth of a black sooty mold is also similar. Evidence of whiteflies may be gained by the presence of whitish, round egg chambers attached to the undersides of leaves. These chambers are no larger than a pinhead and may contain eggs or be merely the remains after crawlers have hatched and moved on. Extreme infestations will be characterized by the black mold mentioned previously. Crawlers are small, greenish, and flattened and are seldom observed unless one pays particular attention. A complete life cycle may take five weeks under typical greenhouse conditions. Adults are easily killed by a number of insecticides but younger stages are difficult to eliminate without resort to specific formulations which kill all stages.

Leaf Miners

Adult leaf miners are small, black flies which vary in appearance depending upon the species. Eggs are deposited under the leaf epidermis by flies. When hatched, the larvae bore between the upper and lower leaf epidermis and consume the soft tissue between veins. Tunnels are serpentine or blotchy and become tan or brown as tissue dies. The serpentine nature of many tunnels and their abrupt termination at hardened major veins distinguishes leaf miner damage from dead tissue caused by other means. Tissue damage is generally the earliest warning one receives concerning the presence of these insects. Adult flies may go undetected if more numerous fungus gnats are present and the larval stage is difficult to observe unless one peels back the upper epidermal layer and observes carefully with a hand lens. Control is much easier when systemic insecticides are applied since larvae are protected from surface sprays by the leaf epidermis. Leaf miner may be seldom encountered until a shipment of contaminated plants is received. The insects may then build up to epidemic proportions before the problem is identified. Chrysanthemums are a prime target of leaf miners and infestations are often imported with the cuttings. Five weeks is the normal duration of a life cycle.

Snails and Slugs

Snails and slugs are related to common aquatic animals such as oysters and clams. Eradication programs aimed at insects have little effect on snails and slugs because the metabolism of the two groups of animals is considerably different. Everyone is familiar with the appearance of snails. Slugs exhibit much the same soft, slimy body shape but have no hard shell; their length is usually ½-1½ inches but large ones up to 4 inches are sometimes found. Slugs and snails damage plants by chewing. They prefer dark, moist areas and are active mainly at night and early morning. Slugs may be detected by the shiny trails of slime they leave behind when crawling over benches and plant tissue. Maintaining dry floors and benches in the greenhouse will inhibit slug and snail populations greatly, as will eliminating vegetation from the outside perimeter of structures.

Miscellaneous Pests

At one time or another almost any insect could become so numerous in the greenhouse as to be considered a pest. The previously discussed major pests are persistent and active at most times of the year. The following pests may cause serious plant damage or customer irritation at certain times but do not seem to be so difficult to control and may develop large populations only at specific times of the year, generally in warmer months.

> Thrips—Damage may become very serious at times. Quite small insects.

> Caterpillars or Worms—Several moths produce larvae which can eat large amounts of vegetation in a short time. Infestations are usually brief and only during the warmer months. Cutworms, armyworms, corn borers, etc.

> Grasshoppers—Serious in summer if air intakes not screened.

Spittle Bug—Recognized by frothy, spit-like excretion on stems or in leaf axils.

Leaf Hoppers—Easily recognized by hopping method of movement.

Ants—May damage small seedlings but also transmit disease and insects from plant to plant.

Sow Bugs, Pill Bugs, Centipedes—Large populations may cause minor damage to root systems.

Earwigs—Will damage any plant structures but especially buds and fruit. Troublesome in summer.

Leaf Rollers—Moth larvae roll themselves up in leaves to pupate. May be serious in summer.

PEST CONTROL

This discussion of pest control will first be directed towards methods and specific pesticides which I have found to be effective through practical experience. Later I will present a selection of pesticides which, although I may have little actual experience with them, are recommended by other experts. All control methods will assume that greenhouse weeds have been eliminated, weeds outside the greenhouse are under control, nonmarketable plants are removed from the greenhouse, and periodic inspections for pest detection are made.

I have used Vapona® (dichlorvos) fog for years as a broad spectrum insecticide application. This compound is recommended for use on aphids, mealybug, whitefly, leaf miners, spider mites, and thrips. Generally little fogging is possible in late fall, winter, and early spring. My personal opinion is that while this formulation may kill the above mentioned pests, it is not particularly effective when used by itself except in the case of aphids. I would characterize Vapona as my principal weapon against aphids but only as a containment mechanism for mealybugs, spider mites, whitefly, and leaf miners.

Plant damage from Vapona fogs has been minimal. Wandering Jews suffered considerably when the fogging program was initiated but damage has now lessened to the point of being negligible. Reduction of damage is perhaps linked to an undetected change in application procedure or to an unconscious selection of plant cuttings which were not damaged and thus resistant to fog burn. Water drip from ceilings can be a problem after fogging when crops with especially tender new leaves are present. Apparently the fogging material is deposited on the ceiling surface and then concentrated in water droplets which fall onto plants below. Young poinsettia leaves develop injured spots quickly from this phenomenon. I have not incurred any flower damage using Vapona fogs during full bloom. It must be cautioned that I have never used these fogs on poinsettias in bloom. The fog blast should be directed away from plants to prevent spraying foliage with hot, unatomized petroleum insecticide carrier. Adequate ventilation must be provided before people re-enter the greenhouse.

Perhaps twice a year, in late spring and especially in late summer, I apply Vapona four times at four day intervals to obtain almost complete elimination of aphids. At other times fogging is done every two to three weeks, weather permitting. Outside temperatures should be warm enough to maintain a 70°-80° F minimum greenhouse temperature while fog is present and to permit at least one hour of rapid ventilation after fogging. Winds must be calm so that fog concentrations in the greenhouse are not diluted by infiltrating air. Fogging when conditions are not suitable for a good kill will most likely result in a greater resistance by the surviving population. In addition, fogging compounds are quite expensive and should not be wasted by careless application.

Additional aphid control is accomplished with Temik® granules and Orthene® aerosols. Both are systemic (absorbed and transmitted through the interior tissues) in action and can be used on problem infestations of aphids. Orthene aerosol bombs are very expensive but are useful when only a few plants need to be treated, when a systemic insecticide is needed and plants are sensitive to Temik, or when plants are to be marketed soon and Temik cannot be applied due to its extreme toxicity to humans. Orthene bombs are most effective if three applications are made about four days apart. This increases the dosage without the possibility of burning leaves and, since Orthene does have some contact killing action, will offer good control with contact properties alone. I have used Orthene aerosols on a broad range of flowering and foliage plants and never suffered any damage, but container labels warn of injury due to repeated applications to chrysanthemums and carnations.

I use Temik sparingly because it is quite toxic to human beings. Two applications are made four weeks apart to all chrysanthemums, cinerarias, calceolarias, kalanchoes, and Christmas peppers. These plants are particularly susceptible to heavy aphid infestation and preventive measures must be taken from the start to insure a clean crop. Dosage is 1/8 teaspoon per 6½ inch azalea pot. Chrysanthemums, cinerarias, and calceolarias are burned easily by Temik so the 1/8 teaspoon measure is leveled when applied to these varieties and carefully spread over the surface to avoid buildup in one spot. A heaping 1/8 teaspoon can usually be applied to 6½ inch Christmas peppers, kalanchoes, and most foliage plants. Dosage is adjusted by soil volume for larger and smaller pot sizes. Water is applied thoroughly after application, making sure that the Temik does not float over the lip of the pot. Heavy watering in is needed especially with those varieties which burn easily. Damage to sensitive varieties seems to be greater when plants are not well established.

Each grower should experiment carefully with dosages before applying Temik to a whole crop since crop damage could be lessened or magnified depending upon the soil mix ingredients. In my particular circumstances, certain crops such as snapdragons are so sensitive to Temik burn that it simply cannot be used on them. I have seen some greenhouses where Temik is broadcast over the tops of plants. Considering the highly toxic nature of the chemical to humans, I think this practice is not conducive to employee health and could result in costly lawsuits. Potted plants must have their last Temik treatment six weeks before sale. Do not apply Temik to plants which must be handled by workers in transplanting. Temik is a very useful insecticide for problem cases of aphids and, as will be pointed out later, several other insects, but its use must be carefully monitored by responsible people.

Mealybugs, scale, and leaf miner seldom become real problems in my greenhouses. When occasional infestations are noted, they are treated with local applications of Temik. Orthene aerosol may be used to provide a quick kill of stages susceptible to contact insecticides while the Temik has a chance to begin working. Boston ferns often become infested with scale and care must be taken when treating the plants with Temik; dosage rates must be kept in the low range and watered in well or damage may occur. The Vapona fog treatments may keep mealybugs, scale, and leaf miners from becoming widespread in my greenhouses, but one should not place a great deal of reliance on this method of treatment alone for control of these insects.

Whiteflies were, until recently, very difficult to control. The introduction of the insecticide resmethrin should make serious whitefly problems a thing of the past if growers will use it properly. I normally use the aerosol form and treat all plants in the greenhouses prior to planting the poinsettia crop. Another application is given after poinsettias have been pinched. This program usually clears the greenhouses of any whiteflies until the following year unless shipped-in poinsettia cuttings were heavily infested. Certain plants such as fushia and lantana may need to be sprayed in the spring if outbreaks occur. Aerosol resmethrin must be directed towards the undersides of leaves and should be applied just before dark since light breaks down the chemical and renders it ineffective. Concentration of the insecticide carrier on tender leaves will cause burns. Temik applied to the soil will also control whiteflies.

Fungus gnats are quite difficult to control unless adults are killed on a regular basis or soil drenches of insecticide are applied to eliminate larvae as they hatch. Insecticide must also be applied to the floor if it is composed of soil. Some growers recommend Temik applications to the floor; this may be quite effective in controlling fungus gnats but is, in my estimation, a hazard to employees. A program I feel is suitable for fungus gnat control is to spray floors, benches, and plants periodically with diazinon. Spraying on the floor may be done quite heavily to ensure the larvae in the soil will be killed. If diazinon alone does not provide suitable control, Temik may be added to individual pots to eliminate the generation of larvae in that soil and resmethrin can be used periodically to kill adults. This combination of the three insecticides should provide almost complete elimination. Diazinon sprays should be used when ventilation is adequate. Diazinon sprayed on the floor and benches will also help eliminate such pests as earwigs, cutworms, sowbugs, etc. which crawl on the floors. Any fungus gnat control program must also include covering bare soil floors with gravel and picking up soil and organic matter left on benches and floors.

Cyclamen mites may be cleaned up at the same time a fungus gnat program is underway. I usually spray two or three times in summer with diazinon as a preventive measure. If cyclamen mites become an obvious problem, spraying should be done four times at five or six day intervals. The spray must be thorough with buds and young tips receiving particular attention.

The best way to control slugs is to maintain greenhouses in as dry a condition as possible on floors and benches. Rock salt under the benches will dehydrate slugs if they crawl over it but care must be taken to keep salt away from metal posts to avoid corrosion. A metaldehyde bait is the pesticide most commonly used on slugs. Bait must not be allowed to get old; for best results change it frequently. Serious slug damage can be avoided by constructing benches so that it is difficult for slugs to reach plants from the floor. Benches attached to sidewalls increase the possibility of slugs coming from the floor to bench tops.

Spider mites are, for many growers, the most bothersome and persistent greenhouse pests encountered. I shared their feeling of helplessness until I made a practice of spraying with Pentac® every three to four weeks through the summer months. During the rest of the year I spray susceptible varieties every eight weeks unless a visible problem occurs; the frequency is then stepped up. Although mites can attack almost any variety of plant they seem to be particularly fond of ivies, hibiscus, diffenbachia, sheffleras, cyclamens, crotons, certain philodendrons, and impatiens. Spray must be directed at the undersides of leaves to be effective. I have tried most other pesticides recommended for mites and never observed any acceptable degree of control. Even Temik at heavy rates did not eliminate infestations. Pentac is degraded by ultraviolet rays and cannot be used under outdoor conditions. I have encountered no phytotoxicity with Pentac.

The specific pest control measures I have mentioned will not work for everyone under all conditions. Soils, weather, and crop programs, will all combine to make every greenhouse a unique environment for particular pests. I feel that most growers could use the programs to effective ends under most circumstances. I must point out again that plant damage due to pesticides can vary greatly with the methods of application and specific environmental factors. Each grower should carefully test pesticides for not only effectiveness but for signs of plant damage. Statements as to effectiveness must not be blindly accepted; several pesticides for each pest should be tested and judged critically for the degree of control achieved. Good pest control rests mainly upon stringent greenhouse sanitation and careful crop management. Effective pesticides cannot be relied upon to achieve control by themselves.

Table 19 lists some common greenhouse pests and popular pesticides used to control them. All compounds listed for a particular pest may not produce equally effective results. Table 20 lists frequently used pesticides and greenhouse chemicals with information concerning their relative toxicity to humans. Growers would be wise to limit their use of highly toxic chemicals to those cases where no other effective control is available. Persons exposed to pesticides must remember that poisoning occurs not only through ingestion but also by skin contact and inhalation of vapors. The chemical family of pesticides is also listed in Table 20. Many experts recommend switching chemical families of pesticides occasionally to prevent pests from developing a resistance to particular classes of compounds. As an example, Vapona and Orthene are in the class of pesticides known as organophosphates. Insect resistance to Vapona should confer some degree of resistance to Orthene and vice versa.

Table 19

Common greenhouse pests and some popular pesticides used to control them. Refer to Table 20 and text before choosing for use.

Pest	Pesticide Trade® or common name	Comments
Aphid	Temik	Systemic action
	Orthene	Systemic action
	Vapona	
	Enstar	Insect growth regulator
	lindane	
	malathion	

Table 19 (con't)

Pest	Pesticide Trade® or common name	Comments
	Meta-Systox-R	Systemic action
	nicotine	
	Pirimor	
	diazinon	
	Isotox	Systemic action
	Sevin	
	Systox	Systemic action
Scale	Temik	Systemic action
	Orthene	Systemic action
	Isotox	Systemic action
	Systox	Systemic action
Fungus gnat	resmethrin	
	diazinon	Suitable for floor soil
	Temik	Systemic action
Mealybug	Temik	Systemic action
	Orthene	Systemic action
	Vapona	
	malathion	
	Dithio	
	Systox	Systemic action
	Enstar	Insect growth regulator
Leafminer	Temik	Systemic action
	Isotox	Systemic action
	Orthene	Systemic action
	Vapona	
	malathion	
	Systox	Systemic action
Spider mite	Pentac	Long residual action, especially effective
	Vapona	
	Temik	Systemic action
	Kelthane	
	Tedion	
	Morestan	
	Omite	
	Plictran	
Whitefly	resmethrin	Especially effective
	Vapona	
	Enstar	Insect growth regulator
	Temik	Systemic action
	Orthene	Systemic action
	Isotox	Systemic action
Cyclamen mite	diazinon	
	Kelthane	
	Thiodan	

Table 19 (con't)

Pest	Pesticide Trade® or common name	Comments
Thrips	resmethrin	
	Temik	Systemic action
	Isotox	Systemic action
	Orthene	Systemic action
	Vapona	
Leafrollers	Orthene	Systemic action
	Isotox	Systemic action
	resmethrin	
Slugs and snails	metaldehyde	Must be replaced as it ages
Ants Cutworms Grasshoppers Leafhoppers Bagworms Cabbageworms Cockroaches Earwigs Sowbugs Millipedes	diazinon	Many insecticides are useful against these pests but diazinon is a good general purpose remedy, especially for any pest which is normally in contact with the soil. Chlordane is very effective but pesticide laws restrict its use under most circumstances.

Table 20

Toxicity and chemical family of common greenhouse pesticides and chemicals.

Trade® or common name	Chemical family	Relative toxicity	Oral LD 50*	Dermal LD 50*
Pesticides				
chlordane	Hydrocarbon	Moderately	283	580
diazinon	Phosphate	Moderately	66	379
Dithio, sulfotepp	Phosphate	Highly toxic	5	
Enstar, kinoprene		Low	4900	
Isotox (mixture of Sevin Metasystox-R, Kelthane)				
Kelthane, dicofol	Hydrocarbon	Low	575	4000
lindane	Hydrocarbon	Moderately	76	500
malathion	Organophosphate	Low	885	4000
metaldehyde	Hydrocarbon	Moderately		
Meta Systox-R, oxydemeton-methyl	Phosphate	Moderately	65	100
Morestan, oxythioquinox	Carbamate	Low	2500	2000
nicotine	Alkaloid	Highly toxic	50	140
Omite, propargite	Sulfite	Low	2200	5000
Orthene, acephate	Phosphate	Low	866	2000
Pentac, dienochlor	Hydrocarbon	Low	3160	

Table 20 (con't)

Trade® or common name	Chemical family	Relative toxicity	Oral LD 50*	Dermal LD 50*
Pesticides (con't)				
Pirimor, pirimicarb	Carbamate	Moderately		
Plictran, cyhexatin		Moderately	180	2000
pyrethrin	Pyrethroid	Low		
resmethrin	Synthetic pyrethroid	Low	1500	3040
Sevin, carbaryl	Carbamate	Low	307	2000
Systox, demeton	Phosphate	Highly toxic	2	8
Temik, aldicarb	Carbamate	Highly toxic	1	5
Thiodan, endosulfan	Hydrocarbon	Highly toxic	18	74
Tedion, tetradifon	Hydrocarbon	Low	5000	1000
Vapona, dichlorvos	Phosphate	Moderately	25	59
Growth retardants				
B-9, daminozide		Low	8400	
Cyclocel, chlormequat		Low	670	
A-Rest, ancymidol		Low	4500	
Soil fumigants				
Cyanogas		Highly toxic		
Chloropicrin		Highly toxic		
methyl bromide		Highly toxic		
formaldehyde				
Vapam, metam-sodium	Carbamate	Low	820	
Herbicides				
diquat		Moderately	231	
paraquat		Highly toxic	150	
Roundup, glyphosate		Low	4320	
2, 4, 5-T		Moderately	300	
2, 4-D		Moderately	375	
Rodenticide				
dicumoral		Low	541	
Fungicides				
Banrot, ethazol and thioallophanate		Low	5000	
Benlate, benomyl		Low	10000	
Lesan (formerly Dexon), fenanainosulf		Moderately	75	
Terraclor, PCNB		Low	15000	
Truban, ethazol		Low	10000	
Daconil, chlorothalonil		Low	10000	

Highly toxic	0-50 mg/kg oral	} Classification may vary somewhat
Moderately toxic	50-500 mg/kg oral	since data is compiled from
Slightly toxic	500-5000 mg/kg oral	several sources.

*LD 50—The lethal dosage for 50% of test organisms expressed as mg/kg (milligrams of toxicant per kilograms of body weight). Human toxicity is inferred from tests with rats. Exact parameters may vary with the data source.

PESTICIDE APPLICATION

Pesticides may be applied in several ways. The method will be dictated by many different criteria, most important of which are effectiveness, economy of labor and materials, possibility of crop damage, and safety to personnel. The criteria mentioned above may change dramatically for the same pesticide, depending on the method of application. As an example, many pesticides are available as either emulsifiable concentrates (EC) in a petroleum carrier or as wetable powders (WP) dispersible in water. Spraying with EC rather than WP formulations usually increases the risk of plant damage due mainly to the petroleum carrier but EC sprays are easier to apply because WP dispersions may clog sprayers and must be constantly agitated to maintain the dispersion.

High pressure sprays have been the most common means of pesticide application for many years. They are economical and effective. Good results hinge primarily upon achieving complete coverage of plant surfaces by having adequate pressure and proper nozzles to produce small droplet size and upon directing spray from several different angles. To prevent spray droplets from beading up on the often waxy surfance of leaves, a spreader or surfactant is sometimes added to mixtures. Spreaders may cause plant damage with some pesticides; check the label. Equipment should be checked regularly to make sure hoses have no weak spots and that on-off valves shut tightly automatically whenever positive hand pressure is not being applied. Motor or engine driven pumps should always be regulated by a pressure gauge. Tanks and lines must be cleaned immediately after use. Leftover spray must be safely disposed of to prevent accidents; in no case should it be saved for later use.

Mist blowers are much the same as sprayers except that the pesticide is delivered to plant surfaces by dilution in a high speed airstream rather than by pressurized liquids. Droplet size is usually smaller in mist blowers than with sprays. Directing the mist to undersides of leaves may be difficult on crowded benches because pesticides are often many times more concentrated than in spray mixtures; close misting between plants may cause damage due to the pesticide strength. Mist blowers can be used for applying insecticidal dusts.

Pesticide dusts are available for some formulations but use in the greenhouse is not widespread because of the visually objectionable residue left on ornamental plants. Dusts are usually a very safe application method from the standpoint of plant damage. Coverage is good on the topsides of leaves but dust is difficult to apply on the underside.

Recent years have seen a large increase in the application of pesticides as vaporized fogs. Ready made formulations are often quite expensive but growers who take the trouble to mix their own concentrates can cut costs considerably. Pesticides diluted with petroleum carriers are injected into hot exhaust pipes or air streams to cause vaporization and subsequently, a fog with exceedingly small droplet sizes. The fog penetrates to every nook and cranny in the greenhouse but little effective pesticide residue is left once ventilation has taken place. Wind and leaks in the greenhouse covering will lessen the effectiveness of fogs. The great advantage of using fogging equipment is that it covers a large area in a few minutes.

Aerosol pesticide bombs function in much the same manner as fogging machines except that small pesticide droplets are carried by gases formed when pressurized liquid propellants are released. Aerosol bombs are expensive because of the packaging and carriers used. It is seldom that a medium or large sized operation would make use of aerosols for greenhouse wide application; less expensive methods would be available. The real benefit of aerosols lies in their handy use for localized infestations. Growers can grab an aerosol cannister as they close up at night and treat small areas without time consuming mixing and cleaning. Very small greenhouses may find aerosols the most economical means of pest control because no elaborate preparations need be made before application and the convenient size will permit frequent purchase of fresh pesticide.

Smoke application of pesticides is very similar to that of fogs and aerosols but the carrier is a combustible material, which when ignited distributes the pesticide with the resulting smoke. Smoke bombs are expensive but convenient for smaller growers. Canisters of material are placed at predetermined locations in the greenhouse and then ignited. Caution should be exercised to prevent accidental fires and to determine if the smoke bomb burned completely. Malfunctions sometimes cause the bomb to go out before combustion is complete and pest control is therefore limited. Application precautions and conditions are similar as for fogs and aerosols. The range of pesticides which can withstand the combustion process is limited. Plant damage is usually minimal because petroleum carriers are not used.

Pesticides are sometimes applied to the soil surface as granules or to the entire soil mass as liquid drenches. This type of application is particularly useful in the eradication of insects, such as fungus gnats, which reproduce primarily in the soil. Systemic insecticides such as Temik not only kill insects in the soil but are absorbed by the roots and translocated to above ground tissue where chewing or sucking insects are poisoned. Application of pesticides to soil should not be made prior to pasteurization or handling by greenhouse personnel.

Methods of application for fungicides are comparable to those for pesticides. Soil drenches are the most commonly used method since several major fungal diseases are soil borne. Pesticides and fungicides must be compatible with one another if two or more are applied at the same time and they must be compatible with other greenhouse chemicals which may be in use. Check the container label for compatibility; if specific recommendations are not made, the material should not be applied at the same time or immediately before or after use of another chemical. Pesticides and fungicides should be purchased in quantities which will insure usage within one year. Any material kept after this period should be inspected for signs of deterioration, especially if the container has been opened. Emulsifiable concentrates may show a tendency for separation of the components or may fail to produce a milky color when added to water if the material is too old. Container labels will sometimes indicate how long the pesticide can be stored. Diluted material often loses its effectiveness quickly.

SAFE USE OF PESTICIDES, FUNGICIDES, AND HERBICIDES

Growers must realize that pesticides, fungicides, and herbicides are chemicals designed to interfere with the life processes of various organisms and many of the chemicals are also toxic to mammalian metabolic systems. Careless use of these chemicals can result in tragic consequences which could have easily been avoided. Poisonous properties may be immediate in action or evidenced only after a long period of accumulated exposure. All pesticides should be handled as potentially life threatening substances; this action will instill a habit of caution in the individual even though some compounds are relatively harmless to humans. Application of chemicals should be delegated only to responsible personnel who have been adequately trained to do the job safely. Failure of employees to follow the common sense safety rules should result in an immediate reprimand and further infractions must be followed by suspension. Misuse of poisons is simply too serious a matter to let slide.

Pesticides should be stored in a well ventilated, locked storage area where extremes of temperature do not prevail. Excluding sunlight from windows will result in a longer shelf life for some compounds. The contents of the room or cabinet must be prominently advertised with warning signs. Periodic inspections of the storage area will insure that all labels are intact and no spills have occurred. Labels are very important to safe, effective pesticide use. The words "Danger-Poison" and the skull and crossbones symbol are required on the labels of all highly toxic compounds. The word "Warning" is required on the labels of all moderately toxic compounds.

The word "Caution" is required on labels of slightly toxic compounds. Containers with no label should be discarded. In most cases it is against the law to store pesticides in any container other than the original one. Pesticides stored in familiar looking household containers may be ingested by children or handled carelessly by greenhouse personnel. Chemicals may corrode containers not specifically intended for them.

Table 20 familiarizes growers with the toxicities of various greenhouse chemicals. It is obvious that, most of the time, growers can design pest control programs without resorting to highly toxic compounds. Especially dangerous material should be employed only in problem cases where no other pesticide will provide adequate results. Absorption of pesticides through the skin is just as deadly as ingestion. Be sure greenhouse personnel realize dermal contact is highly dangerous. Clothing, goggles, and gloves certified as impenetrable to pesticides should be used during application and mixing. Clothing must be adequately washed after each use or discarded if disposable. Employees should take a thorough shower after applying pesticides.

Common sense and caution are the most important ingredients in pesticide safety. Pointing nozzles away from the body at all times, not blowing out clogged nozzles or hoses with the mouth, and dispensing concentrated pesticides carefully without spilling would seem to be self-evident precautions. Any employees who lack common sense and a proper regard for pesticides should never be allowed to handle them. Goggles and a respirator covering the mouth and nose are sufficient for applying low toxicity chemicals. With more toxic compounds a full face gas mask is recommended. Both respirators and gas masks are equipped with cartridges to filter fumes and particles from the air. Gas masks have a more complete filtering capacity than do respirators. Replacement of cartridges must be observed according to the manufacturers' recommendations if they are to be effective.

Application of pesticides should be accompanied by warning signs when work is in progress and afterwards if warranted. If greenhouses are left unattended, they should be locked. Pesticides and empty containers must be disposed of properly when they are no longer useful. Labels will contain disposal information but the local health service or county agent will have more detailed instructions concerning disposal sites.

Although I have attempted to present responsible information concerning the control of various unwanted greenhouse organisms, I will in no way be liable for the application or use of any chemical mentioned in this book. The accuracy and adequacy of information is not guaranteed and the author and publisher specifically recommend confirmation from other sources before chemicals are used. Environmental conditions may alter the activity of many chemicals and the susceptibility of organisms to them. To avoid plant damage, one should initiate experimental treatments before widespread use. In the event of suspected poisonings of humans by pesticides, a physician should be contacted immediately and remedial measures on the label followed. The container may be needed by the physician or treatment center. The local phone book will contain a number listed under "Poison Control Center" which can be called for emergency treatment information.

PLANT DISEASES

The term "plant disease" has traditionally included those disorders which are caused by organisms known as viruses, bacteria and fungi. Chemical control programs for plant diseases are not so well developed and not so effective as are those available for control of insect pests. The lack of control measures is due in part to the extreme resistance of certain life stages of these diseases and in part to the microscopic size of most organisms causing diseases. Even though plant losses due to diseases may outstrip those caused by insects, the lack of a visible agent may tend to cut down on the research applied to develop control techniques. Since effective post infection treatments are often lacking, control of plant diseases is largely limited to preventive measures. The following discussion will first present a description of the various disease organisms and available chemical techniques used to control them. Preventive control measures will be treated as an individual topic.

Viruses

Viruses are the smallest of disease causing agents and are similar in composition to the genetic material contained in plant cells. The diseases caused by viruses may occur because their similarity to genetic material creates confusing signals for the direction of cell processes. No effective chemical means of controlling viral diseases exist and once plants are infected they should be removed from the greenhouse. The spread of viral diseases is predominantly through the feeding of juice sucking insects which insert their contaminated mouth parts into plant cells. Some viruses can be spread by the contact afforded when plants are pinched, disbudded, and propagated.

Plants seldom outgrow or overcome a viral infection but the effects may become masked for periods of time, thus giving the appearance of a cure. This apparent cure or "sleeping" of the virus in many plant varieties leads the grower to propagate vegetatively from infected plants and eventually spread the disease more widely. Virus indexing is a method devised to uncover the presence of specific viruses in plants which show no external symptoms. Indicator varieties which are known to display prominent visual symptoms of particular viral infections are exposed to infection by the plant in question. If no symptoms appear in the indicator varieties, the plant tested is declared free of the particular virus the indicator variety is susceptible to.

The use of virus indexed plants for vegetative propagation is an important method of preventing the spread of viral diseases. Specialist propagators offer these indexed plants at very reasonable cost for growers to either use as stock plants or finish as a crop. Viral diseases are seldom transmitted from one generation to the next through seeds. Growers should take this advantage into consideration when deciding whether to propagate by seed or cuttings when a choice exists.

The symptoms of viral infection are varied. Stunting or dwarfing of the plant is one of the most common manifestations. Changes in leaf shape and color are striking evidence of virus activity. Leaves are usually affected in localized areas of mosaics, streaks, or blotches with light green, yellow, or white colors replacing the normal green color. Leaf shape may be puckered or stretched in appearance. Flowers may show many similar symptoms and may sometimes revert to a semi-leafy structure.

Bacteria

Bacteria are larger than viruses but still very small. Control by chemical means is difficult for most bacteria but some bactericides are available. Bacteria are often spread by water and can be present in soils. Proper sanitation and selecting of disease free plants are the keys to preventing bacterial blights. Important diseases caused by bacteria are bacterial wilt of carnations; bacterial stem rot of various crops, especially geraniums; soft rot of cuttings and bulbs; crown gall, especially on geraniums, roses, and chrysanthemums; bacterial leaf spots of geranium and English ivy; and fasciation of chrysanthemum, geranium, and carnation stems. Plant stock free from bacterial infections may be obtained by purchasing culture indexed material. Cuttings or mother plants declared to be free of particular bacterial or fungal diseases have been carefully evaluated. Sections of tissue are removed from various portions of the plant and placed in a sterile nutrient agar medium. Any sign of bacterial or fungal growth in the agar disqualifies the plant that the tissue was taken from for culture indexing.

Fungi

Fungi are lower plant forms which range in size from only a few cells to very large mushrooms; they are devoid of chlorophyll and must obtain their nourishment from dead or living organic matter. Those forms which derive their nourishment from living plants are the subject of discussion. Fungi produce thread-like filaments called hyphae which when grouped together form a mycelium. More developed fungi, such as mushrooms, may develop several distinct tissues, but lower forms, characterized by bread mold and powdery mildew, are little more than a collection of hyphae. Fungi reproduce vegetatively sometimes by the mycelium's breaking into pieces, but the sexual production of spores (analagous to seeds in higher plants) is more common. Transmission of fungal diseases is by windborne spores or by water and contact transport of spores and mycelia. Mycelia and some forms of spores die readily if environmental conditions are not favorable but certain types of spores are extremely resistant to adverse conditions and can cause reinfection after it appears an outbreak of disease has been cleared up.

Chemical control of fungi is more advanced than for viruses and bacteria but not so well developed as for insects. Much chemical disease control is aimed at prevention, particularly with regard to soil borne fungi. Post infection treatment is often futile because early stages of diseases go unnoticed and plants are severely damaged when visual symptoms appear. Preventive soil drenches composed of two or more compatible fungicides are often used since one formulation rarely controls the full range of harmful soil fungi. All precautions mentioned for pesticides should be taken with fungicides.

Powdery mildew, which is caused by several varieties of fungi, attacks numerous commercial plants. Almost everyone has observed the familiar white to slightly grey mycelia of powdery mildew on the upper or lower leaf surface of garden roses. Stems and flowers may become affected in serious outbreaks of the disease. Infected leaves and growing tips may become severly distorted in addition to being covered with mildew. Chemical control of powdery mildew is impossible if greenhouse conditions are maintained which promote rapid growth of disease organisms. Powdery mildew flourishes when relative humidity is high and temperatures fairly cool. Temperatures lower than 60° F may not be especially conducive to growth of mildew but relative humidity increases as temperatures drop. Lowering the humidity through ventilation and the application of heat is the best way to bring the disease within possibility of control by chemical means. Repeated trouble with serious infections of powdery mildew should cause growers to carefully evaluate their ventilation and heating practices.

Botrytis or grey mold is a serious greenhouse disease particularly in those areas where high humidity prevails. The disease most often attacks leaves and flowers but can affect stems. *Botrytis* outbreaks on flowers are particularly disheartening because a crop has been nurtured along patiently only to be destroyed at the last minute. The course of the disease may proceed with amazing speed when conditions are favorable. Growers unfamiliar with visual symptoms may suffer severe crop losses before the problem is diagnosed and remedial action can be taken. The practice of bringing poinsettias into bloom for early sales and then lowering temperatures to retard development and save on fuel has led to more than a few serious losses from *Botrytis*. The increased humidity brought about by lower temperatures provides ideal conditions for *Botrytis* development.

Botrytis is recognized usually by a brownish, water soaked appearance of affected tissue. Flowers, petals in particular, may appear transparent when held to the light. Grey mold eventually covers the rotted areas if high humidity persists. Development of *Botrytis* on red poinsettia bracts appears as sunken tissue which has a purplish-black color. Similar symptoms may appear on red poinsettias if soluble salts are high or if plants suffer from lack of water; in these cases, damage is confined more to the edges and tips of bracts.

Several fungal diseases attack the roots and lower stems of plants. Control of these diseases is primarily a matter of managing the soil environment and of practicing good soil and plant sanitation. Soils which allow good drainage and air circulation will help prevent extensive damage from these organisms. The spread of these diseases is primarily through contaminated soil particles, water droplets, plant tissue, or utensils.

Damping off disease and stem rot are both caused primarily by fungi in the genus *Rhizoctonia*. Damping off causes young seedlings to fall over because stem tissue at the soil line has rotted. Stem rot due to *Rhizoctonia* has a dry, brown appearance while stem rots caused by *Thielaviopsis* are dry and black. Root rot is primarily caused by *Pythium* which also is responsible for blackleg of geraniums. *Fusarium* and *Phytophthora* are other genera of fungi which often cause rots.

Since root and stem rots may be caused by several different organisms, it is generally best to administer soil drenches composed of compatible chemicals which will control all important fungi likely to be involved. The layman would generally lack the background and instruments necessary to definitely identify the fungus responsible for damage. Certain plant varieties may exhibit a sudden severe wilting condition when root or stem rots have progressed to a critical stage. Poinsettias are particularly prone to this phenomenon. Since transmission of damping off and root and stem rots depends heavily on contaminated soil particles and water droplets, it is very important to remove infected plants immediately.

CHEMICAL DISEASE CONTROL

The fungal diseases just described are the more important and widespread but growers should be alert to possible damage from less common diseases. Various other leaf spots, mildews, wilts, rusts, stunts, and cankers can at times become a problem. Broad spectrum chemical control programs aimed at the major offenders will often reduce damage due to the more exotic diseases. Table 21 indicates some of the chemical control measures which can be employed against fungi and bacteria.

Table 21

Chemicals used for control of greenhouse diseases. Refer to Table 20 for toxicity.

Disease	Trade® or common name of chemical used for control	Organism controlled and remarks.
Root and stem rots	Banrot, mixture of ethazol and 3-thioallophanate	(Systemic action) Pythium, Fusarium, Phytophthora, Thielaviopsis, Rhizoctonia
	Lesan (formerly Dexon), fenanainosulf	Pythium and Phytophthora
	Benlate, benomyl	(Systemic action) Rhizoctonia
	Terraclor, PCNB	Rhizoctonia (Apply only once.)
	Truban, ethazol	Pythium and Phytophthora
Powdery mildew	Benlate, benomyl	Systemic action
	Daconil 2787, chlorothalonil	
Botrytis	Benlate, benomyl	Systemic action
	Daconil 2787, chlorothalonil	
Damping off	Banrot, mixture of ethazol and 3-thioallophanate	(Systemic action) Pythium, Fusarium, Phytophthora, Thielaviopsis, Rhizoctonia
	Lesan (fenanainosulf) combined with Terraclor (PCNB)	Apply Terraclor only once
Wilts	Try broad spectrum fungicide such as Banrot. May control some wilt organisms.	Not effective on bacterial or viral wilts.
Miscellaneous leaf and flower spotting	Benlate, benomyl Daconil 2787, chlorothalonil Exotherm Termil, (chlorothalonil	Several organisms may be responsible. Experiment with different applications to observe results.
Bacterial diseases	Agri-Strep, streptomycin	May cause plant damage.

PREVENTIVE CONTROL OF DISEASES

Controlling diseases with post planting chemical treatments will be much more effective if certain steps are taken to limit pathogen populations in the greenhouse environment. A clean, well organized greenhouse without plant debris lying about or weeds growing inside or out is an absolute necessity for the success of any disease control program.

Soil pasteurization and fumigation will provide a clean medium for plants to grow in. Certain soil ingredients such as clean sphagnum moss, perlite, and vermiculite are essentially free of pathogens and need not be pasteurized. Many smaller growers may find that steam pasteurization or chemical fumigation of soils is an uneconomical process for their operation. If one finds that the soil mix being used results in negligible losses due to stem and root rots, one would have little incentive to pasteurize or fumigate. Each grower must balance the losses suffered from disease organisms with the considerable cost of treating soils. Any grower using natural field soils in the greenhouse soil mix should certainly consider treating it.

Steam is the preferred method for treating soils if there is an available source. Many smaller establishments must rely on chemical fumigants since they lack the equipment for steam generation. Soil treated with chemical fumigants must be allowed to air out for approximately two weeks prior to planting. Because fumigants are dangerous to both humans and plants, soil treatment should not take place in the greenhouse. Chloropicrin (tear gas), formaldehyde, methyl bromide, and Vapam (sodium methyl dithiocarbamate) are common chemicals used for soil fumigation. Methyl bromide is perhaps the handiest to use since it has the shortest aeration period and can be used in greenhouses containing plants but it is extremely hazardous to humans. Aeration periods of soil fumigants can vary with soil characteristics, temperature, and moisture content. Lettuce seed sealed in jars with treated soil should germinate equally well as seed sealed with untreated soil if aeration is adequate. Recontamination of clean soil must be avoided. Locate soil storage areas where crop residue will not accumulate and excess water is not present. If possible, soil piles should be covered.

Old pots and containers are major sources of disease. If containers are used again, they must be sterilized. Growers should analyze whether pot recycling is economical; it is questionable if the labor required to sterilize small plastic pots can be justified. Potting tables and greenhouse benches should be periodically sterilized. All tools and containers used in propagation must be sterilized; cleanliness is more important than ever in the propagation process. Common household bleach (5.25% sodium hypochlorite) in a 1-to-10 dilution with water can be used as a sterilant. LF-10 and

Physan 20 (quaternary ammonium compounds) are commercial brands of disinfectants readily available from greenhouse suppliers.

People working in the greenhouse must be alerted to common sense rules of cleanliness which can reduce the incidence of disease considerably. Soil from the floor or outdoors is almost certainly contaminated with disease organisms; it should never be allowed on benches. Hose ends and shoe soles are obvious means of transport for soil to plant benches. Hanging hoses with hooks at the end of benches will keep nozzles off the floor. Whenever plant cleanup work or disbudding and pinching are done all plant tissue should be gathered up rather than left on the floor. Crop residues and unsaleable plants must be removed from the greenhouse immediately after the last good plant is gone. Do not leave reject merchandise lying around in hopes of a sale.

If cuttings or plants are purchased, suppliers should be put on notice that disease ridden shipments will be rejected. One should not feel obligated to pay for plant material which is not clean.

Some mention has been made previously concerning controlling disease by manipulating environmental factors. The basic strategy is to eliminate excessive relative humidity, condensation, and standing water on floors or benches. Most diseases grow and reproduce more quickly in moist situations. Ventilation and adequate night heat with constant air circulation are the chief means of reducing humidity. When greenhouses are being closed for the night, humidity can be reduced by allowing ventilation to continue for a few minutes after the heat comes on. Constant air circulation at night removes high humidity from the microenvironment around leaves and stems. Watering should always be done before afternoon so that greenhouses are dry by evening. Certain disease organisms flourish at particular temperatures; no universal temperature regime is effective against the majority of diseases. Soil pH can sometimes be used to control particular pathogens. *Thielaviopsis* is seldom a problem when soil pH is lower than approximately 4.5 to 5.0. Good soil aeration brought about by soils with large particle sizes and by proper watering practices reduces disease damage.

PLANT DISORDERS FROM POLLUTION

Strictly speaking, any of the environmental factors treated previously in this book could be considered pollutants if their presence were of a degree or nature to cause harm to plants. Topics which the general public would normally consider pollutants will now be discussed briefly. Dramatic plant losses due to pollution are not encountered frequently except in certain problem areas, but almost every grower has experienced at least one crop failure from this cause. Subtle reductions in crop yield are, however, all too common in many urbanized and industrial areas where smoggy conditions limit light intensity at certain times during the year.

Pollution generated by the operation of the greenhouse itself is more frequently the cause of plant damage than is pollution from outside sources. Natural gas leaks, inadequate venting of furnace burners, plant tissue respiration, weed killer residues, soil fumigant vapors, wood preservative and paint fumes, and equipment exhaust are all sources of potentially harmful materials to plants. Oxidation of carbon compounds, whether occurring naturally in the respiration of plant tissue or as combustion of fuels, produces ethylene and carbon monoxide, both of which can damage plants. Plants are sensitive to ethylene at much lower concentrations than they are to carbon monoxide. Ethylene can be produced in sufficient quantities by respiration in plant tissues to cause plant damage. Carbon monoxide liberated by respiration is not sufficient to cause problems. Fuel combustion in furnaces and gasoline motors generates large amounts of ethylene and carbon monoxide. All furnaces should be vented properly and vehicle engines turned off as they enter greenhouse buildings. Ethylene may be detected in the greenhouse by introducing young, vigorous tomato plants to suspected areas. If ethylene is present, it will cause leaves to grow downward as if they were wilted even though the tissue is still turgid.

The dangers of herbicide residues and fumes to plants have been discussed previously. If the greenhouse has a shallow irrigation well, the possibility of water contamination with herbicides from adjacent properties should be considered. Growers must always keep alert to potential crop damaging chemical fumes or combustion by-products. The best policy is to keep all chemicals, paints, and fuels in an area separated from the greenhouse. All natural gas pipes, furnace vent pipes, and heat exchangers should be checked for leaks before the winter season. Tomato plants will also show leaf distortion in the presence of natural gas. The soil fumigants chloropicrin, formaldehyde, and Vapam are all harmful to plants until complete dissipation has occurred.

Air pollution at great distances from the greenhouse can sometimes cause plant injury. Industrial and urban areas produce ozone, PAN (peroxyacetyl nitrate), sulfur dioxide, ethylene, and other less well known pollutants that damage plants. Air need not always appear smoggy to contain enough of these chemical compounds to cause injury. The toxicity levels of some common pollutants are listed in Table 22. Information concerning concentrations of various pollutants may be obtained by contacting local air and water quality agencies. Constructing greenhouses in a different location would be advisable if pollution injury could be expected to occur frequently. The prevailing wind pattern might be studied if greenhouse construction is planned near major urban or industrial sites. Upwind locations would be more desirable.

Table 22

Concentrations at which common pollutants can cause plant injury. Caution must be exercised because numerous plants which have not been tested could suffer damage at lower concentrations.

Pollutant	Concentrations (ppm) at which damage occurs	Plants tested
Ozone	0.2	Petunia
PAN (peroxyacetyl nitrate)	Less than 1.0 physical damage, 0.15 growth slowed 5%.	Petunia
Ethylene	1.0 or less	Most plants
	0.1	Tomato
	0.017	African marigold
Sulfur dioxide	1.0	Most plants
	1.0 and below	Roses, buckwheat, salvia, tomato
Mercury vapor	0.0083	Rose
Hydrogen fluoride	0.05	Gladiolus
Hydrogen sulfide	40-400	Many plants
	40.0 and below	Aster, salvia, cosmos, tomato; very slight damage.
Chlorine	50.0 or less in water, no damage. Chlorine in domestic water is approximately 0.5-1.5.	

CHAPTER 17

HOW TO GROW
PLANTS THAT SELL

Anyone who has read the preceding chapters of this book should be able to produce attractive plants which consumers will be well satisfied with. I feel it will be advantageous, however, if the essential factors which lead to production of beautiful plants are outlined in a concise discussion. Readers may come away with a better overall understanding if the necessary but sometimes confusing details of previous chapters are forgotten for the moment. All greenhouse managers should periodically evaluate production methods to be certain that the product is attaining the necessary standards and that the standards reflect market demand. Growers can sell many more plants if they know what type of plant is wanted and how to produce it reliably.

PLANNING AND FACILITIES

The first step in producing beautiful plants is planning the crop carefully. If a complete knowledge of crop requirements is lacking, the grower should consult reliable references well in advance. Supplies and suitable greenhouse space can be reserved more accurately if the details of crop culture are known adequately. Scheduling has a direct bearing on plant quality. If crops are propagated without regard to greenhouse space, possible markets, labor available, and seasonal weather factors, one cannot expect to achieve success.

Space and labor must be available to transplant crops at the proper time so that plants grow vigorously without check. When seasonal weather will not permit quality growth of particular crops, growers should find suitable substitutes. Trying to grow crops at the wrong time of year is waging an uphill battle. Well grown crops will deteriorate quickly in appearance and quality if markets are not available at harvest time. Every successful grower must have one eye on the market and one eye on the greenhouse if plants are to be harvested at their peak of consumer satisfaction.

Growers can increase the quality and accuracy of their planning and timing by keeping adequate crop records. It is much easier to produce good plants if one has well documented data from previous personal experience. Cultural and scheduling recommendations from books and articles can never anticipate the growing conditions in a particular greenhouse or location. One can also improve buyer satisfaction by being sensitive to the form and keeping quality of varieties and colors within varieties. It is sometimes the case that certain flower colors in the same variety will last much better; concentrating on these long lasting varieties and colors will result in happy customers.

Sales records by variety and colors will aid growers in planning future crops. Consumer color preferences are very important and as much thought should be put into growing the right colors as is expended in selecting crops and varieties. If men are selecting flowers, red is the most popular choice; if women are selecting, pink or salmon may replace red. The various shapes and size of flowers can also be a large factor in customer preference. Novelty shapes such as spider or anemone mums and smaller flowers are popular at the present time. Tropical foliage plants may exhibit subtle variations of color and form within a variety which will greatly affect sales. Highly variegated golden pothos sells much better than the greener leaved types.

Top notch plants that sell quickly cannot be produced in a greenhouse facility which is not suited to the crop. Short, bushy chrysanthemums are impossible to grow in a structure which has low light transmission but tropical foliage would prosper under the same light conditions. If the facilities are not adequate to produce the crop in a reasonable manner, it is better to search for an alternate crop which can be grown to high standards. Greenhouses need not always be fancy to produce good crops but they must be suitable for the task at hand. Labor must be provided in sufficient quantity and quality to care for crops in a timely manner. A crop may be of particularly high quality until a labor bottleneck occurs, but then quality falls rapidly because an essential task is left undone. Growers can increase quality simply by employing workers who display a genuine interest in plants. These people will always produce better merchandise than those who work only for money.

The methods enumerated above for producing appealing plants do not depend on a high degree of technical knowledge but rely mainly on the good sense of greenhouse managers. These non-technical aspects of growing are probably the most neglected ingredients in profitable production.

HEIGHT AND SHAPE CONTROL

Perhaps the physical feature which most often affects the salability of plants is overall height. Conditions of reduced light, high humidity, warm temperatures, plenty of fertilizer, and close spacing which are present in the greenhouse all tend to make plants grow taller. Plants which are too tall display poorly and their stems are top heavy and weak and tend to fall over, imparting a "used" look to the plant. Tall, weak stems make plants harder to handle without damage and increase shipping costs due to the extra height needed for boxes.

The relatively recent introduction of effective chemical height control compounds has greatly increased the ease with which growers can produce a short, compact plant possessing a pleasing shape. Growers should become familiar with the attributes of major growth retardants and the degree of effect they may have on different varieties. Only by having a reasonable appreciation of their action and applications can one use growth retardants in a knowledgeable manner. Chemical height suppressants should be used as supplementary cultural tools rather than as cure alls for excess height. Plant height can be controlled by proper manipulation of environmental factors in most varieties. Growth retardants cannot take the place of intelligent growing practices. When chemical means of height control are absolutely necessary or prove to be the most economical avenue, their use is justified.

Most greenhouse conditions which promote stiffer, shorter stems also produce a tougher, less succulent plant. When environmental factors are modified to limit stem length, one must make sure plants maintain a fresh, robust appearance rather than becoming so toughened as to look overly dwarfed and dried out. A certain amount of toughening or "toning" will prevent damage during the process of shipping and retail selling. Table 23 outlines those conditions which will lead to shorter, more shapely plants if properly manipulated. Readers should refer to previous chapters for more detailed discussions of these environmental factors.

GENERAL PLANT APPEARANCE

The combination of stem length and shape of plants was discussed separately because it is so often a major detriment to sales. There are

Table 23

Cultural conditions which will result in shorter, more compact plants.

A.	Light	Provide adequate spacing and clean, high quality greenhouse covering.
B.	Temperature	Grow at the low end of acceptable crop temperatures.
C.	Ventilation	Provide adequate air exchange whenever temperature or humidity becomes excessive.
D.	Water	Grow at the low end of acceptable crop requirements.
E.	Flower induction	Induce flower initiation before stems elongate excessively.
F.	Fertilizer	Grow at the low end of acceptable nitrogen requirements.
G.	Containers	Use porous walled containers which will maintain average soil moisture at lower levels.
H.	Plant Material	Choose varieties which naturally grow short and are suitable for the particular season of the year.

numerous other attributes which must be properly attended to before a plant exhibits that near perfect healthy appearance which makes it irresistable to consumers. No physical characteristic can be said to be more important than another in contributing to plant sales because any factor which makes a plant unattractive takes away the buyer's incentive. Any negative attribute can nullify all the positive qualities a plant may possess. Growers must realize they are in the business of selling beauty and not that of producing a certain number of units regardless of appeal.

Yellow leaves may be present on plants for a number of reasons. Too much water, too little water, too hot, too cold, too much fertilizer, too little fertilizer—all these extremes will produce yellow leaves. Yellow leaves are a universal symptom of sick or weak plants and the causative agent is often difficult to determine since so many factors can be responsible. Close spacing results in yellow lower leaves due to shading while intense summer sun may cause upper leaves to yellow when chlorophyll is destroyed. Leaves may turn yellow, especially around the edges, when soluble salts are high in the soil or ammonium toxicity is a problem. Attacks by disease organisms or insects will also cause leaves to yellow in certain cases. A few leaves turning yellow on plants is a natural occurrence as each leaf reaches old age; growers should not become over anxious at the first sight of this happening. Only when the number of yellow leaves is significant should one begin to worry about diagnosing the problem. Diagnosis for the cause of yellow leaves must follow a methodical process of elimination with the grower going over each factor which might be responsible for the problem. High soluble salts are quite often the culprit when soils are tight and the grower is unaware of the need for leaching.

A well balanced fertilizer program with adequate iron and micro-nutrients will keep plants dark green and healthy looking. Feeding slightly less than the optimum concentrations will reduce chances of soluble salt damage and keep plants from becoming overly lush. Very succulent tissue is damaged easily during the marketing and shipping process. Using growth retardants may result in leaves which exhibit a deep green color without the excessive succulence associated with heavy nitrogen applications. Nitrogen is the most frequently oversupplied element and leads to lush growth more so than other elements. An over abundance of fertilizer can often result in plants growing larger than planned and becoming crowded, causing yellow leaves at the base from shading. Fertilizer must contain adequate amounts of potassium and especially phosphorus in proportion to nitrogen if flowering is to be profuse. A well designed feeding program can result in significantly more and larger flowers which will in turn increase the sales appeal of plants.

Many plants will develop flowers under a wide range of conditions but much improvement may be noted if growers are knowledgeable concerning the optimum requirements for flower initiation. Once flowers are developed, employees must take care to avoid getting water or dirt in them since this generally leads to an attack of botrytis. Watering should be done from below the foliage level whenever possible, not only for the above reason but also because minerals in the water leave an unsightly white residue in the leaves and flowers of many varieties. As the crop matures and is ready for market, time should be alloted for a cosmetic clean up of plants as they leave the greenhouse. A small percentage of plants will always have a few minor blemishes which would never be noticed if attended to before merchandise reaches the buyer. Proper maintenance before and at harvest will result in crops being sold to the last plant rather than having a 5-10% or even higher dumpage rate. Many growers make it a practice to lower the temperature a few degrees on flower crops a week or two before harvest. This usually results in brighter, more vividly colored flowers. Caution must be exercised since lower temperatures can lead to botrytis and certain warm crops such as gloxinias do not benefit from this practice. White flowers may tend to "pink" at lower temperatures and render them unsuitable for some uses.

PREPARATION OF CROPS FOR GARDEN AND HOME ENVIRONMENTS

It is not uncommon for consumers to purchase apparently healthy plants only to have them develop problems within a week or two. This situation arises partly because of neglect or lack of knowledge on the part of the purchaser and partly because growers failed to condition plants properly for the environment to be found in the garden and home. Movement to a new environment is always a shock to any living organism. This trauma can be reduced by altering the greenhouse environment a week or two in advance of harvest to approximate more closely the situations found in homes and gardens.

The environment found inside the home is normally less humid and bright than that of a greenhouse. Most foliage or green plants used for interior decoration will adapt quite readily if they make it through the first two or three weeks. The principal cause of unsatisfactory initial performance is the inability of plants to function properly under suddenly reduced light levels. This problem is significantly reduced if growers acclimatize foliage to lower light levels at least two weeks before sale. Many growers are unwilling to provide heavy shade before sale because plants grow slower and because of the extra expense involved. One must realize that dissatisfied customers will not purchase plants in the future and the effect will eventually be a lowering of greenhouse production and profits.

Greenhouse plants destined for use in the garden will be subjected to generally drier, windier, and sunnier conditions. Temperature extremes in the garden are likely to be more pronounced. Growers can improve garden performance by adjusting greenhouse conditions at least ten days before harvest. Night temperatures should be turned down, watering and fertilizing reduced, and maximum ventilation afforded. Care must be taken to adjust these factors only to the point of toughening plants somewhat, not subjecting them to a starvation diet and arctic temperatures. Excessively lush, pampered plants do not perform well in the garden but neither do ones weakened from unsuitable conditions. Maximum sunlight compatible with specific varieties should have been provided throughout the growing period but it is even more important directly before harvest so that plants can withstand outdoor sunlight.

HIDDEN FACTORS AFFECT QUALITY

Several factors which affect consumer satisfaction after the sale should be attended to by growers. Extremes of temperature and moisture just before and during harvest often result in poor plant performance.

Excessive exhaust fumes in shipping areas during busy periods may cause delayed damage due to ethylene gas. Plants should be inspected carefully for unnoticed insects and diseases prior to sale. This is a high priority item because customers are almost certain to be lost if they receive an infested plant. No other plant defect irritates people so much.

Excess soluble salts in the soil is perhaps the number one cause of the long term decline of plant health in the home. Growers can alleviate this problem for at least the first several months by making sure that plants are thoroughly leached periodically so they do not enter the consumer's home with soluble salts at a high level. A responsibility many growers fail to fulfill is disseminating information concerning the care of their product. Whether plants are sold wholesale or retail, greenhouse personnel should be trained to offer well prepared advice whenever questions about plant culture are asked. The people who actually grow plants are the ones best qualified to begin a flow of information to consumers.

A SUMMARY

Growing beautiful plants and flowers which will insure loyal repeat business cannot be accomplished by haphazard methods or by personnel who feel their only responsibility is to provide for the day to day needs of plants. Successful growers must realize the need for careful crop planning and marketing efforts. One can no longer be competitive if the needs of the marketplace and consumer satisfaction are not thoroughly integrated into crop plans. If consumers are not pleased with their purchases of plants and flowers, overall demand will fall. Special effort must be exerted toward insuring that when plants leave the greenhouse they are in a physiological state which will maximize their chances of survival in a new environment.

Cultural practices, which are the traditional province of the grower, must be refined and methodically analyzed so that a generally excellent program is not nullified by one or two mistakes or omissions. Growers today must be knowledgeable in many disciplines to compete in the fast changing horticultural field.

CHAPTER 18

ECONOMICS OF GREENHOUSE PRODUCTION

The following discussion will be aimed primarily at presenting methods which will enable the reader to calculate the costs of crop production and determine prices to charge. Certain related topics will be included to show how prices and costs may change with different modes of production. A chapter concerned mainly with sales and marketing will follow and expand more fully on pricing.

PRODUCTION COSTS

The first step in determining costs of production is to gather up all the expenses of the greenhouse and arrange them into logical categories for later reference. If one has not been in the greenhouse business previously, it will be necessary to estimate all costs as accurately as possible. Costs can be estimated with a reasonable degree of precision if care is taken to be thorough in locating all potential outlays and current prices are used in calculating the actual cost of these outlays. Outlays or expenses are normally split into fixed and variable categories. If an economic model is constructed which has compartments for each possible expense, all that needs to be done to arrive at an up to date growing cost is to feed in current prices for each outlay. Table 24 illustrates a hypothetical model for both fixed and variable greenhouse costs. It should be pointed out that no two greenhouses will have the same costs and some managers may wish to interchange certain fixed and variable costs depending on their operation and inclination.

Table 24
Cost analysis categories and totals for greenhouse crops.

Fixed production costs	$ Per Year
Interest and depreciation on entire cost of machinery, vehicles, and buildings	
Cost of renting, leasing, or owning land	
Property tax, if any	
Insurance, property and liability	
Electricity	
Greenhouse fuel	
Vehicle fuel..	
Labor, includes management and sales	
Fertilizer, insecticides, water	
Repair and maintenance	
Bad accounts...	
Telephone, postage, office supplies..................	
Miscellaneous	
Total fixed costs per year	

Total ÷ 52 = Weekly fixed cost for greenhouse range ÷ Square feet bench space in greenhouse range = Weekly fixed production costs per square foot of bench space

Variable production costs	$ Per Unit
Plant material - cuttings, seedlings, seeds	
Containers	
Soil..	
Labor - above normal use for special labor intensive crops	
Growth regulators	
Total variable costs per unit	

Note: Freight should be included in purchase price of all items. Certain fixed costs could be treated as variable costs if the situation warrants.

The use of fixed costs on a square foot basis is common in the greenhouse industry and allows managers to quickly compute the expense involved in production of a merchandise unit (whether it be a single plant or a multiple plant sales unit). One aspect of fixed costs which seldom receives sufficient scrutiny is the expense of financing land, buildings, vehicles, machinery, and operating costs. All investment by the owner should be charged against the crops at prevailing interest rates. Depreciation according to the useful life of the item should also be charged against crops. If interest and depreciation are not included as costs, the owner will receive no compensation for all the money invested in the enterprise. My own estimate is that during periods of high interest rates the interest and depreciation expenses should comprise 15-30% of total fixed cost. The range of costs is dictated by the difference in investment required for a lower quality greenhouse range and one which is built to meet the highest quality standards.

If actual figures are inserted into a crop production analysis, it will show that interest and depreciation and labor are the major fixed costs. If depreciation and interest are ignored or grossly underestimated, crop costs will appear much lower than they actually are. Labor costs should always include a reasonable salary for the owner if he or she actually works in the business. Labor accounts for 35-45% of fixed production costs in the average greenhouse. Fuel is another important component of fixed costs and would approximate 8-12% in a reasonably energy efficient, year round operation. Fuel would account for much less of fixed costs if the greenhouse was operated only in the spring.

Readers should study the categories of fixed and variable costs quite carefully so that they understand the relationship of these costs to their own particular operation. The importance of certain categories will change with the type of buildings, interest rates, local labor costs, etc. Production costs will vary considerably with the location and type of operation. I prefer to designate most expenses as fixed since this simplifies computation of crop costs. Many experts prefer to assign labor, fuel, fertilizers, and insecticides to variable costs since the cost of these items will change considerably with different methods of operation. Larger concerns which specialize in a few crops and sell in a highly competitive market may wish to detail the cost of each crop more carefully and put more costs in the variable category. It has been my experience that the more complicated an analysis system becomes the less likely it is to be used.

Production costs must be calculated to assure that crops are always priced at a level which will insure recovery of production expenses plus a suitable profit. The following formulas enable growers to determine crop profitability at a glance:

Weekly fixed production costs × per sq. ft. of bench space	Number of sq. ft. of benches × occupied per unit	Number of weeks on bench	+	Per Unit variable costs	=	Product cost/unit

Product cost/unit   ×   Number units grown   =   Total expenses

Total expenses − Total revenue (number units sold × selling price)   =   Profit or loss

Persons new to the greenhouse business will need to refer to these formulas quite often until they become familiar with the cost and pricing schedules of each crop. Growers should compare the profitability of different crops and try to emphasize production of those which are highly profitable.

One can see that the number of weeks a crop is on the bench and the number of square feet of bench occupied per unit are extremely important in producing profits. Growers must recognize that some benches are empty at times but fixed costs for this vacant space continue to mount. If three crops are normally realized during the year, each crop would be charged for 17.3 weeks of bench space. Raising crop production to four crops per year would cut bench time per crop to 13 weeks and greatly increase profits. Of course, every crop does not require the same length of time to grow but vacant space must be assigned to each crop in an equitable manner. A year round grower aiming at seasonal markets for Christmas, Easter, and springtime should easily produce three crops per year and can approach four if hanging baskets are grown to utilize space above aisles and if late bedding plant crops are produced for summer. The fixed costs per square foot of bench space per week will vary considerably with the type of operation but would most likely range between 12 cents and 20 cents in mid 1983. My own basis for cost calculation is 17 cents per square foot per week for facilities which are well run but not fancy.

PRICING

There are several avenues to determine selling prices but, realistically, prices are usually arrived at by a combination of methods. If any one pricing approach has more validity than another it would be the return on investment method. When expenses and the owner's monetary investment are computed and prices are set to recover these expenses plus a suitable return on investment, revenues will certainly exceed expenses unless the crop cannot be sold.

Other methods of determining price, such as a percentage of the sales price, markups related to purchase price, competitive pricing, charging what the market will bear, and pulling prices out of the air, do not assure that the selling price will exceed expenses. One can sell a large volume of merchandise with the latter methods of pricing and still be operating at a loss since the prices charged are not directly related to expenses. If interest at prevailing rates is charged as an expense for all money invested in buildings, land, machinery, and operating costs, a return on investment need not be added to the cost of production since the interest recovered acts as a return on investment. This assumes that the owner is satisfied with a return equal to the interest rate; if not, additional markup would be added to selling price. One should make certain that prices reflect a profit at the production level and at the retail level if both operations are combined in the same business. The costs of retail activity must be included in the expenses.

Inexperienced people should always rely on a cost analysis and check the return on investment when setting prices for crops. As one becomes more familiar with the cost of raising different crops and the prices necessary to make a decent profit, one can make adjustments in price without a detailed analysis. When major price moves are necessary every one or two years, costs and returns on all crops should be analyzed. In reality, it is not always possible to establish rigid prices according to the return on investment one expects. It may be necessary to meet competitors' prices in certain instances or to lower prices if customers exhibit a great deal of resistance. On the other hand, it may be possible to obtain higher prices than necessary on selected crops. Growers should be on the lookout for and concentrate efforts on those crops which exhibit strong demand and a high rate of return while reducing those crops which show a low rate of return due to strong competition or consumer resistance.

I believe strongly that greenhouse owners are successful in large part because of their shrewd approach to marketing and pricing and concentrating on those crops which are highly profitable. It is not unethical to receive returns on investment of three or four times that which most people would be satisfied with. If a person has the capability and does the work necessary to identify and take advantage of rewarding situations, he or she should be compensated accordingly. Most greenhouse owners would be happy to receive a 10-15% return on all money invested in the business in addition to drawing a suitable salary if they work in the company. It is possible to increase one's rate of return markedly through careful growing practices, cost control, effective marketing, and wise business management.

Prices charged will generally have a marked effect on the volume of merchandise a business sells. Other factors will affect volume but price is a major consideration in most cases. Greenhouse owners must sometimes alter pricing to achieve a certain level of production. An example would be where cuttings are shipped in and the minimum order is considerably more than could be sold at desired prices. The grower must decide whether to lower prices to the point where minimum shipments can be sold without loss or to omit this crop. A grower may wish to fill an entire greenhouse with a single crop which requires a particular temperature and cultural practices. It is possible that the price may have to be lowered to sell an entire greenhouse full of one variety rather than a mixture, but the savings in ease of culture may also lower growing costs. There are many cases where the price volume dilemma might need to be addressed. Growers must weigh the advantages and disadvantages carefully so that the most profitable overall course is taken.

Many businessmen become overly cost conscious trying to save a few pennies when their time could be better spent in an effort to realize top prices and increased yield. A simple example will demonstrate the tremendous effect a small rise in prices or yield will have on profits:

10% Price Rise

1 plant sold at $5	— $4.50 production cost	=	$0.50 profit
1 plant sold at $5.50	— $4.50 production cost	=	$1 profit or 100% increase in profits

10% Increase in Yield

10 plants sold at $5 = $50	— $45 production cost	=	$ 5 profit
11 plants sold at $5 = $55	— $45 production cost	=	$10 profit or 100% increase in profits

I have always found it much easier to institute price rises or increase yield than to save a like amount on costs. All growers pretty much buy supplies at the same price as long as they are reasonably careful and purchase in larger quantities, but not everyone sells at the same price or obtains the same yield. Yield and sales price are in large degree determined by the capabilities of the greenhouse manager and grower.

RECORD KEEPING

It should be evident by now that profitable management of a greenhouse depends on knowing how different aspects of the business will affect each other. A capable manager must be able to predict the eventual outcome of actions taken. Good records not only document what took place in the past but they also allow one to prepare models which can predict the future with some degree of success. Even in a very small greenhouse business no one can hope to accurately remember all that needs to be recalled.

Growers and managers should analyze carefully what data needs to be recorded and the most useful system of recording it. Collecting unnecessary data and organizing records in a fashion which prevents easy access is a waste of time and often discourages personnel from performing these tasks. People are more likely to collect information and use record systems frequently if they can see a well organized plan behind their actions.

In a small greenhouse there are two relatively distinct areas about which records should be kept. Important aspects of crop culture must be faithfully registered at the time each task is performed. Inexperienced growers usually think they will remember the important aspects of crop culture. It is true they may recall 75% of the information accurately but the other 25% is rather fuzzy. Acceptable crops may be produced without good records but exceptional quality plants which are timed properly for the market and grown in quantities which will eliminate overproduction losses can only be grown by people who have a proper respect for accurately recorded information.

At the very least, crop records should include the propagation or shipping date, number and size of plants grown, ready-for-sale date, number of plants sold and price received, and any cultural procedures specific to the crop. The correct variety name must, of course, accompany each record sheet. Some growers prefer to collect more detailed data concerning weather conditions, labor costs, spacing dates, photographs of crop progress and quality, etc. There is no end to the details one can keep track of—make it brief!

Financial records must be maintained not only for business use but also for satisfying the requirements of local, state, and federal laws. The minimum amount of information required will be determined by the need to comply with these laws. Data needed for filing federal tax returns will generally be sufficient for most business purposes if records are organized so that information on pricing, sales, and profitability of different aspects of the business can be retrieved at will. Financial records should allow a reasonably capable person to appraise past performance and plan future operations intelligently.

Larger companies may need to keep files on other business areas. Labor or personnel matters become more important as a company grows and managers must evaluate the need for beginning a formal employee file. Governmental regulations can become quite complex in this area and one should become familiar with the important laws concerning employees and working conditions. Periodic evaluation of employee performance must also be kept track of as the business grows beyond the stage where managers have close daily contact with the work force. Repair and maintenance records become necessary when the greenhouse manager cannot accurately recall the necessary details to assure proper care of buildings and equipment.

It should be emphasized that records are merely a business tool and must not become an end in themselves. If the owner or manager of a greenhouse firm is not capable of or inclined to keeping business records, it is possible to have a large part of them handled by accounting or bookkeeping specialists. One should realize that this is another expense and these specialists may often not perform their work as conscientiously as people employed directly by the greenhouse. Taxes are an extremely important aspect of running a business, especially when it becomes successful. Tax planning can greatly affect the after tax profits of a business.

THINK AND PLAN FOR INCREASED PROFITS

Greenhouse profits can be increased significantly by operating according to a well thought out plan which emphasizes cultural, marketing, and management practices conducive to high revenues while minimizing expenses. To devise such a plan, managers and growers must carefully analyze each step of greenhouse production and marketing to determine at what efficiency it is executed. After each step has been investigated individually and adjusted to produce maximum profit, one should assess whether the individual steps will integrate successfully. Many of the practices which lead to higher profits have been alluded to previously; the following information will summarize some of the more important ones.

Success in the greenhouse business is made up of many different facets functioning as an integrated whole. The entire operation must be made to run smoothly and undue emphasis cannot be placed on isolated areas. The business must change with the technological, marketing, and financial environment but change for the sake of change must be avoided. Profitable operations are built upon reproducible crop production and marketing from one year to the next. Sticking to established production schedules from year to year saves time in both labor and management and also reduces the risk of crop failure or unsuccessful marketing. Changes in operation should be made only after careful study and, if possible, test projects.

Market conditions will change periodically and influence the relative proportions of crops which should be grown. Growers must identify trends early so that new crops or changes in emphasis may be phased in gradually. Waiting until trends are full blown and then altering production schedules drastically all at one time is an invitation to disaster. Introduction of new plant varieties should follow the same cautious path. Certain new varieties will become the best sellers of the future but 90% of them will be relegated to obscurity after thorough commercial production and marketing tests. The fortunes of a well run greenhouse will not rise or fall on the basis of being the first to offer a new, highly publicized variety but rather on whether that variety has been trialed carefully enough to insure consumer satisfaction and profitability in production.

Optimum utilization of greenhouse space is a major factor in increasing profits. In addition to growing plants at the most profitable spacing during strong marketing seasons, the greenhouse manager must attempt to sell crops at those times of the year when slack market demand leaves greenhouse benches empty. Summer crops of large outdoor planters and hanging baskets and fall crops of garden mums will help insure a steady cash flow. Many northern greenhouses boost production with a crop of foliage plants in the summer. More plants can also be produced per bench by lessening the length of time a crop spends in the greenhouse. Some growers specialize in buying from other growers plants which will mature in a few weeks. In this manner revenues are increased greatly because of the large number of crops which can be raised in a year. The drawbacks to this program are that purchasing larger plants increases expenses and smooth operation of the greenhouse depends on other growers. Foliage plant crop time can normally be significantly reduced by placing more cuttings in the growing container. Selecting early flowering varieties is another way growers can reduce production time.

Mechanizing greenhouse work is one fertile area for reducing costs. Each step in the production sequence should be analyzed to see if mechanization is possible. A cost analysis of manual labor versus machines will then enable the grower to decide which avenue is most profitable. It should be pointed out that mechanization may sometimes be desirable even though it is slightly more expensive than manual labor. If mechanization permits the grower to go through the busy spring season with only a slight increase in the amount of labor hired, it will eliminate much of the confusion and inefficiency inherent when large numbers of seasonal workers are employed.

Some growers are machine lovers and will buy all types of gadgets without subjecting the purchase to a cost and need analysis. Small greenhouses can seldom take advantage of the numerous automated systems which can be profitable for larger ranges. A small grower will generally be better off to limit the purchase of machinery. One advantage of using manual labor is that when business is slow, employees can be laid off rather than having expensive machinery not operating or operating at very low capacity.

Certain aspects of the greenhouse business may be more profitable than others. Managers should evaluate the plant production field and concentrate their efforts on the most profitable crops possible. Hundreds of United States greenhouses have been forced out of cut flower production in the past decade by foreign competition. Those managers who detected this trend early and switched production to potted flowers, bedding plants, and foliage plants have prospered while their less observant counterparts are out of business. Propagating plants for other greenhouses can be very lucrative but generally requires more skilled labor, more initial investment, and a longer time to establish reliable markets. If growers have the patience and resources to specialize in propagation, it may be more profitable in the long run. Each greenhouse manager should periodically analyze the need for changing greenhouse operations to fit newly arisen business conditions.

Unless greenhouse management is constantly on the alert, there are several potential inefficiencies in production and marketing which can lead to serious problems. Labor is usually the largest single expense in growing plants. Greenhouses which have an industrious and capable workforce are in a strong position to be competitive and successful. I believe the most important knowledge one can possess in building a solid core of employees is that money is seldom the prime motivation for workers to be highly productive. Within the framework of traditional fixed pay schedules, additional wages do not, in my opinion, result in significant increases in productivity as long as the salaries paid are reasonably competitive with similar job opportunities in the area. Incentive and profit sharing programs are probably conducive to increased productivity but require additional bookkeeping and administrative work which many managers feel is not worth the effort when applied to lower level employees.

The pay schedule for horticultural employees has traditionally been on the low end. This makes it difficult for greenhouses to pay high wages and still remain competitive in the marketplace. Workers who do not have a genuine love of plants seldom last long in the greenhouse. Managers must emphasize the positive aspects of greenhouse work as much as possible to make up for generally low wages. If hours can be somewhat flexible and the working atmosphere and conditions pleasant, one will have little trouble in attracting intelligent, hardworking housewives to whom money is not the main objective.

Industrious and intelligent workers do not guarantee high productivity. Their activities must be organized by management into a structure which leaves little room for wasteful practices. Managers who are constantly at odds with the majority of employees over a lack of productivity should look to themselves as the primary cause of the problem. Either the proper people are not being hired for the job or work is not sufficiently organized so that workers can give their best effort. Chronic problems may arise with a particular employee and occasional troubles with most others even when management is excellent.

Communicating objectives and instructions to employees is, in my experience, a particularly troublesome area. As a rule, carefully worded written work orders will result in increased productivity and eliminate acrimonious debate about who should have done what or who did what wrong. This type of communication procedure also frees the manager from constant interruptions during the day so that some productive tasks may be undertaken. For many years I have spent several hours each weekend organizing a work schedule for the coming week. This allows me to get through the coming week without major conflicts between trying to supervise employees and meet immediate business needs. All routine activities have been planned in advance and explicitly written down so that workers may always find something to do without interrupting me.

Maintaining an effective workforce is a never ending job. There is always a certain amount of turnover, even among longtime employees. Training replacements and temporary spring help is an ongoing task. If several good workers are employed throughout the year, one can entrust training of new people to them. Periodic sessions should be held with employees in private and as a group to go over greenhouse policy, introduce new material, and discuss any problems which may have arisen since the last session. These encounters should not be held too frequently or the degree of importance employees place on them will decrease. The people working in the greenhouse are the chief determinants of its success or failure. Supervisors should be judged on their ability to organize work efficiently and motivate workers to accomplish objectives. Workers must display a willingness to work and concern for the future of the company. Anyone who cannot display these qualities must be phased out if the greenhouse is to be successful.

Many greenhouses are operated in an inefficient manner because crops are not tailored to fit the market. The result is a high percentage of unsold plants. Successful greenhouses should dump no more than five percent of their crops. When dumpage rates exceed this level, there is definitely a problem in the planning stages. The problem of unsold plants may be solved by constantly growing too few to meet market demand. This practice reduces revenue considerably and encourages customers to find their merchandise elsewhere. The objective is to satisfy market needs and have as few plants as possible left over.

Once plants are sold one must insure that payment is received. The profits from several sales can be erased by one bad account. Many experts advise that strict collection policies be enforced without fail. This type of policy can lead to the loss of some very good customers who simply do not pay attention to due dates on bills. The best insurance against bad debts is to know your customers well. If one does not have personal contact with customers, a strict collection policy is best. Overdue accounts constitute an additional expense to the greenhouse. This money could be used to finance operations or be put in an interest bearing account. If past due accounts are not charged interest, the cost of carrying these accounts must be reflected in the price of plants.

Periodic reviews of greenhouse costs will enable managers to notice changes in the price of supplies, labor, services, and fuel before there is any serious impact on profits. Cost reviews will also uncover excessive or wasteful use of materials in the greenhouse. Although each individual expense category may affect profits slightly, total greenhouse expenses are a major factor in this regard. Buying supplies at the right price is the first step in controlling costs but even more important is the need to prevent wasteful use in the greenhouse.

Each individual business has optimum sizes at which it is most profitable relative to the capital invested. A small backyard greenhouse may be extremely profitable as long as it can be operated by the owner and overhead expenses are shared with the owner's residence. When overhead is not shared and the owner does not operate the greenhouse, the business must be large enough to make full use of such things as the telephone, soil mixer, etc. The manager's time must also be fully utilized. If profits relative to investment only are considered, the optimum greenhouse sizes are probably small ones where cost sharing and owner management are feasible and medium sized ones where cost sharing may not be feasible but where the owner is able to handle general management responsibilities and still have close personal contact with greenhouse operation. Whenever expansion is considered, one should analyze whether or not this action will contribute to making the greenhouse more of an optimum economic unit.

Many greenhouse owners become obsessed with meeting the price of competitors. It should be understood that plant prices are relative entities and must vary with the quality and services offered. One cannot hope to compete with prices in the flower and garden departments of supermarkets and chain stores. Persons who are knowledgeable about plants should market not only a product but their expertise as well. There are numerous businesses and consumers willing to pay extra for the services and convenience offered as part of the price.

Success in the greenhouse business is achieved through a combination of ingredients. Hard work, perseverance, vision, and luck all play their part but one cannot hope to rely on these qualities alone. A thorough knowledge of the economic principles inherent to the business is also necessary.

CHAPTER 19
SELLING PLANTS
AND FLOWERS

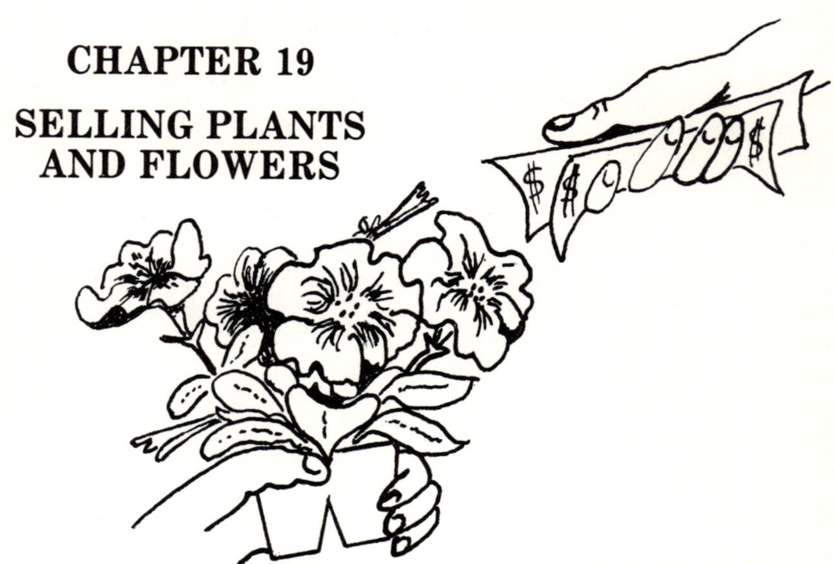

Brief references to selling plants and flowers have already been made in several previous chapters. There is now a need to bring these points together, to expand on them, and to present additional topics which pertain to sales and marketing.

No one who wishes to grow plants and flowers as a business should proceed without a well thought out plan for selling the product. The great majority of potted flowers, bedding plants, and tropical foliage is sold directly by the grower to either retail outlets or the end consumer. These channels of distribution require that the grower become intimately familiar with sales techniques and theory. Direct sales to retail shops or consumers may seem to be an inconvenience to those growers who prefer to concentrate their skills on plant culture, but it is also a blessing in that it gives them a good measure of control over the promotion and pricing of their products. Many cut flower producers sell at auctions or to middle man distributors and consequently have little to say about how flowers are marketed or what price they will receive. They are in a passive market posture, much like the rest of American agriculture.

FUNDAMENTAL MARKETING DECISIONS

Each grower must make some basic decisions about the nature of his or her business before much progress can be made in the direction of developing a coherent sales program. Is the greenhouse to be wholesale or retail or a combination of both? Will the greenhouse emphasize services and convenience to customers as well as plants and flowers or will it be mainly production oriented with customers fending for themselves in the selection and care of plants? The choices made here will affect many aspects of the business.

People who are primarily interested in the technical aspects of plant culture and who have little desire to spend much of their time devising sales programs would most likely be happier as wholesalers. This is not to say that marketing skills are not important to the wholesale trade but sales are confined to one level rather than two and, generally, fewer sales contacts must be made. A person who enjoys contact with consumers and has skills as a salesperson would very likely enjoy managing a retail greenhouse. A mix of the two marketing channels might prove more satisfying to some people.

Whether one would prefer a wholesale or a retail business may have little bearing on what is possible. Wholesale greenhouses usually require more initial capital to begin and considerable risk may be present in raising the first crops in the hope that a few large accounts can be landed. Many more plants and flowers need to be raised in the wholesale business because the markup over expenses is lower than in retail sales; thus operating expenses and investment in buildings and machinery are great. The competitive situation in a locality may dictate whether a wholesale of retail greenhouse should be set up. A mixture of the two levels of sales is very difficult to combine since other retailers are reluctant to depend on their supplies from a competitor. To a certain extent, wholesale and retail businesses have different objectives and doing a good job at one level of sales may preclude successful operation in the other.

Businesses in the United States have tended to diverge into two different categories over the past several decades: those who offer full customer service with their products and those who provide little or no services with merchandise. The owner or manager of a full service outlet is likely to be a professional in the particular product line sold while those businesses offering little service may be operated by persons whose main interest is merchandising.

The horticultural industry has reflected these national trends. At the retail level today approximately fifty percent of greenhouse products are sold in a self service atmosphere. Thirty years ago very few plants and flowers were offered outside the traditional full service store. The result of these marketing trends has been generally lower prices to the consumer but in many cases a serious drop in quality and customer satisfaction. The problem of quality in self service stores is not caused by the sales strategy but rather through most managers' insistence on emphasizing low price rather than quality at a reasonable price. The chain and grocery store personnel handling flowers and plants often have no training at all in buying, marketing, or caring for the product. This situation may be improving.

There are opportunities for flower and plant sales in every level of service and product combination but the operator must be aware that choosing one or the other will affect many phases of the business. The battle between traditional stores and self service outlets has perhaps reached a stalemate where neither is losing or gaining a great deal of market share. I believe the great opportunities in retail horticulture for the next decade will belong to those people who devise sales methods which emphasize top quality and reasonable prices along with competent services when they are asked for. Customers will have the privacy of self service shopping but knowledgeable professionals will be available for those who desire further information or service.

The perishable nature of plants and flowers and the complexities of their proper care and use will always require trained people to handle and sell them if cutomers are to be satisfied. Low price may entice consumers to purchase greenhouse products for the first time but only satisfactory performance of plants and flowers will make them return.

To a lesser degree, people who enter the wholesale greenhouse business must make a choice to concentrate on product or services. Delivery to stores, decoration and pricing, care tags, and display upkeep are some of the services a wholesaler may offer to prospective customers. Other greenhouses may sell strictly plants and flowers for pickup at the greenhouse. Obviously a manager of the first mentioned business would have more diverse problems to deal with.

I have made no attempt to exhaust the ramifications a choice between retail or wholesale and full service or self service may have on the operation of the greenhouse business. I hope that the reader will be stimulated to reflect carefully on his or her psychological makeup before attempting to make any such decision. A common sense evaluation of the possible combinations of marketing strategy will enable potential managers to predict the varied effect such a choice will have on other aspects of the business. One must also base these fundamental marketing decisions on factual observation of the particular market needs in the chosen locality, or choose the desired marketing strategy and discover a locality suitable for implementing it.

IMPORTANT SALES CONCEPTS

A mystery often encountered is why stores with seemingly similar locations, products, and visible presentation of goods can be so dissimilar in the success achieved. I believe salesmanship is comprised of four basic concepts, each of which is essential to the success of a business.

I. A viable product line must be present. The customer must perceive it as being useful (not necessarily utilitarian) and the sales force must "believe" in the product so that enthusiastic promotion to the customer is possible.

II. The consumer's attention must be drawn to the products and service through conventional advertising or other means.

III. Once attention has been drawn to the product, the customers must be convinced it will fulfill a need. Upon purchase, the product or service must indeed satisfy that need, the cost must not exceed the urgency of the need.

IV. A competent sales force must be on hand to transfer goods and services to the customer in as economical and satisfying way as possible.

Readers should take note that the major thrust of these concepts is "people" oriented—customers must be convinced, employees must promote and transfer merchandise, the customer's attention must be drawn, the customer must be satisfied. Adequate sales cannot be assumed simply because good merchandise at a fair price is placed before consumers. Managers must realize that the product is only one of several ingredients in a successful sales effort.

PLANNING FOR MAXIMUM SALES

Owners and managers of greenhouses should evaluate themselves critically to determine if they possess the qualities necessary to formulate and lead a sales program. It often happens that good growers are not especially competent in the sales field. If this is the case, someone else should be placed in charge of sales. In smaller establishments, it may not be feasible to have separate sales personnel and it will be necessary for the manager or grower to become as proficient as possible in this field through careful study.

Some people organize and carry out good sales programs without ever knowing how they did it. Even when sales of a company are adequate or better, an effort should be made to identify the reasons behind the success. This is necessary so that key ingredients in a winning combination are not changed unknowingly and so that the formula becomes formalized for use by future personnel. The essential points of a good sales program should be recorded in the same manner a grower keeps records of plant culture in the greenhouse. Understanding exactly why a business is successful in its sales efforts will help in predicting how new and different lines of merchandise will be accepted.

The appearance of a business is an extremely important factor in promoting sales. Well maintained facilities and displays give customers the impression of success and people prefer to shop at stores they think are doing well. An attractive business setting need not be expensive but it must be neat, clean, and well organized. Sales of flowers and plants are generally much greater in a greenhouse atmosphere than in the "four walls and a roof" type building used for most retail stores. Greenhouse construction is almost always less expensive than that for traditional buildings and presents the product in a most appealing fashion. Spring garden sales are especially enhanced by the greenhouse effect.

Landscaping is of major importance to any business handling plants and flowers but it becomes exceptionally critical when outdoor plants are sold. One cannot expect customers to have confidence in the plants being sold for gardens if landscaping on the business grounds is not well maintained. All dead or sick plants must be removed from the landscape immediately. In addition to instilling confidence in customers' minds, a pleasing landscape for the business creates demand for the product through suggestion. If a garden store has certain varieties planted on the grounds, a perceptible increase in sales will be noted for those plants. A good landscaping job is probably one of the least expensive methods of enhancing the image of a business.

The sales force is the primary contact a business has with the public and employees should be selected and trained to reflect the image a business wishes to establish. The care and use of flowers and plants is sometimes complex and there are many different varieties. Much of the information needed by consumers concerning their purchase can be communicated by means of signs and tags, but selling plants and flowers will always require a high degree of personal contact to insure customer satisfaction. Signs may be adequate for many people but others shop at a particular business because it offers courteous, personal service.

All salespersons need not be experts in plant culture as long as they have been trained to answer the most common questions and to consult reference books when they do not know the answer. One person should always be available in person or by telephone to deal with complex or uncommon inquiries. Ladies who have done a good deal of gardening or make a hobby of houseplants are often ideal for plant sales since they will need little training on the technical aspects. Some of the best advertising a plant and flower store can do is to have knowledgeable sales people. Customers like to shop for plants where competent help is available and they let their friends know about it.

Salespersons should also be trained in basic sales techniques such as how to tie in one sale with another and how to spot a customer who needs help. The most basic qualification for being an excellent salesperson is a genuine enjoyment of being with and helping customers. The good will is immediately apparent to the customer and makes it much easier to make a sale. Managers should select sales personnel mainly for their personality and natural inclination and secondarily for technical knowledge.

The topic of "guarantees" for flower and plant material elicits a varied and vocal response among owners and managers. In my experience, in most cases a guarantee is not justified because the customer has abused the merchandise. Many plant stores will not guarantee their plants for this reason. If this problem is viewed from the standpoint of good business practices, rather than who is responsible for the damage, I feel it is best to be very liberal with guarantees and satisfy the customer except in extreme cases of flagrant abuse.

Most people are fair minded and when a knowledgeable sales person politely explains how the merchandise was damaged, the customer is more likely than not happy without a refund if it is apparent the damage was not the result of poor merchandise. Those people who still feel the store is obligated to some extent will generally be satisfied with a smaller plant or a one-half refund. Full refunds or exchanges should be given when the customer demands it or if it is likely the plants or flowers were at fault. Always attempt to replace the merchandise rather than refund with money and make certain the customer now knows how to care for the product.

A guarantee which is honored grudgingly is as bad as no guarantee. Cheerful refunds and exchanges make a customer loyal and will result in good word of mouth comments about the store. The total cost for guarantees is generally not a major expense and will easily pay for itself in advertising the good will of the company. If refunds and exchanges become too common, the quality of plants and flowers should be evaluated and sales people should check to make certain proper care instructions are being given to the customers. I believe people are more particular about where they buy plants and flowers than they are about where they buy catsup or dish soap. A liberal guarantee policy assures customers of one's integrity and will insure a certain amount of loyalty on their part. Repeat business is the backbone of any sales program and customers will not return if they feel they have been unfairly treated.

Wholesalers need not be as liberal in their guarantee policy. Complaints can normally be handled on a case by case basis because of the limited number of clients. Most retailers are reasonably knowledgeable about the plants and flowers they handle and do not expect any type of guarantee. If the merchandise did not meet their specifications, they should not have accepted it. Growers should not honor complaints unless they are made on arrival of the merchandise or if a problem which appears later can reasonably be attributed to the growing operation.

The degree of emphasis which must be placed on actively promoting sales may differ with general economic conditions and upon the stage of growth the business is in at a particular time. Some people entered the plant and flower business in the early 1970's and had never known the need to really promote sales because a definite boom was taking place in foliage plants, bedding plants, and potted flowers. The severe recession of the early 1980's jolted many owners into the realization that the easy ride was over. Potted flower and foliage sales dropped off and it became necessary to fight for every sale possible rather than waiting for the customers to beat a path to the door. Some people never realized the need for a different sales approach and were not heard from again.

A business just starting out must obviously advertise heavily and devise other means of obtaining sales. After a stable clientele has been established, the chief emphasis may pass from sales to internal organization or refining purchasing and pricing policies to increase profitability. The emphasis placed on each major aspect of the business will change from time to time depending on the manager's evaluation of what is most important at a certain stage. When market demand for plants and flowers becomes reasonably satisfied, it may be necessary for businesses to again stress sales promotion if they wish to expand beyond their present size. The same situation may arise not because of internal expansion but because a competitor expands or a new one arrives on the scene.

There are circumstances where maximum sales promotion and expansion are not valid business goals and money spent on them is wasted. If a business has reached the limit of sales or production which can be carried on in its physical facilities, it would be better to concentrate on means of increasing profit until the decision is made to expand those facilities. Other situations which might weigh against pursuing increased sales are a lack of qualified personnel, the desire to spend more time on personal or other business interests, and a lack of capital to finance business expansion. It should be pointed out that a constant and long term policy of downplaying expansion is likely to lead to the irreversible decline of a business. The old axiom in business is that if you are not going forward you are going backward.

Prices charged will always have an important effect on sales programs. A discussion of pricing was presented in the preceding chapter concerning greenhouse economics. Only a few additional comments which pertain especially to retail sales will be added here. A popular retail markup for plants and potted flowers is to double the purchase price, including freight and packing. This markup should enable most stores to return a profit and assumes that a fair amount of sales personnel are available to customers. Somewhat lower markups would be in order if emphasis was placed on doing a large volume business in a self service setting. Markups of three to four times the purchase price are valid if plants and flowers are artistically arranged or other comparable services rendered. Each manager will have to evaluate the services offered and determine what prices are suitable for the individual business.

A return on investment analysis must be performed at least annually to make certain a true and adequate profit is being generated by whatever pricing formula is used. On the wholesale level one may choose to set all prices through a return on investment analysis but in retail sales the larger number of items handled and the need to adjust prices for clearance and promotional sales will require a simpler method.

A topic which bears some discussion is that of the sales unit price. It has become popular in recent years to talk of reducing the size or number of plants offered as a sales unit so the price would appear to be more competitive. Actual prices of plants and flowers are increased but consumers are offered a smaller and smaller package so that the price per sales unit remains relatively low. The primary causes of this phenomenon are a steady march of inflation and the entry of low priced outlets as a major marketing force. The advantages of such a strategy are quite obvious; the customer is duped into believing the true price is remaining stable and that prices are just as low as those of the competition down the street.

There are some not so obvious disadvantages to shrinking the sales unit. Customers shop not only because they expect to spend an allotted amount of money or because they need a certain number of plants but also because of the size of sales units offered to them. If only a large sized sales unit is offered, many people will purchase it even though they would not have purchased two sales units half that size. A switch to smaller and less costly sales units should be made only when it is deemed likely that sales lost due to people not picking up the larger unit are more than compensated for by the increased incentive to purchase because prices appear to be lower.

An example from my own experience may serve to illustrate the problems one may encounter. I was selling nine petunia plants in a pack for 99 cents each and needed a price increase to maintain profits. In order to keep the purchase price under $1, I followed the conventional wisdom of the day and grew six petunias per pack and sold them for 89 cents. This represented a hefty price increase. I grew the same total number of plants after the price increase but sales were only 85% of the previous year's total number. This happened at a time when sales were normally increasing 10-20% a year. It is quite obvious that either people were buying a good deal by the pack rather than because they wanted a certain number of plants or that they were not fooled by disguising the price rise. Both reasons probably contributed to the drop in total number of plants sold.

In the example, 150,000 petunia plants were being sold at 99 cents per pack of nine plants. Total revenues for the crop were $16,500. If the number of plants sold remained the same, a switch to six plants per pack at 89 cents would have yielded revenues of $22,250. The actual revenue realized after the price rise was only $18,912.50 since 15% of the crop went unsold. The increase in revenue was less than half of that planned for. If one assumes that the trend of increasing sales would have continued at 10% or better, the move to six plants per pack at 89 cents looks even less appealing. As long as there is no extreme urgency to reduce the size of sales units, I favor keeping them as large as the market will accept.

Decreasing sales unit sizes may also have the effect of making the product less useful for the intended purpose. Flowers in the 6 inch pot size have become the general industry standard partially because they represent a convenient size for decorating and they appear big enough for a gift one does not have to be ashamed of giving. Smaller flower sizes may be marketable if decorating needs change or if smaller gifts are appropriate, but sellers should be certain that size changes will provide the desired results. Decreasing the size of outdoor hanging baskets and porch planters may allow the prices and profits to remain steady in the face of inflationary pressures, but a decrease in the container volume will make it harder to keep plants watered during summer weather. If the size were decreased several times, the usability of these baskets and planters would be seriously impaired. When one feels there is a demand for smaller sales units or more inexpensive prices, it may be prudent to add the smaller line and retain the original.

The marketing year for greenhouses and plant stores exhibits several peaks and valleys of sales activity. A great majority of sales are concentrated in the period between Thanksgiving and the end of spring planting season. Devising sales programs which create demand during the summer and fall slack periods should be a prime objective of management. Most overhead expenses continue unabated at these times and any extra income adds greatly to the profit picture. Sales of larger garden plants and container gardens in the summer and of hardy perennials, especially colorful garden mums, offer opportunities for additional income. Greenhouse managers may find that a crop of tropical foliage raised during summer months will find a ready market in fall before poinsettias must be moved to final spacing. The addition of one extra crop can make a marginally successful operation into a super successful operation.

Table 25 recaps some of the important points about selling which have been mentioned throughout this book. Once a sales program has been decided upon, it should be given adequate time to prove its worth. Deviations from the plan should be for good cause and not because of short term market gyrations.

Table 25
Summary of important aspects in the
marketing of plants and flowers.

A.	Quality will always sell. Even if inexpensive items are sold, make sure the quality is there.
B.	Stand behind your merchandise. Repeat sales are the backbone of a sales program.
C.	Business structures and grounds must be clean and well landscaped.
D.	Service commensurate with price should be offered.
E.	Cultural information is a necessity for the eventual satisfaction of customers.
F.	Provide adequate merchandise for maximum sales but avoid waste.
G.	A wide variety of plants and flowers attracts more customers than a limited selection.
H.	Proper surroundings must be provided to display merchandise at its best.
I.	Eliminate insect pests and sick plants; either one of these will completely ruin a display.
J.	Let people know you are in business. Advertise conventionally and by other means.
K.	Be ready for sales peaks. A high proportion of yearly sales in plants and flowers is done in a relatively short time.
L.	Extend the sales season as long as possible.
M.	Budget for daily care of plants and flowers and of displays.

The preceding discussion of sales has been primarily aimed at the retail level. Wholesale marketing is of course somewhat different in emphasis but the general principles are similar. A wholesaler's primary sales tool is usually the telephone. Weekly calls to retailers in the slower times and more frequent contact during rush periods will increase sales considerably. Make sure the retailer has been happy with plants and flowers ordered. Many times, a small misunderstanding can be cleared up before it becomes a serious problem. Growers must resist the temptation to send out the last few rejects of a crop; this can quickly lead to the loss of a customer. When the grower has only a few retail stores to deal with, it is extremely important to understand the personality of owners and managers if maximum sales are to be achieved. The grower must care about the retailers' businesses because if they don't sell merchandise, orders to the greenhouse will drop. If suggestions are made to retailers about how to improve business, it must be done very tactfully since they will resent anyone trying to tell them how to run their business.

CHAPTER 20
BUSINESS MANAGEMENT

Creative, hard working people start their own businesses to achieve goals such as financial success, possession of power, or independence from others. These individuals are the entrepreneurs, the innovators of the business world. Quite often these entrepreneurs lack the aptitude for efficient management which is necessary to carry a project any distance beyond the starting line. Entrepreneurs may also have little time to be concerned with management. The origin and operation of a business involves three general areas of activity: the idea, systems to accomplish the idea (management), and labor or work to carry out the objectives of management.

Entrepreneurs must force themselves to find time for management or allow someone else to fulfill this aspect of business. It is seldom that the founder of a plant or flower business would have the resources to hire full time managers nor would the founder normally be comfortable with other people taking over the idea and ushering it to completion. Most people starting a plant or flower business enjoy playing an active role in management if adequate time is set aside to prevent an overly stressful situation from arising. A good understanding of what management involves and the methods of practicing it will make the duties more efficiently accomplished and enjoyable.

Some form of management is practiced in every business whether the operator knows it or not. If sufficient time is not devoted to management, and an organized knowledge of it is lacking, it is likely that management will be poor and the business will not be overly successful. A well conceived management program does not just happen. It takes many hours of careful thought to delineate objectives and efficient means of reaching these objectives. Many more hours will be spent in making sure all the different goals are integrated into a workable master plan.

It is difficult to define just where management duties begin or end. There will always be some overlap with the province of the entrepreneur and also with labor. Equally difficult is the task of stating hard and fast rules as to what constitutes a good management plan. Managers are paid well because of their individualistic approach toward devising a method of organizing and controlling a company successfully. If the process of devising a management plan for the thousands of unique business situations possible could be codified and set in stone, ordinary workers could look up the formula and apply it as well as anyone. Each business has a unique environment and requires an individualized management program. Only a person who has special capabilities, either as an innate gift or through training and experience, can organize an excellent management program.

Since management requires an individual approach, it is not surprising that several well planned programs for the same business may differ in some respects. The question of right or wrong is answered by the smooth operation and success of the business.

I prefer to look upon management as falling into two broad categories: strategic management which may only be practiced at crucial turning points in the life of a business, and tactical management which includes the more concrete problems of organizing systems to accomplish stated objectives. The following discussions will point out what I feel are the main components of a management plan. Examples of strategic and tactical management decisions will be presented under each topic to familiarize the reader with the concepts. It must be remembered that each individual component must integrate with others when a management program is complete.

BUSINESS OBJECTIVES

Businesses are started by people for different reasons or combinations of reasons. For many the chief objective is financial success but a significant number of people begin in business mainly for a sense of personal satisfaction. Possession of power or recognition may also be important motivations. Most often the founder has several objectives in mind for the new business to satisfy. Business objectives should be enumerated and arranged in the order of importance they will assume in the new business. Objectives must not be in opposition to one another.

Formalizing business objectives involves the practice of strategic management. These goals should be altered only when the needs of company principles undergo fundamental changes. Decisions of this nature may be made only once in the lifetime of a business or they may be made several times over a period of many years.

Tactical management in the area of business objectives is concerned chiefly with the methods and organization used to accomplish the goals. If a person's main goal is financial gain, flower and plant crops and markets would be scrutinized to determine the most profitable combination with little regard for the personal satisfaction derived from working with them. A primary goal of recognition within the community may dictate that tactical management decisions to donate plant material for community beautification be made without concern for possible ill effects on company profits.

Tactical management decisions made to accomplish the major goals of a business must not be allowed to endanger the actual survival of the enterprise. Emphasis on goals other than profitability are valid as long as the business continues to remain in healthy financial shape. The enterprise must maintain at least minimal economic solvency or other goals will have little hope of being realized.

PRODUCTION OBJECTIVES

An example of a strategic crop production objective could be the decision to provide wholesale potted flowers and foliage plants for all retail flower shops in a prescribed area. An alternate decision might be to supply all plant and flower material for a single retail outlet which is a joint venture with the greenhouse. In another example, one greenhouse firm may specialize in a single crop for regional or national distribution while others are committed to a wide variety of crops for local use.

Tactical production management will be altered considerably by the objectives in mind. Greenhouses and machinery installed for a large wholesale operation may not be the most economical choices for a small retail greenhouse. Management of pest control programs can be considerably complicated by the presence of retail customers or by location in a heavily populated area suitable for retail sales. Changing the objectives of crop production will necessitate adjustments in a much larger number of lower level management programs in order to maintain efficient production.

LABOR OBJECTIVES

Instituting a goal of minimizing greenhouse labor by capital investment in machinery would be considered high level management. Tactical management to realize this goal might include organizing a production schedule of crops which lend themselves to mechanization. If maintaining a skilled year round work force is an objective, a system of maintaining reasonably constant sales and production schedules is necessary to keep workers busy.

Much can be accomplished toward profitable operation of greenhouses and retail stores if one manages labor in an organized and intelligent manner rather than simply hiring anyone who comes along. People are the ones who produce and sell plants and little can be accomplished without efficient use of their efforts. Labor is perhaps the most difficult area of management since one is dealing with people who have a variety of rather unpredictable emotions and needs. Understanding people is more difficult than organizing production schedules or devising a financial records system.

MARKETING AND PRICING OBJECTIVES

The inter-relatedness of objectives is demonstrated by the obvious effects different production goals would exert on marketing and pricing objectives. One could seldom have an objective of maximum possible production and also realize a goal of maximum price per unit sold. Businesses often develop a strategy of marketing to particular segments of the population based on such attributes as economic class, sex, and age. The theory is that one cannot be all things to all people. Management decisions made as a consequence of such a strategy must organize marketing efforts to appeal to the group selected.

Marketing strategies, once conceived, may be very difficult to change since the perception the public has of a business is influenced in great part by marketing efforts and vice versa. When an image is sufficiently implanted in the public mind, it may be impossible to successfully change the marketing strategy unless it agrees with this image. Changes in production, labor and investment strategies can normally be made reasonably easily if one is willing to exert the effort and incur additional expenses sometimes associated with radical change. A change in the nebulous area of public perception is, however, sometimes elusive no matter how much effort and money is spent.

FINANCIAL OBJECTIVES

The idea of financial objectives seldom concerns inexperienced business persons. Most people entering business for the first time would think the goal of making a profit is enough. This is perhaps a valid approach when the business is young and not making much money. After a reasonable degree of success has been attained and the business is generating good profits, financial objectives generally need to be more sophisticated. When funds are accumulated in excess of what it takes to operate the present business, a decision must be made as to how this extra money will be utilized. It could be reinvested for expansion of the business, invested in other business interests, used for personal enjoyment, or set aside for children or charitable purposes. The choices must be carefully weighed to prevent expensive mistakes which arise through improper money management.

Financial objectives will usually change as a person matures. More emphasis may need to be placed on providing for retirement through conservative investments and less money allocated for business expansion if a sale of the operation is expected when the owner retires. Older owners may wish to set aside much of the business profits as gifts for children and grandchildren. The continued existence of the business after the owner's retirement or death must be carefully planned to avoid costly tax consequences and disruptions in management.

Tactical financial management must be tuned to the main objectives. Taxes, for example, will vary greatly with the uses business income is allotted to. Money reinvested in the business is generally taxed differently than dividends or salaries distributed to the owner or shareholders. Careful watch must be kept on the everyday financial workings of the company to make sure there will be adequate resources available to accomplish the selected goals.

INTEGRATION OF MANAGEMENT DECISIONS

In the previous discussion of management objectives, only a few examples were presented to acquaint readers with the general types of problems which may be encountered. It should be apparent that a great number of management decisions will be made in even a small plant and flower business. An essential feature of management duties is the integration of separate objectives and decisions into a compatible whole. All parts of a management plan must function harmoniously together. Much effort and expense can be saved by designing a management program before commencing operations.

PART II
INTRODUCTION

Cultural notes for specific crops will be presented in the following chapters. The information will be drawn mainly from personal experience and, as such, will represent a distillation of the author's own cultural programs. Certain varieties will be left out entirely in the interests of brevity to enable the author to expand more fully on major crops. In some cases, such as azaleas and poinsettias, the details of propagation will be minimized or eliminated since these plants are generally purchased from specialist propagators.

It will be assumed the reader has thoroughly studied Part I of this book so that a detailed explanation of terms and environmental relationships is unnecessary when discussing each crop. Information pertains specifically to culture in the peat-sand growing mix and with the calcium nitrate and potassium nitrate fertilizers detailed earlier. Growers using different soil mixes and fertilizers should reflect upon the possible effect these changes may have on crops. Schedules represent what can be expected at a northern latitude of approximately 43° with high winter light conditions. Temperatures recommended are for night time unless otherwise stated. Growers are cautioned not to rely blindly on published schedules.

Recommendations of specific varieties will not be given for a crop unless it seems justified. New and better varieties are introduced at such a fast pace that much of this information would be quickly out of date. Details on size of containers to grow in and how many plants to use per pot will be given only when it is deemed necessary. Different markets will require different container and plant sizes.

CHAPTER 1

BEDDING PLANTS

No segment of the floral industry has shown such sustained market strength in the past decade as have plants used for outdoor gardening. Growers generally have difficulty producing enough plants to meet demand during the spring gardening season. Profitability of each crop must be carefully analyzed since space will be limited and should be allocated to those crops which provide the greatest return on investment. Every effort must be made in the spring to increase the number of crops produced when market demand is high. Prices charged during this strong seasonal market may be somewhat over the amount needed for a good return. Such a practice will make up for periods when market demand is slack and lower prices are the norm.

Bedding plant culture must reflect the fact that plants are to be used outside. Crops grown with too much heat, fertilizer, and water are likely to suffer severe damage on store shelves and in the garden. Careful selection of varieties, especially vegetables, which will prosper under local conditions is important for continued good sales in future years. Business during the spring can become very hectic and growing containers must be chosen to protect plants from abuse and excessive drying out. Small plants must be offered in sales units to minimize damage caused by customers handling them. Growing several crops of each variety at weekly intervals will provide fresh plants throughout the season and increase sales appeal.

Success in the spring season often hinges upon the ability of staff and management to react quickly to changing market and growing conditions and to get critical work done on schedule. A few busy days in the spring may represent a large part of yearly revenue and every effort must be made to move merchandise at these times. Not only must harvesting crews work at top speed but new crops must be planted to fill the benches as quickly as possible. Profits can be greatly improved by those growers who are able to prolong the selling season with fresh plants.

The past several years have seen the introduction of two new concepts in bedding plant culture. Flats are now often seeded directly with automatic seeders. These seeders have been available for some time but only recently have they been improved to the point where acceptance is widespread. Specialists have begun to offer a wide variety of half grown "plug plants" which can result in additional crops for the spring producer. These plugs also cut down the labor needed to transplant from seedling flats. Each of these new production methods should be evaluated for its applicability to particular operations. Most bedding plants are raised in flats containing individual packs as a sales unit. Each pack has a number of containers fused together. Unless otherwise mentioned it can be assumed that plants are normally grown in these. There is much controversy as to whether bedding plants should be sold in bloom or green. Growers will profit more if plants can be sold green but maximum sales volume is seldom reached unless plants are in color. The controversy will be solved by each individual grower assessing what the most profitable course is for the particular market conditions present. Garden performance is generally increased when plants are set out in an actively growing stage before blooming. My experience, however, is that consumers will choose a blooming plant ten to one over non-blooming ones.

Schedules mentioned assume that plants will be in bloom unless they are varieties traditionally sold green. Some plants would become too tall if allowed to bloom in the packs or they may not bloom until midsummer or fall. Propagation is by seed unless otherwise noted. The preferred fertilizer for all bedding plants is 6 ounces of potassium nitrate per 100 gallons of water unless an exception is mentioned.

Ageratum

Customers in need of short border plants will appreciate ageratum. Newer varieties seldom reach a height of more than 8 inches. The powder blue colors available are an asset not frequently found in other flowers. White varieties are less popular. Ageratum presents a very neat appearance in packs because of its short stature but several crops must be grown to avoid their having dead flowers, which do not drop off easily.

After transplanting, temperatures should be maintained at 60° F until plants are well established to avoid root and stem rot. Temperatures can then be dropped to 50° F to harden or delay crops. Full sun is preferred but some shade will not harm the appearance of the plants. Special care to avoid overwatering must be practiced when plants are young because of the rot problems mentioned.

Packs sown March 1 will bloom near Mother's Day at an average temperature of 55° F.

Alyssum

Alyssum is the most widely used border plant. Height seldom exceeds 6 inches and blooms are very fragrant. Well grown packs of alyssum are attractive but can become overgrown quickly in hot weather.

Alyssum performs best if a cool 50° F is maintained after one week of establishment at 60° F. Pink and purple varieties especially need an initial warm period to start because they grow somewhat more slowly than white. Full sun is a must to bring on profuse blooms. Over application of water, nitrogen or heat will result in grassy plants with fewer blooms. Diseases and pests are seldom a problem after establishment but damping off occurs quite readily in the seedling stage.

Flats become saleable quickly if clumps of seedlings are transplanted to each container. Easy germination and inexpensive seed make alyssum a prime candidate for direct sowing of multiple seeds. Seedlings left in the heat of germination chambers are quickly ruined. Alyssum is a very profitable crop due to the short bench time and low priced seed. White varieties are much more vigorous with purple making the slowest growth.

Sow April 1 for Mother's Day plants. Pink and purple varieties will require progressively longer growing periods.

Alyssum (Perennial)

Masses of brilliant yellow color in early spring make perennial alyssum a show stopper. Plantings around the retail store will stimulate good demand for green plants in packs. Large pots sown in the fall and carried in unheated cold frames will bloom profusely for instant sales. Heavy sales will last only as long as the blooming period since few customers are familiar with these plants.

Culture is much the same as for annual alyssum but cooler temperatures will be tolerated. Sow February 15 for Mother's Day sales as green plants grown at 50° F.

Asparagus

Asparagus sprengeri is useful for outdoor plantings mainly as a green, feathery foliage mixed with flowering plants in porch planters and hanging baskets. The varieties meyeri and plumosous are cultivated as foliage plants and arrangement greens along with sprengeri.

Growth is slow below 60° F. Plants can be grown in full sun but will remain very compact and may yellow during midsummer. Light shade in summer and 65° F temperatures will produce plants suitable for combination pots and arrangement work. Lower temperatures are better when compact foliage specimens are desired. Excessive drying will yellow plants permanently but excess water for short periods is seldom harmful when plants are well established. Aphids love the succulent new tips and must be watched for very carefully. Fertilizer of 6 ounces calcium nitrate and 3 ounces of potassium nitrate per 100 gallons of water is recommended.

Seed sown in late summer will yield heavy 3 inch plants by May 1. Seeds lose viability quickly and should not be stored for long periods.

Asters

Gardeners looking for an exceptionally nice color range in cut flowers or tall background plantings will enjoy asters. Dwarf and perennial varieties are available in addition to the popular long stemmed plants. Few cut flowers will last as long in the home.

Asters may be grown straight through at 50° or 55° F and should receive full sunlight. Excessive water may bring about outbreaks of stem rot on young plants but when foliage covers the pack, copious amounts of water will be used on bright days. Asters are quite profitable because of their rapid growth to saleable size in the green stage. Customers should be warned to move aster beds at least every two years to prevent outbreaks of stem rot resulting from contaminated soil.

Seed sown April 1 will produce heavy packs of green plants Mother's Day. Summer potted flowers can be obtained using dwarf strains sown in the late spring. Stem rot in these pots is a difficult problem unless soil is sterilized.

Balsam

Balsam is one of the undiscovered plants useful for shady areas. It is in the impatiens family and can be treated in a similar manner. Rose-like double flowers in soft pastel shades are produced in mid May from a March 15 sowing. Excessive fertilizer will result in tender growth with few flowers and eventually to soluble salt damage. A very well drained soil mix such as that recommended earlier for rooting cuttings will help prevent salt buildup. Seed is large and germinates easily; in contrast, there are sometimes problems associated with impatiens seed germination.

Begonia

Everflowering or waxed leaved begonias have achieved outstanding acceptance as garden plants in the past few years. Extensive breeding has resulted in a wide range of varieties to please the consumer. These plants will perform well in sun or shade if they are not exposed to excessive sunlight without being conditioned to it. Growers shifting plants from moist, shaded houses to full sun must choose a period of cloudy weather to avoid severe damage to succulent leaves. Fibrous rooted or wax begonias make an excellent show in pots or packs. Small, inexpensive blooming pots are very popular for gifts and table decorations on Mother's Day at church and nursing home celebrations. Three or 4 inch pots are also useful in combination work for planters and baskets.

Begonia seeds are very fine and take extra care for proper germination. The seed bed should be pressed firm and seeds left uncovered. Water is applied as a fine spray to avoid puddling and consequent aggregation of seeds. High moisture levels must be maintained since the seed is lying exposed on the surface. Germination is poor in the dark. Growing temperatures should be no lower than 60° F until plants are well established, at which time they can be lowered to 50°-55° F if necessary. Growth is slow at these lower temperatures but flower color is enhanced. If plants become overgrown, they can be sheared back and will return to flower in three or four weeks. Dwarf strains are by far the most popular and are essential in pack production. Packs with larger compartments should be used when growing begonias if they are to be sold in flower.

January 1 sowings grown at 60° F will make heavy 3½ inch pots for Mother's Day. Packs require approximately three weeks less time. Good demand also exists for large specimen plants in the spring. A monthly sowing schedule will provide growers with nice 4 to 6 inch material through the winter when there is a need for inexpensive window plants.

Recent introduction of the Nonstop tuberous rooted begonia varieties has led to inexpensive production of large flowered tuberous rooted plants. The flowers are impressive both in form and and color. Four inch pots and hanging baskets sell well through the spring and summer for use in shady outdoor locations. Six inch pots make an excellent seasonal potted flower for indoor use from May through September.

Mid December sowings will yield good 4 inch plants on Mother's Day. Hanging baskets and 6 inch pots should be started four or five weeks earlier. A 62°-65° F temperature is necessary through mid winter but established plants may be carried at 55° F in March and April. Four hours of additional light is needed until March 15 to ensure early blooming and to encourage branching. Young plants must be transplanted to the rooting soil mix formula for mid winter growing in small pots but the final shift to larger containers can be made in the growing soil mix. Growers should consider planting 6 inch pots and hanging baskets with several smaller plants to produce heavy flowering in very short order. Single plants in large containers can tend to be somewhat skimpy if basal branches have not been heavily produced.

Carnation

Carnations may be offered in annual and perennial varieties. Annual strains will survive mild winters but northern gardeners prefer the fully hardy perennial Grenadin cultivar. Both annuals and perennials will bloom from seed the first year but flowering is much heavier in the annuals. Carnations are widely known because of their popularity as cut flowers and can be sold green in the packs. They remain compact and neat on display if grown at 50° F or less. A full range of colors is available and cut flowers will last a considerable length of time in the home. Carnations make ideal perennial backgrounds and are one of the few perennials to remain in bloom through the summer.

Plants grown warmer than 50° F or with excessive fertilizer become grassy easily and will fall over. Full sun helps maintain sturdy stems. Aphids love carnations and will be sure to attack the crop unless preventive measures are taken.

Green plants of perennial strains will be ready in packs May 1 from a February 1 sowing. A Christmas sowing of the annual Knight varieties will produce blooming 4 inch pots for mid May. Cyclocel can be applied to prevent excessive height in blooming plants but will restrict growth after transplanting to the garden. The Knight series also produces very nice 6 inch flowering pots if high potassium, low nitrogen fertilizer is applied and if light levels are high. Customers are particularly drawn to the spicy fragrance of these flowers. Seed is sown at Christmas for 6 inch Mother's Day pots with six plants per pot—no pinch. May 1 sowings will bloom in mid August.

Chrysanthemum

Perennial chrysanthemums can be sold in quantity from early spring through the fall. Spring and fall crops are especially easy to grow while summer crops will require artificial manipulation of the daylength to bloom. Chrysanthemums provide late summer and fall color in the garden when other flowers have spent themselves or succumbed to frost. Light frosts only serve to intensify color in chrysanthemums. Many varieties are available in a complete range of height, flower color and shape, and bloom dates. Growers in areas where severe frosts come early should offer seven or eight week cushion varieties that bloom in August and September. Chrysanthemums are classified by the number of weeks needed for plants to flower from the onset of short days. Chrysanthemums have become the premier floricultural species because of their unequaled lasting quality and vigor of growth. Mass displays of chrysanthemums in bloom are a sure sale.

Manipulating daylength for flowering garden chrysanthemums in summer becomes quite detailed and no precise schedule will be presented here. Readers may refer to manuals published by Yoder Brothers and Pan American Plant Company for excellent timetables. Daylength control at this time of year means a short period of long days to encourage vegetative growth and establishment and then a long period of short days provided by shading to induce flowering. Unless a definite market exists for a good volume of summer plants, it is usually best to omit crops at that time and concentrate on no light-no shade crops for spring and fall when the great majority of sales are made.

Mums require a temperature of 62° F to set buds evenly. After buds set, temperatures may be dropped to 55°-60° F for growing on and even to the freezing point for conditioning or storage when flowers are opening. Garden varieties will generally form suitable buds at 55° F but better crops are obtained with a 62° F initial temperature. Full sun is essential to avoid tall, skimpy plants. Two applications of B-9 growth retardant at 0.25% are necessary to control height. When plants become established they will use large amounts of water on sunny days. No disbudding is practiced on garden mums.

Mums are prone to aphid attacks and if the pests are not eradicated before flower buds open, it may be almost impossible to control them. On 6 inch pots a level 1/8 teaspoon of Temik when plants are established and a repeat treatment six weeks before sale usually controls aphids very well. Leafminers, which can sometimes be a problem, are controlled at the same time. Most varieties are somewhat susceptible to leaf burn from Temik and overdoses can be avoided by watering plants heavily after application and placing granules away from the base of the stem.

Spring garden mums are usually planted one cutting per 3 or 4 inch pot, pinched one week later and grown under a no light-no shade schedule. Seven week varieties will flower at the end of April while eight week plants bloom the first part of May. No light-no shade programs are not reliable after a planting date of approximately March 10 although some growers plant two weeks later with good results on selected varieties. If cuttings are already showing buds, the pinch should be very hard so vegetative growth is forced from the base. Three and 4 inch pots will become crowded and weak if soft tip pinches are given which allow too many breaks to appear. The first B-9 application should be made when new breaks are ½ - ¾ inches long.

The cuttings which result from pinching can be stuck and rooted easily if they have not set bud and if they are large enough. Patented varieties cannot be propagated in this manner without a license agreement. Cuttings rooted from the original plants will bloom well in 2¼ inch pots with no pinch.

Spring mums are usually grown in flats with no spacing so control of height with B-9 applications is essential. Fertilization with potassium nitrate as recommended for other bedding plants will also check lush growth. After buds have appeared, crops can be split into two or three temperature regimes so that a succession of bloom dates occurs. Choosing an assortment of varieties and including some six week, seven week, and eight week varieties will also insure that the crop does not bloom all at one time. Customers should be warned that spring is not the normal blooming time for mums. Inexperienced gardeners may become upset if plants do not flower the next spring.

Fall mums are grown on a one or two pinch schedule for heavy 6 or 7 inch pots and as a no pinch fast crop in 5 and 6 inch pots. Pinched crops are planted in May and June and allowance must be made for about three weeks between pinches for new growth to elongate. No pinch should be made after July 10. Published schedules recommend planting the no pinch fast crop about July 23. I experience better production with a July 5 plant date. Fast crops bloom a few days later than pinched plants. Unless exceptional quality is desired, the fast crop is more economical since less time is spent caring for the crop and an inexpensive plant may be offered to gardeners. A B-9 application is made when breaks are ½ to ¾ inches long after the final pinch or about ten days after no pinch cuttings are planted. A second application should follow in 10 to 15 days. Plenty of space is usually available in the fall for wide spacing so that the calcium nitrate-potassium nitrate fertilizer should be used to promote maximum growth.

In areas where hard frosts come early, growers must choose varieties with the earliest natural flowering date. Certain varieties are more reliable in no light-no shade spring schedules and some varieties produce a better plant under fall fast crop conditions. Propagators will supply this information on request for their current offerings. Growers must evaluate performance under their particular conditions since propagators' recommendations do not always work out under all circumstances. Cuttings are normally ordered from specialists since it is uneconomical for most greenhouses to maintain stock plants of the many varieties needed.

Coleus

Bright colored foliage and a tolerance of shade and warm temperatures make coleus a favorite for garden and indoor use. There are numerous colors, sizes, and leaf shapes available. The market for coleus includes packs, pots, hanging baskets, and planters. Plants grown for the garden are usually from seed while hanging baskets and indoor pots are often propagated from cuttings as well as seed. Spring packs remain neat and saleable for extended periods if compact varieties are used and temperatures are lowered to 60° F. Hanging baskets sell very well even through the winter months. Several asparagus sprengeri plants at the edges of coleus baskets make a particularly nice combination.

Vigorous growth of coleus takes place only above 60° F but plants may be lowered to 55° F in order to keep crops from becoming overgrown. Although coleus is classified as a shade plant, the nicest greenhouse crops are obtained with light shade only in summer. Plants grown under shade and high temperatures (65° F) from October through March will be excessively tall and colors will appear faded. Coleus wilts quickly when water is deficient and a slight wilt between waterings will discourage stem rot and excessive succulence. The appearance of flowers from early fall through late winter is somewhat of a nuisance and can be overcome to a certain degree by careful selection of those varieties which have the weakest and shortest flowering response. Soft pinches of terminal shoots at three to four week intervals will eliminate the remaining flowers. Combination baskets with asparagus sprengeri should receive the calcium nitrate-potassium nitrate fertilizer formula to encourage sufficient growth of the sprengeri.

With year-round schedules it is best to take the majority of cuttings before and after heavy flowering occurs because both cutting production and rooting will be slow at this time. Five hours of additional light starting four weeks before flowers normally appear will keep stock plants in a vegetative stage if cuttings must be taken during winter. Seedlings can be treated in a similar manner to prevent flowering. Cuttings root very easily and many growers stick them directly to the finishing pot.

Mid March sowings will be ready for sale in packs by mid May at 60° F. Four inch pots are saleable in six weeks in summer and nine weeks in winter when four cuttings are stuck directly to the pot and pinched once when established. Ten inch baskets take approximately six weeks longer with eight cuttings per basket and two pinches. Varieties for hanging baskets should be selected so that growth is spreading and compact rather than straight up. A good supply of 4 inch pots in the taller varieties is valuable for centerpieces in spring shade planters having begonias and impatiens around the edges.

Dahlia

Dwarf dahlias are the main concern of bedding plant growers, the taller, giant flowered varieties being generally unsuitable for pack and small pot production. Bedding varieties range from 10 to 24 inches in height and display a wide assortment of colors with either single or double flowers. Three or 4 inch pots of dahlias can be used for inexpensive Mother's Day gifts or for use in planters. If packs are to be sold in bloom, a maximum of 48 cells per 11½ inch x 21 inch flat should be grown to avoid spindly plants.

Dahlias prefer warm temperatures of 60° F to start out but excellent plants will result from temperatures as low as 45° F for finishing, Full sun is required to prevent stretching and promote flowering. Aphids are particularly fond of dahlias.

A mid February sowing will produce flowering plants in mid May. Dahlias germinate and grow very fast and extra late season crops can be turned by selling them green in 72 cell flats approximately four weeks after sowing at 60° F. Flowering seems to be inhibited somewhat either by the days' becoming shorter after the summer solstice or by high summer temperatures.

Daisy, Shasta

This old favorite perennial can be offered in economical packs as green plants or in larger pots in flower. Traditional varieties are 24 to 36 inches tall but dwarf varieties no taller than 15 inches are more appealing when flowered in pots and are increasing in popularity. White flowers with double or single forms, depending on the variety, are produced from July through the summer and are widely used as cut flowers because of their long lasting qualities.

Shasta daisies are best if grown at 55° F or less. Higher temperatures promote luxuriant soft growth which is undesirable. Plants started the previous fall and sold in larger pots when in flower require exposure to light frost during winter months to bloom profusely. Light shade will not harm green plants but results in a grassier growth. Plants must receive full sun for proper flower production. Aphids can become a problem if adequate preventive measures are not taken.

February 15 sowings will produce good green plants for late April at 50° F. Seed sown September 1 will make heavy 6 inch blooming plants the following summer if subjected to cold during winter. These flowering specimens will increase sales during a normally slow period and a goodly number can be sold because of the widespread popularity of daisies.

Dianthus

Dianthus is made up of a large number of useful garden flowers. Carnations, treated previously, are a member of this genus as are annual dianthus, annual sweet william, and their perennial counterparts. Varieties are quite variable as to height, ranging between 6 and 18 inches. Colors heavily favor the pink and red shades (hence the common name "pinks") mixed with white.

Gardening emphasis in the past has been upon the perennial forms of dianthus and gardeners still associate the name with them. Improved strains of annual dianthus have been introduced recently and are rapidly displacing the perennial forms in popularity because of the increased color they produce. My own experience is that many annual dianthus will survive harsh winters for several years and customers accept them as the equal of a perennial. Packs or 4 inch pots of the newer annual varieties are brilliantly colored when in bloom and draw immediate customer attention.

Dianthus grow best when 50° F or lower temperatures are maintained. Higher temperatures or excessive fertilizer promote lush growth with weak stems and few flowers. Full sun is essential to keep plants compact and promote branching.

A March 1 sowing will produce packs of blooming plants in mid May with annual dianthus. Perennial sweet william can be started at the same time but will remain green. All dianthus can become overgrown quite easily and temperatures and watering frequency should be lowered if crops are not moving out quickly enough.

Fushia

Well grown fushia pots or hanging baskets always draw more than their share of attention. People are taken by the unfamiliar bell shaped flowers and rich colors. When they discover fushias will do well in shade, a solid repeat business will develop from year to year. Six inch pots of the more compact varieties are sometimes produced as spring and summer flowering plants but acceptance as an indoor decorative has been limited because flowers drop off quickly. Both trailing and upright varieties are used in hanging baskets.

Fushias are normally propagated from tip cuttings. Extremely succulent or overly mature tissue should be avoided. Cuttings must be kept moist and turgid until they are stuck and placed in a shady location. Propagation during hot dry weather is often difficult unless mist is used. The cuttings root rapidly with bottom heat of 75° F.

Fushias prefer cool temperatures of about 55° F but where compactness is not a critical factor (hanging baskets) 60°-62° F will produce acceptable plants in a shorter time. Full sun should be given to pots at all times of the year except mid summer to prevent weak stems. One cutting is usually placed in 3 or 4 inch pots and pinched when established. Six inch pots will require at least two pinches and 10 inch baskets will need two or three pinches if five cuttings are used.

Stock plants of fushias must be meticulously inspected for the presence of spider mites and especially white flies. Either one of these pests can render an entire crop worthless in short order. Plants will remain pest free during the spring season if no eggs or adults were present on stock plants.

Cuttings taken in mid January will yield good 4 inch pots in early and mid May with one pinch. Baskets for early April sales can be propagated around Thanksgiving. Plants should receive the last pinch approximately eight weeks before sale in early spring and six weeks before sale at later dates.

Geranium

Geraniums are one of the most important crops in floriculture today and their popularity increases yearly. Many greenhouses rely on them as the number one spring crop. Well grown geraniums can generate a great deal of traffic in plant stores since it is often difficult for customers to locate high quality plants. The widespread use of geraniums has come about because of their free flowering habit and ability to tolerate adverse conditions. In addition to being excellent performers outdoors, geraniums are present in the window sills of millions of homes, schoolrooms, and businesses. They are truly the all American plant.

Geraniums are sold in all sizes up to large planters and hanging baskets. The standard size for outdoor use is the 4 inch pot. Recent introduction of improved seed propagated varieties has led to sales in packs. Growers have perhaps neglected important sales which can be made in the 6 or 7 inch pot price range. Well branched plants of this size with several large flowers are valuable merchandise for retail flower shops in the spring and particularly Mother's Day and Memorial Day for garden centers. A large stock of geraniums is necessary over and above individual sales to fill the need for them in planter and basket combination work.

The recent renaissance in geranium production is the result of improved varieties from plant breeding programs, disease free stock plants and cuttings produced by specialist propagators, and improved cultural programs made possible by the two previous advancements. Thirty years ago the typical 4 inch geranium might have been started in November and been sold at Memorial Day. Today it is possible to begin with disease free rooted cuttings and market a well done plant in six weeks. The development of acceptable seedling varieties has led to more widespread use of geraniums in the garden. Consumers could seldom afford to make mass plantings with 4 inch pots but this practice is now feasible with seed geraniums in packs.

Vegetatively propagated geranium varieties are numerous and there is considerable variation in their resistance to diseases, habit, flowering performance, rate of growth, and adaptability to garden conditions. It is necessary for growers to select carefully varieties suitable for the particular production and market conditions prevailing. Certain varieties have flowers which shatter or fall apart easily; these are especially unsuitable for shipping long distances. Customers seem to prefer plants whose leaves are marked with distinct reddish green zones. The following varieties have performed very well and will be suitable for neophyte growers until they gain the experience to select ones perhaps more suitable for their conditions. A suggested crop percentage is listed after each color.

Sincerity	Reddish orange flowers, good zonation in leaves, compact and well branched, grows quickly. An exceptional variety which combines all the good traits a grower needs. Some customers may prefer a true red but if only one red is to be grown, Sincerity should be it. 55%
Didden's Improved Picardy	Salmon-pink flowers, good zonation in leaves, compact and well branched, grows more slowly than Sincerity, flower color superb. 20%
Cherry Blossom	True pink with whitish undertones, some zonation in leaves but not especially pronounced, compact and well branched, slow growing. This is not an exceptional variety but neither does it possess objectionable traits. 10%
Snomass	Pure white, no leaf zonation, tends toward legginess and weak flower stems, fast

	growing and easy to root. Not exceptional but it is the best white. 5%
Springfield Violet	Neon-purple, no leaf zonation, becomes leggy and sparse, fast growing, easy to root. Not a grower's dream but it does offer an unusual color. Do not grow this variety unless demand exists for the color. 10%

Each of these varieties has also been selected for good garden performance and resistance to flower shatter and botrytis.

The many new seed varieties introduced each year make it difficult to offer recommendations since the information may be out of date quickly. Some varieties are especially suited to pack production while others will do better in pots. Consult seed catalogs for up to date varietal selection.

Much production has been shifted to seedling varieties, especially in larger, more mechanized operations. Seed geraniums lend themselves to automated production more so than do cutting varieties. This economy in production has made seed geraniums popular at chain stores and super-markets. There are some indications that seed geraniums will, in general, out perform vegetatively propagated plants in the garden. My own customers prefer cutting geraniums by a five to one margin mainly because flowers are larger, more double, and resistant to shatter. This preference is manifested even though a premium price is charged for cutting varieties. Growers must evaluate their own market conditions to determine what proportions of the two types to grow. Low price-low service outlets will likely move a large proportion of seed geraniums while full service garden centers may sell mostly plants from cuttings since they cannot compete with prices at low service stores. Development of seed varieties with double flowers and shatter resistance will certainly increase their popularity.

If stock plants are saved from year to year, a rigorous selection of only the best plants should be practiced rather than starting next year's crop from leftovers. Plants left at the end of the season are often late bloomers or have hidden diseases which delayed their development. Selection of stock plants like this year after year can lead to a large percentage of slow growing, late flowering plants in a crop. Many growers nowadays purchase disease free stock plants from specialists each year to assure good crop performance. These plants are grown in larger pots through late summer and fall, with tip cuttings being taken periodically to shape the original plant and to accumulate additional stock. Depending on market dates, cuttings for 4 inch material are usually taken January through March for the spring season.

Either stem or tip cuttings may be used. Stem cuttings will require an additional two weeks to bloom. A large crop of stem cuttings may be taken on the last cut when stock plants are cut completely up or trimmed severely to stimulate new growth. If stock plants are to be sold and have been in the same pot for an extended period, they should be removed from it after trimming the tops and planted in new soil. Roots may be cut back at this time and watering must be reduced greatly until new growth is evident. This method of treating stock plants ensures that new growth will be vigorous and plants will produce large flowers rather than being hardened, woody plants with few and undersized blooms.

Geranium cuttings must be handled with care to prevent contamination by diseases. Clean knives and containers must always be used. Any plant which appears odd or malformed should be culled immediately. When cuttings are taken, stock plants should be cleaned of all old leaves to prevent conditions conducive to disease growth. Cuttings are stuck in the root mix with enough space to assure air movement; crowded cuttings will inevitably lead to mold. Geraniums root with less loss to disease if the medium is kept a little on the dry side, with just enough moisture to allow rooting. Different varieties must be rooted in separate trays since rooting time may vary considerably between them. Rooting hormones may be used to increase rooting speed and uniformity but are not necessary.

Cuttings planted to the final containers when roots are less than a half inch long will suffer fewer broken roots and lessen the chance for entry of diseases into wounds. If the soil was moist at planting, irrigation should be done sparingly until plants are established. Overwatering is the nemesis of young geraniums. Temperatures of 62°-65° F will help newly potted cuttings off to a fast start after which 55°-60° F will suffice for growing on. The growing on temperature may vary with the needs of the grower. Closely spaced plants will be more compact at the lower temperatures while plants that are given adequate space will be saleable even at temperatures of 65° F. At times it will be necessary to grow at 65° F to meet a particular time schedule for markets.

My own geranium program consists of growing on in 4½ inch square pots without spacing at temperatures of 55° F. Only potassium nitrate fertilizer is used and irrigation is heavy but infrequent after establishment. When about a third of the crop is sold, plants are then spaced evenly in the vacant areas. No pinching is done except on a few extra skimpy plants. Sales per square foot are maximized because no spacing is used until the last two or three weeks of crop time. Square pots are easy to handle in flats and hold more soil than round ones so that watering frequency is reduced. With this method the number of pots handled at spacing time is reduced by one third.

About ten days crop time can be saved by spacing plants to begin with and growing at 62°-65° F. The increased space used is balanced off by the reduced production time but fuel consumption is higher and more plants are handled at spacing time. The choice of programs should be determined by market objectives and timetables. Some growers prefer very heavy plants for exclusive markets. Spacing plants more widely and giving them a pinch will accomplish this objective but flowering will be delayed two to three weeks by a soft pinch and four to six weeks by a hard pinch. This method of growing increases the selling price greatly.

My preference is to market heavily branched plants in 6 inch pots rather than in 4½ inch pots. The increased soil volume makes caring for the plants easier and customers feel the same size plant in a 6 inch pot is worth quite a bit more. Six inch pots are also a more acceptable size for florist shops and as gift items. Cutting and repotting of 6 inch stock plants should be done eight weeks before intended sales. Plants which have not been severely trimmed or repotted may return to flower in three or four weeks.

In areas where sunlight is intense, geraniums will benefit from full sun in all but the brightest summer months. Reduced light results in stretched plants with large thin leaves and in reduced flowering. A no space program cannot be utilized if light is limited.

Pests seldom become a great problem with geraniums unless control programs are poorly handled. Insects and mites will usually show up on other species long before they become numerous enough to attack geraniums, Fungal diseases must be constantly guarded against to prevent excessive losses. Blackleg or stem rot is the main disease contributing to losses. Blackleg is recognized by black, rotted areas appearing on the stem, usually at the soil line but lesions higher up the stem are not uncommon. Roots may also be affected but are less often diagnosed. Pythium and fusarium fungi are usually the agents of this disease. Botrytis on leaves and flowers is also common when proper control of humidity in the greenhouse is not exercised.

Virus diseases of geraniums such as crook-neck, crinkled leaves, and mottled leaves are not controlled by any chemical means. Plants showing evidence of viral diseases must be culled immediately. Using culture indexed stock plants and practicing careful sanitation will eliminate serious losses due to diseases. Fungicides will need to be used only as a preventive measure on young plants. A condition known as oedema sometimes occurs on geraniums under conditions of high soil moisture and excessive humidity. Cork-like eruptions occur on the undersides of leaves and sometimes on the petioles. Less frequent but heavier waterings and good ventilation help in controlling this physiological aberration. Certain varieties also seem to be more prone to damage.

Similar temperatures and light conditions are applicable to seed geraniums. Diseases are usually of much less concern since a carryover from generation to generation is not likely. Seed geraniums must be given a Cyclocel spray or drench at 3,000 ppm when plants are about the size of a fifty cent piece. This produces a well branched, compact plant. Some leaves may discolor to yellow after treatment but plants will soon grow out of this condition. Seed geraniums should be timed carefully to prevent flower shatter from becoming a problem. It is best if plants can be sold before flowers are more than a fourth open. There has been some success in preventing flower shatter with applications of silver nitrate but procedures are not well enough established to recommend. Seed geraniums are seldom raised in pots larger than 4 inches.

Representative examples of schedules for 4½ inch flowering geraniums will be given for a temperature of 55°-60° F. It is assumed that stock plants have been renewed each year with disease free, culture indexed cuttings. Cuttings taken February 1 will be flowering for Mother's Day if no pinch is given. Add two to three weeks if plants are soft pinched and four to six weeks if hard pinched. Pinched plants must be spaced. Memorial Day no pinch plants may be cut March 1. If good 2¼ inch plants are purchased from propagators and a pinch is not given, an April 1 planting will easily be ready for Memorial Day. A 10° F rise in temperature will save 10 to 14 days crop time on 4½ inch unpinched plants. Cuttings started at Christmas and given two hard pinches will be heavy blooming 6 inch plants for Mother's Day.

Seed geranium varieties vary as to flowering dates but Smash Hit will be ready in late May from a February 10 sowing at 55°-60° F. Packs of 32 or 48 cells or 4 inch pots may be used. Green plants in packs will be ready three to four weeks earlier.

Gerbera

Gerbera as a bedding plant is a recent introduction. Cultural directions are included only because it seems the plant is destined to become a fairly large crop. Customers are attracted to the soft pastel colors exhibited by handsome daisy-like flowers. Sales are mostly in 4 inch pots. Gerberas have long been a minor cut flower crop but until plant breeders introduced the dwarf variety Happipot, growth was too vigorous and tall to bloom in small pots. Four inch pots of Happipot will have flower stems of 8 to 15 inches and the leaves are reasonably small. Serious gardeners will appreciate having these beautiful plants offered to them. Cut flowers last very well in the home.

Plants will flower in late May when sown January 1 at temperatures of 60° F. Full sun is necessary to keep the leaves small and reduce flower stem length. Plants may be grown without spacing in 4 or 4½ inch pots during late spring. Aphids should be monitored since they love the flower buds. If whiteflies are present in the greenhouse, gerberas will be susceptible to attack but plants will be clean to start since the are grown from seed.

Hanging Baskets

Cultural recommendations for the major hanging basket plants are discussed under the varietal headings. The purposes in a separate treatment of the topic are to present an overall view of the place hanging baskets should have in bedding plant operations and to suggest some additional varieties for use. Hanging baskets have become increasingly popular with consumers and show no sign of market weakness. They offer a significant opportunity for local greenhouses to increase sales since long distance shipping is especially impractical for larger specimen plants. A well done display of heavily blooming hanging baskets will generate impulse sales and set a plant store apart from competitors.

It is important to have a large number of hanging baskets ready for Mother's Day, but the majority will be sold at other times during the spring and early summer, especially after gardeners have completed their main plantings. Baskets must be shaped and allowed enough growing time to develop into heavy floriferous specimens. Skimpy plants with few blooms simply will not move. Having an adequate supply of baskets striking enough to sell well but not overbloomed takes careful scheduling. Enough labor must be available to care for the plants in a timely manner. Hanging baskets, like any other specialty crop, should be planned in detail to develop a good cultural and marketing program.

Many growers, in order to have an inexpensive line, offer hanging baskets in container sizes too small for plants to grow and bloom in without constant watering by the consumer. This practice may result in good sales for a few years but the ultimate outcome is customer dissatisfaction and a declining market. I feel that plants for sunny areas must be in at least 10 inch baskets and those for shady spots in at least 8 inch baskets. Containers with porous sidewalls, such as moss lined types, will require extra watering in dry climates. Cultural instructions should accompany each basket since customers will often fail to realize that these plants must be cared for on a more timely basis than similar varieties in the garden.

Hanging baskets warrant special emphasis by the grower since they can be grown in the ceiling where potted crops are impractical. The extra revenue afforded by this opportunity to utilize space more effectively cannot be ignored if the greenhouse is to be successful. Judgment must be exercised to prevent undue shading of crops underneath the baskets and excessive weight stress to structural members of the greenhouse roof. Extra production of hanging baskets is of little use when other crops are reduced in value or buildings damaged. Placement in the ceiling must also be guided by the need to water and care for the baskets on a regular basis. If the location will not permit reasonable access, it is better not to locate plants there.

Irrigating hanging baskets presents some problems. Automatic watering tubes do not allow the flexibility of mixing different sizes or varieties of baskets on a particular line, and, unless tubes deliver a sufficient water volume, water tends to drain in a straight line through the soil and out the bottom with no wetting to the sides. When the conditions of plant uniformity and large volume water delivery can be met, automatic watering is a real benefit. Hand watering of hanging baskets must be done by experienced and conscientious workers to prevent excessive moisture being applied to plants below the baskets. The location of baskets overhead makes it harder for personnel to determine when water is needed and also increases the chances that the task will be forgotten entirely on busy days. Growers must exercise extra vigilance to assure watering is being done properly. It is definitely recommended that baskets remain on benches where they are easily viewed until they are well established. When the plants are growing vigorously, water should be applied heavily and then withheld until the soil dries somewhat. There will be less chance of overwatering if saucers are removed from baskets while they are being grown.

Hanging baskets will generally benefit from a little more fertilizer than is given to the same variety in packs. This can be accomplished without altering fertilizer schedules by incorporating a small amount of slow release fertilizer in the soil. The danger of overgrowth is considerably less in baskets. Most plants will make better baskets if they are pinched at least once. Some varieties may require two or three pinches to produce specimens. This is assuming that six small plants are planted per basket. It is difficult to generalize for all varieties but flowering usually occurs about six weeks after a soft pinch. It is better to be a little ahead of schedule than to miss the market. If flowering occurs too early, it may be necessary to clean old blooms off before putting baskets on display. Pests may be more of a problem on hanging baskets simply because they are in the greenhouse longer than pack annuals and, if grown higher than eye level, infestations may remain undetected until damage is severe. It is important to completely eradicate pests before the baskets are hung.

The choice of containers for hanging baskets is considerable but most growers choose an inexpensive plastic type. If there is a market for more expensive containers, redwood, clay, ceramic, or moss lined wire baskets may be used for at least a part of the crop. Saucers, if present, should be detachable and easy to re-attach. Careful attention must be focused on the strength of hangers and the rim or lip of the basket where the hanger is attached. It is not uncommon to find that some brands under certain conditions will fall because of structural weaknesses. This is both dangerous and costly. Ask container salesmen to submit samples so the strength of baskets can be tested before ordering large quantities. Be sure the soil is soaked with water when tests are made. Almost any flower can be planted in spring hanging baskets but certain varieties lend themselves better to this than others. The decision as to which varieties should be planted must not be left in question or guided by what is in surplus. Only first quality material and suitable varieties will produce the desired result. Baskets which do not perform well will result in customer dissatisfaction and an eventual decline in sales. Perennials which bloom once a season should specifically not be used in hanging baskets. Blooming garden mums may be an attractive basket but when the flowers are gone in late spring no more are produced for summer color. Mixing appropriate varieties is fine but the bloom dates may not correspond exactly to produce the most striking display. Fillers of foliage such as asparagus sprengeri or vinca vine can be advantageous with flower varieties which do not display a cascading effect. Table 26 lists flower varieties most commonly used in hanging baskets.

Table 26

Flower varieties commonly planted in hanging baskets. Those suitable for shaded areas are followed by an (S).

Ageratum	Lobelia (S)
Begonia (S)	Nasturtium
Coleus (S)	Petunia
Cuphea	Portulaca
Fushia (S)	Salvia
Gazania	San vitalia
Geranium	Snapdragon
Ice plant	Strawberry
Herbs	Thunbergia
Impatiens (S)	Verbena
Ivy geranium	Vinca
Lantana	Viola

Herbs

The use of home grown herbs has increased greatly as a result of the numerous articles about them in magazines devoted to ecology and natural foods. The recent popularity may be enduring but the wise grower will stay alert to signs of declining demand if publicity does not continue. Unless one intends to promote herb sales extensively, it would be best to grow only those varieties which have wide public recognition and may be counted on to generate an adequate volume of business. Herbs are usually offered as 2¼ to 4 inch pots with informational name tags attached.

Both perennial and annual herbs are available but perennials are in more demand. A growing temperature of 50°-60° F and full sun will suffice for the more common varieties. Perennial herbs grown in 2¼ inch pots at 55° F will be saleable in early May from a March 1 sowing. Annual varieties will require 2 to 3 weeks less crop time.

Impatiens

Growers have been increasing impatiens crops faster than any other bedding plant in recent years. It is the gardener's number one choice for shady spots. Sales may not be so spectacular in areas of the country where summer sun is extremely intense or in newly built up neighborhoods where shade from large trees is negligible. Every house, however, has a shady north side. Newer varieties of impatiens are tolerant of somewhat higher light levels. Impatiens is particularly useful in hanging baskets and planters which are used in covered patios. Indoor use in sunny windows, atriums, and home greenhouses ensures steady demand for plants through the winter.

Few plants will exhibit more color to entice customers than properly grown impatiens. Hanging baskets and large pots are particularly showy. Plant breeders have contributed to the impatiens success story by introducing many fine varieties in the past decade. Taller types reaching 14 inches in height are available as well as varieties only 8 inches tall. A wide range of colors from soft pastels to intense reds and purples is offered.

Germination of impatiens seed can be difficult because it is very sensitive to moisture stress. Since light is required, seed will not germinate if covered heavily with a medium to retain moisture, but a very fine covering will help to keep seed from drying out. Germination problems are particularly acute in late spring and summer when temperatures become warmer. Impatiens seed is expensive and if germination problems persist, it may be best to order seedlings from specialists. Damping off is frequently encountered in the seed flat and shortly after transplanting. Impatiens is sensitive to many fungicides so applications should be made at half strength if used. Removing the seed flat after germination to a slightly shaded area with plenty of air circulation will reduce the possibility of damping off. Seedlings must be handled carefully when transplanted; their succulent nature renders them easily damaged.

Impatiens is quickly damaged by excess soluble salts. Growth will be enhanced if seedlings are transplanted to the rooting mix formula since it drains more easily than the growing on soil. Once plants are growing well in packs, they may be transplanted to larger containers of growing on soil as long as heavy fertilizer applications are not made and leaching occurs every four weeks. Ammonium forms of nitrogen are reported to damage impatiens. Nitrogen of any form should be applied cautiously because excesses will result in lush vegetative growth and few flowers.

A temperature of 65° F after transplanting is recommended but the best temperature for further growth is 55°-60° F. Temperatures lower than 55° F for extended periods will result in yellowish, constricted growth. In plastic or older fiberglass houses, impatiens should be grown in full sun to promote flowering. Glass houses may need to be shaded lightly for best results. Watering should be heavy but infrequent to reduce the possibility of soluble salts damage. Wilting is not desirable but more compact plants are obtained if the soil is allowed to dry before irrigation. Impatiens is not difficult to grow but attractive plants are obtained only if growing procedures are followed carefully. These plants react wonderfully to proper care but will not tolerate abuse as some other varieties will.

Impatiens is not especially susceptible to pests unless problems already exist in the greenhouse. Growers who operate year round may find that spider mites and cyclamen mites can become established on plants if sources of infestation are not cleared up before spring crops are put in. Particular care must be exercised since these two pests may escape notice until populations are beyond control. Crops are often completely ruined before visual confirmation of cyclamen mites occurs.

Packs sown in late March will be flowering in late May at 60° F. Three inch pots which have been pinched will require an additional three weeks. Three pinched plants per 6 inch pot will be ready at the same time as 3 inch pots. Seed for 10 inch Mother's Day hanging baskets must be started in early January. Six plants are planted per basket and sheared heavily when foliage covers the surface. If the season is warm and bright, these baskets may be one to two weeks early but plant quality will not suffer. Time schedules are for the variety Super Elfins Mix.

Ivy Geranium

The increased popularity of hanging baskets in recent years has led to more interest in ivy geraniums. They are also useful as trailing plants on the edges of planters. Garden use is limited to varieties which exhibit a more compact habit. Light purple, pink, red, white, and peppermint colors are available. Most ivy geraniums are decidedly trailing and have flowers which shatter. Sybil Holmes is the most widely grown variety because it is compact and has fully double pink flowers which do not shatter. Well grown hanging baskets on display will ensure a brisk demand for 3 and 4 inch pots. Ivy geraniums are often not offered at chain stores and supermarkets so a premium price can sometimes be realized.

Care of stock plants, cutting production, and establishment should be guided by the same considerations as were mentioned previously for geraniums. A temperature of 55°-60° F is ideal for growing on. Higher temperatures will contribute to the legginess of plants and nullify the good done by pinching. All varieties must generally be pinched but acceptable pots and baskets of Sybil Holmes may sometimes be produced without a pinch in high light periods. If flowers are desired for Mother's Day, no pinch should be given after April 1. Ivy geraniums are basically sun lovers but Sybil Holmes will continue to bloom under slight shade. Most varieties are more or less susceptible to heat stall in midsummer and should be located near coolers at that time.

Fungal diseases are not a special problem with ivy geraniums when reasonable care is taken with sanitation. Spider mites can sometimes cause extensive damage if the pests are not completely eradicated from stock plants prior to cutting production. Oedema, a physiological disorder, is the chief production problem. The petioles and undersides of leaves may be seriously disfigured by the cork-like eruptions which characterize oedema. Excessive soil moisture and humidity are thought to be the chief causes of this disorder. My experience is that if extremes of temperature and soil moisture are avoided and good ventilation is practiced, oedema will be relegated to the status of a minor inconvenience. Oedema is not transmitted from one plant to another.

Cuttings taken in mid January make flowering 3½ inch pots for early May at 55° F. One hard pinch will be necessary. If 6 or 7 cuttings are planted to a 10 inch basket, the same schedule will be appropriate for Mother's Day. Baskets pinched more than once should have 3 to 4 weeks added to the schedule.

Lobelia

Short varieties of lobelia are used extensively as edging in gardens and the trailing varieties are often used in planters and hanging baskets. Blue is the color most in demand but white and reddish varieties are also available. Packs grown very cool will bloom at a height of 3 to 5 inches with a solid mass of purplish tinged foliage. Crops sold in mid and late spring should be sown in progression since lobelia can become overgrown quickly as warm weather approaches.

Lobelia is best if grown at 35°-45° F because it will remain short in the packs. At higher temperatures plants become overgrown before they reach the flowering stage. Temperatures of 50°-55° F will produce acceptable green plants if they are sold quickly. Good hanging baskets can be grown at the higher temperatures but plants are not so compact. Lobelia will tolerate light shade in the garden but greenhouse plants do best in full sun except at mid summer. Small clumps of seedlings are usually transplanted to packs since seed is inexpensive.

Plants sown January 1 will bloom May 1 if grown at 40°-45° F. Heavy green plants may be sold June 1 from an April 1 sowing if grown at 50°-55° F. Hanging baskets grown at 50° F for mid May must be sown in early December. Six plants per basket are used and no pinch is necessary. If hanging baskets are offered, some trailing varieties should be grown in packs for those customers who prefer to plant their own baskets. Heavy fertilization, especially with nitrogen, should be avoided in packs to prevent lush growth.

Marigold

A continual growth in marigold sales has taken place because they are one of the most easily grown and floriferous annuals. All heights are available from 6 inch dwarfs to 3 foot background varieties. Yellow, orange, and deep reddish-bronze are the prevalant colors in marigolds but the patterns these colors are arranged in are numerous. Flower form and size also has a wide range. The number of varieties in marigolds is large and increasing every year. Some attempt must be made by the grower to limit offerings to 2 or 3 basic colors in each height and flower form class.

The tallest background marigolds are always sold green at about 2 to 5 inches of height. Crackerjack is an example of this extremely fast growing class with fully double carnation-like blooms. A medium height group of marigolds (14 inches) with fully double, carnation-like blooms is represented by such varieties as Sunshot and Apollo or the Inca series. This latter group may be sold green or grown on to flower. Flowering plants are most often sold as 3 to 4 inch pots. The smaller edging and bed type marigolds such as the Boy series (8 to 10 inches) and Bolero or Honeycomb (10-12 inches) are generally sold as packs in bloom. Properly grown marigolds in flower can seldom be matched for consumer appeal. Large displays of them are very effective in producing good sales of this profitable crop and providing a bright spring atmosphere for the shopping area. Information should be available to customers so that the correct use of each variety is clear.

Marigolds are a grower's dream. They are quick to germinate, fast to reach saleable size, easy to grow, and they have a sizable market demand.

They are one of the most profitable spring crops available and every effort should be made to maximize their sales. Marigolds are especially useful in sun planters and a large supply should be reserved for this purpose. Garden performance is as superb as it is in the greenhouse.

No problems are normally encountered in germination but mice are especially fond of marigold seed and one mouse can destroy an entire sowing overnight. Seedlings must be transplanted from the seed flat quickly or plants will become stunted and flower in the packs before sufficient vegetative growth has occurred to make them appealing. Seedlings will also develop excessively long stems if they are subjected to the warm, shady conditions of germination chambers only a few hours too long.

Marigolds will grow reasonably well at temperatures from 45°-65° F but 50°-60° F is the most acceptable range. Lower temperatures may be used to slow crops. When summer temperatures become excessive, growth and flower production are lessened. Full sun should always be given to develop adequate flowers and compact plants. Flowering of marigolds is enhanced by short days so that crops grown into mid summer may tend to be less floriferous and require extra time to bloom. No daylength manipulation is necessary. A few growers have used shadecloth to flower Sunshot and Apollo types at earlier dates than would be possible with the normal daylengths of late spring and early summer.

Proper fertilization is the key to exceptional marigold crops. Many growers become accustomed to withholding nutrients to prevent petunias and cool temperature bedding plants from becoming lush and overgrowing the container. Marigolds must receive the potassium nitrate formula at every irrigation to maintain sufficient vegetative growth for an excellent crop. No pure water should ever be given. Faster growing varieties such as Sunshot, Apollo and Crackerjack are especially susceptible to potassium deficiencies. The calcium nitrate-potassium nitrate formula can be used if heavier vegetative growth is desired, but in my opinion plants are in better shape for garden use when they receive only potassium nitrate. Consumers must be informed that marigolds require adequate feeding to realize their full potential.

Marigolds will use copious amounts of water when they become larger and weather is warm and dry. Slight wilting on occasion is not harmful, but, if it occurs too often, plants will be more restricted in growth than necessary for their best appearance. Pests and diseases are seldom a problem with marigolds when reasonable care is given. The old wives' tale that marigolds repel aphids is, in my experience, not valid. Severe infestations may occur if aphids are allowed to increase without check.

The schedule related here refers to specific popular varieties. Growers must realize that a change in varieties may require timing adjustments. For mid May sales the following seeding dates are applicable at growing temperatures of 50°-55° F: March 10 for packs of of the Boy series in bloom; March 1 for packs of Bolero in bloom; March 20 for packs of Apollo or Sunshot as green plants or February 20 for 3½ inch pots in bloom; April 7 for packs of Crackerjack as green plants. An additional week of growing time could be added if plants are desired in full bloom rather than a third bloom.

Martha Washington Geranium

These old time favorites have been neglected for many years but recent interest in them may reactivate widespread commercial production. Martha Washington geraniums do not flower well when night temperatures are over 50°-55° F in the garden or home. The modern practice of heating homes to 60° or 70° F at night has no doubt led to a decline in using Martha Washington geraniums as flowering house plants. Energy cost hikes have forced consumers to lower thermostats at night so that in many homes these beautiful plants will now flower again if sunny areas are available. Greenhouse production of Martha Washingtons must also be geared to those seasons when garden temperatures are not over 55° F for prolonged periods. Outdoor sales will be limited in regions that do not have growing seasons with cool nights.

The flowers of these plants are exceptional, coming in many colors and having the general appearance and size of azalea blooms. Martha Washingtons make excellent 6 inch pots for the floral shop trade from late winter through spring. Both 4 and 6 inch material for garden use will find strong demand in cooler regions or where mild winters permit gardening with cold tolerant plants. A Mother's Day crop is particularly valuable since many other 6 inch gift flowers are either out of season or require special conditions to produce good quality at this time. If holiday sales are not as good as expected, plants can be sold for garden use, thus eliminating some of the risk associated with holiday crops such as gloxinias. Because of their extraordinary beauty and relative novelty, these plants can often realize a premium price.

I find cuttings of Martha Washingtons hard to root unless they are placed in a cool, lightly shaded spot and allowed to take their time. In spring and fall the ideal spot is in front of the cooling pads. All attempts I have made to speed rooting by means of bottom heat have led to failure. Rooting at 45°-55° F should be accomplished in 50-70 days. The propagation medium must never become waterlogged. Authorities vary in their recommendations for the proper temperatures necessary for flower induction. I make certain flowers are initiated by subjecting plants to 50° F for a period of eight weeks. Plants can then be finished between 45° and 62° F depending on the time available until marketing. Full sun is necessary until summer when plants can be grown under light shade.

Pests are not normally a problem with Martha Washingtons but growers should be on the alert for whitefly attacks if there is any reason to suspect their presence. Botrytis on flowers can become very serious; this problem is the main reason I suspend summer production. Crops in winter and spring have shown no inclination to develop botrytis. Summer botrytis probably occurs because artificial heat is unnecessary at that season and humidity builds up quickly in tight polyethylene houses as temperatures cool down greatly from the heat at mid day.

Cuttings taken in October and rooted before Christmas will make good flowering 6 inch pots by April 15 at 50° F. Plants must be pinched once when transplanted. Four inch pots for April and May sales should be cut at Christmas; no pinch is necessary.

Pansy

Gardeners can seldom resist purchasing at least one pack of blooming pansies even if they are not needed. Their flower colors are some of the most interesting and beautiful encountered in the plant world. An early blooming habit and cold hardiness make pansies a natural for heavy promotion when frost first leaves the ground and gardeners are looking for something to plant which tolerates late snows and frosts. The color provided by pansies in early spring and late fall is especially welcome since most other plants are out of bloom at these times. Most gardeners still believe that pansies should be planted in shaded areas but this notion has been outdated by the introduction of new varieties which will tolerate summer heat. Although pansies are annuals, they will overwinter in mild climates and also in northern areas if some protection is afforded by a loose mulch cover.

The traditional method of producing pansies has been to start seed in the late summer and carry well established plants through the winter in cold frames insulated with straw or similar materials. Frost protection is removed at winter's end and plants are in bloom after the first week or so of moderate temperatures. During the past twenty years a shift to sowing seed in winter and marketing plants without overwintering has occurred. This method greatly decreases production costs. Although the best pansies are those from early seedings, growers in very cold climates may sow seed into mid April for summer gardeners. These late crops must be sold quickly or plants will become overgrown.

Pansies develop an undesirable lush growth whenever temperature, fertilizer, or water is excessive. After establishment, temperatures between 35° and 45° F will result in excellent plants. If no heat is available, plants can be allowed to freeze lightly when they have had a week or two of cold temperatures to become adjusted. Greenhouse culture when nights exceed 50° F is impractical. Fertilizer, particularly nitrogen, should be withheld as long as plants maintain a healthy green color. Slight wilting between irrigations is permissible to check excessive growth. Plenty of ventilation to prevent high daytime temperatures and reduce humidity is necessary. Night-time ventilation is also advisable when the danger of heavy frost damage is past. Full sun must always be given in the greenhouse.

Many growers move pansy crops outside after the harsh weather of early spring is over. These plants must be carefully monitored for water each day and protected from wind damage to maintain quality. The full sun, good ventilation, and generally cooler nights afforded by outdoor conditions can result in a longer selling season. Aphids must be kept in check or they can become a serious problem. Infestations will be easily apparent to customers since the pests congregate on flower stems and flowers. Control of aphids should be taken care of early since many insecticides will damage open flowers, and as plants become grown together it is almost impossible to achieve a satisfactory kill.

Packs of Majestic Giant hybrids sown in mid December will be heavy flowering plants in early April if transplanted to 55° F for establishment and then lowered to 45° F for growing on. Two more weeks should be added if plants are to be sold in 3½ inch pots. Pansies make especially colorful hanging baskets at Mother's Day. These baskets can be sold at very reasonable prices since no pinching is required and containers can be spaced closely. They may even be grown outdoors if wind and severe frost protection is provided. The variety Universal Mix is especially useful in baskets because it produces a large number of medium sized blooms. Early January sowings grown at 45° F result in a fairly small finished product if 6 plants per 10 inch basket are used. Two weeks growing time may be added if heavier material is desired.

Perennials

A discussion of all the perennial varieties which can be included in greenhouse programs would be beyond the scope of this book. Several of the more important ones have been treated. Gardeners are always asking for perennials but their enthusiasm is often dampened when they are shown a clump of green leaves. If large amounts of perennials are to be sold, they must be brought into flower. Certain of the more well known perennials can be sold reasonably well in the green stage because people have a good conception of what they look like in bloom.

Readers should refer to the discussions of shasta daisies and primula for basic culture of most perennials. Plants may be sold in bloom after exposure to cold winter temperatures or as green plants when they are sown in late winter and early spring. A few perennials such as violas are exceptions in that they are very floriferous even without cold exposure. In general, high temperatures and fertilizer levels are the enemy of perennials.

The length of time perennials must be handled to be sold in flower dictates that prices be relatively high. Growers and retailers who wish to realize the greatest potential profits from this group of plants must embark on a well planned sales program which will include both blooming specimens and less expensive green plants. The green plants will usually be more profitable to growers even though prices are lower. Displays should be arranged so that blooming plants will lead customers to purchase green plants and colorful tags must be placed in nonflowering containers. Perennials are a largely untapped market in many locations and offer people willing to implement a careful growing or selling strategy the opportunity to increase profits in a low competition market. Acceptance of the program will be gradual and overnight success must not be counted on.

Germination of some perennial seed is slow and erratic and growers may benefit by ordering small plants from specialists. If 3 inch and larger pots are to be flowered for spring, it is often possible to buy dormant plants in late winter for potting up and eliminate the need to germinate seed and overwinter plants. The particular program used for perennial production will depend greatly on other fall crop schedules and upon the facilities available for overwintering plants. Any grower who holds plants through the winter must be certain to add enough to the selling prices to compensate for the use of facilities and risk of winter kill even though plants may require no care for several months.

Some of the more popular perennials which have not been discussed previously are aquileja (columbine), English daisy, campanula (bell flower), delphinium, gaillardia, geum, lupine, phlox (creeping and tall), poppy (oriental and Iceland), painted daisy, rudbeckia, snow in summer, and various sedums and hen and chicks.

When varieties for the growing program are being selected, the physical habit of plants must be considered since some perennials may be extremely tall and unsuited for blooming in containers. Container sizes must also be chosen carefully to match the expected size of plant at marketing. Dormant perennials often surprise neophyte growers with their speed of growth when dormancy is broken and plants are sometimes potted in too small containers. Schedules must be meticulously coordinated so that the entire supply of plants does not bloom at one time.

Petunia

Petunias are synonymous with flower gardening in many people's minds and every garden shop must maintain an adequate supply to meet demand. The dominance of petunias in gardens has perhaps been brought about more by chance than any other factor. There are certainly other flowers which demonstrate equal beauty and performance in the garden but flower breeding technology was first focused in a concentrated and successful manner on petunias. Consumers and growers alike recognized the value of the improved varieties and began planting petunias in increasing numbers. Petunias soon became the number one garden flower. Their relative popularity has been slipping in the past few years as plant breeding efforts have been concentrated on other groups of flowers. Petunias ushered in the beginning of the modern bedding plant industry and it is unlikely that their number one spot will be relinquished until the growers and gardeners who grew up with them pass on.

Modern petunias are available in five basic types: multiflora singles (small flowered), grandiflora singles (large flowered), multiflora doubles, grandiflora doubles, and California giants. Multiflora singles were the first truly popular petunias and are contrasted with the grandiflora singles by having smaller flowers, smaller leaves, more branches, and earlier and more blooms. Grandiflora singles replaced the multiflora singles in popularity not because they are better plants (in fact many authorities rate the multiflora as superior overall), but because the flowers are much larger and attract consumer attention. Grandiflora singles comprise the great majority of petunia production today. The difference between the multiflora and grandiflora double flowered petunias is much the same as for single petunias but, in this case, no real predominance in popularity is evident. California giants were an early class of extremely large flowered plants with a coarse habit. They enjoyed a brief period of success but, because of inherent weaknesses, were replaced by the multiflora and grandiflora singles.

The number and diversity of petunia varieties is large and no specific recommendations will be made here. Neophyte growers will generally do well to start with the most popular varieties a seed company offers and build upon this base as they gain experience. A cropping program of approximately 18-25 varieties will allow two varieties each for red, white, true pink, purple, and a good selection of more exotic colors. This variety range may be too much for the small grower and perhaps too few for extremely large operations. Grandiflora doubles are in good demand for pots and special locations but are ineffective in massed beds because they are not as floriferous as the single flowered varieties. Growing more varieties than warranted by market conditions decreases productivity.

Color preferences will certainly vary from market to market but I will offer some generalizations based on my own experience. Red is far and away the most popular color, followed by white and the many shades of pink available. Not far behind pink and white are deep burgundy, red and white bicolors, wine (represented by Sugar Daddy), and purple. Yellow (represented by Summer Sun) is increasingly popular since its introduction a few years back. Other color combinations represent only a small percentage of my total production but are valuable in that they please customers who are looking for something different. Many growers produce a large number of mixed color flats which I do not emphasize because only one flower may be open on a pack and customers purchase it believing the entire pack is a solid color. They become irritated when the color scheme of their garden is upset.

Distinguishing between varieties according to their adaptability to greenhouse culture is fraught with uncertainties since conditions from one greenhouse to another will differ considerably. It is my definite opinion, however, that true red colors are much more susceptible to serious damage from botrytis during rainy humid weather and when humidity builds up in the greenhouse because artificial heat is no longer required at night. Some other attributes I have observed in varieties I grow are that pinks and purples bloom earlier, sky blue colors are exceptionally tall, and yellow (Summer Sun) and grandiflora doubles need more fertilizer than other varieties to develop properly.

Petunia seed is quite small but germinates more quickly and easily than many other types of flower seed if reasonable care is given. The seed should never be covered and must not be allowed to dry out. Because petunia seed is round and small and rolls out of the packages easily, it is often sown too heavily. As soon as a good stand of seedlings is visible, the seed flat should be removed to a 55°-60° F location in full sun. Excessive stem elongation and damping off will occur if seedlings are left in warm, moist germination chambers.

The debate over methods of petunia culture waxes hotter than for other bedding plant groups, perhaps only because more petunias are grown than any other flower. One faction advocates higher temperatures and plenty of feed and water to produce a softer, actively growing plant at the time of sale. A central tenet to this philosophy is that the plant should go into the garden without any check in growth. The opposite faction believes in withholding water and fertilizer and lowering temperatures to produce a short, tough plant which will hold up under rough harvesting, sales, and transplanting treatment. The perfect petunia for marketing and gardening probably lies somewhere in between.

I believe the best petunias are raised by maintaining a moderate 55° F temperature, irrigating heavily only when water is definitely needed, and fertilizing only to maintain an acceptable green color on foliage. Water and fertilizer must not be withheld to the point where foliage becomes yellow. Severe checks in growth generally lead to rotting tissue after the next heavy watering. I recommend establishing plants with potassium nitrate fertilizer at every irrigation, then reducing it to every third irrigation during growing on. About ten days before sale, I increase the frequency of fertilizing to green up plants a little more.

Fast growth undoubtedly increases the profitability of petunias but anyone who has visited a garden center full of tall, lush plants falling over in the packs after being handled a few times will understand the need for a cultural program which toughens up plants. On the other side of the coin, customers will not buy dwarfed, starved plants either. Growers who monitor growth carefully, follow a middle course, and refrain from cultural extremes will have excellent crops. An ability to anticipate the needs of plants is essential to a good petunia crop.

Growers should be aware of several factors which can influence petunia production greatly: petunias reportedly do not initiate flowers at less than 55° F; lengthening the light period increases flowering and internode length of stems; petunias generally require less fertilizer (especially nitrogen) than most other bedding plants; excessive daytime heat will greatly reduce flower size; botrytis will attack flowers and even basal foliage if humidity is too high, so some heat should always be left on at night and fresh air drawn in if necessary; and petunias grown on bare soil will root into the ground and produce wild, uneven growth caused by some plants' roots reaching the rich soil and others' roots remaining confined to the flat.

Full sun is absolutely necessary to good petunia production. Aside from botrytis, petunias are relatively free of diseases and pests in the northern United States. Southern humid areas may be plagued to varying degrees with rots which attack plants. Growing on raised benches will decrease the incidence of botrytis and other rots by permitting air flow underneath the plants. It will also lead to somewhat shorter plants in most cases.

A recap of cultural conditions which result in shorter, tougher plants is in order: keep temperatures cool, down to 55° F; go easy on the fertilizer, especially nitrogen; irrigate heavily but only when plants definitely need water; never allow any shade on plants; grow on raised benches, if possible, and provide plenty of air circulation. Application of B-9 at concentrations of 2,500 ppm have been recommended for height control but this is an added expense which should be unnecessary for the careful grower.

There are many people who advocate selling petunias in the green stage. This would increase profits while eliminating almost all the problems associated with production. Petunias are among the easiest plants to grow until flowering occurs. The argument is also made that these plants will perform better in the garden. I have no defense against these proposals except that customers will not readily accept green petunias. I have provided beautiful green plants with adequate color tags on several occasions at my retail stores; each time the response has been disappointing. People pick flowering petunias ten to one over green ones. Armchair experts recommend an educational program to convince consumers of the benefits of green petunias. My response is that few small businessmen can afford the tremendous short term losses entailed in this program when the outcome is by no means certain.

Single grandiflora petunias sown on March 1 and grown at 55° F will begin to flower in packs in mid May. Single multifloras should be sown a week later and double grandifloras two weeks earlier. Double multifloras will respond with double grandifloras. Two weeks can be added to this schedule for production of 3½ inch pots without a pinch. Later sowings will require less time to flower as daylength and temperatures increase. Extra fertilizer and water should be applied to the double petunias if full realization of their flower form and size is to be reached.

Hanging petunia baskets are very popular and easy to produce. Most seedsmen recommend use of Cascade series in these baskets, but I do not feel this choice is critical; any good petunia is suitable. Seed for Mother's Day baskets grown at 60° F should be planted January 15. Six plants are transplanted from packs to baskets and pinched shortly after establishment. A second pinch five weeks before Mother's Day should bring a fresh full bloom for the holiday. This schedule produces very heavy baskets but ones which are neat and not yet cascading. A small charge of a slow release fertilizer with a high nitrogen content should be added to hanging basket soil so a more luxuriant growth of these plants will be possible. Potassium nitrate is also applied at every irrigation.

Planters

A considerable market exists for large outdoor planters for porches, patios, and apartment balconies. These items are seldom handled by plant stores unless produced locally since they are generally unsuitable for long distance shipping. Garden centers that handle large planters may increase slow summer sales and tap a market in which little competition exists.

Planters must have a large enough soil volume for plants to grow vigorously and not require constant watering. In drier climates it is my opinion that containers less than 12 inches in diameter are too small for customer satisfaction. Containers must be chosen carefully to compliment the plants yet be economical enough to attract customers. I have used 12 inch wooden fruit baskets for many years. These baskets are reasonable in cost and present a rustic look. Baskets treated with green tinted wood preservative last a full season and are quite attractive. The main crop of planters should be in inexpensive, standardized containers but a few more exotic models might be included for those customners willing to pay a little extra.

In order to develop significant sales volume, growers must schedule planters like any other crop and present them to the public as a pick up item rather than relying on customers to special order. Individually prepared planters require too much sales time for taking the order and too much production time in the greenhouse. A special order planter will take four or five times longer to produce than ones scheduled as a crop and planted in quantity.

Sufficient plant material of the proper size, variety, and maturity must be available to meet planter schedules. The quickest way to make a failure of this program is to fill planters with left over or sick plants. A certain amount of fill in work with excess plants may be possible but only first class material which will add to the appeal of the product should be used. If the material used was in the bud stage, planters generally look their best for market two to four weeks after planting.

Planters for shady areas will require large supplies of impatiens, coleus, and begonias. Taller coleus varieties or dracena spikes can be placed in the center to add height. Lobelia and balsam are two other plants which will stand some shade. Although the choice of plant material is rather limited for combining in shade planters, sales of them are rather good because of the large number of covered patios in suburban areas. Some growers even add inexpensive foliage items such as purple wandering Jew or Swedish ivy to shade planters.

The range of flowers which can be grown in sun planters is large so that many interesting combinations are possible. Marigolds are my favorite choice as planter material. The taller Sunshot and Apollo types are nice for height in the center with lower growing varieties being useful near the edges. A showy geranium is the preference of most customers for a center plant. Dracena spike, dahlias, zinnias, or other appropriately tall plants can also be used for height. Lobelia and alyssum are especially good at the edges of sun planters. The different combinations of plants are endless and growers will discover by experience what sells in a particular locality.

Workers who create planters must be instructed in the proper use of different plants and given a good idea of colors which will compliment one another. Depending upon what the selling price is to be, some guidelines should be set down concerning the number and value of plants to be used. A thorough soaking of all plants prior to transplanting will allow them to become established somewhat before watering of the larger containers is necessary. A real danger of overwatering exists if planters are irrigated heavily too soon. Greenhouse personnel will generally do very nice work on planters if one spends sufficient time teaching them how to go about the job.

Planter soil should be fortified with a small charge of slow release fertilizer and customers must be instructed in the proper methods of fertilizing and watering. The development of a good business in planters, hanging baskets, perennials, or any other specialty item takes time and will only come about if care is taken to provide a quality product which satisfies consumers. Happy customers spread the word quickly.

Portulaca

Sunny hot spots where it is too dry for other flowers are ideal for portulaca. It is a short, creeping plant which can be used for groundcover. Portulaca is becoming a more important bedding plant as population shifts to the hotter and drier regions of the United States. Colors are very bright and made up predominantly of red, rose, orange, and yellow. The double flowered varieties are selected most frequently for pack production but there is some use of the single flowered variety Wildfire in hanging baskets. Packs of portulaca are attractive and will remain short for a long period. Sales displays must be in a sunny area because sunlight triggers the blooms to open each day.

Portulaca can be grown as low as 50° F after it has been well established. Better crops are produced, however, if temperatures can be maintained at 60° F for the entire period. Soil should be kept moist after transplanting but once plants have rooted it is advisable to lean toward the dry side so that serious problems with rot will be avoided. Dry soils will delay the crop a bit but excessively moist conditions can result in crop failures. Portulaca is relatively pest and disease free except for the rot problem mentioned above. Some fertilizing may be done with the calcium nitrate-potassium nitrate formula if more luxuriant growth is desired since overgrowth is not normally a problem.

Varieties with less expensive seed can be sown heavily in the seed flats and the seedlings transplanted as small clumps to packs. Portulaca seed germinates quickly and the new seedlings are difficult to see. Inexperienced growers may fail to notice germination has occurred and leave the flat in the shade and high humidity a few extra days. This practice results in excessively long stems and an increased incidence of damping off.

When plants are grown at 60° F, a March 1 sowing should result in flowering packs by the end of May. Packs sold green will be ready three to four weeks earlier if several seedlings are transplanted to each cell.

Primula

Perennial primroses are an old favorite with gardeners and considerable sales can be made of flowering or green plants. A wide range of extremely vibrant flower colors make primula a close second to pansies in consumer appeal when plants are in bloom for early spring. Numerous florets in clusters are borne at the tip of a naked stalk with a neat rosette of leaves at the base. Flower stalks are seldom more than 10 inches high so that primula makes a nice perennial border.

The high cost of seed and the need for cold exposure to initiate flowers has led to most primula being sold in 2¼ inch or larger pots when in bloom. Green plants in packs can be profitable if less expensive seed of the Colossea strain is used. Many growers offer primula in 3 or 4 inch pots from late winter until Mother's Day for small gift or impulse sales in supermarkets. They do not hold up well under the 70° F temperatures of home or store.

Primulas to be sold as small flowering pots in springtime should be sown in late summer and overwintered in protected cold frames or in unheated greenhouses where temperatures will dip slightly below freezing at times. Because light aids in germination, seeds should not be covered. I have had good luck in producing flowering packs and 2¼ inch pots by sowing seed December through January. After establishment, these plants must be grown in a house where night temperatures will approach freezing at times. The latter schedule can lead to plants with few or no blooms if temperatures are not low enough for at least one month. December 1 sowings flower in late April. January 15 sowings grown at 50°-55° F can be sold as green plants in mid April without cold exposure.

Watering and fertilizing of primula should be somewhat on the lean side if plants are to be sold in bloom. A combination of high fertilizer and temperatures can lead to grassy growth with few flowers. Plants to be sold as soon as they are large enough in the green stage do not require the same restrictions of temperature, fertilizer, and water. Spring crops of primrose will require no shade in the greenhouse but if plants are grown in summer, they will benefit from a light sunscreen. Aphids may infest flowers and stalks if precautions are not taken but primula is seldom bothered by other pests and diseases.

Rose

Garden roses are not widely grown by larger wholesale greenhouses but they constitute a significant crop for a great many retail establishments. The market for roses started in pots and sold green or in flower is considerable even though dormant plants can be sold for less than half the cost. Potted roses extend the selling season through the summer instead of limiting sales to springtime. A well done potted rose display is a major attraction at plant stores since roses are the favorite American flower.

Facilities needed for starting roses are minimal. Essential to success is a shaded, humid area where 50°-55° F temperatures can be maintained until sprouts have appeared. Many growers start their roses outdoors under a burlap cover or in sheds without provision for good light. Either of these latter methods will result in reduced productivity due to substandard growing conditions. When plants have sprouted well, the shade is removed and humidity lowered to normal greenhouse levels. Depending upon the time remaining until sale date, plants may be grown on at 40°-60° F. The lower temperature is usually preferable 10 days before sale or if plants are to be moved outdoors to make room for greenhouse crops. Roses will tolerate a very light frost if they have been conditioned.

Dormant rose plants are purchased from specialists and potted in mid February if large plants with some blooms are desired for Mother's Day. The stems or canes should be pruned back to approximately 8 inches and roots are pruned slightly so that they will fit easily into a 2 gallon container without crowding. Larger containers may be used but will increase the selling cost. Soil is lightly tamped around the roots to eliminate air pockets. The graft unions must always remain above the soil level and roots should never be allowed to dry out during the potting process.

Soil is soaked heavily after planting with the calcium nitrate-potassium nitrate fertilizer formula fortified with micro nutrients and iron. No further fertilizer is applied until vigorous growth has begun. Many growers incorporate slow release fertilizers into the soil but I feel it is safer to limit early fertilizer applications until the plant can use nutrients rapidly. Roses do not like soggy soil and it is easy to overwater when plants are still dormant and the weather is cool. Full sun is best for roses after they have rooted in.

Aphids and spider mites can cause serious damage on roses unless a good control program is carried on. Spider mites seldom become a problem until the weather warms up. Mildew will appear with warm weather and is almost impossible to control through chemical means. If plants remain in the greenhouse, the grower must employ the standard practices for lowering night time humidity. The best cure for mildew is often to move plants outside and make sure irrigating is done in the mornings.

Many growers schedule crops of small woody shrubs to be planted with their roses. The market for any one variety is not so large as for roses but if 10 to 15 varieties are grown they will certainly be more important than the rose crop. Shrub culture is much the same as for roses but a generally lower humidity will be tolerated by shrubs and they are not quite so susceptible to aphids, spider mites, and mildew. Certain shrubs such as lilacs should not be pruned back since the flowers are already formed in dormant buds.

An alternative schedule may be followed with shrubs by potting in late fall and allowing plants to root in a cold greenhouse through the winter. In northern areas, some mulch protection must be given to pots stored outdoors so that tender roots do not freeze severely. Shrubs planted in the fall are generally superior to spring plantings and a premium price can be obtained. An added bonus is gained by transferring a job from the busy springtime to a slower season.

Both shrubs and roses should be checked carefully for damage caused by freezing or drying out in transit and an immediate claim filed if damage is apparent. When plants are frozen, they must be allowed to thaw out gradually. Quick thawings will damage cell membranes extensively.

Salvia

Midwestern and eastern gardeners are especially fond of salvia and it is an important crop in these regions. Growers in other areas of the United States may experience only moderate demand. Salvia varieties range from 10 to 30 inches in height. Red is by far the most popular color but blue and white are available. Plants are generally planted to the garden in full sun but will also perform well in partial shade. The bright red, shorter varieties are among the showiest of annuals when flowered in packs or pots.

Salvia seed is left uncovered on the germination medium. It must be kept constantly moist at a temperature of 70° F. Poor germination is perhaps more of a problem with salvia than other plants because the seed will not tolerate less than optimum conditions. Seedlings are susceptible to damping off and must be moved to an area that is well ventilated at a temperature of 55°-60° F. Salvia is very sensitive to damage by methyl bromide and soils fumigated with this chemical must not be used for growing on or germination.

Salvia can be grown at 55° F but I prefer to maintain temperatures at 60° F until plants are setting flower buds. I also like to use the cutting mix soil formula for growing on, the combination of lighter soil and higher temperatures to dry out plants faster seems to cut down losses due to various stem rots. These diseases are the main cultural problem encountered with salvia. It has been reported that salvia is sensitive to high soluble salt levels; a lighter soil would also reduce the possibility of salt buildups.

After establishment, irrigations should be more thorough to avoid salt buildups but the soil must dry out between waterings if stem rots are to be controlled. Shaded conditions in the greenhouse will reduce flowering and cause plants to be taller. A March 15 sowing will bring packs of the earlier, shorter varieties into bloom for late May if grown at 60° F. Salvia makes nice 3 or 4 inch pots and is quite useful in planter combinations.

Snapdragons

An improvement in snapdragon varieties has been the major impetus in making them an important spring crop. A full range of heights and colors is now available in these delightfully fragrant flowers. Since the introduction of the dwarf (6-8 inch) Floral Carpet series and medium height plants, snapdragons are more popular for edging and bed use than they are for background and cut flower purposes. The snapdragon lasts well as a cut flower in homes and offers an unusual form for incorporation in arrangements. Plants which have been conditioned may be set out in early spring and will tolerate light frost.

The key to appealing, husky snapdragons is cool temperatures. Plants may be subjected to light frost if heat is lacking but the most economical crops are produced at 45°-50° F. Full sun and plenty of ventilation will help keep stems strong. The height of plants in packs will remain under control better if water and fertilizer are applied somewhat sparingly. Aphids are the most common pest to afflict snapdragons and several fungal stem rots may become problems if plants are overwatered frequently.

Tall snapdragons of the Rocket series will be ready for sale as green plants in packs by mid April from a February 15 sowing if grown at 45° F. Many authorities recommend pinching these plants to 3 or 4 leaves to produce a bushy habit, but I find plants are quite acceptable if left single stem. The cost of pinching in terms of labor and extra bench time is prohibitive in most markets.

Packs of edging varieties such as Floral Carpet will bloom in mid April from January 15 sowings when grown at 45° F. Green plants are ready 3 to 4 weeks earlier. The dwarf varieties make very nice 3 or 4 inch pots. Crops of snapdragons for late May and June sales must be planted in weekly progression to avoid having too many ready at one time. The plants become weak stemmed easily as warm weather arrives.

Thunbergia

Thunbergia or blackeyed susan is especially useful in hanging baskets and as a climbing vine which will quickly provide shade or act as a screen if given support to climb on. The variety having orange flowers with a black eye is most popular but white and yellow flowered varieties are also available. Blackeyed susans will vine to a considerable height in the course of a season and bloom freely without interruption until frost. Many consumers are unfamiliar with these plants since they are not commonly offered at garden stores. Displaying a large number of hanging baskets in bloom will lead to a good demand for green plants in 3 or 4 inch pots.

Thunbergia seeds germinate and grow quickly so plants must be transplanted from the flat before growth is restricted. A minimum temperature of 60° F should be maintained until plants are well established. Temperatures of 55° F will suffice for further growing on but the speed of growth is much less satisfactory than that obtained at 60° F or above. Blackeyed susans require full sun to remain compact and flower profusely. the plants are heavy feeders and must be given supplemental fertilizer in addition to the usual potassium nitrate formula. A small charge of slow release fertilizer is adequate. Iron chlorosis is common in thunbergia and an application of this element is essential to maintain a dark green color. Stem and root rots will plague the young plants if they are overwatered but more mature containers use copious amounts of water.

Spider mites can cause serious damage to thunbergia if sources of infection are not eliminated. Control of these pests is very difficult when the plants become densely twined together. Spider mite damage should not be confused with dark brown specks or blotches which may appear on leaves when potassium is deficient.

Early January sowings grown at 60° F will result in heavy 10 inch flowering baskets for Mother's Day. Plants to be used in hanging baskets are normally grown in 2¼ inch pots and pinched once before transplanting 4 or 5 of them to baskets. Two more pinches are needed to produce good quality, the last one 5 weeks before sale. Green plants in 3½ inch pots for mid May are obtained from a March 1 sowing with two soft pinches.

Vegetables

Many customers who view flowers as a luxury item will readily purchase vegetable plants because some economic value can be realized from them. Plant stores stocking a full line of healthy vegetables will attract an added segment of the gardening public. There has been a nationwide trend for people to grow more of their own vegetables. Gardens are even springing up in the centers of large cities. The growing popularity of vegetable gardening seems assured since more young people are being introduced to the delights of fresh home products.

Growers should concentrate on this increasing demand for vegetable plants because these crops often command a premium price while being less expensive to produce. Production costs are generally lower for vegetables than for flowers because less time is spent on the bench and culture is often easier. Vegetable seed is large and easy to germinate and the plants grow rapidly. The selling season for vegetable plants is lengthening because larger plants are more popular than before and varieties suitable for growing in patio planters have been developed. Developing a thriving business in vegetable plants is based upon selecting the proper varieties for the local climate and providing adequate cultural information to consumers. Healthy, strong plants are, of course, the beginning of any sales program.

A discussion on the greenhouse culture of vegetable transplants may be conveniently divided into two sections based upon the temperatures required for production of quality plants. Broccoli, brussel sprouts, cabbage, cauliflower, celery, chives, onions, lettuce, and strawberries all thrive with rather cool night temperatures while cucumbers, eggplant, melons, peppers, pumpkins, squash, and tomatoes prosper under somewhat warmer temperatures. Vegetable plants will generally be better products if subjected to the same slower than maximum growth and final hardening process as was recommended for floral bedding plants. A middle course should be followed with neither lush growth nor excessive hardening being allowed to take place. Chemical applications to control pests and diseases on vegetable plants must be more carefully monitored since the products are intended for human consumption.

The selection of varieties to grow will revolve mainly about the expected maturity date. It is especially important to offer early maturing plants in areas where the growing season is short. The number of days until harvest quoted in seed catalogs is the growing time required from setting out small plants in the garden. Certain varieties may exhibit characteristics such as resistance to specific diseases which make them more suitable for growing in one geographic area than in another.

Garden stores located in ethnic neighborhoods may need more of some plants than others. People of Italian descent will favor eggplant while German and Polish cooks make heavy use of cabbage. Greenhouses in areas where Hispanic culture is strong should raise adequate quantities of jalapeno, chili, and other hot peppers. Catering to ethnic tastes will ensure that these customers return when other plants or flowers are purchased. There are numerous varieties of vegetables and care must be taken to grow the ones which will satisfy the use to which they will be put. Cucumbers may be picklers or slicers, tomatoes for juices or salads, cabbages for sauerkraut or fresh use, squash for winter or summer. The choices are almost endless.

Vegetables which prosper under cool greenhouse conditions are usually grown at 45°-50° F. Lower temperatures for prolonged periods will cause premature flowering or "bolting" in cabbage, broccoli, brussel sprouts, cauliflower, and celery. Higher temperatures lead to weak grassy growth. Cool vegetables, excluding onions and chives, grow to market size very quickly and therefore, return good profits. In regions where autumn weather is mild, customers will sometimes plant a second crop. Except for strawberries, plants are not often sold in larger pots. Cool vegetables may be grown in cold frames and customers may set them out early since a light frost will be tolerated.

Full sun is recommended for all cool vegetables. Fertilizer should be on the lean side to guard against weak grassy growth. The cabbage family can become infested with aphids unless precautions are taken but other pests and diseases are not normally a problem. Seed of cool vegetables germinates quickly and seedlings must soon be moved to cooler temperatures to avoid spindly growth. If plants must be held back severely by restricting water and fertilizer, small heads or other unwanted side effects may be evident in the garden. Careful scheduling will eliminate the need to hold back plants in this manner. At 50° F most cool vegetables are saleable six to seven weeks after sowing or, in the case of strawberries, planting the dormant roots. Lettuce will be ready one to two weeks earlier and onions, chives, and strawberries from seed require several extra weeks of growth.

Strawberries grown from dormant plants are saleable earlier than those grown from seed but the initial cost is higher. Because seed is available for only one variety, propagation in this manner is restricted. Strawberries are generally sold in 2¼ inch or larger pots and sometimes as fruited hanging baskets. These baskets are not especially practical for fruit production and serve mainly as novelties.

A temperature of 55°-65° F is used to grow warm vegetables. The lower range is employed only when plants are to be hardened for market or held back for a short period. Temperatures below 55° F will halt growth in most varieties and cause leaves to become yellowish. Tomatoes are by far the largest selling vegetable and special attention should be given to selecting the proper varieties and growing an adequate mix of fruit types and container sizes. Peppers and cucumbers are the next most important warm vegetables. Larger pots are becoming more and more popular with this group of plants as pack sales have declined. Most crops are now produced in 3-5 inch containers but tomatoes especially are in good demand even in 8 inch pots with blossoms and green fruit. Five gallon pots with ripe tomatoes are profitable in summer if greenhouse space is not being used for other purposes.

Tomatoes are one of my favorite crops because they return a high profit. Growth is quick and easy and sales volume is high. Tomatoes and petunias in heavy supply are absolutely essential to good spring sales. Greenhouses that make a special effort to grow excellent tomato plants will draw additional customers for other products. Preparations must be made to move large volumes of plants in a short period of time. Significant tomato plant sales can be made past the main gardening season by offering 6 and 8 inch plants in quantity. These larger plants can be ready in 2 to 4 weeks from 2¼ inch material if water and fertilizer are at high levels.

Scheduling for tomato plants must be precise to take advantage of optimum sales yet prevent overgrowth. The main marketing season is short and furious with no mercy for the grower whose crop is late. Crops should be sown to be saleable every 5 to 6 days during the main season and timed one week early. If growth is normal and plants are ahead of schedule, the greenhouse can be cooled and water restricted somewhat to slow development.

Eggplant and peppers grow best a few degrees warmer than tomatoes and can be placed in the warmer areas of a vegetable house. Neither of these plants is usually grown in larger than a 4 inch pot. Eggplant will grow at approximately the same speed as tomatoes while peppers require 2 additional weeks to reach marketable size in 4 inch pots.

Cucumbers, squash, cantelope, watermelon, and pumpkins are all sown directly into the finishing pot. Typically 3 seeds are planted in a 3½ inch pot, covered with soil, then watered in. At 70° F seed will germinate in 4 to 7 days with squash and pumpkin being the earliest. If space is at a premium, the flats of pots may be stacked until germination occurs. These direct seeded plants are undoubtedly the most profitable greenhouse crop available. Marketable size is reached in 3 to 5 weeks from sowing. Cucumbers and squash are quite popular while cantelope, pumpkins, and watermelon are minor crops in most areas. Watermelon and cantelope are very sensitive to cool temperatures but the other varieties may be held back by lowering the temperature to 50°-55° F. Squash and vine plants must be handled carefully when transplanting to the garden, They will not tolerate root damage. All three plants in the pot should be planted together.

Warm vegetables thrive in full sunlight. Water and fertilizer can be restricted somewhat to maintain sturdy growth but not to the point where plants lose good green color and lower leaves become yellow. Peppers and eggplant are especially vulnerable to aphids with peppers also being subject to heavy damage by slugs. The most bothersome pests to tomatoes are whiteflies. Cutworms can damage all 3 crops when plants are grown on the floor. Clean pea gravel or plastic on the floor will usually eliminate trouble from cutworms. Allowing weeds to grow on floors during the summer is asking for cutworm problems. Melons and vine plants are seldom in the greenhouse long enough to be infested by pests. All warm vegetable seeds are favorite foods of mice and only one mouse can cause several hundred dollars damage overnight. Peppers, cantelope, and watermelon are susceptible to stem rots if greenhouse temperatures are low and excess water is applied.

A schedule for warm vegetables is presented in Table 27. Crop time lessens as the season progresses toward longer days.

Table 27

Schedules for marketing on May 20 with a growing temperature of 60° F. Latitude 43° north.

Crop	Sowing date	Pot size (inches)
Tomato	4/4	2¼
Tomato	3/20	3½
Tomato	3/5	6
Tomato	2/20	8
Pepper bell	3/21	2¼
Pepper bell	3/10	3½
Eggplant	3/22	3½
Cucumber	4/20	3½
Squash Zucchini	4/29	3½
Pumpkin	4/29	3½
Cantelope	4/20	3½
Watermelon	4/20	3½

Viola

These cheery "baby pansies" have been a favorite perennial through the years. Violas prefer full sun but will tolerate light shade in the garden. A good selection of colors is present, with apricot being one of the more exotic and popular. Most varieties have flowers a quarter the size of pansies but there is one group, called Johnny jump ups with flowers much smaller than this and possessing a more compact habit. Jump ups are one of the first harbingers of spring in the greenhouse and few customers can resist choosing a pack or two to plant out on the first fine days. Violas look very nice in the packs if the heat is kept to a minimum; late season displays may become tall and ragged quickly as the nights warm up. Jump ups bloom profusely.

Viola culture is the same as that for pansies except flowering occurs sooner and plants will generally overwinter in cold frames more easily than pansies when seed is sown in the fall. The majority of crops are now handled as conventional bedding plants without an overwinter stage. January 1 sowings of the larger flowered violas will bloom in early April and plantings of the jump ups must be delayed two weeks to flower at the same time. No cold treatment is necessary for flowering to occur but the quality of plants declines as temperatures rise with plants becoming very grassy and having few blooms.

Zinnia

Although zinnias are easy to plant from seed, gardeners increasingly prefer to buy started plants. Zinnias come in all sizes and colors and have been a favorite flower for many years. No other flowers seem to love the hot days of summer more. The taller, larger flowered types are still the most popular but short varieties with small flowers are being used increasingly for foreground planting. Zinnias are quite nice as cut flowers in the home. Short varieties such as Thumbelina can be flowered in packs but taller varieties must be sold green unless offered in 3 or 4 inch pots.

Zinnias prefer temperatures of 60°-65° F with full sun. Plants grow extremely fast and must be transplanted out of the seed flat quickly. Seeds can be sown directly to packs if a warm spot is available for germination. Overwatering will certainly lead to losses from stem rot; plants should be allowed to dry out well before the next irrigation. The major portion of zinnia crops can be transplanted after Mother's Day and still be saleable by June 1. They are one of the most profitable crops because of the short time necessary to reach marketable size.

Tall varieties for packs should be sown May 1 for late May sales as green plants. Short varieties will benefit from an extra week of growth if they are to be sold green and will require four more weeks from the green stage to flowering. State Fair is a popular tall variety whose seed is inexpensive. Dwarf varieties with larger flowers than Thumbelina sell well in 3 and 4 inch flowering pots. The seed for these short varieties with medium sized flowers is quite expensive and they are seldom offered in packs because of this. An April 1 sowing will provide 4 inch flowering pots in early June.

CHAPTER 2

FLOWERING POT PLANTS

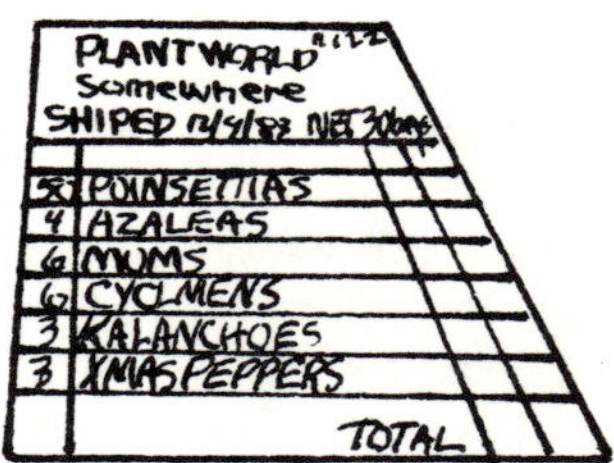

The greenhouse owner who develops a good trade in flowering pot plants will enjoy a reasonably stable year around business. Potted flowers can be raised as the main crop through the year or as a fill in crop for those who specialize in bedding plants. Year around crop schedules result in a more efficient use of buildings and equipment and also permit establishment of a permanent work force. The bedding plant producer who continues to operate for holiday potted flowers is ready to go in the spring without the need for re-opening greenhouses and cleaning away trash which has accumulated during the winter.

Growing potted plants through the year requires more technical and marketing knowledge than is necessary for temporary operations in the spring. More attention to detail must generally be given to individual potted flowers since people purchase them as gifts or for decorating and expect each plant to be perfect. The greenhouse environment in mid winter when most flowering pots are grown is not so conducive to easy growth as it is when sunlight is more abundant and temperatures higher. It is necessary for the grower to be an expert in manipulating cultural conditions to achieve good quality at this time of year. Choosing varieties which grow well at various times of the year and are the most labor efficient is an important task of the flowering plant grower. High fuel bills may cause winter operation to be unprofitable unless production is efficient and prices are maintained at levels which will compensate for increased energy use. Pest control in this season can be more difficult because weather conditions prevent adequate ventilation.

Year around growing does not fit the objectives of all people. The responsibilities entailed in caring for crops and physical facilities will prevent a person from having any extended free time unless the business is large enough to employ a responsible and capable manager. Anyone with a little knowledge and ambition can usually turn a profit in the spring when plants grow easily and market demand is tremendous. Flowering pot plant culture is more exacting and, except for holidays, demand is not overwhelming. Competition for the market is heavier and the individuals involved are generally more competent on both the growing and marketing levels. There are significant opportunities for profit in flowering pot plants but only people who develop a high degree of horticultural excellence will be assured of success. The year around market is for those individuals who desire to become professionals in the field and devote full time activity.

Marketing a limited number of flowering pot plants can be easy if a retail store is part of the greenhouse business. Developing a wholesale market is generally more difficult because most retail outlets will already have suppliers they are reluctant to abandon. Chain stores can be a source of business but they are often not authorized to buy from local growers and will be unlikely to pay top prices since the have the ability to buy on the national market at the lowest prices. Local florists and plant stores are excellent prospects because they are accustomed to paying high prices. If there are no local suppliers, these smaller shops have to pay for transport and packing. There is also an advantage in having revenues dependent upon several smaller customers rather than one or two large accounts. No one customer has a great deal of bargaining leverage. The marketing plan one develops for flowering pot plants may include a mixture of company owned stores, florist accounts, and chain stores, or anything in between.

Company stores and florists will generally create a more even flow of business while chain stores will be heavily oriented toward holidays. Florists may be difficult to sell to if the greenhouse maintains its own retail outlet since they are reluctant to buy from a competitor. It will take persistence and a good product to overcome this prejudice. The busy season for flowering pot plants begins at Thanksgiving and ends after Mother's Day. The time between these holidays becomes rather slow with the low point being reached from mid July through mid September. Thanksgiving, Christmas, Valentine's Day, Easter, and Mother's Day are the prime marketing periods but daily demand through this period is also strong. Timing crops for holidays is, needless to say, extremely critical. Secretary's Day is becoming more important every year. Other special days may bring a small increase in sales.

African Violet

The African violet has been a favorite of plant lovers for many years. Although the display of flowers and plant size are small in relation to most other blooming pot plants, the African violet lends itself to good growth and flower production in the home. A discussion of African violet culture could as well be treated under foliage varieties since the plants will continue to bloom and grow for years if given the proper care. Thousands of individuals have made hobbies or part time businesses out of growing African violets. Many people are active in breeding new varieties and will readily purchase any new types which appear on the market. The most common market size is the 4 inch pot although 3 and 5 inch pots are not uncommon. Sales of greenhouse grown plants is substantial but not so large as would be expected because so many plants are propagated at home and sold or traded by individuals. An ability to flourish under the warm, low light conditions of most homes is the reason African violets are so popular.

Temperatures for commercial production should be no less than 65° F. Plants grown cooler than this are subject to mildew, have hardened, brittle growth, and develop slowly. Light intensities in the greenhouse should be in the range of 1,000-2,000 foot candles and shading is necessary in all but the darkest winter months. Plants that receive too little light will have elongated petioles and flower lightly or not at all. Bleaching of the foliage and overly compact growth are signs of excess light. Inexpensive light meters will eliminate much of the guess work about when to shade African violets. Excellent plants can be grown under artificial light at 600 foot candles for 16 hours a day. Exposure to 24 hour lighting is not harmful but there is some question as to whether the additional length promotes further growth. Two flourescent light fixtures 4 feet long with 2 tubes each can be hung 12 inches high over a 4 foot square bench to approximate 600 foot candles. Tubes must emit the proper wavelengths of light for best growth.

Water spots and rings will form on African violet foliage when plants are irrigated overhead with water having a temperature less than 65° F. Water should be applied thoroughly after plants have been allowed to dry out. Many growers eliminate the leaf spot problem by subirrigating pots with capillary mats. The advantages of this system are sometimes outweighed by a lack of leaching and a greater chance of transmitting disease between plants. Fertilizer should be applied at half to three-quarters of normal rates since African violets are not heavy feeders and can be damaged easily by excessive soluble salts. The calcium nitrate-potassium nitrate fertilizer mix is suggested to maintain plants in a less hardened state. Plants will respond better if the rooting mix formula is substituted for growing mix when potting to final containers. African violets prefer a highly organic soil with good drainage assured by the addition of granular particles such as perlite. They will not grow well in clayey, tight soils.

Pests and diseases are not excessive if proper culture is given to plants which are clean initially. Root rot and soil nematodes can become troublesome, particularly when water is applied from a common subirrigation system. Clean soil and planting stock will control these infestations. Mildew was mentioned as being a problem when temperatures drop below 65° F. Several types of pests can affect African violets but the most devastating is the cyclamen mite. Infestations are seldom noticed until serious damage has occurred since the pests are only observable with difficulty when a 10X hand lens is used. Outward manifestations of cyclamen mites are hard, dwarfish growth of new leaves, flower buds which are malformed and fail to open, and a dense, whitish pubescence on dwarfed leaves. The hairiness of these leaves occurs because leaves fail to grow to normal size but hair growth is not restricted, thus increasing the amount of pubescence relative to surface area. On casual observation this pubescence is sometimes confused with mildew. Diazinon sprays are effective in controlling cyclamen mites but heavily infested plants are often beyond recovery.

Propagation of African violets is commonly by leaf cuttings. Seed is available for some varieties but is not often used. Leaves with an inch or two of petiole are excised from the mother plant and stuck into rooting mix with the base of the leaf slightly elevated from the soil. Roots form within a few weeks and small plantlets suitable for transferring to 2¼ inch pots will be ready within two to three months of cutting. When these containers become restrictive, a final shift can be made to 3, 4, or 5 inch pots. Multiple plantlets may have formed by this time and they can be separated if 3 inch pots are to be planted or lighter 4 inch material is desired. Some growers space cuttings more liberally and allow plants to develop in the rooting flat until potting to the final container. Flowering plants are ready from cuttings in six to eight months. Seed propagation will require ten or more months until flowering.

Violets are often a very profitable crop on a square foot basis and lend themselves more readily to local production than some other flowers since they do not ship easily. Tender leaves are readily damaged and soil particles become attached to the hairy leaves when boxes are jumbled. Cold temperatures during winter shipment can affect later growth considerably. Those growers not wishing to propagate their own plants will find a large number of suppliers capable of shipping a complete range of sizes from small plantlets to budded plants.

Azaleas

High production costs have prevented the azalea from challenging for the number one sales position in flowering plants. Azaleas remain a major crop because they are exceptionally beautiful and last for long periods in the home. Customers demand them even though the retail price may be double or more that of other potted flowers. The primary colors are red, pink, and white. There are many varieties of azaleas but only a small proportion are commonly used in the floral trade, the rest being grown by nurserymen for outdoor planting. Azalea varieties should be chosen for their suitability to bloom at particular times of the year and for larger, more desirable flowers. The better varieties will also have glossy, dark green leaves and a compact habit. For each season there will be only a few truly superb varieties which perform well under a grower's individual circumstances. To select azalea varieties for a program, one should obtain descriptive literature from suppliers and then grow a limited number of each variety to evaluate performance.

The woody cuttings of azaleas are difficult to root unless conditions are naturally optimal or special rooting beds are prepared. Some azaleas are propagated by grafting. Propagation and the early growth stages for floral trade azaleas are usually left to specialists. The present discussion will focus on culture of dormant budded plants for immediate forcing with only an outline of the earlier steps from rooted cuttings to the budded stage. Very few greenhouses propagate their own azaleas, a somewhat larger number grow them from rooted cuttings to budded stages, and the great majority purchase dormant budded plants to force.

Azaleas are graded or classed according to the diameter of the plant. A head size of 6/8 means the plant diameter is between 6 and 8 inches. The latter size is the most popular for marketing in 6 inch pots. Plants in the 6/8 range have generally been grown two years or more if only one cutting is used. Many growers have begun to use two cuttings per pot in an effort to shorten the crop cycle. The length of time capital is invested in the crop is the primary cause of azaleas being high priced. Cuttings propagated in the spring are rooted by fall. The following fall they could be sold as 4 or 5 inch pots of 4/6 head size, but most plants are grown to the second fall and sold as 6/8's in 6 inch pots.

Pinching is practiced to shape the plant and develop numerous branches for bud formation. No pinch should be given to plants after July 1 if they are to be forced for early winter flowering. This time span is necessary to allow bud formation and conditioning. Buds are formed in azaleas when temperatures remain above 65° F for at least eight weeks. A period of four to six weeks at temperatures of 40°-50° F after buds have set is necessary to condition plants for even flowering on the plant and uniform forcing of the crop. Plants must never be exposed to freezing temperatures. The conditioning phase also induces the production of multiple buds. Every effort should be made at this time to keep temperatures uniform and prevent the greenhouse from reaching more than 60° F during the day.

Major azalea producers are located in areas where these autumn conditions prevail naturally. The Pacific Northwest is especially favored for growing plants to be forced in early winter. Certain southeastern states are major producers of plants for later forcing. The cooling treatment may be artificially produced by placing plants in refrigerated structures where light is supplied to prevent leaf drop. Growers invest in this equipment so that their crops will be better timed and also to produce plants which will bloom earlier in the season. Early azalea varieties grown under natural conditions in the Pacific Northwest can normally be forced by December 1 but a few growers can supply plants which have been refrigerated to force by September 1. Year around azalea forcing is possible with plants grown and conditioned under artificially controlled temperatures, but these plants become quite expensive. Natural season azaleas are forced from Christmas to Mother's Day with plants for the later dates often being supplied by southern growers.

Chemical growth retardants and pinching agents are sometimes used on azaleas to eliminate the costly process of hand pruning. The reaction of the chemicals varies considerably with the variety and application procedure, so careful tests should be conducted before any large scale use of these materials is contemplated.

Soils for azaleas are normally composed of at least 50% sphagnum peat; many growers use pure sphagnum as a growing medium. A grade of sphagnum with chunks the size of fingertips is best for good drainage and aeration. Perlite, sand, and wood particles are sometimes mixed with sphagnum to produce an acceptable medium. Azalea soil must be acid in nature (4.0 - 5.5 pH) and low in soluble salts.

Fertilizers should be acid in reaction and have as low a salt index as possible concurrent with other required characteristics. Azaleas are light feeders and over applications of fertilizers are dangerous from the standpoint of excessive soluble salts. No more than one-half normal fertilizer concentrations should be applied during the active growing season and even less when plants are semi dormant. Leaching must be thorough at each irrigation. Applications of chelated iron will prevent chlorotic new leaves. Chlorotic conditions may arise because soil pH is high, making iron unavailable, or because the soil is too wet, preventing proper root growth. The standard calcium nitrate and potassium nitrate fertilizers recommended earlier in this book are not generally suitable for prolonged azalea growth because they are not acidic in nature. They are, however, all right to use when plants are only being forced into flower. If the forcing period is short, no fertilizer at all may be needed.

Water quality, especially as it relates to soluble salts, is extremely important in azalea culture. Long term growing of azaleas with water having a soluble salt content of more than 500 ppm should not be attempted. Forcing can be accomplished with water considerably higher in soluble salts if plants are leached at each irrigation. The content of specific minerals may also be of importance since certain of them will tend to spot the leaves of plants more so than others. Water low in soluble salts usually is not overly basic in pH but a safety check should be made to confirm this as fact. Pest and disease problems are no more acute with azaleas than other plants but the length of time they are grown until the forcing stage enhances the chance that some calamity of this nature will befall the crop if stringent precautions are not taken. Plants that are clean when received for forcing seldom experience any disease or insect problems.

Dormant azaleas should be checked carefully for signs of damage caused in transit. Drying of the root ball and freezing are the most common problems. Frozen plants may be thawed very slowly with no damage when frost is light but a claim should be filed with the transport company to assure compensation if damage becomes apparent after several days. Immediate planting will prevent a decline in quality which might occur if plants are left in the packing box too long. Much labor is saved if the pots are exactly the right size to slip plants into without removing a portion of the root ball or without adding extra soil around the edges. Plants should be watered in heavily after planting. Early fall plantings in high light areas will benefit from a light shade for several days or as long as excessive light persists.

Forcing is normally accomplished at temperatures of 60°-65° F but plants may be subjected to temperatures of 40°-70° F to slow down or increase the speed of forcing. Azaleas stored at 40° F for long periods will often develop a reddish-brown tinge to the leaves, especially on the tip. Alternating very cool night temperatures with warm day temperatures will sometimes lead to more than ordinary leaf drop. Azalea roots must never be allowed to dry out. Moisture stress, excessive soluble salts, and too high a soil pH are the leading causes of failure in the forcing process. Christmas plants are sometimes difficult to bring to flower early enough while plants for later holidays often present the problem of too rapid development. Suppliers should be asked to make certain the proper varieties are shipped for each season. Late flowering varieties simply will not force for Christmas while it is difficult to hold early flowering varieties back if they are forced for Valentine's Day and Easter.

Growers should manipulate temperatures carefully to maintain azalea crops at the proper stage for harvest. Plants are best for customers when color is showing the full length of the bud but flowers have not yet opened. Heavy shade applied to retard development will result in washed out colors when flowers are open under the shade. If soluble salt levels in irrigation water are over 500 ppm, care should be exercised to avoid spraying water on the leaves since this will result in unattractive water spots. Vegetative shoots may begin to grow around the buds of some varieties; these shoots must be removed so that flowering vigor is not reduced and flowers are not hidden by vegetation. Plants may force differently each year because growing conditions prior to shipment vary considerably from year to year. Growers should plan on plants flowering slowly; if development takes place too rapidly the temperature can be lowered. An experienced eye can be of help in judging the amount of time required for forcing. Early forcing may require four to six weeks while spring flowerings may be accomplished in as little as one week.

Begonias

The begonia family is quite large and only a few of the more popular potted flower types will be discussed. Their attraction as blooming plants in the home is due, in part, to an ability to prosper under less than full sun and at temperatures common to most homes. Fibrous rooted varieties will bloom constantly without regard to daylength or temperature while tuberous varieties generally require special cultural treatments to flower profusely. Begonias have not become a highly important crop because their succulent, brittle nature does not lend itself well to shipping long distances and both growers and consumers often consider the plants somewhat tempermental. Tuberous begonias are perhaps more demanding in their requirements and susceptible to fungal diseases than other common flowers, but for some growers they are quite easy to grow.

Local growers may find begonias a welcome addition to their program since they can be propagated easily by seed or cuttings. A well done begonia is a very attractive plant if shipping damage can be avoided. Tuberous begonias of the Reiger and Non-stop series are quite popular, as are the Lady Frances fibrous rooted types. The culture of Non-stop and fibrous rooted garden types has been dealt with in the bedding plant chapter of this book.

Reiger tuberous begonias are very showy plants with both single and double flowered varieties available. Two general types of Reiger begonias have been developed: the Schwabenland series, propagated by leaf cuttings, and the Aphrodite series, propagated by stem cuttings. Schwabenland varieties are more suitable for pot plant production while the generally less compact Aphrodites are commonly used in hanging baskets unless Cyclocel growth retardant is used. Production of 2 inch plants for transplanting to larger pots requires 8-12 weeks, depending upon growing conditions. One of these plants per 6 inch pot will flower 8-10 weeks after short day treatment begins at 65° F.

Manipulation of the daylength is essential for year around production of Reiger begonias. Photoperiodism is not especially strong or absolute but is used to allow small plants to grow to sufficient size before flowering. To prevent flowering, one additional hour is added to the natural daylength starting September 1 and an additional half hour is added every two weeks until November 15, when there should be a total of six hours artificial daylength until January 31. The artificial daylength is then reduced every two weeks in the same manner it was increased. When sufficient vegetative growth is made, plants are subjected to short days with blackcloth from 5 p.m. to 8 a.m. The critical daylength for flowers to be initiated appears to be 14 hours or less, but most growers begin a short day program in early September as is done with mums. Full sun is given in winter and light shade during summer.

Reiger begonias are not heavy feeders and will benefit if the usual calcium nitrate-potassium nitrate fertilizer is skipped every third irrigation. Slightly hungry plants will produce more flowers and the leaves will be more flexible so that they are damaged less during handling. Bacterial and fungal diseases are a major complication in Reiger begonia culture. There is no effective chemical treatment against bacterial oil spot sickness. Mildew and botrytis can be controlled chemically only when relative humidity is reduced through careful cultural practices. Waterings should not be done from overhead or late in the day. Common greenhouse pests may infest plants but their significance is negligible in comparison with the diseases just mentioned. I would recommend that, whenever possible, crops of the Non-stop series from seed be substituted for Reiger begonias. Culture is very similar but bacterial and fungal diseases are not a major problem. Exact schedules for growing winter crops of Non-stops are not available but one could perhaps adopt a similar lighting program, as for Reigers, and observe the results in test plantings.

An everblooming, fibrous rooted type of begonia known as the Lady Frances is a good year around crop for local growers. The flowers are fully double and the foliage is dark bronze. Flowering plants are produced from rooted cuttings in 12 weeks at 62° F during winter. Cuttings are planted three or four to a 6 inch pot and pinched once to produce heavy material. Many growers prefer to put their main production into 4 inch pots. Full sun is beneficial at all times except mid summer. Pests and diseases are seldom troublesome. A lack of branching can sometimes be encountered if cuttings are taken from flowering stems which lack side shoots. This problem is eliminated if only cuttings with a small vegetative shoot present in the leaf axil are taken.

Bulb Plants

Tulips, hyacinths, crocus, and daffodils are cheery reminders that spring is not far away. They have been important pot plants for many years but their popularity is declining as longer lasting crops, such as chrysanthemums, take a greater share of the market. The main advantage of bulb plants to a greenhouse program is that they can be forced in a short period of time. If a grower can schedule successive plantings of bulb plants or has only a limited block of time available, these crops can be profitable. The initial cost of bulbs is quite high and is compensated for in the selling price by the relatively short time greenhouse space is occupied. To flower properly, bulb plants require a cool temperature regime prior to forcing. The time honored way of providing these conditions was to bury potted bulbs in ground beds outside in the fall and dig them up as needed. This method is laborious and not conducive to profitable production. Controlled temperature rooms either under or above ground now are used to provide the cool, dark conditions necessary in a more efficient manner.

Spring bulbs normally arrive in the fall with flower parts already formed inside the bulb. The cooling period is not necessary to form flowers, as many people believe, but rather to allow formation of a large root system and bring about physiological changes which will assure rapid forcing, longer stems, and larger flowers. Bulbs must be stored at 55°-65° F when they arrive. Extremes of temperature in storage or transit can seriously affect bulb performance later. Large bulb forcers rely on elaborate temperature schedules and cooling rooms for precise control over their crops. The following discussion will assume that the cooling room is located underground and cools naturally to a point just above freezing during mid-winter; no special temperature control is used unless the room is in danger of freezing.

Bulbs are planted in mid October in azalea pots or shallow bulb pans. A sufficient number should be used to give the pot a full appearance at flowering. Six inch pots of tulips will require six or seven bulbs, hyacinths three or four, and daffodils three or four. Crocus in 4 inch pots will take four or five bulbs. Only larger bulbs should be used for forcing and varieties must be chosen carefully for their suitability to force properly as pot plants at the designated flowering date. Bulbs must be planted rather than pressed into the soil. Pressing the bulb in compacts soil underneath and when roots form they push the bulb out of the soil because they cannot grow into the compacted soil easily. Heavy soils are unsuitable for bulb plants. The nose of bulbs should be above the soil line.

Pots are watered in heavily and then placed in the cooling room. Light must not be admitted on a continuous basis or shoots will become too long. Pots should be kept moist but excessive water will cause rotting of the bulbs. If mold appears on the nose of bulbs, a drench of fungicide can be applied. Cooling room temperatures should be at approximately 45°-50° F by early November. If the autumn has been particularly warm, some night air may be admitted to cool underground rooms sufficiently. Forcing may begin after January 1 on early varieties. If they are ready to force, tulips will be one or two inches tall and exhibit a small bulge at the shoot base where the immature flower is. Other varieties will exhibit at least one inch of growth. Mid winter temperatures in the cooling room should be low enough to hold further growth to a minimum for those plants intended for later blooming.

The following forcing temperatures are suitable: crocus 55° F, daffodil 62° F, hyacinth 65° F, and tulips 62° F. More or less heat may be applied to meet schedules but drastic lowering of temperatures to hold plants back should be practiced only after buds are visible. Shading is sometimes applied if stem length is not sufficient. Spring bulbs seldom need fertilizer since they have sufficient stored foods to flower properly. Crops of tulips and daffodils brought into the greenhouse in early January will require three to four weeks to become saleable and hyacinths and crocus about two weeks. A week of extra time is often allowed for safety. Plants maturing too early can be stored slightly above freezing for several weeks.

Diseases are seldom a major problem with spring bulbs if they were not infected prior to receipt. All bulbs showing evidence of rot or being shriveled should be discarded. Botrytis is troublesome unless adequate ventilation is given and proper watering practices are followed. Aphids will become established on succulent new buds if sources of infestation are present. Customers enjoy bulb plants more if they are marketed as soon as slight color is apparent in the most advanced buds. Flowers already open at the time of sale have but a short life span.

Bulbs should be purchased only from reliable suppliers to lessen the chances of crop failure due to improper handling or disease. Suppliers will also be able to advise growers concerning the proper varieties to force for particular dates. The list of varieties is enormous, especially in tulips, with relatively few being suitable for pot plants.

Calceolaria

Ladies' pocket book plant or Japanese lantern are the common names for these cool loving shade plants. The distinctively shaped flowers provide some relief from other more common potted flowers in mid winter and early spring. Lasting quality of calceolarias in homes and flower shops is not especially good unless room temperatures are less than 60° F at night. Mother's Day crops are often of poor quality since greenhouse temperatures in late spring are generally too high. An ability to prosper under low temperatures and light conditions make calceolarias a natural for winter weather. Common flower colors are yellow, red, and orange shades. Yellow flowers are less susceptible to sun burn and hold up better under late spring conditions.

Calceolaria seed is fine and should not be covered with the medium. Seedlings are transplanted to 2¼ inch pots after germination and grown at 60° F until potting to 5 or 6 inch pots. Calceolarias will not initiate flowers at 60° F or higher. Heavy bud set is assured if temperatures are dropped to 50° F at the time plants are transferred to larger pots. When buds are apparent, temperatures may be raised to speed forcing if necessary. Flowering can be speeded by artificial lighting, but plants may become spindly and soft under these conditions. Full sun is given in northern greenhouses except during early fall and late spring. Some light shade should be kept on hand to prevent flower burn if abnormally clear, warm weather arrives early.

Irrigation of calceolarias must be carefully restricted to prevent stem rot, but plants should not be allowed to wilt. The rooting mix formula for growing on will provide a more porous medium to reduce the incidence of overwatering and soluble salt buildup. Poor growth is frequently encountered when water sources are high in soluble salts unless plants are grown in a porous soil mix and periodic leaching is practiced. The potassium nitrate fertilizer mix should be used after plants have attained good size to prevent the luxuriant growth which can occur with high nitrogen fertilizers and to lower the amount of salts added to irrigation water. Aphids love calceolarias and careful control must be practiced from the very beginning. Temik applied at the rate of 1/8 level teaspoon per 6 inch pot twice during the growing period will eliminate serious outbreaks. Granules must be watered in heavily to prevent foliage burn since calceolarias are somewhat sensitive to Temik. Early infestations are detected by looking for aphids on the undersides of leaves rather than waiting until the pests are apparent on flowers and stems. Heavily infested plants should be discarded.

The variety Brite and Early mix can be flowered for Valentine's Day in 6 inch pots from a late August sowing if temperatures are returned to 60° F after buds have appeared. Growers who wish to flower in 4 inch pots should germinate seed later and subject plants to cool temperatures at an earlier stage. Crops blooming after April 15 may require special provisions to keep them cool and shady.

Christmas Cactus

The literature concerning variety names and flower initiation is very confused for this group of plants. Basically, there are those plants which begin to bloom in mid October (Thanksgiving cactus) and those which begin flowering shortly after Christmas (Christmas cactus or sometimes referred to as Easter cactus). These blooming dates assume natural daylengths and 60° F temperatures at latitudes in the northern United States. Those plants commonly sold for the Christmas holidays are Thanksgiving cactus and their leaves have sawtooth like margins with the teeth pointed somewhat forward. Christmas cactus have rounded points on the leaf margin.

Most plants are sold at the Christmas season in 3 or 4 inch pots. Hanging baskets and 6 inch pots are less common. Demand for plants in October, November, and after Christmas is steady but not exceptional. The Christmas cactus with rounded points on the leaves is more spreading in habit and looks better in hanging baskets. Blooms last only a few days but a steady succession keeps plants saleable for several weeks. After buds have become visible on Thanksgiving cactus, plants may be moved to cooler locations to hold them until nearer the Christmas season. Growers who wish to experiment might start Christmas cactus on short days September 1 to observe if these plants will be more acceptable for Christmas sales than Thanksgiving cactus which are held back.

Both daylength and temperature affect flower initiation. Some authors cite temperature as the major `inductive factor while others favor daylength. The only program which should be depended on until practical experience dictates otherwise is growing at 60° F with natural daylengths. The two factors are likely to be interrelated in their action and may have different effects on the two groups of plants.

Both Christmas and Thanksgiving cactus are natives of Brazilian tropical forests and do not flourish under excessively dry or bright conditions. It has often been suggested that the plants be kept on the dry side during flower initiation but adequate moisture should be provided at other times. Light shade is helpful during the summer months. The rooting mix soil formula is suitable for these plants with the calcium nitrate-potassium nitrate fertilizer program being used infrequently since the plants grow slowly. Pests and diseases are seldom troublesome unless precautionary measures are neglected.

Both groups of plants root very easily and can be stuck directly into the final container if weather is warm. A joint of three or four leaves is detached from the mother plant and the lower leaf is inserted into the medium about half its length. Flowering 3 inch pots should be propagated in early spring or at the latest by early summer if bedding plants are not yet gone. The later propagations must include several plants per pot since little vegetative growth can be expected before flower initiation occurs. Pots larger than 4 inch may need to be grown more than one summer season to develop a suitable shape. The need for large numbers of stock plants to be carried over in the greenhouse often renders production of Christmas cactus unprofitable unless the climate is such that stock plants can be grown outside.

Christmas Pepper

These easy to grow plants become covered with bright red and cream colored fruits shortly before the Christmas holidays. Demand is rather limited and does not hold up after the holiday season. There are numerous varieties with different shapes of fruit but all require similar culture. Small white blossoms and deep green foliage contrast nicely with the red fruits.

Christmas peppers grow well in the warm days of summer and fall without additional heat, but as cold weather approaches they should be maintained at a minimum of 50° F when fruits have already become visible. If fruits have not yet formed, a 60° F temperature will be necessary. Full sunlight is required at all times. Plants will use large amounts of water in the summer but care must be taken to reduce irrigations as light levels decline in fall. The calcium nitrate-potassium nitrate fertilizer formula is used until plants have reached adequate size; after this stage the potassium nitrate formula will prevent excessive vegetative growth from covering up fruits. Two applications of B-9 growth retardant at concentrations of 0.25% are usually required to develop a nice bushy shape. Attack by aphids is troublesome if Temik is not applied on a regular basis. This treatment will also guard against whitefly infestations.

The variety Holiday Cheer has unusual round fruits and a compact growth habit. Sowings of this variety in early June will produce well colored plants in 6 inch pots by November 1 if fall temperatures are maintained at 60° F. Some growers prefer to start plants later and offer inexpensive 4 and 5 inch pots. No pinching is required for either program. Fruits on other varieties are more often cone shaped or tapered in the manner of edible peppers. Ornamental pepper can also be offered as small bedding plants in the spring.

Chrysanthemum

Chrysanthemums now reign supreme as the most important year around potted flower crop. The mum, like petunias in outdoor plants, has been the catalyst for a revolution in floriculture. Mum plants are vigorous growers, are predictable in flowering response, last a long time in bloom, ship well, and come in a large number of flower colors and shapes. Few other flowering pot plants can match the degree of favorable characteristics possessed by chrysanthemums. Even so, it is doubtful if such a level of popularity would have been reached if it were not for the commitment several large propagators made in making quality mum cuttings available on a year around basis.

The majority of mum plants are produced by medium to large greenhouses which have substantial wholesale business. The necessity of shipping cuttings in and providing artificial daylengths dictates that this crop is more suited to situations where a large number of pots can be grown on a regular basis. Small retail growers will find that mums, especially on a year around basis, may prove less profitable than other crops. Plantings of less than 50 pots every two weeks are often considered uneconomical by trade experts. I will show readers some methods whereby cuttings can be shipped on a less frequent basis with acceptable results. Smaller growers should deliberate carefully before beginning a mum program. Although these plants are the mainstay of the industry and are admirably suited to production line methods, they are not recommended for every operation.

Production figures may also be somewhat misleading. Supermarkets and chain stores are the premier marketers of mum plants while traditional florists and garden centers generally place less emphasis on them. Depending upon the type of market, a grower may wish to specialize in mum production or forego their culture altogether. In many cases, it is more sensible to contract with another grower to purchase mums for the limited number needed and concentrate efforts on crops more suitable for the situation at hand. Traditional retail outlets may find that their customers avoid mum plants because of their association with mass market outlets and because people simply get tired of looking at them day in and day out. Every retail florist will have a significant demand for mums but it may be much less than would be expected from national production figures.

The literature and cultural details concerning chrysanthemums is voluminous. An entire book could be written to cover their production in a thorough manner. It will be the objective of the present discussion to acquaint readers with basic cultural practices and alternatives. Growers wishing more information on scheduling and the fine points of culture under specific programs will do well to contact the mum planning department of horticultural supply houses or request the technical bulletins available from major propagators.

Chrysanthemums are a joy to grow because they respond wonderfully when proper environmental conditions are provided. Growing facilities for mums must have high light conditions, the ability to manipulate daylengths, and a capability of maintaining 60° F minimum temperatures at all times in the growing season. Plants grown under good conditions with attention to detail are predictably of high quality while those suffering from poor conditions will fail to bloom altogether or be of such poor quality as to render them unmarketable. Mum growers must educate themselves about cultural details if they expect to produce high quality at minimum cost. The number of varieties offered by propagators is bewildering and thorough study should precede selection of varieties. If salesmen or mum planning services are relied upon to recommend specific varieties, they should be given adequate information about objectives of the program and the facilities available, Final responsibility for approving a selection of varieties will always rest with the grower and poor crops cannot be blamed on mistakes made by someone else.

The cultural requirement which affects the timing and occurrence of flowering in chrysanthemums most significantly is daylength. It is appropriate that mum growers have a good general understanding of this important topic. Chrysanthemums are known as short day plants; that is, they initiate flowers when day lengths are shorter than a certain critical length. The true critical daylength differs with the variety but, as a practical matter, 12 hours or less has been adopted by the trade as the effective meaning when this term is applied to chrysanthemums. Short days are needed both to initiate and develop flowers; exposure to long days before buds have begun to show color can cause serious problems with flowering. Development of crown buds is caused when short days are given to initiate flowers but not continued long enough for flowers to fully mature. Crown buds are merely buds which have differentiated to the point where the floral center is present in a semi developed stage but petals are not.

Interrupted lighting of the type just described is sometimes used as a cultural practice to modify the shape of flower heads, mostly in cut mum programs where spray varieties are concerned. In these cases short days are used to initiate flowers, then a series of long days is given, followed by a return to short days. Interrupted lighting is not to be confused with the practice of cyclic lighting. Cyclic lighting programs have been developed which enable growers to switch lights on for brief moments during a specified period instead of leaving the lights on for the entire duration. This practice reduces the amount of energy consumed in providing artificial long days.

Mum varieties are described according to the number of weeks required for flowering after the start of short days when grown at 60° F. Rapidly flowering varieties initiate and develop flowers at longer daylengths than do slower flowering varieties. As an example, 6 week garden mums have a critical daylength of 16 hours or less while 15 week cut flower varieties have a critical daylength of 11 hours or less. Knowledge of the variance in critical daylengths may sometimes enable the grower to understand apparently abnormal flowering behavior. Blind acceptance of the widely publicized 12 hour critical daylength for mums can occasionally lead to misunderstandings, particularly when one is dealing with extremely fast or slow flowering varieties. The vast majority of pot mums are of the 9 and 10 week varieties and their critical daylength closely approximates 12 hours.

Provision for proper daylengths is made by following the lighting and shading methods described earlier in this book when light factors were discussed. The important practical consideration to remember is that mum flowers initiate and develop when the daylength, either artificial or natural, is less than 12 hours. This means shading for daylength control starts March 15 and ends September 15. The period between September 15 and March 15 has naturally short days. When shading is not to be used after March 15, the crop in progress must have flowers to the point of color or development may be arrested. Shading is normally done from quitting time at 5 or 5:30 p.m. to 8 a.m., but, if at all possible, shading in hot weather should be delayed until 6:30 or 7 p.m. to prevent heat buildup under the blackcloth. Pulling the blackcloth may be omitted one day a week without serious consequences or delays.

Artificial lighting must be practiced if the objective is to keep plants vegetative. Recommendations vary concerning the optimum length of light periods and the time of year they must be provided. The following light schedule will be adequate: four hours for October through March, three hours for April through May and August through September, and two hours for June and July. Several of these months are technically long day, but lighting is recommended to prevent any possibility of premature bud set. The lighting period should occur as close to the middle of the night as possible. Be sure lighting does not affect other crops in the same greenhouse or adjacent ones. Lighting is practiced so that plants will remain vegetative while becoming established. Especially short varieties can be given a longer light period to increase stem length before short days are permitted to induce flowering. Stock plants must, of course, be kept in a vegetative state at all times.

Mum propagators have made life simple for growers by compiling detailed schedules to follow during each calendar year. These schedules can be obtained by contacting the propagators or the plant broker. Caution should be exercised in relying on these timetables. Crop maturity can be altered considerably by latitude, light conditions, season of growth, and general growing practices. Informed growers will modify the schedules to fit their particular circumstances.

The temperature mums are exposed to not only affects the speed of vegetative growth but also the initiation and development of flowers. Some authors are of the opinion that adverse temperatures only delay flowering while others state that flowering can be totally prevented when temperatures depart too far from the generally accepted 60°-62° F growing range. Small variations from the optimum temperatures generally result in uneven bud set and development. Lowering of temperatures affects flowering more seriously than does an equal upward adjustment, but higher temperatures can cause spindly growth which renders plants unsaleable. The temperature the cuttings were grown at can also alter the speed of flowering.

The interaction of temperature and photoperiod probably is considerably more complicated than commonly thought but need not trouble the practical grower if suggested daylength schedules and temperature regimes are followed. An ideal temperature program is to start cuttings in the first week at 65° F then grow on at 60° F until a strong flower color develops. The temperature can then be dropped to as low as 50° F to intensify and brighten colors. Certain varieties may react in an adverse manner to lowering temperatures as color develops. White flowers often tend to "pink" under cool conditions and yellow flowers may take on a bronze hue. Petal and flower shapes may also change somewhat under cool finishing temperatures.

Higher light intensities for mums translate into better quality. Shade is sometimes applied at the flowering stage in mid summer but maximum light is essential at all other times. Quality chrysanthemums simply cannot be grown in houses with poor light transmission or if plants are spaced too closely. Mums grown under low light situations will be tall and spindly and lack sufficient size. Some mum varieties perform well in winter while others do better in summer. A great deal of this differenece in performance results from a particular variety's ability to prosper under the lower or higher light intensities prevalent during a season. Descriptions of mum varieties in propagator's catalogs will indicate which months of the year a particular variety may be grown with success.

Most growers put newly potted cuttings in full sunlight. Several light waterings a day for the first week will keep cuttings turgid until roots become established. Winter crops will need only an initial watering to prevent wilting. Mums grow rapidly and require large amounts of water. Summer crops may need two or three irrigations a day if the soil is porous. Water must be kept out of the blooms if botrytis is to be avoided. The calcium nitrate-potassium nitrate fertilizer formula should be used. Potassium nitrate applied alone will reduce height but overall plant and flower size is reduced to an unacceptable level. Growers who apply higher levels of nitrogen in relation to potassium than is contained in the calcium nitrate-potassium nitrate formula may find that growth is overly lush and plants could require some form of support. Fast growing mum plants love heavy applications of potassium and will quickly develop characteristic necrotic spots on older leaf margins if sufficient quantities of this element are not present. The large amounts of water and fertilizers given to mums will require that some leaching takes place at each watering or that heavy leaching be done at least twice during each crop. High soluble salt damage shows up first as a yellowish scorch of lower leaf margins which quickly progresses to brown as the tissue dies. To the neophyte potassium deficiency and soluble salt damage may appear similar in mums, but potassium deficiency is characterized by localized dead spots on the leaf margin rather than generalized death of the edges.

Chrysanthemum crops generally develop few disease problems if propagators ship clean cuttings. Stem blights and wilts can be troublesome when stock plants and rooting areas are not free of these diseases. Any grower having an appreciable number of wilted or stunted plants should first make sure sanitation in the greenhouse is adequate and, if the problem persists, contact the propagator so that the disease may be tracked down. High humidity at flowering time may lead to outbreaks of botrytis on the flowers. Many common greenhouse pests will attack chrysanthemums, but aphids and leaf miners are the most persistent threats. Preventive application of Temik at the rate of a level 1/8 teaspoon per 6 inch pot will eliminate both aphids and leaf miners. Plants should be well rooted before Temik is applied and watered heavily afterwards. Mums are sensitive to Temik and lower leaves will burn severely if procedures are not followed carefully. The practice of broadcasting Temik over the tops of plants creates a serious health hazard and should be avoided.

Cuttings must be planted and established in the proper environmental conditions immediately. The basic 6 inch pot of pinched mums is planted four or five cuttings per pot. Three cuttings may suffice if the variety is extremely vigorous and light conditions are excellent. Cuttings are pointed slightly outward and arranged in a circle at the edges of the pot. This arrangement allows plenty of light and air to enter the center so that inside branches develop well. Slanting the cuttings outward tends to broaden the plant's shape. Firming the soil more than is necessary to assure proper anchoring will result in reduced growth, particularly in the early stages.

Most pot mums are grown as pinched plants. The date of pinching after planting is governed more by plant growth than it is by any specific date. Roots should be well established and at least one inch of new top growth made before pinching. A fourth to a half inch of the stem tip should be removed when a pinch is made. It is important to remember that this measurement refers to the stem tip rather than the immature leaves. Unless the actual growing tip enclosed by leaves is removed, the plant will continue growing without branching. A delayed pinch is sometimes made in an effort to reduce plant height. Plants pinched long before short days begin will be taller than those pinched closer to or after the start of short days. Delayed pinches made after the start of short days result in longer crop cycles.

Excessive height is a common cultural problem in mums. The height of many otherwise fine varieties cannot be controlled by normal greenhouse practices and chemical growth retardants must be administered. B-9 is the most commonly used growth regulant on chrysanthemums but the brand A-Rest has been used successfully. Applications of B-9 are usually made on pinched plants when new growth is one to two inches long or approximately two weeks after pinching. Propagators may recommend delayed applications of B-9 for those varieties which are especially sensitive to its effects. The normal B-9 concentration applied is a 0.25% spray. A second treatment may be required right after disbudding on especially tall varieties. It is important that overhead watering not take place for 24 hours after application to avoid dilution or washing off of the chemical.

Disbudding of mums is a tedious process and adds considerably to the cost of production. All side buds are removed on most pot mums, leaving only the terminal bud on each branch. This is done so that the terminal bud develops a large exhibition bloom and is not crowded out by competition from side buds. Daisy mums and certain small flowered varieties are often treated in the opposite manner; the terminal bud is removed and the side buds are left. This practice results in a more attractive pot and considerably reduces labor costs for these varieties.

A modification of this center bud removal technique is sometimes practiced when too many flowers remain on the plant or flower stems do not elongate enough and a "club" of flowers develops at the stem tip. Removal of multiple buds reduces the number of flowers and if done early, when buds are only slightly visible, will result in an opening up of the flower head by allowing flower stems to grow longer. This technique also saves labor since the tip buds may be pinched off in one movement rather than being rolled out individually. Multiple bud removal can be practiced on some varieties of larger flowered mums which do not have a pleasing appearance when only the terminal or center bud is removed.

Descriptions of mum varieties refer to plants as being adaptable to a short, medium, or tall treatment. In general, what this means is that varieties are planted and, as a consequence, pinched at different dates in relation to the beginning of short days. Tall varieties are planted later in relation to the beginning of short days and subjected to the delayed pinching discussed earlier. Varieties listed for tall treatment will require two B-9 applications at most times and must be spaced well. It should be obvious that a continuation of long days after pinching on pinched plants or after planting on single stem plants will result in taller plants.

Many growers include a substantial number of 4 inch pots in their production program, especially if they market to chain stores. Some demand also exists for plants larger than 6 inch. Several different flower forms are grown. Large decorative type blooms are the most common and represent what most people think of as a mum. Daisy and spider flowered types are frequently grown to provide variety. Varieties with large incurved flowers (often termed football mums) are sometimes included in programs where plants are grown single stem. Yellow is the most popular flower color on a year around basis, but each holiday will require alteration of color proportions. White is popular at Christmas, but purple and lavender are preferred during the Easter season. All shades of bronze, red, and yellow are grown extensively for autumn. Selecting the proper varieties for the season and for the particular mum program can make the difference between success and failure. One variety may be absolutely beautiful under certain conditions while another is unsaleable.

Large growers have little trouble in developing a profitable mum program but smaller greenhouses may need to consider some of the options presented below to reduce shipping and labor costs and to stagger the flowering period of a crop. Air freight is a large part of the small grower's cost in purchasing cuttings. More cuttings can be shipped at one time for the same total freight cost by planting some cuttings as single stem pots and subjecting them to short days immediately, growing a second group of cuttings on a normal pinched plant schedule, and growing a third group as delayed pinch plants. If one half the last group planted is moved to cool conditions once color is evident, the cutting shipment will have been broken up into four different flowering dates rather than the customary one.

Staggering the bloom date may be accomplished by manipulating daylength, pinching dates, disbudding methods, storage temperatures at the bloom stage, and variety selection. Multiple bud removal will delay flowering at least two weeks over leaving only the terminal bud and one week over removing the center bud. The mum program of a small grower may be considerably more complicated than that of a large grower and variety selection will have to be done carefully to fit some of the optional treatments mentioned.

Previous references to single stem plants may require an explanation. Some mum varieties, particularly those with large flowers, are suitable to grow as pot plants without pinching. Generally only the terminal bud is left. Single stem 6 inch pots require at least six cuttings and preferably seven. Single stem growth usually results in very large exhibition flowers which make up for the lack in numbers. Crop time is shortened by one or two weeks over pinched plants and this compensates for the extra cuttings required. Labor is reduced because 7 stems are disbudded rather than the 12 to 15 stems on pinched plants. Pinching costs are eliminated. A new wrinkle in single stem cultures would be to grow smaller flowered types but practice multiple bud removal and perhaps cut back on the number of cuttings to five.

Small growers may wish to include production of potted spray mums for cut flowers in their program. This option will also increase the number of cuttings shipped at each date and thus reduce freight cost per cutting. Five cuttings for single stem crops or three for pinched crops are arranged at the edge of a 6 inch pot. B-9 may or may not be needed. Some support for plants will be needed if long stems are required for the market. Center bud removal is practiced. Standard mums (single large exhibition cut flowers) can be grown in the same manner with normal disbudding but spray mums are much more useful in everyday floral work.

Cineraria

Cinerarias are an important crop in winter and early spring when their ability to prosper at cool temperatures is an advantage over other crops which require more heat. The plants are received by consumers quite well and will last for two to three weeks in the home at 65° F. Cinerarias are very colorful, becoming covered with a mass of daisy like flowers. Blue shades are most common but many other flower colors will be encountered. Flowers with white eyes seem to be more popular than solid colors. The quality of plants begins to suffer as greenhouse temperatures become warmer in late April and May. Well grown cinerarias will find a ready market which, combined with their ease of culture, makes them a profitable crop.

Cinerarias require exposure to temperatures of less than 60° F for approximately six weeks in order to develop flower buds. Temperatures before and after flower initiation may be higher. Typically, seedlings are transplanted to 2¼ inch pots and grown at 60°-63° F until they are shifted to 6 inch pots when the temperature is dropped to 50° to 55° F. After buds have become visible, plants may be forced at 60°-63° F, if necessary, to meet time schedules. Excessive heat will result in soft growth and washed out colors in the flowers. Lighting to provide long days accelerates flowering but growth will become spindly unless high intensities are provided.

Cinerarias require full sun in winter but will benefit from light shade in early fall and toward the end of April. Late crops are difficult to keep watered on sunny spring days. Heavy plants have a large leaf area and transpire generous quantities of water. Bright, sunny days after periods of dark weather cause cinerarias to wilt even though the soil is saturated; plants will recover overnight and will cease to wilt after becoming accustomed to brighter weather.

The calcium nitrate-potassium nitrate fertilizer formula should be used on young plants until they cover the surface of the final pot. Potassium nitrate may then be used alone to prevent excessively lush vegetative growth which can partially obscure flowers. Being too generous with fertilizer and failing to initiate low temperatures early enough can result in extremely large plants which are unprofitable because they occupy too much bench space. This situation most often occurs with early crops because temperatures have not dropped low enough in fall to begin flower initiation. If leaf color is not green enough it may be beneficial to make light applications of chelated iron in conjunction with the regular fertilizer program. Heavy irrigations are necessary when plants have become established but soil should be allowed to dry out somewhat before repeating. Although cinerarias use large quantities of water they do not enjoy wet feet. Constantly wet soil will result in stem and root rot. Neophyte growers often overwater cinerarias when wilting occurs on sunny days. If the soil is wet, no amount of irrigating will cause plants to become turgid. Only a reduction in sunlight will be of benefit.

Aphids can become very troublesome if early precautions are not taken. Young plants should be sprayed often with a systemic insecticide such as Orthene. After roots are well established in the final pot, Temik may be applied at the rate of 1/8 level teaspoon per 6 inch pot. Cinerarias are sensitive to Temik and must be watered heavily after applications. Some lower leaves will generally develop dead spots one to two weeks after application and should be removed. Damage to a few lower leaves is not serious since it is usually of benefit to remove large, succulent first leaves anyway; they occupy a great deal of bench space and do not add to the appearance of the plant. Lower leaf removal should take place when plants are relatively immature so the remaining leaves have a chance to cover the holes before marketing.

Aphids establish themselves on flower stalks and the lower surface of leaves. When plants become heavily infested, it is best to discard them quickly before pests move to adjoining pots. It is absolutely necessary to have cineraria houses completely free of aphids before the crop is moved in. Careless handling of the aphid problem can lead to an entire crop's being unsaleable.

Some growers advocate the use of B-9 to cut down the size of cineraria plants and allow closer spacing. The same objective can be achieved by dropping temperatures earlier to induce flowering and by using straight potassium nitrate fertilizer sooner to reduce vegetative growth. These same cultural procedures can be used if one wishes to grow plants in 4 inch pots for mass market sales. Large 6 inch pots of Improved Festival will be ready for Valentine's Day if seed is sown August 21 and temperatures are raised to 62° F after buds are visible in the growing tip. Blooming plants may be ready sooner if earlier maturing varieties are used. If large plants are desired, care must be taken to allow adequate vegetative growth before lowering temperatures on later crops.

Cyclamen

Few potted flowers have undergone such radical changes in growing procedures as have cyclamens in the last decade. Cyclamens have always been popular at Christmas but the market for them has now been extended from early November through March. Their increasing popularity can be traced to two factors: a general lowering of home temperatures which favors cyclamen's keeping quality, and a reduction in the time necessary for growing which makes their price more competitive with other flowers. The first energy crisis in 1973 induced homeowners to lower their thermometers and at the same time spurred growers to emphasize winter crops which could tolerate cooler greenhouse temperatures. New hybrids which flower seven to nine months from sowing with careful culture eliminated at least six months from the traditional cyclamen schedule.

Cyclamens have a distinctive flower with reflexed petals which is very attractive. Flower color ranges from white through pink, red, and some deep lavender strains. The colors are generally very soft and some strains exhibit two tone patterns. Many people consider the leaves of cyclamens almost as attractive as the flowers. Leaves are fleshy and rounded with a green background coloration. Light green or greyish-green zones interrupt the green background to produce pleasing patterns. The low, rounded habit of cyclamens makes them a favorite for coffee tables and other locations where a compact form is necessary.

Cyclamens will tolerate a wide range of temperatures and still produce acceptable crops. The optimum regime for fast crops with F_1 hybrids is to carry seedlings at 65° F through the spring and summer months until transplanting to 6 inch pots when temperatures are dropped to 60° F. Winter crops should be scheduled so that essentially all major growth has taken place by December and plants may be kept at 50° F or even lower. Colder temperatures do not harm the plants but may subject them to a shock when moved to 65°-70° F flower shops. If the greenhouse warms up to 60° F in the daytime, there should be no problem. Plants grown at cold temperatures must also receive plenty of space for ventilation and must be watered carefully. Rotting of leaf and flower stems will occur quickly if humidity is not controlled.

Cyclamen plants form a roundish, fleshy corm from which leaves and flower stalks originate. The top half of this corm should be above the soil line when planted so that water does not collect at the base of leaf and flower stems. Soft rot will be troublesome if corms are planted deep, especially at colder temperatures.

Summertime day temperatures over 85° F are not conducive to good growth but the intense sunlight is even more damaging. Medium shade is beneficial in high light areas. No shade is recommended from late September through March. Cyclamens prefer a moist but not waterlogged soil; good porosity is therefore essential. Overhead irrigation with water high in mineral salts will result in dull leaves with a mineral film covering their surface. It is best to water from below the leaf surface. Waterings should be thorough but infrequent to lessen the humidity around the crown of the corm. Using the calcium nitrate-potassium nitrate fertilizer formula will result in a good amount of well colored leaves without harming flower production. Cyclamens are not heavy feeders.

Flowering may be, in part, controlled by daylength since even large plants fail to flower much in summer but return to bloom in late fall. The flowering mechanism is generally of no consequence to practical growers since plants bloom well in the growing season without special treatment. Large growers may benefit by spraying plants one or two times with gibberellic acid at 100 ppm. Flowers are produced in a heavy flush by this treatment and flower stalks become longer to elevate blossoms well above the foliage. Care must be exercised to limit overexposure since flower stalks can become excessively long and fall over. It is reported that crops will flower more speedily and evenly with gibberellic acid applications.

With the exception of crown rot, which has been mentioned as being troublesome when humidity levels rise during cold weather, cyclamens are not especially prone to diseases. Spider mites and cyclamen mites can cause serious problems unless growers keep a careful lookout. Both of these pests are likely to cause irreparable damage before being noticed unless a preventive spray program is instituted. Spider mites are controlled by periodic treatments with Pentac; the spray must cover the undersides of leaves. Diazinon spray will prevent cyclamen mite infestations. Both of these spray programs are best administered when plants are young so that the active ingredient can easily reach all parts of the plant. Treatments when plants are large with a dense leaf cover are ineffective.

March 1 seedings will produce 6 inch flowering pots by November 1 if fast crop varieties and temperature schedules are utilized. Sowings every two to three weeks over a 2½ month interval will ensure a progression of bloom dates through March of the next year. Finishing temperatures of the second and succeeding plantings are lowered to 50° F as winter arrives.

Cyclamen seed is not easy to germinate and the seed of newer F_1 hybrid varieties is very expensive. Good germination can be obtained if the following practices are followed. Place seed in a vial of hot tap water and allow to soak overnight; this removes germination inhibitors present in the seedcoat. Plant in rooting mix with 1 inch spacing between seeds. Cover seeds with ¼ to ½ inches of medium; germination will not occur if light penetrates to the seeds. Keep the medium constantly moist at 70° F for 45 days. Germination occurs over a period of time but at the end of three months approximately 80% success should be obtained. Seedlings are allowed to grow in the flats until they become crowded. Plants are then transplanted to 3 or 4 inch containers with the top half of the corm above the soil.

Some growers offer 4 inch flowering pots for market. Dwarf strains are better for this purpose but regular size varieties can also be used.

Many wholesale greenhouses offer 3 or 4 inch cyclamen plants for sale to other growers as growing on stock in the fall. The beauty of producing plants for this market is that space is occupied almost entirely in the slow summer season when heating costs are low. Small growers may wish to purchase these young plants rather than bother with germinating a few seeds and carrying plants through the summer.

Gloxinia

Gloxinias are a highly profitable crop when grown under proper conditions. Local growers will find a ready market because gloxinias are difficult to ship. The large leaves and delicate flowers damage easily when being sleeved or boxed. A profusion of large, bell shaped flowers make gloxinias very showy. Colors are deep and rich and occur in all shades of red, pink, blue, and white. Two tone colored strains are also available. Gloxinias last well under home conditions due to their tolerance of temperatures over 65° F and low light conditions. Traditional florist outlets are particularly fond of gloxinias since they are not commonly found in chain store displays because of their poor shipping characteristics.

I believe gloxinias are one of the most satisfactory crops for local growers, whether small or large. Execellent quality plants can be flowered year round with no special treatments or complicated environmental manipulations. The only requirement is a house which can be maintained at

65° F or higher. Once the crop is potted, there is very little labor involved until market time. The low labor aspect of the crop more than compensates for the higher cost of heating to 65° F. For the grower who can provide the temperature requirements and has substantial potential demand locally, there are few crops which will be as suitable for continuous profitable production. Retailers who have not handled large numbers of gloxinias previously may need to be educated as to their desirability when shipping damage is not present. Several orders of beautiful local plants will make regular customers of any doubters.

Seed of gloxinias is very fine and is sown on seed mix which has been lightly firmed on the surface to prevent seeds from falling between soil particles. No covering of soil should be applied. Watering must be done carefully so that seed is not disturbed. Germination takes place easily in three to four weeks if 75° F temperatures and constantly moist soil is maintained. Seedlings are slow to develop and are transplanted to 2¼ inch containers when their diameter is at least that of a dime. Plants are then shifted to 6 inch pots when they begin to crowd. Excessive crowding at any stage is detrimental to growing dense, well shaped plants. Gloxinias can be grown from tubers more quickly but initial costs are higher and the resulting plants are usually not so attractive as those grown from seed.

Maintaining temperatures no lower than 65° F at all stages of growth is absolutely essential to success with gloxinias. Small plants will benefit from 70°-73° F temperatures but more compact growth is obtained when finishing temperatures do not exceed 70° F. Development almost ceases at temperatures under 65° F and the little growth that is made is yellowish and brittle. Excessive heat is translated into large floppy leaves and elongated flower stalks which may not stand erect. Night temperatures are much more important than day temperatures but if summer days regularly exceed 90° F in the greenhouse the same symptoms may be noted. Plants moved to retail outlets and to consumers' homes in winter must be protected from the cold.

Most authorities cite 2,500 foot candles as the optimum light intensity for gloxinia growth. Growers may wish to use this as a general guide but test crops grown with higher light intensities may be in order if plants continually develop oversized, soft leaves. Heavy shade is necessary during summer months with little shade being needed in the winter at northern latitudes. Except for brighter days, plants could be grown without shade in mid winter. Some experts recommend the use of mum lighting to speed maturity in gloxinias. My experience is that any shortening of crop time is offset by the plants' becoming less compact under this type of lighting. Larger gloxinia growers might find that variable shading, depending on light conditions, would result in significantly faster growth. Plants receiving excessive light will turn yellow and be undersized.

Proper spacing is critical to profitable gloxinia production. The high energy costs of this crop dictate that as many plants as possible be raised per square foot. One square foot per plant is entirely adequate if compact plants are raised with proper levels of heat, fertilizer, and light. One and a half plants per square foot may be harvested if they are sold at first bloom and the market will tolerate a few less than perfect plants. If the latter spacing is used, extremely good air circulation is necessary to prevent various rots and mildews.

Gloxinias will not thrive if allowed to dry out regularly. Irrigation should be heavy and applied before any appreciable water stress takes place. Watering from overhead with cool water has never caused any damage in my experience. Water left in the crowns and on leaves for extended periods will result in rotting of the leaves and stems. Healthy gloxinias are reasonably heavy feeders but excessive nitrogen will result in soft growth and large, brittle leaves. The calcium nitrate-potassium nitrate fertilizer formula is used exclusively. Potassium nitrate alone will result in small plants and, in my opinion, causes premature flower drop in some varieties. Small amounts of iron chelate added to the fertilizer mixture and applied to plants at least a month or two before blooming will prevent iron chlorosis. I have encountered some damage to leaves when 10% iron chelate was applied at rates exceeding 2 ounces per 100 gallons of water. The margins become a dark brownish green color and plants may die if the overdose is severe. Mild cases sometimes improve if leaching occurs. Gloxinias will not tolerate a heavy, tight soil. The soil must be well drained and include a large percentage of organic matter.

Diseases are not especially prevalent in gloxinias if air circulation is good and water is not standing on plants or benches. Spider mites and cyclamen mites can cause serious damage if not kept in check. The reader should refer to the preceding discussion of cyclamen culture for information about treating these pests.

Some variation in maturity can be expected between varieties but crops sown in the spring may require as little as four and a half months to flower while those seeded in October can take seven months. Mother's Day is a particularly good market for gloxinias and seed should be planted in late October to assure flowers for that date. This schedule assumes a high light, northern United States location. In order to produce excellent winter quality, I have made it a practice to plant two 2¼ inch plants per 6 inch pot for all crops sown July 15 through November 1. Single plants which flower from mid October through Mother's Day simply do not seem to reach sufficient size to command a premium price. The Ultra series of F_1 hybrid varieties produces very nice single flowered plants and seed costs are reasonable. Some double flowered varieties may be added to the program for novelty.

It cannot be emphasized too strongly that gloxinias must be compact to be attractive and profitable. The correct form is achieved by providing adequate light and spacing and by not overdoing nitrogen fertilization and growing temperatures.

Hydrangea

The importance of hydrangeas as a floral crop has been declining for many years. There are several reasons for this decline. Hydrangea production costs are high because the crop requires a good deal of greenhouse space per plant and a previous summer-fall production phase is needed before forcing. Consumer satisfaction is often minimal since plants wilt easily in the home if not watered heavily. Introduction of new varieties and production techniques has been slow compared to the activity with other potted plants such as chrysanthemums, kalanchoes, and poinsettias. The result has been a loss of market by the hydrangea to the other plants.

Hydrangeas are still in fairly strong demand for Easter and Mother's Day, even though a well done plant should retail for a third to a half more than most potted flowers. Lasting quality in the home is excellent if proper directions are given for watering. The flower heads are extremely large and showy when in full bloom. Flower colors are mainly soft blue and pink shades. If the market will accept a price necessary to provide adequate profit margins, growers may wish to produce hydrangeas to include variety in their spring crops.

The summer and fall requirements for hydrangeas will be outlined only so that the ultimate forcer will understand how prior growth and storage conditions may affect greenhouse performance. Most greenhouses, especially smaller ones, order ready to force plants from hydrangea specialists. Cuttings are taken from late winter through spring and, after establishment, are generally grown outdoors. Nights below 65° F for six weeks are required for plants to set flower buds properly. Frost must be avoided to prevent bud injury. After buds are developed, plants are stored at 33°-45° F for another six weeks to complete a necessary dormant period. The length and temperature of storage can alter forcing schedules. Failure to develop flowers during forcing can be attributed to several factors during summer and fall preparation: temperatures over 65° F, early frosts, severe disease or pest injury, pinching too late in the fall, shifting to cold storage too early, and improper storage temperatures.

Hydrangeas for forcing should be ordered from reputable suppliers to assure proper pre-conditioning. Dormant plants are started in the greenhouse at approximately 65° F until midway through the forcing schedule when temperatures are dropped to 55°-60° F. The lower finishing temperature instensifies flower color but cool temperatures throughout forcing will result in taller plants. Greenhouse forcing requires about three months, depending on temperature and variety. Full sun is given until flowers are opening; a light shade is then necessary on bright days or some burn of petals may occur. Hydrangeas use large amounts of water and will wilt quickly if sufficient supply is not present. They do not, however, tolerate water logged soil; drainage must be good. In general, flower buds should be the size of a pea eight weeks before flowering, nickel sized six weeks before, and show slight color two to three weeks before well blooming plants are desired. Plants for Mother's Day may develop slightly faster while those for an early Easter could require a few extra days.

If plants are consistently too tall, B-9 may be applied after active growth is well started. Pests are not normally a problem during forcing unless sources of aphids are abundant. Botrytis and mildew can become troublesome if extremely high humidity is present at flowering.

Fertilization of hydrangeas is important not only to proper growth but because management of fertilizer and soil pH greatly influences flower color. Basically, flower color is determined by the amount of available aluminum present in flower cells. High available aluminum results in blue flowers while a low content produces pink or reddish flowers. A medium concentration will cause flowers to be in between; those midway colors are often unsightly but occasional shades may be pleasing. Pink or red is generally assumed to be the natural color of varieties and certain of them are more suitable for color change. White hydrangeas contain essentially no pigment and cannot be changed to either pink or blue.

High levels of phosphorus in the soil make aluminum unavailable to plant roots. A high soil pH accomplishes the same result. If clear pink flowers are wanted, soil should be amended with limestone to a pH of 6.0-7.0 and heavy application of phosphorus made when fertilizing. Neutral or basic reaction fertilizers should be used. Blue flowers will be obtained when little or no phosphorus is added to the soil or fertilizer and soil pH is adjusted to 4.5 - 5.0. Only acid reaction fertilizers should be applied. It may be noted that both potassium nitrate and calcium nitrate fertilizers are unsuitable to produce blue hydrangeas.

One cannot normally make blue flowers appear simply by restricting phosphorus and maintaining an acid soil reaction. Additional aluminum is generally required since most soils do not contain enough aluminum to accomplish a distinct color change. If no aluminum has been added to soil prior to receipt of plants for forcing, five or more applications of aluminum sulphate will be required. A solution of 1.5 pounds per ten gallons of water is applied. Maintaining soils at a high pH for pink flower color often results in iron chlorosis. This may be remedied by light applications of chelated iron. Fertilization programs used prior to forcing will affect flower color since dormant plants are normally received with a considerable soil ball and only minimal new soil is added when potting up for forcing.

Kalanchoe

Kalanchoes offer an example of the benefits a strong selection and breeding program can offer. Until a few years ago, kalanchoe production was light and limited to one or two red varieties around Christmas time. Plants are now flowered heavily from October through Mother's Day and summer crops are not uncommon. Production has not yet reached the stage of truly major crop status but this distinction could be attained within relatively few years if more attention is given to educating consumers concerning the favorable qualities of kalanchoes. Their blooms are probably the longest lasting of any commercially grown crop and plants will survive under drought conditions which would completely desiccate other potted flowers. The impetus to kalanchoe production has been spearheaded by several large propagators making a major effort to improve the selection of varieties offered as cuttings and small plants on a regular schedule.

The cultural aspects of kalanchoe production are not difficult and very nice plants may be produced if attention is paid to environmental factors and variety selection. Perhaps the biggest mistake which has been made in this crop is that many growers fail to control excessive height through chemical, cultural, and variety selection techniques. Excessive succulence brought about by poor control of fertilizer, heat, and light intensity has also been troublesome at times. The amount of acceptance gained is somewhat surprising in light of the number of tall, floppy plants growers have turned out. The kalanchoe is not inherently especially showy but is quite attractive if grown properly. Poor plants will not sell, as will some potted flowers which have a large colorful flower to cover up defects. The vigor and habit of vegetative growth in kalanchoes must be emphasized particularly since heavy flowering will not obscure imperfections. Perhaps more emphasis should be placed on producing the relatively few superior varieties.

Kalanchoes can be grown under a wide spectrum of temperatures but the most suitable range is 58°-63° F. When buds are evident and vegetative growth is sufficient, plants may be held back at temperatures as low as 45° F. Initiation of flowers is inhibited below 50° F and above 86° F. Plants stored below 55° F will develop a reddish tinge to leaves in some varieties and intense flower colors. Watering will need to be severely reduced at these low temperatures. High temperatures produce washed out flower colors. The number of crops necessary may be reduced by subjecting half of the plants of each crop to cooler temperatures when buds become evident.

Watering must be carefully monitored to obtain adequate and speedy growth but prevent undue succulence or stem rot. Growers should lean toward the dry side since less harm will be caused by intermittent water stress than by overwatering. Heavy but infrequent irrigation will result in much nicer plants than light waterings. Although kalanchoes are succulents, they do not benefit from being kept dry during production. Smaller leaved, naturally dwarf varieties will grow best if the calcium nitrate-potassium nitrate fertilizer formula is used until plants are of sufficient size to begin use of potassium nitrate alone. Excessively succulent or large leaved cultivars will benefit if only potassium nitrate is applied after establishment in the finishing pot.

Kalanchoes are grown under full sun but some shade is beneficial when flowers are present in summer. Light shade from May through August will still produce suitable plants. Several pests can become established on kalanchoes but aphids are the most persistent problem. Temik applications will eliminate any losses due to this insect. Kalanchoes are not especially sensitive to Temik so a heaping 1/8 teaspoon dosage is recommended for 6 inch pots. Botrytis in the leaves and stem may become a serious problem when temperatures are lowered for strorage or at any time when humidiy is excessive. Especially robust varieties may require one or more treatments with B-9.

The most common method of propagation is by tip cuttings. Seed is seldom used in newer production methods. Cuttings for Christmas crops are taken in early July and will root easily directly in the finishing pot without bottom heat if shade is applied. Three cuttings per 6 inch pot are sufficient. Cuttings taken after August 15 for later crops will benefit from bottom heat and should be planted four per 6 inch pot. The number of cuttings per pot can be reduced if they are taken earlier and pinched to produce a bushy plant. No pinch is necessary with the above Christmas schedule. Short days are initiated August 15 for a Christmas crop. Stock plants must receive long days at all times of the year if cuttings are to be taken earlier than mid June. Most desirable varieties are patented and require a license to propagate.

The critical factor in kalanchoe scheduling is daylength. These plants are similar to chrysanthemums in their photoperiod requirements. Varieties will differ somewhat in their response but generally plants should receive a 14 hour dark period each night for six weeks to initiate flowering.

Plants can then be returned to long days if necessary. Most varieties will flower 10 to 12 weeks after the start of short days in summer and in 14 weeks during winter. Plants should, of course, be given long days until they have reached sufficient size to finish properly. A rule of thumb might be to continue long days until the plant is a third the desired market size. It is generally assumed that days are naturally short enough to initiate flowers in kalanchoes from October 1 to March 1; blackcloth shading is necessary from March 1 through September 30. When vegetative growth is desired, mum lighting schedules may be used from early September to late March. Crops grown without artificial daylengths bloom shortly after Christmas in the northern United States if grown at 60° F. When temperatures and light levels are high, some varieties may bloom shortly before Christmas under natural daylength.

The following schedules may be used as a guide for fall and winter crops under average conditions: shade July 20 through September 20 for mid October flowers; shade August 15 through October 1 for early December flowers; shade September 1 through October 20 for Christmas flowers.

Kalanchoes are also popular as 4 inch plants. One cutting per pot without pinching is sufficient if the previous propagation schedule for Christmas is used. Blooming plants in 2¼ inch pots will find a ready market from florists at Christmas for use in dish garden arrangements. To prevent overgrowth, these small pots should be subjected to short days as soon as cuttings are taken.

Lily (Easter)

No crop presents more challenge in timing than does the Easter lily. Not only does the holiday come at a different time each year, but also weather in the lily fields the previous fall can have a significant impact on forcing speed. The relatively short shelf life of lilies is another complicating factor. Supplies of lilies change significantly from year to year. An extremely late Easter will cause many growers to forego lily production in favor of spring bedding plants while some greenhouses may lack sufficient heating facilities to force especially early lily crops. The Easter lily has, in the author's opinion, not shown strong market performance in the flower shop trade in the past decade when compared with other potted flower varieties sold at the same time. Sales of lilies have shifted heavily to mass market outlets at the expense of traditional florists, perhaps to a greater degree than with other varieties.

Lily bulbs may be purchased in a precooled state ready for forcing or as raw bulbs which must be conditioned by the grower to force properly. Care should be taken to state specifically which type of bulbs are wanted. Bulbs are graded by the circumference around their girth. In inches, they are termed 6/7, 7/8, 8/9, 9/10, and 10 and up. The lower grades will produce significantly smaller plants with fewer flowers. Only two varieties are in widespread use, Ace and Nellie White. Ace lilies are generally not so heavily foliaged and short as Nellie White but occupy less bench space.

There are three widely used methods of preconditioning bulbs for forcing. Regardless of which early treatment is used, the final forcing temperature is approximately 60° F. Early Easters may require a higher temperature while late dates could be met with 58° F. The first preconditioning method is to subject bulbs to at least six weeks of 33°-38° F temperatures in the packing box with slightly moist peat packing. Longer treatments result in bulbs that force faster. These precooled bulbs generally arrive in late November or early December and are placed at forcing temperatures approximately 120 days before Easter. The second preconditioning procedure consists of potting up raw bulbs a few days after they are harvested from the field and placing them in a cool greenhouse or coldframe where temperatures do not rise above 50° F. Freezing must be avoided. Forcing conditions and duration are the same as for precooled bulbs.

The third preconditioning method is termed CTF, controlled temperature forcing. Non-precooled bulbs from the field are immediately potted up and placed at 63° F for three weeks; the temperature is then dropped to 35°-40° F for Ace and 40°-45° F for Nellie White for approximately six weeks. The plants are then subjected to the normal forcing temperature for about one hundred days. Day and night temperatures during the first four weeks of CTF forcing should not be allowed to go below 60° F or above 65° F. A long day treatment is sometimes given to plants after emergence. Growers wishing to use the CTF method should contact their bulb broker for specific details concerning the year in question.

Precooled bulbs generally yield a smaller plant with fewer buds than do either of the methods where raw bulbs are potted and then conditioned. A 7/8 precooled bulb is often suitable for mass market sales while a 6/7 bulb which is potted and then conditioned will produce equal quality.

Lily bulbs left lying around in packing sheds or greenhouses can be damaged by temperature and moisture extremes. They should be potted immediately. Six inch standard rather than azalea depth pots are used so that the bulbs can be covered with several inches of soil. Roots developing on buried stems will add more vigor to plants. Soils must be well drained and uncompacted. Lilies will not flourish in tight soils. Bulbs must be removed from the packing case carefully to avoid injury to shoots which may have formed; they are placed on one to two inches of soil already in the pot. Covering soil must be firmed slightly to prevent bulbs from shifting during movement. The bulbs' not remaining straight up and down will cause shoots to emerge at the sides of pots.

A heavy watering and treatment with fungicide drench is given after potting. No large amounts of fertilizer should be mixed in the soil or given as liquid feed until vigorous growth begins. It has been suggested that tip burn of leaves is associated with high phosphorous levels so phosphorous is normally omitted from liquid feed and incorporated into soils at reduced rates, perhaps a third of normal concentrations. Several experts recommend that soil pH be adjusted to 6.5 to 7.0. I have had no problems with an initial pH of lower than 5.0 when the calcium nitrate-potassium nitrate formula is used exclusively in conjunction with the growing on soil mix.

Overwatering must be carefully guarded against, especially before vigorous growth begins. Constantly wet soil can result in crop failure due to severe root rot but the most common result is survival of plants in a state of reduced vigor and loss of lower leaves. If a mistake is to be made, it is better to water slightly on the dry side. Lilies do not wilt easily from water stress and good judgment must be exercised not to dry plants out excessively. Each irrigation should be thorough with light touching up to drier pots in between times.

Lilies must always be grown under full sun to prevent excessive stem length and to assure maximum growth rates so that flowering schedules are met. Adequate spacing is also necessary to reduce height and prevent yellowing of lower leaves. The amount of space given will vary with the size of bulbs, but a rule of thumb might be to allow one square foot for each two and a half to three plants in northern high light areas. This would assume 8/9 size bulbs are potted. Growers whose greenhouses are oriented east and west will often encounter a bending of some plant stems southward. This crooked stem condition can be alleviated somewhat by turning pots late in the forcing schedule. Greenhouse space is in strong demand at Easter and lilies cannot be grown profitably unless spacing is as close as possible consistent with acceptable quality.

Problems with root rot are considerably reduced by the post potting fungicide drench recommended earlier. Many growers will apply a second treatment at the mid point in growth. Aphids are the major pest. If greenhouses are clean of these insects, there should be little more than scattered outbreaks, which can be controlled by spot spraying. When aphid populations have been troublesome in the greenhouse, Temik may be applied after vigorous plant growth has started.

Chemical height control is practiced by using Phosphon or A-Rest growth retardants. The amount applied will depend on the degree of trouble that has been encountered in controlling height. More plants per square foot may be grown if height is reduced so that many growers producing for mass markets will prefer to reduce height more than would be consistent with sales to traditional floral outlets. Some degree of chemical height control will normally be desirable irrespective of the market. Each grower must evaluate local conditions to determine the expected deviation in scheduling from the widely accepted 120 day forcing period at 60° F . This 120 day time span does not apply to CTF growing methods. Flowering times may vary considerably depending on geographical location, cultural practices, and condition of greenhouse facilities. Ninety-five days before Easter the shoot should be above the soil, ten days later it should be two to four inches tall. Buds should be visible in the growing tip perhaps fifty days before Easter in low light areas while forty days may be sufficient in higher light localities. Three weeks before Easter the largest bud should begin to turn downward. When it is swollen and creamy white, only a few days remain until blooming. With a late Easter, plants may progress quite rapidly at the end while early Easters present the opposite problem. One holiday with green plants will convince any grower that it is better to be early than late. A more complicated leaf counting method may be utilized to estimate crop progress. Bulb brokers should be contacted to supply details of this method for the year in question.

Careful manipulation of temperature is the most important tool the grower has in timing a lily crop. Progress of the crop must be monitored periodically and temperatures turned up or down to speed or slow flowering. Early anticipation of progress is much better than waiting until two or three weeks before Easter to adjust temperatures drastically. Severe alteration of the temperature is not good for plants but even the most experienced grower will occasionally have need to "sweat" lilies at high temperatures or store them near freezing to assure Easter blooms. During the forcing period, more advanced plants can be sorted out and moved to the cooler spots in the greenhouse. Subjecting lilies to night temperatures over 75° F defnitely lowers crop quality and can result in abortion of smaller buds. Plants ready too early can be stored at 33° F in the dark for approximately two weeks. Wilting may occur if these stored plants are returned to bright sunlight or warm temperatures without being acclimatized. Plants to be stored should have one or two buds which are large and creamy white but none in the open stage. Botrytis and mildew must be guarded against during storage.

Poinsettia

More poinsettias are now grown in the United States than any other potted flower. Their present popularity demonstrates the potential market for other plants when excellent new varieties are introduced and major horticultural firms lead the way in cultural research and promotion of the product. In the case of poinsettias, consumer demand was most likely always there but never fulfilled because a product which was both beautiful and long lasting was not available. The market for potted flowers, poinsettias in particular, should continue to grow in the Christmas season. Few competing merchandise lines can offer comparable perception as a tasteful, high quality gift for such a low price. A tremendous increase in poinsettia sales has been accomplished even with the large number of substandard plants produced each year.

Poinsettia production would be considerably less were it not for the introduction of long lasting and shorter varieties. Early varieties were tall and lost their leaves shortly after leaving the greenhouse, if not before. At the present time, there is no excuse for informed growers to offer plants which are not acceptable to the consumer in every respect. Introduction of the variety Paul Mikkelsen in 1963 revolutionized poinsettia marketing and culture. It possessed the traits of good foliage retention and stiff stems. The revolution was hardly well established when new, long lasting, shorter varieties known as Eckespoint C-1 and Annette Hegg were made available in the United States in 1968. These later varieties are characterized by the ability to produce plentiful side branches when the growing tip is removed. Thus if a grower wants four blooms per pot, a single plant is pinched so that four leaf nodes remain. One can readily see the economy of this production technique over the traditional practice of planting four plants to obtain four blooms.

Annette Hegg derivatives have become the overwhelming favorites of American growers. These plants are generally considered easier to grow than Eckespoint C-1 and they require less heat to grow properly: 60° F plus versus 64° F. Many southern greenhouses grow C-1 because heating costs are not so large a concern there as in the northern United States. Annette Hegg is ready for sale eight to nine weeks after the start of short days while C-1 has a 10½ week response. The newer Gutbier series has a heavier leaf texture and strong stems as does the C-1 but is reported to respond in eight to nine weeks at 60° F in unison with Annette Hegg. Gutbier varieties could combine the good traits of both earlier introductions; more extensive production will be needed to confirm initial results. Each of these variety groups is attractive. Available facilities, market demand, and grower preferences will determine what particular ones are grown. There are several other varieties available but their market share is small in comparison to the ones just described. Mikkell Rochford and Mikkel Scandia are perhaps the most widely grown varieties of secondary importance.

The keeping quality of poinsettias has progressed so greatly that customers will often have flowers until Mother's Day. The ability of plants to last a long time and their initial sales appeal is sometimes seriously impaired by shipping conditions. Temperatures under 45° F will cause wilted looking plants as will prolonged periods (two to five days) of confinement in shipping containers. Cold temperatures can also result in plants' losing their leaves. The colored bracts (actually leaves) of poinsettias are easily bruised and torn in transit. Bruised spots will develop an unsightly black color within a short time. Difficulties encountered in shipping poinsettias make it imperative that handling and packing operations be carefully supervised. Local growers will be at a distinct advantage in marketing their crops because their plants are likely to suffer almost no damage and the supply to florists is not subject to shipping delays and mishaps due to weather.

Many bedding plant growers have entered the poinsettia market in recent years with the result that, in some regions, there has been an oversupply. Poinsettia crops fit in very well with bedding plant schedules, especially in the North. A second crop helps defray the cost of equipment and greenhouses. The inexperience of some of these growers with poinsettia culture has led to a wide variation in plant quality. Inadequate facilities for cold weather growing has often contributed to the quality problem. As many of these growers become experienced or eliminate poinsettia production because they pack proper facilities, the reputation of the poinsettia will increase greatly.

The grower who makes poinsettias a major crop should plan growing methods and marketing strategy carefully to assure a profit. Only one chance a year is available and mistakes in culture, timing, or market planning can lead to failure. Colors and varieties should be selected to match the market and growing conditions. Maturity dates need to be in line with expected demand at different periods of the holidays. The intended market, whether retail florist or mass market, will generally influence the amount of space given and number of blooms planned per plant. Above all, planning should be done long in advance. Early orders of cuttings and supplies will often result in appreciable discounts and contacts with customers may assure sales of all or part of the crop before it is planted.

Poinsettia stock plants are grown through spring and summer and managed so that a large number of cuttings will be available from late July through September. Tip cuttings are rooted with a soil temperature of 70°-75° F and must be under mist. If adequate bottom heat and mist cannot be supplied, it is fruitless to attempt propagation. Shade is generally required. Cuttings root in about four weeks and should be planted soon afterwards to ensure uninterrupted growth. Shade and mist are gradually reduced as rooting progresses so that the new plants are toughened up to withstand normal greenhouse conditions.

Poinsettia propagation has become big business for some greenhouses. The efficiency connected with this specialization in one crop generally means that it is more economical for smaller growers to purchase 2¼ inch plants rather than becoming involved in propagation. If plants are purchased, investigation into the reliability and integrity of the supplier is a prerequisite so that crop schedules and quality are not compromised by late delivery or poor condition of small plants. Contamination of plants by diseases and pests can be a major problem if suppliers are not chosen carefully. Shortfalls in quality should not be tolerated for any reason since the ultimate profitability of the crop is, in large degree, determined by planting healthy stock.

The planting date chosen in August and September can significantly alter the cultural practices needed to produce a good plant. The ultimate height and size of early plantings is generally greater than in later plantings if environmental conditions are similar. To obtain well proportioned 7 inch pots using one plant per pot, I favor a mid August planting. The planting date is then delayed one week for each 1 inch decrease in pot size. Planting different sizes on different dates can be inefficient when small numbers are involved; in this case all plants can be potted early and the form and size of plants regulated primarily by the pinch date and secondarily by temperature. It is difficult to obtain larger specimen plants for exclusive markets when pinched plants are grown with late potting dates.

Poinsettias are one crop which I have always preferred to grow in porous walled pots of clay or wood fiber. Good plants can certainly be grown in plastic pots but will require more skilled labor for watering. When plastic pots are used, a lighter, quick draining soil mix is recommended. The use of porous walled pots also has the advantage of reducing dependence on chemicals for height control. Plants just naturally grow a little shorter and stiffer in this type of container. For potting, the recommended growing on soil mix is amended with two cubic feet of vermiculite per standard batch. The vermiculite provides a reservoir of potassium which, in my experience, generally becomes deficient as plants approach flowering. Small plants should be irrigated heavily before potting. As pots are moved to the greenhouse, they are drenched thoroughly with an appropriate fungicide to prevent root rot and stem rot.

Foam blocks have recently come into widespread use for poinsettia propagation and plants potted from these blocks must be handled differently than those potted from small pots or peat pellets. The latter plants may be irrigated heavily when drenched and then kept reasonably moist until they are established; shade is not essential unless light intensity is extreme. Pots planted from foam blocks must be kept saturated until roots spread into the soil (about ten days). Misting several times a day is also helpful. Shade is absolutely necessary. Cuttings rooted in foam blocks may be efficient for the propagator but they certainly make life more difficult for the ultimate grower.

Management of soil fertility is very important in poinsettia production. The calcium nitrate-potassium nitrate fertilizer formula is applied for the first two heavy irrigations after potting and perhaps once or twice again during the vegetative growth period. Potassium nitrate alone is used at all other times. When color first begins to show, it may be necessary to increase the potassium nitrate by one half for several applications to prevent a potassium deficiency from occurring. The visible symptom of this disorder is necrotic (dead) spots on the leaf margins, especially on older leaves. When plants are fully mature, clear water may be used for irrigation to lessen the possibility of salt buildup in the soil.

Minor elements are applied soon after potting at the rate of 3 ounces of Peters Soluble Trace Element Mix and 1 ounce 10% chelated iron per 100 gallons of water. The same solution is again applied mid way in the growth cycle. Minor elements may be mixed with the normal fertilizer. If leaching occurs at each watering, it may be necessary to increase the concentrations of all fertilizers used throughout forcing. When leaching does not occur it is absolutely necessary to leach heavily at least twice during growth to remove excess salts. For early plantings, leaching is suggested at the end of September and October. Symptoms of high soluble salt damage are a general yellowing of leaf margins, slow growth, and death of root tips. Leaf margins eventually take on a scorched appearance as they turn brownish-yellow and die.

These recommendations for fertilizers are specific for the growing on soil mix formula presented earlier. While it is likely that similar artificial soil mixes would require somewhat the same fertilizer regime, adjustments may be needed. I have found that exceptional quality poinsettias are heavily dependent upon proper soil and fertilizer management and seemingly small alterations can produce large variations in plant growth. Artificial soil mixes require the grower to make certain all mineral elements are present in proper quantities. Molybdenum deficiencies are often encountered with poinsettias grown in artificial mixes. This element should be provided in sufficient quantity by the suggested applications of trace elements. Poinsettias are particularly susceptible to the phenomenon of ammonium toxicity which is more likely to occur in artificial mixes. Symptoms of this disorder are quite similar to those shown when soluble salts are excessive.

Fertilizers of the ammonium type should be avoided in favor of those supplying nitrogen in the nitrate form.

Poinsettias can be grown in the general growing mix with the calcium nitrate-potassium nitrate fertilizer formula but plants will be taller, leafier and more subject to potassium deficiencies. Using potassium nitrate alone most of the time reduces the need for chemical height control. If satisfactory results are being obtained with a particular soil mix and fertilizer regime, growers should be reluctant to change. Fertilizer and soil recommendations for poinsettias by different experts vary considerably; the ones presented here have worked well together for me but are no magic formula to success under all conditions.

Poinsettias are short day plants. They initiate flowers when days are shorter than a critical length and proper subsequent development of flowers requires that the days continue to become shorter for a period of time. Photoperiod requirements differ for varieties and can be influenced significantly by temperature. In general, plants initiate flowers at daylengths less than 13 hours. Flower initiation with natural daylengths occurs towards the end of September and early October in most areas of the northern hemisphere. Christmas crops normally require no daylength manipulation but varieties which mature slightly too early can be lighted to delay flowering. Early flowering plants of late varieties can be had by using blackcloth shade to speed up initiation. Stock plants for propagation must be subjected to a 14 hour photoperiod to maintain vegetative growth. The temperatures plants are subjected to during flower initiation alters the critical daylength. Temperatures higher than 60° F generally require shorter photoperiods to initiate flowers. It is common practice to lower temperatures to 60° F for two to three weeks when flower initiation is to take place. Growers must be careful to prevent extraneous light from causing plants to remain vegetative. Busy highways, street lights, and lighted signs can prevent flowering if the intensity is great enough. Neophyte growers need not worry themselves about a few street lights or neon signs a block away. New lighting installations in the neighborhood should always be a source of concern to growers.

Poinsettias grow best at slightly warmer temperatures than most flowering plants and will not tolerate exposure to cold. I have found it much easier to produce a quality crop if temperatures are maintained 2°-3° F above the generally accepted growing temperatures of 60° F for Annette Hegg and Gutbier varieties and 64° F for C-1 types. Growth at these elevated levels is rapid through September, October, and November. Temperatures can then be turned down to 60° F for C-1 and 58° F for Annette Hegg and Gutbier. With this heating schedule, most development takes place when nights are warmer. Less heat is needed during December when fuel costs are at their peak. Growers should remember to lower temperatures to at least 62° F when flower initiation is taking place. Temperatures above 75° F during initiation can seriously delay flowering.

Much larger bracts are developed, in my opinion, if good heat is supplied during their expansion in November. My experience has been that developing large bracts is difficult after weather becomes cold and dark in December. The trend toward marketing large numbers of plants near Thanksgiving and in early December makes these heating plans work well. Those growers who are troubled by botrytis and root rot may be well advised to plan heating schedules so that higher temperatures are maintained in December to help prevent losses from these diseases. Cool temperatures normally increase their incidence. One often sees crops of poinsettias with healthy looking leaves but very small bracts. I believe much of this condition is caused by too little heat during bract formation. Another factor which may contribute to this problem is too much nitrogen in relation to potassium in the soil. Bract color in red and pink varieties is deepened by exposure to colder temperatures while white varieties tend to become more cream colored.

Poinsettias should be grown at the highest possible light levels to develop stiffer, shorter stems and prevent over expansion of leaves. I prefer to remove all old leaves from pinched plants after new shoots begin good growth. This allows more light to young leaf tissue. There has been some mention that new leaves of certain varieties become yellowish green under high light intensities. I have noticed this problem with new shoots shortly after pinching Annette Hegg varieties. At times it can become quite worrisome but there is no firm evidence in my experience to link the problem with high light intensities. Plants generally grow out of this condition in two to three weeks. Growers in high light areas who encounter this trouble with Annette Hegg varieties may wish to investigate further. High light levels have sometimes been suggested as being responsible for burning of the edges and tips of fully developed bracts. I feel the actual cause of this phenomenon is a high soluble salt level in the soil restricting water uptake. Bright days naturally intensify the problem.

Spacing the poinsettia crop is very important both to profits and quality. The widely quoted rule of thumb allowing one half square foot per bloom is, in my opinion, completely outdated unless plants are being grown single stem. I have consistently produced excellent quality 6 inch pinched plants averaging five blooms in slightly less than one square foot per plant. Gross returns for this crop in 1983 were $5.50 per square foot. Annette Hegg varieties are used and light intensity is high. Plants are thinned to approximately 1 for every 1.25 square feet before bract development is maximized since a large number of the most advanced ones are sold shortly after

Thanksgiving. Growers who suffer from botrytis problems and low light will find such close spacing impossible. Plants spaced too closely become taller and develop yellow lower leaves.

Irrigation of poinsettias must be carefully monitored, particularly in early and late stages when overwatering is most prevalent. Thorough waterings with a drying out period in between are best. Heavy leaching must take place two or three times during growth or soluble salts will damage plants. Poinsettias are susceptible to root rot if the soil is overly moist for long periods but plants should never be allowed to wilt for want of water. Watering from overhead when bracts begin to color will leave objectionable salt spots on them, particularly red varieties. Heavy irrigations late in the season should be timed to coincide with periods of sunny weather. Plants which are soaked in dark weather may develop serious botrytis problems on the bracts and could lose lower leaves because of fungal diseases attacking the petioles. Both diseases thrive under high humidity. If plants are watered heavily and cold, damp weather comes on unexpectedly, the temperature may be turned up for a few days until some drying out takes place. Botrytis and leaf drop make progress with alarming speed and growers must think ahead rather than reacting to damage as it occurs.

Pinching of poinsettias must be planned to make sure it is done properly and on time. The following schedule may be taken as a guideline when one plant per pot and natural daylengths are used with Annette Hegg varieties: 7 inch pots, pinch September 1 leaving 7-9 leaf nodes; 6 inch pots, pinch September 7 leaving 4-6 leaf nodes; 5 inch pots, pinch September 13 leaving 3 leaf nodes. Any leaf node which is appreciably above the soil line should be counted even if the leaf has fallen off. The pinch is made slightly above the topmost leaf node to prevent unintentional damage to the embryonic bud contained in the leaf axil. Growers who wish more flowers per pot may increase the number of leaf nodes left but more space must be allowed. Increases of more than 25% in flower number will generally result in significantly weaker stems and smaller flowers even if more bench space is given to the plant. Soft pinches leaving large numbers of potential leaf nodes are completely unacceptable. The plant becomes a mass of weak, tangled stems which cannot hold flowers upright.

Several authors have stated that C-1 types fail to branch as freely as Annette Hegg types. I have not found this to be the case; no problems with branching have been encountered in either the C-1 or Gutbier varieties. Gutbier and C-1 types generally develop somewhat larger bracts when compared to Annette Hegg varieties and should be given more space if the same number of flowers per pot is desired. Pinching date seems to affect the flowering date even though the pinch is made several weeks prior to the start of short days. Plants pinched early mature sooner. Final plant height can be significantly affected by the pinch date. Those plants pinched early to allow more vegetative growth before flower initiation will be taller. Care must be taken to pinch soon enough before flower initiation so that plants can develop a desirable amount of vegetative growth. Delaying the pinch more than one week past the dates mentioned above will result in very short, dwarfy plants unless daylengths are artificially lengthened.

Poinsettias often become too tall or the stems are not strong enough to hold the flowers upright. Manipulation of cultural factors such as pinching closer to the start of short days, using potassium nitrate fertilizer alone, and spacing adequately is often sufficient to reduce plant height to the desired level. In those cases where further height reduction is needed the grower may employ the chemical growth retardant Cyclocel. Cyclocel is applied as a spray or drench. The frequency and concentration of Cyclocel applications will vary with the degree of height reduction wanted but the following recommendations may serve as a guideline for medium effects: spray once before October 15 when new shoots are one to two inches long with one quart Cyclocel to 10 gallons of water over 2,000 square feet of bench; or drench 6 inch pots with approximately 6 ounces of the same concentration of solution.

Some undesirable effects of Cyclocel applications which may occur are reduced bract size, yellowing of leaves, delayed flowering, and marginal leaf burn. Soil drenches are less likely to produce these adverse reactions. The yellowing of leaves caused by spray application generally disappears after a few weeks. Late treatments with Cyclocel are more likely to cause plant damage. Many growers are of the opinion that Cyclocel makes leaves a deeper green color. Treatment with Cyclocel is an added expense and can result in some unwanted side effects; if height can be controlled adequately by cultural methods, then it should be done in that manner.

Diseases and pests can quickly cause havoc with a poinsettia crop. No major problems should be encountered when reasonable care is extended to plants which were clean when potted in disease free soil and containers. Losses to stem and root rot should be minimal if fungicide drenches are applied. A general loss of vigor, leaf yellowing, and leaf drop are characteristic of these diseases but the sudden collapse and subsequent death of plants is also common. Botrytis and sudden lower leaf drop due to fungi are caused primarily by high humidity; modification of watering, ventilating, and heating practices to reduce humidity is the only practical solution to these disorders. Botrytis can completely ruin a crop in a few days by disfiguring the bracts. Remedial action must be swift and decisive at the first signs of this disease. Some relief may be gained by the use of fungicides, but one must be certain no damage will result to the bracts from chemical use. Botrytis is characterized on the bracts by blackish areas caused from rotting of the tissue. This damage can be easily confused with that resulting from bruises or edge burn due to chemical use or high soluble salts in the soil.

While many greenhouse pests can become established on poinsettias, white flies are the most troublesome. Resmethrin aerosols or Temik will quickly control white flies. Whitefly control should be complete before bracts begin to expand so that there is no chance of chemical damage to them. Tomatoes, peppers, fushias, and lantanas left over from spring crops are a prime source of whitefly infection. Poinsettia growers must be certain all these plants are removed or completely clean of adult whiteflies and eggs before the crop is planted.

Latex eruption on tissue surfaces will be noticed on some plants. This phenomenon poses no threat to the health of plants but extreme cases, especially when located in the flowers, can cause disfigurement. As the latex dries, it turns a greyish brown color and is commonly termed "crud." It is thought that excessive soil moisture and rapid variations in temperatures are the chief causes of this problem. Bract burn due to high soluble salts has been discussed previously. Bract burn may also be brought about by improper use of chemicals, especially pesticides. Extreme care must be exercised with any pesticide applications after color begins to show on plants.

Table 28 outlines the more important cultural steps in producing a crop of Annette Hegg poinsettias using my crop schedule. C-1 types may be substituted in the schedule if temperatures are raised 3°-4° F and flowering is expected to take place one to two weeks later. Gutbier varieties, in my limited experience with them, can be substituted with no change in the schedule. Neither Gutbier nor C-1 types seem to suffer much from yellowish new growth after pinching and both can be expected to finish appreciably shorter than Annette Hegg types. Extra large specimen plants in 10 inch pots can be started in June and pinched in mid summer to five or six leaves and then again August 29. When a few of the weaker branches are pruned out, 15-20 flowering stems will remain. Large pots can also be produced by planting multiple plants and growing single stem. Slightly earlier flowering should be expected with the latter method. Several other production techniques for poinsettia trees, pixie poinsettias, mum-settias, and hanging baskets are described in brochures available from major propagators. Current variety offerings and up to date information on the cultural requirements are also available.

Color percentages of plants to be grown will vary from market to market but the following proportions may serve as an initial guideline: 75%

Table 28

Suggested timetable for a Christmas crop of Annette Hegg poinsettias. Based on author's experience with the artificial soil mix described in the text. No Cyclocel is applied unless extra short plants are desired or local light intensities are low. Natural daylengths are assumed.

Heavy shade and mist 2-3 times a day if planted from foam blocks.	20 August	Plant all pot sizes to clay or fiber pots. Drench heavily with Banrot at 8 ounces per 100 gallons of water. Greenhouse temperature 62°-63°F.
	1 September	Pinch 7 inch plants to 7-9 leaf nodes.
	7 September	Pinch 6 inch plants to 4-6 leaf nodes.
	13 September	Pinch 5 inch plants to 3 leaf nodes.
New growth may be yellowish on Annette Hegg varieties—plants should soon grow out of this stage.	14 September	First application of trace elements and two heavy irrigations with calcium nitrate-potassium nitrate fertilizer combination should now be complete. Switch to potassium nitrate fertilizer alone unless more vegetative growth is desired.
	23 September	Leach heavily.
	25 September	Reduce temperature to 60°F for flower initiation. Make sure extraneous light sources are not present.
	10 October	Raise temperatures to 62°-63°F.
	23 October	Leach heavily and apply trace elements for second time. First hint of color becomes evident; potassium deficiencies may appear.
Very rapid growth.	29 October	Increase potassium nitrate concentration by one half for two irrigations then return to normal.
	23 November	Leach heavily if weather permits, if not then begin use of clear water for two out of three irrigations. Apply Banrot again if any signs of root or stem rot are present.
	27 November	Many plants can be sold, especially those pinched first.
Watch carefully for signs of botrytis or leaf drop.	1 December	Turn down temperature if most plants have well developed bracts; do not expose to lower than 57°F.
	25 December	Sold out.

red, 12% pink, 8% white, 3% pink and red bicolor, 2% pink and white bicolor. Those growers wishing to be more conservative would be better advised to increase the red at the expense of other colors.

Rose

Potted roses are a traditional gift for Easter and Mother's Day. The plants are not especially suited to keeping well in the home but at this time of year they can be planted outside when frost danger has passed. Roses kept inside quickly develop yellow leaves due primarily to the low light intensities. Floribunda roses are commonly used for greenhouse forcing because they have numerous smaller flowers as compared to hybrid tea varieties which produce large flowers but not nearly so many. Three grades of greenhouse roses are sold: XXX, XX, and X. Grade X is not suitable for forcing unless small promotional plants are wanted.

Initial procedures for forcing roses are similar to those described for spring crops intended for garden sales. Once plants are well started the temperature is generally raised to 58° F for forcing. Appreciably higher temperatures are not recommended because plant quality will suffer. It is much better to have plants ahead of schedule and cool them down for market timing than it is to apply extra heat. Mother's Day roses should be planted the first week in February and Easter crops are potted at least three months before the holiday. Pinching is sometimes used to time crops more precisely. Plants flower for Easter approximately eight weeks after pinching. Mother's Day plants are pinched seven weeks before marketing.

A method I have used to have Mother's Day roses is to select the most vigorous and well shaped plants from my spring garden crop when new growth becomes abundant. These plants are then forced at 58° F instead of being conditioned at lower temperatures for garden use. The majority will be hybrid teas roses, of course, but this does not seem to diminish their appeal appreciably. Further cultural information can be found in the bedding plant chapter of this book.

CHAPTER 3
FOLIAGE PLANTS

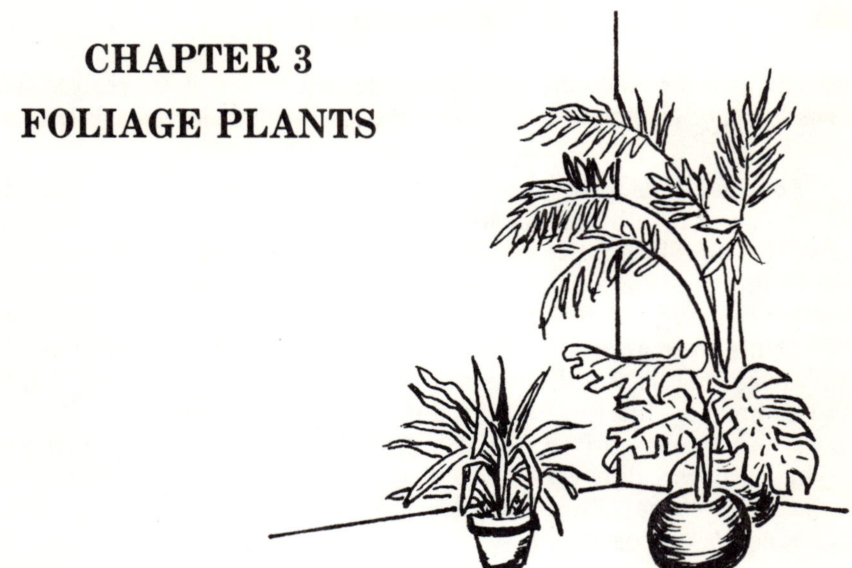

A generalized name for this group of plants is difficult to arrive at. Some of them may exhibit very little foliage and a great number are not tropical in origin. There are three rather broad categories which most foliage plants fall into: those plants originating from tropical forest regions, those native to temperate (cooler) climates, and succulents and cacti which are most often found in dry, subtropical deserts. These categories cannot encompass every type of foliage plant but it is useful if growers are familiar with the environmental conditions naturally present in these habitats. Certain plants such as hibiscus and bougainvillea do not fit into a particular category. They are tropical or subtropical in origin and do not flourish particularly well in the forest or desert but rather in conditions somewhat in between. Many other plants will also defy placement in the groups mentioned above.

Those foliage plants native to tropical forests usually prefer low light intensities, organic soils, warm temperatures, and high humidity. Most plants from these areas grow on or near the forest floor and are shaded by a dense canopy of trees. Foliage plants from temperate regions require cooler temperatures. Most of them have been collected originally from shady habitats along stream bottoms or in the forest but some temperate zone foliage plants originate from fairly sunny habitats. The majority of cacti and succulents are natives of rather dry, sunny regions where days are hot and nights cool. Optimum growing requirements of this rather diverse group of plants termed "foliage" are quite varied and both the commercial grower and ultimate consumer will do well to realize that a knowledge of each variety's preferences will lead to increased success.

Foliage plants in the home, office, or public place have probably been around since man began constructing shelters to make life more comfortable. The first decorative plants were undoubtedly those which were present in the immediate geographical area and possessed some capability to survive the shady conditions normally present inside a structure. More exotic plants were gradually added to the pool of suitable varieties as Man's knowledge of the world increased through travel for conquest, hunting, and commerce. Interior landscaping very likely progressed little or may have even regressed from the fall of the Roman empire until that period when European discovery opened up the new world and many Pacific regions. A surge of new and exciting foliage plants was then made available for the leisure classes to enjoy.

STATE OF THE FOLIAGE INDUSTRY TODAY

Another great expansion of interest in foliage plants began in the 1970's. This increased interest was brought about primarily because of society's perception that preoccupation with material, especially manmade, objects was wrong. Plants became the "natural" way of decorating to enhance the indoor environment. Wholesale foliage plant sales multiplied by more than ten times from 1970 to 1977. A general slowdown in demand became apparent toward the end of the decade and some shrinkage in sales occurred as the faddish buyers became interested in newer pursuits and a great worldwide recession crippled people's ability to afford decorative items. In 1984 the market seems to have stabilized at a healthy level of sales, and slow but steady growth can now be expected if growers and retailers offer consumers a quality product.

Established growers and retailers may find that future sales in foliage plants increase rapidly because marginal producers and street corner retailers have been shaken out during the recent market decline. In boom times some growers were more worried about quantity than quality and retail stores were hard put to keep up with the volume and still maintain high standards of service and handling. Many people in the foliage plant business have re-evaluated their methods during the slowdown and have, we hope, improved their standards so that the groundwork for a steady market resurgence has been laid. Foliage plants are still a very large and profitable market for those who plan ahead and manage carefully.

PRODUCTION AND MARKETING CONSIDERATIONS

The majority of foliage production in the United States is centered in Florida and California. Texas is also an important producer. Most large wholesalers are located in warmer states because of the high fuel consumption necessary to keep foliage greenhouses at 65°-70° F in northern areas. Growers in the north can profitably produce the types of foliage which require cooler temperatures and those exhibiting fast growth rates. Even tropical foliage may be grown profitably in the north if the majority of development takes place during warm summer months. Summer crops of foliage are an excellent way to fill normally empty benches if a market can be found for them before the onset of winter. Northern summer production is usually dominated by smaller plants but nice 10 inch specimens of faster growing plants such as sheffleras and Japanese aralia can be grown. Certain local growers may find that foliage production is profitable on a limited scale even in winter. If transport facilities are poor and the area is at considerable distance from southern production areas, a program of heavy summer growing coupled with holding at minimum temperatures through the winter may be the only way of assuring reliable supplies. High fuel costs may be compensated for by avoiding delivery charges from the south and damage which normally occurs to plants in shipment. I am a firm believer that at least 5-10% of a plant's value is lost in routine packing and shipping. This does not include the occasional heavy losses incurred from freezing or heat damage for which many carriers will not assume responsibility. The benefits of assured supply and quality are added incentives for northern growers to produce their own foliage. One must also consider the labor involved in receiving and unpacking shipments. Growing of most specimen plants in 10 inch containers and larger should certainly be left to southern producers but there are a few varieties which can be grown to this size profitably by northern growers in one summer.

The most common marketing system for foliage plants today is the movement of southern plants to independent local distributing greenhouses north of the growing areas. These distributing greenhouses then sell to chain stores, florists, and smaller greenhouses. Although the distributing greenhouses may produce a considerable amount of the faster growing types and small tropical foliage, their main emphasis is on shipment of material from southern production areas with a quick sale after receipt. Most of the cuttings used for small tropical plants are also imported rather than propagated at the greenhouse. A few of the ultimate retailers may move sufficient quantities of tropical foliage to ship direct from the growing areas rather than obtain their plants from a middleman.

Smaller greenhouses often follow a marketing pattern similar to that of the distributing greenhouses but they are as likely to obtain their plants from distributors as from the initial grower. Any firm acting as a distributor or re-distributor must make certain that an adequate markup is obtained to cover all expenses and yield a suitable profit. An important aspect of this business to remember is that inventory must be turned quickly to compensate for the relatively low markups generally accepted. Some smaller establishments could well be advised to specialize in only those foliage crops which are profitable for them. A certain critical size must be attained by greenhouses before importing cuttings and larger plants becomes feasible.

The type of foliage plant program a greenhouse ultimately settles into will generally vary more greatly than the common practice in flowering pot plants and bedding plants of growing all your own needs. The foliage grower must evaluate all impinging factors and devise a program of growing and buying plants which is most profitable for the circumstances at hand. The present discussion of foliage plants is mainly oriented towards those greenhouses located outside of the main production areas since growing operations in the latter locations are generally quite large and will require more specific cultural information than is possible in this book. Three reference books which will be indispensable to anyone involved appreciably in foliage plants are *Exotica 4—Pictorial Cyclopedia of Exotic Plants From Tropical and Near Tropic Regions, Tropica,* and *Exotic Plant Manual* by Alfred Byrd Graf. Details of identification and culture are well presented in these volumes.

Whatever approach is taken toward marketing and growing foliage plants, it must be carefully planned ahead and implemented vigorously. Constant vacillation from one hastily contrived plan to another will be a waste of effort. Accurate scheduling is certainly as important to profitable foliage plant production as it is in the case of potted flowers and bedding plants. Each crop must be timed so that a steady supply of high quality merchandise is available for market. One must realize that foliage crops reach a point when marketability and profitability interact to produce an optimum marketing period. Plants may sell quickly when they are allowed to become oversized for the price range, but profitability decreases because they remain in the greenhouse too long and are gradually occupying more space. Attempts to market plants before they have reached an acceptable size may increase the profitability of each pot sold, but total profits for the crop will decrease because most customers refuse to purchase an undersized product. Determining the optimum marketing period for foliage plants is not so easy as it is with potted flowers and bedding plants. Most of the latter two crops are sold when flowers appear and price is adjusted according to the amount of time and space consumed in reaching this stage. A definite physical characteristic is usually not apparent in foliage plants to signal the beginning of marketability.

This lack of definite criteria to initiate sales leads many growers into the complacent state of mind that there is no urgent need to work toward a finely tuned balance of sales and production. Their attitude is that if a plant does not sell today it will get larger and be sold in the future. This attitude may be justified somewhat if a higher price is charged for the extra size, but letting crops grow to the next size on a regular basis will upset plans made for larger containers. When plants frequently become too large and must be transplanted to the next size container or if shortages are often encountered, efforts should be made toward developing an improved schedule.

Foliage plant sales are, in general, less of a feast or famine proposition than are potted flowers and bedding plants. Sales of foliage definitely increase in the winter and spring months and especially near Christmas and Mother's Day but continue at a good pace throughout the year. Production is normally on a more or less regular schedule without the exaggerated peaks and valleys associated with spring plants or potted flowers. Small individual crops are often the result of this marketing pattern since large amounts of each variety are not needed at any one time. No particular method of scheduling foliage plant crops is any more correct than another for all situations. The main criterion of suitability is whether or not the scheduling method works to produce plants acceptable for the intended market without serious oversupplies or shortages becoming commonplace.

I have made a practice of growing foliage plants by a rather informal scheduling method. Inventory estimates of each variety are tabulated every week and cuttings are then taken whenever the supply of cuttings and pots already started fall below a certain level. The new cuttings will bring inventories of that variety to somewhat more than the critical level. This method of scheduling requires an experienced eye to estimate quantities quickly and compute the number of cuttings required. Realizing that perhaps 100 different varieties with three different container sizes for each variety are involved, one can appreciate the need for speed. I inventory each week so that supplies will be more finely tuned to sales, but there is no reason why crops cannot be made somewhat larger and inventories estimated every two weeks or monthly.

Growers supervising large wholesale foliage plant greenhouses would be unable to use a manual inventory system efficiently since the time required to inventory crops regularly would be prohibitive. Computerized inventory and marketing records could enable large growers to work with the same methods. This system of frequent inventory and crop scheduling works quite well with smaller plants and those which grow rapidly. When large specimen plants and those which grow slowly are considered, it is best to schedule far in advance on the basis of estimated needs. The crop cycle for these plants is so long that one cannot schedule on the basis of immediate inventories. Most northern greenhouses will be little concerned with growing larger specimens and slow maturing varieties, preferring rather to purchase them from southern sources.

Foliage plant production is, in some respects, less difficult than other greenhouse crops but the large number of varieties grown and the diverse environmental conditions these varieties require places a burden on the grower to devise cultural programs that can encompass this diversity. It is obvious that different growing environments cannot be created for each variety except in operations where that variety is a major crop. It is incumbent upon the grower to create as few cultural programs as possible which will permit economical growth of the varieties to be produced. Limiting the number of cultural requirements, when possible, will increase greenhouse efficiency. A balance must be created between the physical requirements of the plants and a need to simplify growing procedures for the sake of efficiency. Certain varieties may have to be eliminated from the program because their cultural requirements do not coincide with greenhouse conditions.

PROPAGATION

Most foliage plants are propagated commercially from cuttings although a significant number are most efficiently started from seed. Cuttings of most varieties root readily and will often exhibit small roots on the stem before they are separated from the mother plant. Seeds of foliage plants are, as a rule, more difficult to germinate than common greenhouse flowers and bedding plants. The time required for germination is often quite long and temperatures needed are perhaps higher than most growers are accustomed to providing. This long germination period leaves more time for occasional improper conditions and practices to eventually reduce the germination percentage. Most growers would be well advised to leave germination of the more difficult varieties to specialists and concentrate their efforts on those such as schlefferas and asparagus which are relatively easy. Growers wishing to begin a propagation program for foliage plants should review Part I, chapter 7.

A great amount of cuttings and seedlings are started in southern areas and shipped to northern growers for potting up. This is often the most economical method of operation, especially with those varieties which require tropical conditions for excellent growth. Northern growers simply cannot justify the energy costs required to maintain abundant winter growth on tropical mother plants so that cuttings may be taken. Some cuttings may be profitably taken to shape plants as crops grow and summertime cutting production can be significant. Greenhouses isolated from main transport arteries and those which are too small to accommodate the minimum shipments often required may find that tropical foliage plant propagation is practical on a year around basis if high enough prices can be obtained for the finished merchandise. The cooler growing foliage plants are, of course, adaptable to propagation in northern greenhouses.

Rooting of plants directly into the finishing container is often practiced with easy to root varieties. This method is particularly well suited to summer crops of cooler growing varieties. No extra heat is usually given. Growers must remember that not all foliage plants thrive under warm conditions and some varieties, such as piggy back plants, will root more readily next to the coolers.

PHYSICAL REQUIREMENTS

Greenhouses in which tropical foliage is grown must be capable of maintaining a temperature of at least 65° F. Temperatures of 15°-20° F above this level are not harmful and daytime temperatures in the 90°-100° F range are acceptable if the humidity is high. Growth of tropical varieties is negligible below 65° F and plants will begin to yellow. Development is more satisfactory at 70° F and the final appearance of plants will be better. Those varieties which are native to more temperate regions will generally do well at 60°-62° F but most of them will develop into satisfactory merchandise at 65°-70° F. Temperatures below 60° F are satisfactory for some cooler growing varieties although growth is slower and plants may appear hardened. Many growers have only one shaded greenhouse and must therefore maintain the temperature in a suitable range for tropical foliage if these crops are grown. The 65°-70° F temperatures required for tropicals may not be the most economical level for temperate varieties but it is an acceptable compromise in most cases. Cooler areas present in most greenhouses should be reserved for temperate varieties.

An understanding of the light intensities different varieties require is perhaps the most important technical information a grower needs in order to maintain foliage crops in good condition. Light intensity is one environmental factor which can be easily modified within a single greenhouse. If the entire greenhouse is shaded to the point where those plants requiring the most light are happy, additional shade can be applied inside or outside, to those areas where plants needing low light intensities are located. Low light plants can also be placed in those parts of the greenhouse which naturally receive less sun, such as the north side of greenhouses oriented east and west. Foliage plants needing full sun can generally be located in potted flower houses. Old greenhouses that no longer transmit sufficient light for full sun crops can be given a new lease on life when transferred to foliage production.

Most foliage plants will make efficient growth in light levels of 1,000-2,000 foot candles. Particular crops such as Chinese evergreens will do better if light intensities are much reduced from this level while hibiscus are happiest in full sun. Light intensities for general foliage production may be allowed to reach 3,000 foot candles during the brightest part of the day but prolonged exposure to this level is normally detrimental. In summer, when natural light intensities are expected to reach 10,000 foot candles in the afternoon, more than ⅔ of the light should be shaded out of the greenhouse. Winter shade should intercept no more than ⅓ of the light in the northern areas. These greenhouse light levels are based on the needs of relatively high light plants and considerably shadier spots must be found for those which prosper under low light. A very heavy whitewash application is required on the greenhouse to filter out ⅔ of the light rays in summer.

A simple test to determine proper light levels can be administered by observing certain plants carefuly. Plants such as sheffleras and aralias which prefer light near the upper levels mentioned will begin to take on a slight yellowish color when light levels are too high. Chlorophyll in the leaves is being destroyed by excessive light. Leaves will be smaller and harder than those exposed to proper light. If the same plants are subjected to excessive shade, they will become tall and spindly with sparse foliage. Chinese evergreens and spathiphyllum, which are low light plants, will exhibit the same yellowing of leaves when light intensity is too high for plants in this group. Light levels being too low for the latter plants is seldom a concern in the commercial greenhouse unless the plants are located under benches. It should be stressed that the light intensities being suggested are those considered optimum for rapid, profitable commercial production. Most varieties will tolerate much lower light if feeding and watering are reduced and rapid growth is not expected.

The duration of light exposure can, to a certain extent, modify the intensities needed for good growth. Some authors have suggested that 20 hours of 500 foot candles exposure is equivalent to 10 hours of 1,000 foot candles exposure. While the longer exposure can certainly compensate to some degree for reduced intensities, it cannot be considered an equivalent situation. Plants requiring high light levels will generally be taller and spindlier at the reduced intensity for the longer duration, while low light plants may exhibit some leaf yellowing at a higher light intensity with reduced duration.

Light duration is important not only because of its effect on the total energy given to foliage crops but also because it may affect the flowering response in many varieties. Plants native to tropical regions do not normally exhibit such distinct photoperiodic responses as do those from temperate regions. This phenomenon is generally ascribed to the fact that many plants near the equator have not evolved photoperiodic mechanisms simply because the daylength is essentially equal all year long. Most tropical plants are thought to bloom in response to the accumulated amount of radiant energy received, not how short or long the day is. Certain cooler growing plants such as Swedish ivy, wandering Jews, and coleus have a distinct flowering period related to daylength, which begins in the fall and continues through the winter. Vegetative growth is usually reduced at this time so that a marked decrease in crop production occurs. Growers will be well advised to concentrate on growing strains of these varieties which exhibit a less pronounced flowering tendency. The small but profuse flowers on coleus and Swedish ivy may initially be attractive but soon leave objectionable, bloomed out flower stems cluttering the plant.

Soil for foliage plants should generally be highly organic and drain well. Few foliage plants will tolerate soggy soil. The general growing mix described earlier is suitable for most varieties but the cutting mix is recommended if one has an appreciable problem in growing a certain plant. These two soil mixes have produced acceptable results with all foliage plants I have had experience with. The calcium nitrate-potassium nitrate fertilizer formula is applied at each irrigation. Potassium nitrate alone is unsuitable to produce the desired amount of luxuriant vegetative growth.

Watering of foliage plants is not appreciably different than for any other greenhouse crop. Plants should be irrigated and then allowed to dry to a point where soil aeration is good before further watering occurs. It is essential that a leaching schedule be set up for foliage houses if some leaching does not occur at every watering. The long term nature of some foliage crops and the often piecemeal harvesting of crops can lead to soluble salt buildups in the soil if the grower is not careful. High humidity is beneficial to the growth of most tropical foliage plants but continually high humidity will often lead to an increase in leaf diseases. Some growers make a practice of spraying plants down as they are watered. This is not harmful as long as water does not stand on the leaves for appreciable lengths of time and if the mineral content of the water does not lead to spotting of the leaves. Most water sources, especially if fertilizer is injected, will cause unsightly salt buildup on the foliage when overhead irrigation is used.

Diseases are as common with foliage plants as with any other crop. The same sanitary precautions must be practiced to achieve good results. High humidity in foliage houses often leads to soft rot of leaves. Lowering the humidity slightly will generally eliminate the need for fungicidal sprays. Several bacterial and viral diseases can cause leaf spots and there is little the grower can do to control these diseases other than to remove infected tissue and be certain only clean plants are brought into the greenhouse. Root and stem rot are controlled by the use of clean soil and the application of fungicidal drenches when necessary.

All greenhouse insects can infest foliage plants but aphids, spider mites, cyclamen mites, scale, and mealy bugs are especially troublesome. The reader should refer to the chapter on plant pests for detailed discussions of these pests and measures used to control them. It will become readily apparent, with some experience, that certain pests favor particular plants. Efforts at control of individual pests should be concentrated on the appropriate plant varieties. Very few foliage varieties are susceptible to damage by Temik in approved dosages and it is often helpful in the control of problem cases. Foliage plant houses often become pest ridden because unsold plants from previous crops are allowed to remain on the benches and because stock plants are often kept from one year to the next without sufficient vigilance for the pests they may harbor. Timely inspection for and control of pests is especially important in greenhouses when mixed foliage is grown on a continuous schedule.

FOLIAGE PLANTS IN THE HOME OR OFFICE

Greenhouse persons having contact with the consumers of foliage plants will often be subjected to horror stories of how plants died quickly or never performed as they were expected to. It is the responsibility of the horticultural trade to educate consumers concerning the proper care of foliage plants and to provide high quality merchandise which will respond to that care. Plants growing actively in the greenhouse often perform poorly when they are moved quickly to the relatively low light conditions present in the average home. Growth takes place slowly under low light conditions and plants must adjust to this change in growth rate. The adjustment process has come to be referred to as "acclimatization." If consumers are to receive maximum satisfaction from their plant purchases, it is incumbent upon the grower or distributor to make certain acclimatization has taken place before plants are offered for sale.

Acclimatization is accomplished by subjecting foliage plants to lower light, fertilizer, and humidity levels than are optimum for luxuriant growth. The plant is being prepared for the likely conditions to be found in the average home or office. Foliage plants will be better able to face the perils of the world outside if they are placed under one half the light levels necessary for fast growth and fertilized at a reduced rate for approximately four weeks prior to sale. A thorough leaching should take place before acclimatization. Plants treated in this manner will be much less likely to begin dropping leaves and turning yellow after the first week or two in the home or office.

Foliage plants which do poorly after leaving the greenhouse are often the victims of poor care by their new owners. Improper light, fertilizer, and moisture conditions are the chief culprits responsible for the poor performance of most plants. Consumers must be alerted to the fact that plants will grow slowly in their new environment and consequently will require much less fertilizer. The beneficial effects of a regular leaching program must also be stressed. A slight deficiency of fertilizer elements is much preferable to an oversupply. Watering practices of consumers are often erratic. The value of thorough irrigation with a drying out period before the next watering must be made obvious. Most consumers would be well advised to maintain foliage plants slightly on the dry side. A regular program of checking for water needs is essential.

The light requirements of different foliage plants are variable and little understood by retailers and customers alike. A concentrated effort by the trade should be made to address this problem. Light levels in the average home will vary dramatically, depending chiefly upon the distance from windows and the size and compass orientation of these windows. Artificial lighting may affect light levels significantly if the duration is long enough and intensity high. Approximate winter light intensities of locations one foot away from north and south windows are 400 foot candles and 5,000 foot candles, respectively, on a bright day. East and west windows will exhibit light intensities intermediate to the values mentioned above. Available light drops off quickly as one moves away from the windows. Three feet away from a north window the light intensity could be expected to read only one third of the value at a distance of one foot.

Many foliage plants will survive quite well at light intensities below 200 foot candles, but most will not grow actively in this situation. Low light plants such as Chinese evergreens, spathiphyllum, cast iron plants, diffenbachias, philodendrons, dracena marginata, dracena warnecki, and dracena sanderiana will prosper nicely even below 50 foot candles. The trend toward homes with large window expanses and perhaps even atriums or small greenhouses has increased the need for foliage plants which can withstand higher light intensities. Hibiscus and bougainvillea have become very popular for sunny areas in recent years. Jade trees, yucca, citrus trees, crotons, wandering Jews, portulacas, ice plants, cacti and succulents, and asparagus ferns will do fine in well lighted locations. Small flowering plants such as impatiens and begonias will add color if used with these high light plants. A well planned atrium or small greenhouse can accommodate plants which prefer different light levels by using high light plants as a canopy to filter out bright sunlight.

It must be remembered that light levels will change with the seasons and plants which prospered in one location during winter may receive excessive light during the summer. The duration of light exposure will also change dramatically with seasonal daylength. Duration must always be considered when deciding upon the correct placement of plants indoors. As was mentioned, longer durations can make up, to some degree, for low light levels.

Reference is often made in the literature to "long lasting" and "temporary" foliage plants. This distinction probably occurs because many plants which prefer relatively high light have performed poorly under the low light conditions of the average home. In truth, they are no more temporary than lower light varieties—they simply have not been grown under proper conditions to ensure long term growth. High light plants often grow vigorously if light is available and they may need frequent pruning and transplanting to remain healthy.

Temperatures encountered in homes and offices are generally suitable for foliage plants if the extremes near doorways, heat vents, and window sills are avoided.

There is some question about the advisability of using leaf polish compounds to remove water spots and other material from leaf surfaces. A few authors are of the opinion that leaf polish can clog the stomates (passages through which air enters the leaf) and prevent proper air entry to the plant. Some concern is expressed that the waxy substances used may collect dust and lint over the long term. Each grower must decide the controversy individually in the absence of definitive evidence. Leaf polish should be tested on each variety before widespread use is begun.

SPECIFIC FOLIAGE PLANT
VARIETIES AND FAMILIES

A discussion of all foliage plant varieties is beyond the scope of this book. They have been treated exhaustively in *Exotic Plant Manual* and *Tropica* by A. B. Graf. A few of the more important families and varieties will be described in the following text to acquaint readers with the diversity of material available and to illustrate the conditions necessary for good growth.

The Aroid Family

Those plants known as aroids are the backbone of the foliage plant industry. They dominate sales and production much as petunias do in the bedding plant market. Most aroids are tropical in origin and exemplify what the majority of consumers and growers would consider a good foliage plant. They tolerate the warm, dry, low light conditions found in homes and offices and should be the core of any low light interior landscape. If one is familiar with the distinctive flowers exhibited by anthuriums, calla lilies, spathiphyllum, and Jack in the pulpits it will be easy to visualize the flower characteristices which are the basis of categorizing individual plants into the aroid family. Aroids range in size from those suitable for small pots to large, tree-like varieties. They may be of an upright habit or climbing vines. Many aroids make their home climbing through the branches of tropical forest trees and are well suited to hanging basket culture. Perhaps 1,000 species of aroids have been domesticated but the groups listed below account for the vast majority of sales and production within the family.

PHILODENDRON—The most important and diverse group within the aroid family are the philodendrons. Older varieties are familiar to most consumers and will be accepted as dependable performers but labor under the disadvantage of being considered "old hat" or common. Philodendron cordatum (heart leaf) is particularly common on poles and in small pots and hanging baskets; it is unchallenged in its ability to survive under the most trying conditions as long as the roots remain on the dry side. The larger varieties are often attached to wooden slabs or grown as bushy floor plants. Many varieties will develop long aerial roots in time; these may be removed without danger to the plant if they are considered unsightly. New varieties of philodendron have been introduced but the group as a whole has been declining in popularity relative to other foliage plants simply because many other groups lend themselves to the more "open" light conditions of modern homes and because of the perception of philodendrons as being common. Monstera is a series of philodendron-like varieties which is characterized by perforated or split leaves which lead to the common names of "split leaf" and "Swiss cheese."

DIFFENBACHIA—Diffenbachias are broad leaved plants with well defined stems, often becoming tree-like. The leaf color is green, variegated with various white patterns. Those varieties with high proportions of white in the leaves and bushier habits have become more popular in recent years. Diffenbachia is commonly called "dumb cane" since a poison in the tissue will paralyze throat and tongue muscles and can lead to suffocation in extreme cases. Spider mites love diffenbachias.

CHINESE EVERGREEN—This variety, known scientifically as *Aglaonema,* is characterized by a bushy habit, tolerance of very low light intensities, and slow growth rates. It was originally popular as a plain green variety, but now is most often cultivated in variegated forms. Chinese evergreens are the premier plant for poor light locations and where a plant which will stay within bounds is wanted. The slow growth rate makes them expensive to produce.

SPATHIPHYLLUM—This is a plant with broad, elongated, green leaves which are borne on a long stem originating at the plant base; a definable primary stem is lacking. A graceful, vase-like effect is produced as the leaves flare out from a common origin. This is one of the few tropical plants which is prized as much for flowers as it is for vegetation. The white, Jack in the pulpit type flowers are borne in the same manner as leaves and are very attractive and long lasting.

POTHOS—Pothos, also known as "devil's ivy" or scientifically as *Scindapsus,* is commonly used in small pots, poles, and hanging baskets; this vine is similar to philodendron cordatum in appearance except the foliage is variegated with yellow or white and the stem is coarser. Pothos will not tolerate the extremely low light conditions under which philodendron cordatum will survive but is otherwise almost as tolerant of adverse conditions.

ANTHURIUM—Travelers to tropical regions have no doubt seen their share of bright red anthurium flowers displayed in hotel and airport flower shop windows. The waxy texture and bright color combine to give an artificial appearance. Anthurium flowers are important in the cut flower trade but plants have not become commonly available as potted specimens. My limited experience with them has been favorable if an extremely porous, organic soil is used for potting. The flowers are very long lasting and considerable market for these plants should exist if suitable production methods were developed and the cultural requirements needed in the home or office were fully explored.

SYNGONIUM—Most commonly known as arrowhead plant and used in small containers or hanging baskets, syngonium is sometimes grown on wooden slabs. Varieties with a good deal of white coloration are the most popular. These plants are climbers, although they may not appear so as small plants, and quickly become overgrown unless grown as hanging baskets or provided support. Syngonium may often be referred to in the trade as nephytis.

The Lily Family

Plants in the lily family are quite varied in their tolerance to environmental conditions and originate from many widely differing habitats. Several succulents from dry deserts are in the lily family, as are some dracenas from shaded, moist tropical regions. A few foliage varieties in this family will tolerate fairly cool temperatures with no ill effects. There is some debate whether or not dracenas, cordylines, and sansevieria belong to the lily or to the agave family; this dispute need not concern the present discussion, where all will be treated as lilies. Members of the lily family are often subject to tip burn of the leaves. This condition may be caused by fluorine and chlorine in the soil and water and some authorities recommend raising the pH of the soil above 6.5 with limestone to eliminate the problem.

DRACENA—This is perhaps the most important group of lilies used as foliage plants. The leaves are typically long and narrow, originating from a well defined stem. Young plants may be bushy and appear to have no stem until it becomes distinguishable with age. Some varieties develop naked, contorted stems which add character to the plant. Most dracenas will tolerate low light conditions reasonably well. Some dracenas are often termed "dragon tree."

CHLOROPHYTUM—Chlorophytum is commonly known as the spider plant. The long narrow leaves of this plant originate at a common source and no main stem is apparent. New stems elongate from the mother plant and are predominantly naked of leaves until the tip, where a small plantlet develops. Spider plants like good light but will grow well in north windows. Commercial production is most profitable at 60°-70° F but the plants will prosper at 55° F in the home. They are particularly well suited to hanging baskets where the long stems with new plantlets can hang down. Plantlets with air roots forming can be detached and will quickly establish themselves in soil.

SANSEVIERIA—This is an old favorite which has seen the inside of almost every American home. Snake plant and mother-in-law's tongue are the most frequently used common names. Sansevieria will tolerate almost any amount of low light and neglect given to it but is actually native to rather bright habitats. Small plants are not especially useful except in combination dish gardens but large plants with many new plantlets in different stages of growth are very attractive if the leaves are not allowed to become damaged.

ASPARAGUS—The members of this group are most widely used as greenery in spring combination plantings and cut flower arrangements but serve also as inexpensive foliage plants. They will tolerate temperatures of 50° F and full sun but grow most efficiently at 60°-65° F with light shade. Asparagus sprengeri and asparagus plumosus are the varieties commonly planted from seed.

CORDYLINE—These plants closely resemble the dracenas in habit and growing requirements. Several varieties of the Ti plant have been selected which have highly colored leaves.

SUCCULENTS—Many varieties of succulents are members of the lily family. The average person would be hard pressed to see any resemblance between most lily succulents and the more familiar lily type plants of the temperate zone. Succulent lilies are generally residents of dry, sunny regions. Aloes are perhaps the most numerous representatives of this group and include the recently popular aloe vera (burn plant). Several agaves are also useful as decorative succulents.

YUCCA—Yuccas have a general appearance much like that of the dracenas but the leaf texture is much heavier and stiffer. Some less commonly used yuccas have very stiff, sharp pointed leaves and could be included as succulents. The green, rather coarse yucca which is widely produced for indoor use today does its best in good light and mildly dry conditions but will survive and remain attractive under low light. Older specimens will develop a thick, naked cane with a tuft of vegetation at the top.

ASPIDISTRA—This is a dracena-like plant with tough, leathery foliage. Cast iron plants are renowned for their durability under almost any conditions. They were used frequently in earlier years when homes were dark and likely to be cool but are seldom seen commercially today.

PONY TAIL PALM—Scientifically known as *Beaucanea recurvata*, this is not a common foliage plant but is interesting because of the large bottle shaped stem which is topped by a tuft of long, coarse leaves that are recurved. It is not a member of the palm family but is one of the many exotic lilies.

The Aralia Family

A diverse family which is comprised of both tropical and near temperate varieties. The tropical representatives do not tolerate poor light as does the aroid family. Fifty foot candles of light is the minimum which most varieties will accept and they would generally do much better at several times this intensity. Sheffleras, Japanese aralias, and ivy trees are fast growing in summer daylengths and profitable 10 inch specimen pots can be produced in one season by northern growers if small plants are transplanted in late spring.

SHEFFLERA—The Queensland umbrella tree is one of our more important foliage varieties. When given sufficient light it grows as a dense, spreading bush and can become quite large. Specimens subjected to light levels near the minimum 50 foot candles are more open and appear tree-like since the lower stems will possess few leaves. If fast growth is not desired, plants may be held on the dry side. Spider mites are particularly fond of sheffleras, as they are of other members of this family, and constant vigilance must be observed to prevent outbreaks. Sheffleras are easily grown from fresh seed; old seed loses viability quickly.

FATSIA JAPONICA—Japanese aralias share the same general characteristics as sheffleras except they are much wider leaved and even bushier and will tolerate slightly cooler locations.

FATSHEDERA—A hybrid variety with the Japanese aralia and Irish ivy as parents, fatshedera is known in the trade as "ivy tree" or "botanical wonder." It combines the large leaves and vigorous growth of the Japanese aralia with the vining habit of ivies. The predisposition towards vining may not be apparent in young plants or if growth is restricted by pinching and reduced nutrients and water. Older stems are thick and tree-like. Ivy trees can be quite attractive if they are given extremely good light and trimmed frequently; under these conditions and slightly reduced nutrients, they will develop as trees rather than coarse woody vines. Rooting is more difficult than with ivy but should be successful if slightly woody tissue a few inches below the tip is used. Tip cuttings are often too succulent on fast growing plants and wilt immediately when removed.

DIZYGOTHECA—False aralia, split leaf maple, and spider aralia are common names of this plant. The palmate, brownish-red leaves are very graceful and are borne on woody stems. False aralia has an interesting form and color and should be used more when good light is available. It is easily propagated from fresh seeds and the young plants are well suited for dish garden use.

POLYSCIAS—These have been named the "ming aralia" because of their resemblance to the Chinese ming tree. Not widely grown but useful where an oriental tree effect is needed. The finely divided leaves are unusual among foliage plants.

IVIES—It is difficult to imagine close genetic relationships between large, tree-like sheffleras and vining ivies but they are both in the aralia family. Ivies are native of subtropical and temperate regions. Subtropical varieties are more adapted to indoor use since they enjoy warm temperatures. Cooler situations are ideal for the more temperate varieties. Ivies are grown the world over as vines and ground cover. Many varieties are available. The problem of growers is to limit their program to a few outstanding selections. Propagation is easily accomplished from slightly woody cuttings and every foliage greenhouse should have a steady supply of small pots and hanging baskets as a staple item. Ivies do well from

60°-70° F but will not maintain compact growth if light levels are low. Spider mites and cyclamen mites will be a continuing problem on ivies unless preventive spray programs with Pentac and diazinon, respectively, are instituted.

The Fig Family

Plants of this family are especially useful when tree forms are needed for interior landscapes. Light levels of at least 50 foot candles are necessary for maintenance; much higher intensities are required for good growth. Most figs used as ornamentals are in the botanical group *Ficus*. All members of this group have a milky latex for sap which accounts for one of the common names applied to them, "rubber trees." This appelation applies in particular to the common, broad leaved *Ficus elastica* and its variants.

In modern decor, the weeping fig (*Ficus benjamina*) is replacing the rubber tree (*Ficus elastica*) as the most popular member of the group. Weeping figs are graceful and their small, leathery leaves lend a more refined aspect than is accomplished with the coarser habit of the rubber tree. Weeping figs are sold as multistemmed bushes or they can be trained to a single stem tree. They are notorious for dropping leaves when not properly acclimated to lower indoor light levels before installation. Exposure to sudden cold drafts or extreme drought will sometimes cause total defoliation. New leaves will generally grow back after a period of time if suitable conditions for growth are present. When weeping figs have become accustomed to their new home they are durable and maintain an excellent shape. Variegated forms of both the weeping fig and rubber tree are available.

Ficus retusa nitida (Indian laurel tree) is similar to the weeping fig but the branches do not hang and the leaves are not so pointed on the tips. It is attractive when sheared to produce a globe of foliage at the top of a naked stem. *Ficus lyrata* (fiddle leaf fig) has large, generously spaced leaves which resemble a violin and are wavy. This plant is very nice if properly grown but good specimens are seldom seen because leaves are often damaged and stems too weak to support themselves. There are other figs used as ornamentals but their commercial importance is negligible.

The Palm Family

Palms are a large family but only a few varieties are important as indoor specimens. They are generally sold in 10 inch or larger containers since their usefulness does not emerge until some size is reached. Many people consider them to be the most graceful of all indoor plants. They convey the atmosphere of tropical paradise more readily than any other type of vegetation. A trunk is seldom discernible on smaller plants but as they become large most will develop a type of stem which is fibrous rather than woody. The majority of palms prefer shade and those which do not will generally tolerate it. They are not, however, considered low light plants. Palms are often categorized by their leaf shape into the feather palms and fan palms. Feather palms have leaflets arranged on either side of a long axis in the manner of a feather while fan palms have the blades radiating out from a central point in the shape of a hand. Fan palms are not especially popular for interior decoration at the present time. Many palms which are native to deserts or highland areas will tolerate cooler night temperatures. Some varieties are native at considerable distances from the tropics and many varieties are resident in situations which are not typical of a jungle environment.

The following are the more important commercial varieties for indoor use:

kentia palm (*Howeia forsteriana*)
neanthe bella palm (*Chamaedorea elegans* "bella")
parlor palm (*Chamaedorea elegans*)
lady palm (*Rhapis excelsa*)
pygmy date palm (*Phoenix roebelenii*)
areca palm (*Chrysalidocarpus lutescens*)

Palms are important for outdoor landscaping in warmer regions of the United States and constitute a considerable crop for nurserymen in those areas.

The Peperomia Family

Perhaps no family of indoor plants is grown so widely for use in small containers as the peperomias. Because of their adaptability to use as small plants, they are a favorite crop in northern greenhouses. Rooted cuttings can be planted in 2¼ inch pots and sold in a matter of weeks. Cuttings may be shipped in or taken from stock plants grown at the greenhouse. Most peperomias yield a large number of cuttings per stock plant and are not space hogs so that propagation is often profitable for northern growers. Stock plants which are pinched for cuttings generally regenerate a new flush of growth in several weeks. Peperomias require a 65° F temperature but will grow more vigorously at 70° F. Unlike philodendrons and pothos which do little more than survive at 65° F, the peperomias will make considerable growth. Light levels for profitable growth should be in the medium range of intensities mentioned earlier for foliage plants. In the home they can be subjected to 50 foot candles and still maintain their appeal.

A limited number of varieties make good hanging baskets and a few are suitable for low profile 6 inch pots. Any variety which is grown in a 2¼ inch container will also make acceptable 3 or 4 inch material. The number of cultivars is extensive and often the grower is in the happy circumstance of needing to cull out varieties which do not perform or sell well under the particular growing program. Peperomias are my choice to utilize as the backbone of a 2¼ and 4 inch foliage plant program; they grow easily and quickly, propagate economically, are not susceptible to extraordinary pest problems, and will tolerate reasonably low light levels in the home. Many of the other groups of plants which can be raised economically for small pots by northern growers are adapted only to the brighter situations found indoors.

Propagation of peperomias is by leaf and stem cuttings and by division of the crown. Stem cuttings are the most common method but certain varieties are more profitably reproduced by leaf cuttings. Stem cuttings of most varieties root within three to four weeks and will make acceptable 2¼ inch pots in an equal amount of time after transplanting. Some varieties may attain good size with this schedule when only one cutting per pot is used, but the majority will require two or three cuttings. Leaf cuttings will require additional production time. Rooting is accomplished easily if the medium is not excessively moist and water is applied only when absolutely necessary. Rotting of stems and leaves is a persistent cause of losses in peperomias during propagation when excessive water is present. Most peperomias will withstand considerable drought and less damage will be done when cuttings and plants are kept slightly on the dry side than if they are overly moist. Good drainage is essential to avoid trouble with rot and growers may wish to transplant peperomias to the cutting mix formula if losses are heavy in the normal growing mix. Cleanliness is mandatory for success in propagating peperomias. Experience will soon educate the grower as to which varieties are especially prone to leaf and stem rot. Plants that are intended for 4 inch and larger pots may be established in 2¼ inch containers and grown to good size before shifting up so that large, actively growing plants will be capable of utilizing the extra volume of water present in the larger pots.

In my experience, peperomias are remarkably pest free although almost any insect or mite will establish on them if heavy infestations are present in the greenhouse.

A description of the numerous varieties of useful peperomias is not possible in this book and the reader is referred to the *Exotic Plant Manual* for complete varietal information and illustrations.

Cacti and Succulents

Cacti and succulents come in a wonderful array of forms and colors. While cacti are all members of the Cactaceae family, the succulents are composed of many families. Cacti, especially, produce some of the most beautiful flowers in the plant kingdom when conditions are appropriate for floral initiation and development. Unfortunately, flowering is generally infrequent. The majority of cacti and succulents are native to rather arid regions with hot days, cool nights, and plenty of sunshine. Many varieties will withstand freezing if they are gradually exposed to cooler temperatures since they grow naturally in climates where winter freezes are frequent. There are a few cacti, including the Christmas cactus, which grow as epiphytes (on the branches of trees) in tropical forests. Cacti and succulents are generally raised and sold in 2¼ inch pots but 4 inch and larger containers are not uncommon. The slow growth rate of these plants increases the cost of larger sizes tremendously.

The ideal environment for most cacti and succulents is one where temperatures are warm, light plentiful, and water available on demand. Although the desert plants can survive extreme drought, maximum growth will be made when they have all the water they can use consistent with proper soil aeration. Low temperatures, shade, and infrequent irrigation and fertilization may not be conducive to quick growth but they will be tolerated with a minimum decrease in quality by most cacti and succulents when they are placed in an indoor environment. These plants will survive a tremendous amount of abuse but excessive soil moisture is one condition which almost always leads to death. Roots lack enough oxygen to function properly and stem and root rot flourish when the soil is waterlogged. Soils must be well drained yet supply adequate mineral nutrition. The growing mix soil formula will be suitable for occasional use but growers who handle appreciable quantities of cacti and succulents may wish to increase the soil pore space by adding extra sand. A sunny south window is an excellent location for these plants. If the window receives no ventilation it may be advisable to provide light shade in summer.

Propagation of most cacti and succulents is easy while others may be extraordinarily difficult. Succulents are often referred to as "soft" varieties and "hard" varieties. The hard ones generally have a much slower growth rate, are more difficult to propagate, and more sought after by collectors. Soft succulents such as jade plants, kalanchoes, sedums, hen and chicks, and euphorbias root quickly from stem and leaf cuttings and exhibit a reasonably fast growth rate. Production of such varieties can be profitable in northern greenhouses if most growth takes place in the summer so that plants can be sold by late fall. Seed, leaf cuttings, stem cuttings, and division of the plant are all commonly used to propagate cacti and succulents. More than one method may be equally feasible, depending on the circumstances. Irrespective of the propagation method, excess water and humidity will usually lead to rot and result in failure. Growers must remember that these plants have considerable water stored in their tissues. Leaves or stem portions of some varieties may be observed sprouting roots even when left lying on dry, hot bench surfaces. It should not be surmised that water is not beneficial during propagation—the key word is **excess.** Any water applied must have ample opportunity to drain off quickly.

Culture of the slower growing cacti and succulents is generally better left to specialists located in areas where fuel consumption is low and good sunlight is assured. Damage during shipment is minimal and transport costs are relatively low due to the small size and durability of the plants.

The hard, tough appearance of most cacti and succulents sometimes leads the uninitiated to believe they are impervious to attack by pests and diseases. Their susceptibility to root and stem rot when excess moisture is present has already been stressed. Cacti and succulents are not especially prone to pest infestations but they are not immune either. Mealy bugs and spider mites are perhaps the two most frequently troublesome pests. Aphids are often the number one offender on soft succulents.

Illustrations and descriptions of numerous varieties of cacti and succulents are presented in the *Exotic Plant Manual.* The number of varieties now in use has grown tremendously so that the avid collector or specialist may need to consult even more specialized works than the one mentioned above.

The Fern Family

Ferns are one of the most widely distributed families of ornamental plants. They are found from the Arctic to tropical rain forests. A good fern habitat is shaded and damp. Even in the tropics ferns will be found in the cooler locations. Soils are usually highly organic so that even though humidity and moisture are abundant, the root zone is well drained. Ferns are diverse in size and shape. Tree ferns of the tropics may reach heights of 50 feet while smaller varieties of colder regions are no more than a few inches tall. The leaves of staghorn ferns are broad, flat, and leathery while the typical ferns have delicate leaflets arranged on a long axis in the manner of a feather. The beauty of most ferns lies in the delicate arrangement of leaflets into a graceful, airy frond (leaf) which is in turn arranged with other fronds into a refreshing, cool oasis of green.

Although there are many varieties of ferns utilized for indoor landscaping, the vast majority of production is made up of the Boston fern group. The several cultivars of Boston fern originated from selections of the sword fern (*Nephrolepis exaltata*). The most popular members of the group are dwarf Boston, fluffy ruffles, Whitmanii, lace, and Rooseveltii ferns. These descendants of the sword fern have monopolized fern production because they are attractive, are easy to grow, and will thrive under the low humidity conditions found in the average home. Other ferns are produced commercially but their importance is minor. Most of them are difficult to grow easily unless humidity levels are high.

Boston ferns can be a profitable crop for northern growers if small plants are vigorously growing by July. Good 3 inch plants transplanted at that time one per pot to 6 inch containers or two to a 10 inch basket will make excellent specimens for Christmas. Temperatures for Boston ferns should be maintained at 60°-80° F with light shade in the winter and heavy shade in the summer. Plants are best if allowed to grow pot bound until it is a real necessity to transplant them. Being pot bound allows frequent heavy irrigations without waterlogging the soil. My experience has been that Boston ferns will grow vigorously in late spring, summer, and fall but fail to make appreciable progress in winter even if proper conditions are provided. Unless the crop is made by late fall it seems to stall until spring arrives.

The common dwarf Boston fern has perhaps been overdone in supermarket produce departments. It is offered on a constant basis, often at reduced prices which few northern growers could profit at. Smaller growers for traditional outlets may find a more exclusive market for lace, feather, and Whitmanii varieties which are not so commonly seen but are just as easy to grow and care for. Large specimen hanging baskets are also an item which is not commonly available at mass outlets.

The propagation of ferns is by spores (very tiny reproductive bodies which are analogous to seeds), division of the crown, or meristem culture. The brown or black dots which are regularly spaced on the underside of fern leaves at certain periods of the year contain millions of microscopic spores. Spores are released from these small capsules at maturity and will germinate if proper conditions are present. The most persistent problem in obtaining good germination of spores is maintaining adequate humidity. Few commercial growers propagate Boston ferns by spores at the present time. Growers who need only a few plants will usually divide the crown of stock plants into sections, each having a small portion of root and vegetation. These are inserted into moist rooting mix and allowed to root and grow until suitable for 2¼ or 3 inch pots. Larger growers will generally find that obtaining small pots from specialists who propagate by crown division or meristem culture is preferable to maintaining a supply of stock plants.

The most persistent pests to attack ferns are the scale insects. Outbreaks are not often encountered if young plants are scrupulously inspected for the pests and if sources of infestation are not present on other crops in the greenhouse. After an outbreak of scale is discovered on larger plants, it is often almost impossible to clear up because of the dense foliage and difficulty in getting control agents to the insects. Temik is useful in this respect but the dosages must be tested carefully and it must be watered in heavily since serious damage can occur to plants through improper application. Tests for damage to plants should be initiated at 1/8 teaspoon of Temik per 6 inch pot and general applications should not be made until test pots show no damage after two weeks.

The Wandering Jew Family

This family contains some of the most profitable and easily grown foliage plants for the northern grower. Its members are generally well known to the public and have been grown in window sills for generations. The ease of propagation and culture leads many consumers to produce their own plants but there is significant demand for quality, professionally grown specimens. Most members of the wandering Jew family make excellent hanging baskets in a short while and some varieties are marketable as 4 and 6 inch pots. Wandering Jews in the home prefer a sunny spot in winter and light shade in summer. Cool rooms will not cause quality to decline. The best greenhouse specimens are grown at 60° F with full sun in winter and light shade in summer although higher and lower temperatures and light levels will be tolerated with amazing impunity.

Propagation is accomplished by sticking tip cuttings directly to the finishing containers. No bottom heat is required. When cuttings are spaced widely, pinching is essential after establishment if heavy plants are desired. I find that crops are more uniform and profitable if the finishing container is filled with enough cuttings to result in good plants without pinching. Roots form in one to two weeks and 4 inch plants can be ready for sale in less than five weeks from cutting when weather is warm and sunny. Many varieties of wandering Jew exist and growers will do well to begin a collection of the more useful types to use as stock plants.

Many wandering Jews exhibit a tendency to flower as winter approaches. This phenomenon is pronounced in certain varieties and almost unnoticed in others. Vegetative growth slows and production may be severely curtailed in those cultivars which bloom profusely. The Tahitian bridal veil plant seems to have the capacity to bloom well in all seasons and vegetative growth does not suffer appreciably. The flowers on this plant are the main attraction but flowers on the familiar "inch plant" are unsightly.

Wandering Jews are exceptionally disease and pest free but rotting out of the cuttings can occur if excessive moisture is applied during root formation. Most of these plants will tolerate a surprising degree of drought and freshly harvested cuttings are best left slightly on the dry side. I have experienced severe damage to some varieties when Vapona fog insecticide is used in the greenhouse. Whether damage is due to the insecticide or to the petroleum carrier is unknown. Certain varietes in my greenhouses have developed a resistance to fog damage while others have not.

The Pineapple Family

This family will be more readily recognized in the floral trade when referred to as bromeliads. Most members are characterized, as is the pineapple plant, by a basal rosette of tough, fibrous, lanceolate leaves. The central cup formed by these leaves serves as a storage reservoir for water. Bromeliads are seldom grown in northern greenhouses, being shipped in from southern growers in most cases. Their crop time is too long and their culture too specialized for inclusion in most greenhouse programs. The bromeliads exhibit a wide range of attractive leaf colors and flowers. In some varieties the leaf is prized while in others the flower is the object of attention. The cost of growing bromeliads to specimen size is the major factor in limiting their market share. If they could be sold at prices competitive with other indoor plants of similar size they would undoubtedly be very popular.

Bromeliads will tolerate a wide range of temperature and light conditions. Even if no growth is made, the tough nature of their tissue prevents any obvious decline in quality from occurring quickly. Ideal conditions would be 65°-70° F, filtered sunlight, porous soil, and soil water in adequate supply but never excessive. Water should be kept standing in the central leaf cup. Fertilizer is applied infrequently to match the slow growth and any fertilizer water put in the central cup must be very dilute. Certain members of the family, including pineapples, have no actual need to hold reserve water in the cup.

Wherever cost is not the main objective and plants are desired which are both unusual and easy to maintain, bromeliads should certainly receive consideration. The selection of varieties available is fairly extensive so that plantings of bromeliads may be made quite interesting using different colors and shapes.

The Grape Family

This family is represented by only one important group of interior ornamentals, the grape ivies. They are entirely unrelated to commonly known ivies described earlier under aralias. The importance of grape ivy is centered primarily upon one variety (*Cissus rhombifolia*) and its variants which are responsible for the great majority of commercial production. Grape ivy is a favorite plant for hanging baskets and trellis arrangements. Because of its grasping tendrils, it can be used for indoor arbors and room dividers. It is particularly useful when a very dark green leaf color is desired.

Grape ivy will flourish at temperatures of 60°-70° F with medium shade in summer and light shade in winter. Propagation is by tip or stem cuttings. I have encountered some difficulty in obtaining good growth with the growing mix soil formula. Better results are obtained when plants are grown in rooting mix. Powdery mildew can prove troublesome when temperatures are low and humidity high.

The Mint Family

The importance of this family is accounted for by several rather "weedy," easily grown varieties. Coleus, Swedish ivy (*Plectranthus australis*), and silver nettle are grown in almost every general purpose greenhouse in the United States. They are highly profitable crops because they grow quickly and easily and enjoy favorable market acceptance. Coleus culture has been described in the bedding plant section of this book.

The mints are considered by many people as temporary plants and perhaps less than full fledged members of the foliage plant fraternity. My answer is if they make money for the grower and retailer and satisfy the customer's needs, who cares about their legitimacy. These plants are no less permanent than others; they simply need different growing conditions and care to remain attractive. Light levels for the mint family in the interior landscape should be good. They will not thrive in dark corners. Cool temperatures of 65° F are ideal for compact growth but higher and lower temperatures will be tolerated. Regular pruning may be necessary to keep them within bounds.

Swedish ivy has become one of the most important modern day foliage plants. Greenhouse production is highly significant and millions of plants are propagated at home. Perhaps no other plant pleases consumers so much; it roots easily and produces large amounts of attractive vegetation without special care if exposed to strong, filtered light. I have realized more profit from Swedish ivy than any other single crop. The demand for it has been tremendous and shows no signs of lessening. Propagation in the home certainly reduces demand for commercially produced plants, but impressive hanging baskets from the greenhouse will always find a ready market. Smaller material also moves at a steady pace.

Greenhouse production is almost fool proof. Tip or stem cuttings will root in one to two weeks at 70° F. Growers may wish to stick cuttings directly to finishing pots in warm weather and resort to rooting in flats with bottom heat in winter. Excellent plants are obtained at 60°-70° F with light shade in winter and medium shade in summer. Large plants will require heavy amounts of water in the summer to prevent yellowing of older leaves. Watering at the time of transplanting cuttings must be restricted to prevent losses due to stem rot and root rot. Pinching must be practiced unless a sufficient number of cuttings is planted in the container to produce a full plant with single stem growth. The following schedule should serve as a guideline for summer production with direct rooting in the container: 4 inch pots, no pinch—4 weeks; 6 inch pots, no pinch—5 weeks; 10 inch baskets, one pinch—9 weeks. Winter schedules should allow ⅓ more growing time if cuttings are rooted with bottom heat.

I have never observed pest infestations on Swedish ivy in over ten years of continous production. This in itself would recommend the plant to any consumer or grower. Swedish ivy blooms in the northern United States from November through March. The numerous elongated clusters of small pale blue flowers are quite attractive but can become a nuisance when they drop on plants below or on carpeting in the home. The mature flower stalks are unsightly after flowers have dropped. Flower production reduces the rate of vegetative growth so that cutting production in winter is somewhat restricted.

The variety of Swedish ivy in heaviest production has totally green leaves with a heavy, slightly wrinkled texture. Mature leaves are ovate and generally one and a half to two inches broad. A similar cultivar with white variegations in the leaf is also available but I have had difficulty in maintaining a good variegated pattern over a period of time. The variegated form grows more slowly. A coarser variety with larger, brownish-purple leaf color enjoys limited sales but it quickly becomes woody and is generally a less desirable plant.

Silver nettle vine (*Lamium galeobdolon variegatum*) is winter hardy outdoors in most areas of the northern hemisphere but will perform admirably if given good light in the home at 60°-70° F. The leaves are slightly longer than broad and may reach two inches in length. They are green with silver markings on either side of the mid rib. Plants in hanging baskets can quickly reach several feet long and frequent pinching is necessary in the early stages of growth to produce a bushy habit. Silver nettle also finds a market in 4 inch pots. These vines make excellent filler in spring flowering baskets when a trailing effect is needed. They will grow in sun or shade when acclimated. Culture and propagation is much the same as for Swedish ivy except that cooler temperatures and more sun will be tolerated. Silver nettle is relatively pest free but cyclamen mites and red spiders can become serious if infestations are not treated immediately.

The Norfolk Pine Family

These tropical and subtropical trees are closely related to the pine and fir trees of the northern hemisphere. The Norfolk island pine or star pine (*Araucaria exclesa*) is a major foliage variety in the United States, particularly in larger containers. Bunya-bunya or monkey puzzle trees are produced commercially but are not frequently seen. The Norfolk pine looks very much like our pine trees but is perhaps more formal with regularly spaced whorls of five to seven branches on the main stem. The needles are soft and awl-shaped. Monkey puzzle trees have much the same general shape but the needles are much larger, flattened, and quite sharp.

Araucaria trees are generally shipped to northern greenhouses from southern production areas but 6 inch pots can be produced in the greenhouse for Christmas from strong 2¼ inch containers if grown through the summer and fall under good conditions. Norfolk pines do well under a wide variety of environmental conditions. They tolerate occasional cold almost to the freezing point and will survivie light intensities of less than 50 foot candles or amost full sun. Ideal conditions would be light shade at 65°-70° F. Diseases and pests are seldom a problem but an occasional inspection for spider mites is recommended. Araucarias are one of my favorite foliage plants to suggest for consumers who want a specimen plant that is easy to care for.

Some Families for Sunny Locations

Numerous homes, offices, and public buildings constructed in the last decade have been designed to admit higher levels of daylight. Not only are these structures more airy, but also they often have specific planting areas set aside in sunny locations. As a consequence, there has been a corresponding increase in demand for decorator plants which will thrive under full sun. Several of these varieties have already been described under headings pertaining to other families: yucca, Norfolk island pine, aloes, cacti, wandering Jews, and some palms. There are an additional few sun loving plants which deserve special consideration because they are so well adapted to these locations and they are especially striking because of their flowers and/or fruit.

Citrus, bougainvillea, and hibiscus are all excellent plants in full sun with plenty of water applied to well drained soils. Each of them flower almost year round with short rest period between heavy bloom production. Temperatures of 60°-70° F are most suitable but higher and lower ranges are tolerable. All of these varieties seem to benefit from occasional applications of 10% chelated iron at rates of 2 ounces per 100 gallons of water. Spider mites are a perennial problem but may easily be eradicated with sprays of Pentac. Aphids are also troublesome, especially on hibiscus and bougainvillea. They may be controlled with Temik applications to these two varieties but Temik or any systemic insecticide should never be used on citrus trees. Poison will enter the fruits and pose a danger to persons tasting them.

Citrus plants are normally grown in the south and shipped to northern markets. The same procedure is common for bougainvillea and hibiscus but both of the latter can be profitably grown in northern greenhouses as summer crops. Cuttings of hibiscus and bougainvillea can be rooted at any time of the year from half hard wood. The rooting process is slower than for more succulent greenhouse ornamentals but should be accomplished in six to eight weeks. Misting is essential to good results although a 20-30% success rate may be obtained if cuttings are simply sprayed occasionally with a hose and left in the shade. It is important that cuttings be taken at a cool time of day and watered in immediately; wilted cuttings will not recover turgidity easily.

Well branched 6 inch hibiscus plants will produce 5 gallon specimens for Christmas if they are transplanted June 1 and pinched hard one month later. These will be truly impressive plants and should command a premium price. Six inch plants for Christmas must be rooted by June 1 and pinched for the last time by August 1 to attain good size. Commercial production of hibiscus for flowering pot plants has increased tremendously in the last few years and small plants are now available from several specialists. The hibiscus seems to be a plant with an unlimited future if current architectural styles persist.

Production methods for plants destined primarily for flowering plant markets may differ from those employed when plants are to be used as foliage specimens. The difference will lie in the emphasis placed on height control by chemical means. Hibiscus for flower markets are normally treated with Cyclocel to give plants a short, very bushy shape with maximum flower buds per square foot of foliage area. These plants are very attractive but can prove disappointing to the buyer who expects a vigorously growing foliage plant. My experience has been that it takes about one year for the effects of Cyclocel to wear off. Plants will not put on appreciable new growth until that time and are more susceptible to a decrease in quality due to poor growing conditions since they are not in an active metabolic state. Plants intended as actively growing foliage specimens should not be treated with Cyclocel. Their height can be controlled sufficiently by allowing plants to suffer slight water stress and by switching to the use of potassium nitrate fertilizer alone to reduce nitrogen uptake.

Hibiscus flowers do not last more than a day or two but are produced constantly over the flowering period. Most varieties have very large flowers. The predominant colors are from pink to red with yellow and white being less common. Few plants can boast a flower which is so striking and yet exquisitely refined. A hibiscus with several full blooms will always be sold within the day if it is placed where customers can see it easily. There are many varieties to choose from. One of the major characteristics to be considered when selecting varieties for the greenhouse program is strength and length of stem. Shorter cultivars with strong stems are generally more suitable for both potted flower and foliage plant production. Production of tree forms with a single naked trunk is better left to southern growers since the crop time is greatly extended.

Bougainvilleas are woody shrubs which develop long, slender branches that may sometimes appear almost vining. Growth is rapid under good conditions and plants may be produced under the same schedule as hibiscus except that at least one extra pinch is needed to finish a reasonably bushy plant. One drawback of bougainvilleas in greenhouse production and for home or office is the unwieldy, clambering growth habit. The length of branches can be controlled to some degree by making sure plants have full sun with only enough nutrients and water to sustain healthy growth. Luxuriant production of vegetation does nothing for flower production and increases the tendency of plants to ramble. To my knowledge the use of chemical growth retardants with bougainvillea has not been investigated thoroughly.

Flowers of bougainvillea are inconspicuous; the real color is provided by paper-like leaves surrounding the flower. Numerous groups of these colored leaves are arranged on short stalks at the ends of branches. A bougainvillea in full bloom is, in my eye, the most striking ornamental plant available. Colors are extremely vivid and some varieties exhibit a neon-like iridescence. The blooms of bougainvillea are long lasting and it is not uncommon for a branch to maintain good color for more than a month. There are many excellent varieties.

Citrus plants offer a unique combination of very fragrant flowers, beautifully glossy foliage and interesting and edible fruits. The wonderful, almost overpowering aroma of citrus plants in bloom is the characteristic which pleases my senses the most. Northern greenhouses may profit from purchasing large one gallon plants in late spring and growing to 8 or 10 inch container size through the summer. Only a moderate amount of growth should be expected and this program is not cost effective unless the starter plants are obtained at excellent prices. Lemon, lime, and orange plants are available in dwarf varieties suitable for container culture. The Calamondin orange is far and away the most popular and readily available because it maintains a compact shape and produces fruit and flowers almost continuously through the year. Calamondin fruit is small and tart but edible if allowed to ripen fully; it is more suited for marmalade production. Other varieties yield sweeter fruit and some lime and lemon trees yield full sized fruit of good quality.

GLOSSARY

Abscission—The process whereby various plant parts become separated or detached from the plant. Abscission usually refers to a passive separation due to a modification of cell structure at the separation point rather than an active detachment by man, animals, or other physical causes.

Acclimatize—The process of subjecting plants to environmental conditions in the greenhouse which will help them withstand being placed in home or garden conditions with as little stress as possible.

Acid—Acid conditions are said to exist when the pH of a solution is below 7.0.

Alkaline—Often used interchangeably with the term basic. This usage is not technically correct but is commonly accepted outside the chemical profession. Alkaline soils or solutions are those which have a high concentration of alkali group chemical elements present and almost always have a basic reaction (pH higher than 7.0).

Ammonium Toxicity—A physiological disorder of plants which arises due to the presence of an excess of ammonium (NH_4^+) forms of nitrogen in the soil. Characterized by scorching of the leaf margins and loss of roots. Occurs more frequently in artificial soil mixes. Different species of plants show a high degree of variability in their reaction to ammonium levels

Annual—A plant which completes its life cycle and dies after the end of one growing season.

Basic—Basic conditions are said to exist when the pH of a solution is above 7.0

Bedding plants—A common term referring to those plants used in flower beds. An expanded meaning often includes all the herbaceous plants marketed for outdoor or patio use.

Biennial—A plant which requires two years to complete its life cycle. The first growing season is spent in vegetative growth and seed is produced during the second season.

Bracts—Modified leaf tissue which sometimes appears as if it is a part of the flower. The colored bracts of the poinsettia are commonly referred to as the flower.

Break—New growth which appears from the leaf nodes after a plant has been pinched.

Chlorophyll—A molecule which plays a dominant role in the conversion of light energy into chemical energy during photosynthesis.

Chlorosis—A physiological disorder which is characterized by yellowing of the area between the veins on newer leaves. Tissue near the veins remains a darker green. Chlorosis is due to a lack of available iron.

Compatability—Generally refers to the ability of two or more greenhouse chemicals or fertilizers to be used together without altering the intended purpose when used separately and without damaging plants which the chemicals used separately would not have harmed.

Culture indexed plants—Plants which have been carefully evaluated in a laboratory and declared free of the particular bacterial or fungal diseases for which the indexing procedure was designed.

Cutting mix—A soil mix composed of peat and perlite which is recommended in this book as a medium for rooting cuttings and germinating coarse seed. Sometimes used as a potting mix for certain species.

Daylength—Refers to the length of light period (either natural or artificial) which is given to plants to induce or prevent flowering in plants. Can also be used in a more general sense to describe the period of irradiation plants are subjected to during a 24 hour time span without any particular connection to the flowering process.

Disbud—The process whereby certain flower buds are removed from the flowering stem to manipulate various characteristics of the flowering stem and flowers.

Fixed costs—Those greenhouse operating expenses which continue regardless of what crops are being grown. Examples: land and building costs, insurance, and real estate taxes. Certain fixed and variable costs categories may be interchanged depending upon the manager's viewpoint of what category it should be placed in.

Flat—A tray used to hold soil or various sizes and designs of plant containers. Many sizes and configurations are available. The most common flat in present day use is made of plastic and measures approximately 11½ by 21¼ inches. It is used primarily for bedding plant production.

Foot candle—A standard measurement of the intensity of visible light. Originally formulated as the light intensity generated by a candle at a distance of one foot.

Genetic—A term encompassing those characteristics of living organisms which are transmitted from one generation to the next by groups of messenger molecules called genes.

Germination—The process seeds go through when they are changing from a dormant state into a newly sprouted seedling.

Growing on—A commonly used term in the greenhouse industry meaning the growth of smaller plants on to the desired marketing stage. This term may be used as an adjective.

Growth retardant—Any chemical which is used to restrict the height of ornamental plants.

Hybrid—Technically, a plant which has been produced by mating a male and female from two different species. In horticulture and agriculture it is common to use this term even when more closely related groups of plants, such as varieties of the same species, are mated to produce offspring with characteristics of both parents.

Induction—The process whereby a life function of plants is caused to begin by the presence of absence of a factor or combination of factors.

Initiation—Generally used synonymously with "induction" but may sometimes be used to describe the beginning of life functions which needed no direct causative factor or factors.

Leach—Application of water or fertilizer solutions in excess of what the soil can hold so that some portion of the applied liquid exits through the drain holes of pots. Dissolved mineral elements are carried out with the drainage. Leaching is important to prevent a buildup of mineral salts in the soil.

Leaf node—That point on the stem of a plant where the leaf is attached.

Long day—A term used to describe the duration of light required to induce a flowering response in a particular plant variety. Can also be used as an adjective to describe that variety. Plants are termed long day when flowers are initiated as succeeding days become longer after a critical threshold duration is reached.

Medium—The material plants are grown and anchored in, eg. soil or artificial soil mixes.

Micronutrients—Those mineral fertilizer elements which are required by plants in very minute quantities.

Necrotic—Dead.

Nitrogen depletion—The using up of nitrogen in the soil by micro-organisms. Nitrogen depletion occurs when a large supply of undecayed organic matter acts as a source of food for micro-organism growth. The organisms also require nitrogen so they use up what is present in the soil and leave little or none for plant growth unless more nitrogen is added than the micro-organisms are capable of using.

Packs—A trade term used to describe a generally shallow, rectangular container in which bedding plants are grown and sold. The container may or may not have individual compartments and several packs are usually grouped to fit into a flat.

Pasteurization—The process of subjecting soils to steam heat to kill pests or disease causing organisms in the soil.

Perennial—A plant which does not die within a specified number of growing seasons but maintains the capacity to grow anew each year from dormant tissue.

Petroleum carrier—Oil base compounds which are used to dilute certain pesticides.

pH—A scale of measurement which denotes the degree of acidity or alkalinity. pH reflects the concentration of hydrogen ions in solution. Acidity or alkalinity changes by a factor 10 for each unit change in the pH scale. Readings below 7.0 are acid while those above 7.0 are alkaline.

Photo oxidation—The degradation of materials caused by light energy incident upon them.

Photoperiod—The duration of light periods to which plants are subjected.

Photosynthesis—A biochemical reaction which is unique to green plants. Transient light energy is converted to the chemical energy contained in plant compounds.

Physiological drought—A deficiency of water in plants caused by the inability of plants to take up water for various reasons even though sufficient water may be present.

Phytotoxic—Poisonous to plants.

Pinch—The action of removing the growing tip of plant stems. The actual tip of the stem is removed rather than just the enclosing leaves. Usually performed to promote branching and sometimes to reduce height.

Propagation—The process of producing new plants from the previous generation.

Relative humidity—A measure of the amount of water present as vapor in the air.

Respiration—A biochemical reaction in which energy is released through the oxidation or "burning" of chemical compounds by plants and animals.

Return on investment—Profits divided by the total capital invested in a business. The quotient is then expressed as a percentage.

Rooting mix—The soil mix composed of peat and perlite recommended in this book for use in rooting cuttings and germinating coarse seed. Occasionally utilized for growing on varieties which require especially well drained soil.

Salt index—A measurement of the amount of soluble salts a fertilizer adds to the soil solution when compared with equal amounts by weight of other fertilizers.

Shade—Refers in general to the condition existing when some portion of the sun's rays are prevented from striking an object. Applied in a more limited sense to the use of blackcloth to alter daylengths for manipulation of the flowering response in plants

Short day—A term used to describe the duration of light required to induce a flowering response in a particular plant variety. Can also be used as an adjective to describe that variety. Plants are termed short day when flowers are initiated as succeeding days become shorter after a critical threshhold duration is reached.

Single stem—Plants which are not pinched to promote development of side shoots. Only one stem is allowed to grow and flower on each plant.

Soluble salts—The chemical salts or compounds which are dissolved in a solution. The liquid film surrounding and present between soil particles is a not so obvious solution containing soluble salts which can greatly affect plant growth. Soluble salts are contributed by the mineral salts naturally present in soils and irrigation water and by fertilizers and chemicals applied to the soil.

Sowing—The process of planting seed to a suitable medium where germination will occur.

Tissue culture—Propagation of new plants by nurturing one or more cells taken from a mother plant to the stage where they have grown and differentiated enough to be self supporting under normal growing conditions.

Turgid—Refers to the condition of plant cells when they contain enough water to be in a normal expanded state. When water is lacking to fill the interior of cells the plant becomes wilted.

Turgor pressure—The pressure which water contained in plant cells exerts against the cell wall in an outward direction. Turgor pressure causes cells to be turgid.

Variable cost—Those greenhouse expenses which change appreciably depending upon the particular crop being grown and upon the level of greenhouse utilization. Examples: cuttings, seed, soil, chemicals. Certain fixed and variable costs categories may be interchanged depending upon the manager's viewpoint of what category it should be placed in.

Vegetative—Refers to the maintenance of plants in a non-sexually reproductive state. Often used in a general sense to denote the green growth made by plants as opposed to production of flower organs.

Vegetative propagation—Producing new plants by means of cuttings, tissue culture, bulbs, corms, and tubers. The sexual process of mating male and female plants to produce seed is avoided and all resulting new plants are genetically identical.

SOURCES OF SUPPLY

No endorsement is intended by listing the following companies as sources of supply. They are presented only because their catalogs are especially complete and a national audience is reached. Many of these companies offer services and literature in addition to the products listed in catalogs.

Greenhouses and Greenhouse Equipment

Acme Engineering and Manufacturing Corp., P.O. Box 978, Muskogee, OK 74401 (918) 682-7791

IBG International, P.O. Box 100, Wheeling, IL 60090 (800) 323-5203

Ludy Greenhouse Manufacturing Corp., P.O. Box 141, New Madison, OH 45346 (513) 996-1921

National Greenhouse Co., P.O. Box 100, Pana, IL 62557 (217) 562-3919

Rough Brothers, Inc., P.O. Box 16010, Cincinnati, OH 45216 (513) 242-0310

X. S. Smith, Inc., Drawer X, Red Bank, NJ 07701 (800) 631-2226

Plants and Cuttings

Mikkelsens, Inc., P.O. Box 1536, Ashtabula, OH 44004 (216) 998-2070

Pan American Plant Co., P.O. Box 64, Parrish, FL 33564

Paul Ecke Poinsettias, P.O. Box 488, Encinitas, CA 92024 (619) 753-1134

Yoder Bros., P.O. Box 230, Barberton, OH 44203 (800) 321-9573

Seed and General Greenhouse Supplies

A. H. Hummert Seed Co., 2746 Chouteau Ave., St. Louis, MO 63103 (800) 325-3055

Al Saffer and Co., Inc., Corner of Pearl and William Sts., Port Chester, NY 10573 (914) 937-6565

Ball Seed Co., West Chicago, IL 60185 (800) 323-3677

B.F.G. Supply Co., 14500 Kinsman Rd., Burton, OH 44021 (216) 834-1883

Brighton By-Products Co., Inc., P.O. Box 23, New Brighton, PA 15066 (800) 245-3502

Burpee Seed Co., 300 Park Ave., Warminster, PA 18974

Cassco, P.O. Box 550, Montgomery, AL 36101 (800) 633-5888

Florists Products, Inc., 2242 N. Palmer Drive, Schaumburg, IL 60195 (312) 885-2242

Geiger Corp., P.O. Box 2852, Harleysville, PA 19438 (800) 443-4437

Geo. W. Park Seed Co., Inc., P.O. Box 31, Greenwood, SC 29647 (800) 845-3366

Gloeckner and Co., Inc., 15 E. 26th St., New York, NY 10010

Harry Sharp and Son, 420 8th Ave. North, Seattle, WA 98109 (800) 426-7766

Henry F. Mitchell Co., P.O. Box 160, King of Prussia, PA 19406 (215) 265-4200.

Joseph Harris Co., Inc., 3670 Buffalo Rd., Rochester, NY 14624 (716) 594-9411

Northrup King Horticultural Supplies Div., 1500 Jackson St. N.E., Minneapolis, MN 55413 (800) 328-2420

Stuppy Supply, 1212 Clay St., North Kansas City, MO 64116 (800) 821-2132

Vaughn's Seed Co., 5300 Katrine Ave., Downers Grove, IL 60515 (800) 323-7253

SUGGESTED LITERATURE

The following books will prove to be excellent background reading for those who wish to pursue additional studies. This list is certainly not complete but contains some of the more comprehensive works in several subject areas.

Baker, Kenneth F., Editor. 1957. *The U.C. System for Producing Healthy Container Grown Plants.* Univ. Calif. Div. Agr. Sci. Exp. St. Ext. Ser. Berkeley, CA.

Ball, Victor, Editor. 1977. *The Ball Bedding Book.* Geo. J. Ball, Inc. West Chicago, IL.

Ball, Victor, Editor. 1984. *The Ball Red Book.* 14th ed. Geo. J. Ball, Inc. West Chicago, IL.

Berninger, Louis. 1982. *Profitable Garden Center Management.* Reston Pub. Reston, VA.

Boodley, James W. and R. S. Sheldrake. 1972. *Cornell Peat-Lite Mixes for Commercial Plant Growing.* Cornell Univ. Plant Science Information Bul. 43:148p. Cornell Univ. Ithaca, NY.

Boodley, James W. 1981. *The Commercial Greenhouse.* Delmar Publishers, Inc. Albany, NY.

Ecke, Paul Jr. and O. A. Matkin, Editors. 1976. *The Poinsettia Manual.* Paul Ecke Poinsettias. Encinitas, CA.

Graf, A. B. 1978. *Exotic Plant Manual.* 5th ed. Charles Scribner's Sons. New York, NY.

Graf, A. B. 1981. *Tropica: Color Cyclopedia of Exotic Plants.* 2nd ed. Charles Scribner's Sons. New York, NY.

Graf, A. B. 1982. *Exotica Four-Pictorial Cyclopedia of Exotic Plants from Tropical and Near Tropic Regions.* 11th ed. Roehrs. East Rutherford, NJ.

Joiner, Jasper N., Editor. 1981. *Foliage Plant Production.* Prentice-Hall, Inc. Englewood Cliffs, NJ.

Langhans, Robert W. 1980. *Greenhouse Management.* Halcyon. Portland, OR.

Larson, Roy A., Editor. 1980. *Introduction to Floriculture.* Academic Press. New York, NY.

Laurie, A., D. C. Kiplinger, and K. Nelson. 1979. *Commercial Flower Forcing.* 8th ed. McGraw-Hill. New York, NY.

Mastalertz, John W., Editor, 1976. *Bedding Plants.* 2nd ed. Pennsylvania Flower Growers. University Park, PA.

Mastalertz, John W. 1977. *The Greenhouse Environment.* John Wiley and Sons. New York, NY.

Nelson, Kennard S. 1980. *Greenhouse Management for Flower and Plant Production*. Interstate. Danville, IL.

Nelson, Paul V. 1981. *Greenhouse Operation and Management*. 2nd ed. Reston Pub. Reston, VA.

Pirone, P. P. 1970. *Diseases and Pests of Ornamental Plants*. 5th ed. John Wiley and Sons. New York, NY.

Sullivan, Glen H., Jerry L. Robertson, and George L. Staby. 1980. *Management for Retail Florists*. W. H. Freeman. San Francisco, CA.

Ware, George W. 1978. *The Pesticide Book*. W. H. Freeman. San Francisco, Ca.

Each of the following periodicals has a nationwide distribution. Numerous other horticultural magazines and newsletters are published by state and regional trade groups.

American Nurseryman. American Nurseryman Pub. Co., 310 S. Michigan Ave., Suite 302, Chicago, IL 60604 (800) 621-5727.

Florists Review. Florist Pub. Co., 310 S. Michigan Ave., Suite 302, Chicago, IL 60604 (800) 621-5727.

Grower Talks, Geo. J. Ball Co., 250 Town Rd., West Chicago, IL 60185.

Interior Landscape Industry. Florist Pub. Co., 310 S. Michigan Ave., Suite 302, Chicago, Il 60604 (800) 621-5727.

INDEX

This index will lead the reader only to the more important references to a particular subject. Especially significant page numbers are printed in bold face type. Part II of *Plants for Profit* is indexed so that discussions of cultural programs for specific crops will appear in bold face. General topics such as fertilizers, insect pests, growth retardants, etc., are not indexed for particular crops since this would result in a more tedious search by the reader and seldom results in finding information applicable to situations other than the crop being presented.

PLANTS FOR PROFIT

by Francis X. Jozwik

This book may be ordered from Andmar Press by sending $39.95 plus $1.95 for postage and handling to:

Andmar Press
Order Dept.
P.O. Box 217
Mills, Wyoming 82644

Remember to include zip code for prompt delivery.
Payment by check or money order—please do not send credit card numbers or cash.

ISBN 0-916781-00-3